WOMEN, ISLAM AND THE STATE

In the series
Women in the Political Economy,
edited by Ronnie J. Steinberg

Women, Islam and the State

Edited by

Deniz Kandiyoti
Senior Lecturer, Richmond College, London

Temple University Press
Philadelphia

Temple University Press, Philadelphia 19122
Introduction, Chapter 2, editorial matter and selection
© Deniz Kandiyoti 1991
Text © Macmillan Academic and Professional Ltd. 1991

First published 1991

Printed in Hong Kong

Library of Congress Cataloging-in-Publication Data
Women, Islam, and the state / edited by Deniz Kandiyoti.
p.   cm. — (Women in the political economy)
Includes bibliographical references and index.
ISBN 0-87722-785-3. — ISBN 0-87722-786-1 (pbk.)
1. Women, Muslim.   2. Women—Government policy—Middle East.
3. Women—Government policy—South Asia.   I. Kandiyoti, Deniz.
II. Series.
HQ1170.W595   1991
305.48′6971—dc20

90-40855
CIP

Contents

Acknowledgements

This book has its origins in a shared dissatisfaction with studies about women and Islam, in particular with their ahistorical tendencies and their neglect of the state as an important agent informing policies, ideologies and institutional practices which have a direct bearing on the condition of women. As such it is the product of an ongoing dialogue among scholars who feel some urgency about moving the debate forwards towards a non-essentialist, more historically grounded perspective.

I am grateful to Richmond College for facilitating this dialogue by sponsoring the workshop on 'Women, Islam and the State' in May 1987. I would like to thank all the participants of the workshop for their valuable contributions. I am also indebted to the Sociology Department of Manchester University where my time as a Simon Fellow in the spring of 1988 enabled me to work on the conceptual framework of the volume. I would like to thank the members of the Middle East Study Group for listening to preliminary expositions of some of the ideas in this book, offering comments and sharing their own work with me. I am also very much indebted to Michele Cohen, Sarah Graham-Brown, Nels Johnson and Rifat Kandiyoti for their incisive comments on my drafts as well as for their moral support. Finally, I owe an older debt of gratitude to my friends and colleagues in Turkey whose formative influence I wish to acknowledge and to whom I dedicate this book.

DENIZ KANDIYOTI

Notes on Contributors

Margot Badran is a historian of the modern Middle East specialising in women's history. She has translated and edited *Harem Years: The Memoirs of an Egyptian Feminist, Huda Shaarawi* and is co-editor with Miriam Cooke of *Opening the Gates: A Century of Arab Feminist Writing.* She is a member of the American Research Center in Egypt and currently resides in Cairo.

Amrita Chhacchi is Lecturer in Women's Studies at the Institute for Social Studies, The Hague. She has published numerous articles and continues her research on women and industrialisation, and on the state and fundamentalism in South Asia. She is also involved in action research projects with women industrial workers and feminist networks in South Asia.

Ayesha Jalal is at the Harvard Academy for International and Area Studies and is Assistant Professor at the Department of Political Science, University of Wisconsin-Madison. She is the author of *The Sole Spokesman: Jinnah, the Muslim League and the Demand for Pakistan,* and *The State of Martial Rule: The Origins of Pakistan's Political Economy of Defence.*

Suad Joseph is an Associate Professor of Anthropology at the University of California, Davis. Most of her research has been carried out in her native Lebanon, with several co-operative works on Iraq. Her publications include studies of Muslim-Christian relations, local development, state and local community, women's networks, women and politics and family dynamics.

Naila Kabeer is a Research Fellow at the Institute of Development Studies, University of Sussex, and specialises in gender and development issues. Her present research project is entitled 'Islam, gender and economics in the labour market', and is a comparative study of Bangladeshi garment workers in London and Dhaka.

Deniz Kandiyoti is Senior Lecturer in the Social Sciences Division of Richmond College, London. She also taught at the Middle East Technical University in Ankara and Bogazici University in Istanbul between 1967 and 1980. She is the author of *Women in Rural Production Systems: Problems and Policies,* and of numerous articles on women in the Middle East, feminist theory and gender and development issues.

Maxine Molyneux is Lecturer in Sociology at Essex University, England. She is the author of numerous articles on women and socialism, of *State Policies and the Position of Women Workers in Democratic Yemen*, and is co-author of *The Ethiopian Revolution*.

Afsaneh Najmabadi teaches Sociology at Wellesley College. She is the author of *Land Reform and Social Change in Rural Iran* and co-author with Nahid Yeganeh of *In the Shadow of Islam: The Women's Movement in Iran*.

1 Introduction

Deniz Kandiyoti

This book examines the relationship between Islam, the nature of state projects and the position of women in the modern nation states of the Middle East and South Asia.

Placing the state at the centre of our analysis may require some justification. Despite the growing interest in recent 'Islamisation' policies adopted by a wide range of governments and in their implications for women, studies of women in Muslim societies have by and large neglected the role of the state and remained relatively untouched by the growing body of feminist scholarship on the subject. The latter highlights the reproduction of gender inequalities through various dimensions of state policy, through 'gendered' constructions of citizenship and through the dynamics of incorporation of national and ethnic collectivities into modern states.[1]

Instead, the treatment of women and Islam has for a long time been dominated by ahistorical accounts of the main tenets of Muslim religion and their implications for women. A predominantly exegetical approach is shared by fundamentalist apologists defending what they see as the divinely-ordained inequality of the sexes,[2] Muslim feminists attempting a progressive reading of the Quran, the *Hadith* and of early Islamic history,[3] and a few radicals who argue that Islam is intrinsically partriarchal and inimical to women's rights.[4]

This tendency has produced a rather paradoxical convergence between Western orientalists, whose ahistorical and ethnocentric depictions of Muslim societies have been the subject of an extensive critique,[5] and Muslim feminists and scholars with a genuine interest in radical change. Whatever the strategic merits of engaging with conservative ideologues on their own terrain, this approach is ultimately unable to account for the important variations encountered in women's conditions both within and across Muslim societies. Nor is it able to conceptualise the possible connections between Islam and other features of society such as political systems, kinship systems or the economy.

There is, on the other hand, a substantial body of research on Muslim societies which addresses the changing condition of women in specific geographical locations and historical periods, dealing with material issues such as women's labour force participation, education, demographic behaviour and political activity.[6] Such studies do not necessarily privilege Islam as an analytic category but insert gender into broader discourses about social transformation. These include modernisation and dependency theory, and incorporate elements from a variety of feminist perspectives. However the specificity of Islam, whether it appears in the form of local cultural practices justified in religious terms, as items of legislation derived from the *Shari' ah* (the canonical law of Islam) or as a more diffuse ideology about cultural authenticity, is seldom explored systematically.[7]

There is at present a growing recognition that the subordination of Muslim women can neither be read off solely from Islamic ideology and practice, nor be entirely derived from global processes of socio-economic transformation, nor for that matter from the universalistic premisses of feminist theory.[8] None the less current scholarship continues to reflect a genuine difficulty in conceptualising the role and specificity of Islam in relation to the position of women. While we cannot pretend to resolve this complex issue, we aim to address a limited but crucial aspect of it.

The unifying argument of this volume is that an adequate analysis of the position of women in Muslim societies must be grounded in a detailed examination of the political projects of contemporary states and of their historical transformations. In this respect, the countries covered illustrate very different paths of evolution. Some have emerged from declining empires (Turkey, from the Ottoman empire), or dynastic rule (Iran, from the Qajar) and others from direct colonial domination (Egypt, Lebanon, Iraq, the People's Democratic Republic of Yemen and the countries of the South Asian sub-continent). Some, like Turkey and Egypt, have a long history of modernisation of state and society, while others are relatively new territorial entities. Their current political regimes likewise cover a wide spectrum. However, they have all had to grapple with the problems of establishing modern nation states and forging new notions of citizenship. This has led them to search for new legitimising ideologies and power bases in their respective societies. It is around these common concerns that we situate our individual analyses, with the ultimate aim of contributing to the development of a comparative agenda.

We propose that the post-independence trajectories of modern states and variations in the deployment of Islam in relation to different nationalisms, state ideologies and oppositional social movements are of central relevance to an understanding of the condition of women. The ways in which women are represented in political discourse, the degree of formal emancipation they are able to achieve, the modalities of their participation in economic life and the nature of the social movements through which they are able to articulate their gender interests are intimately linked to state-building processes and are responsive to their transformations. The case studies presented in this volume illustrate important variations on these themes. They also suggest elements for a comparative exploration of four central issues to which the remainder of this chapter will be devoted.

ISLAM, NATIONALISM AND WOMEN'S RIGHTS

In a broad survey of feminism in the Third World, Jayawardena links the emergence of feminist movements to anti-imperialist and nationalist struggles, a general move towards secularism, a new concern with social reform and modernity and the ascendence of an 'enlightened' indigenous middle class.[9] Muslim societies certainly share in these general tendencies.[10] At the turn of the nineteenth and the beginning of the twentieth century, reformers of women's condition in the Muslim world emerged from the ranks of an educated, nationalist, male elite. Their concern with women's rights, centering around the issues of education, seclusion, veiling and polygyny, coincided with a broader agenda about 'progress' and the compatibility between Islam and modernity.

It is customary to present the reformist zeal of the modernisers and the defensive entrenchment of the conservatives as two sides of the same coin: a reaction to the economic and cultural penetration of the West. Some reformists sought to transform their societies by emulating the West, although more often than not the preferred device was to argue that the principles enshrined in the Western model are compatible with a 'modernist' reading of Islam.[11] The conservatives, on the other hand, perceived such reformism as a wholesale attack on the integrity of the Islamic polity and a capitulation to Western cultural imperialism. Cole also points out that the controversy around the status of women in turn-of-the century Egypt was characterised by fairly clear class divisions, Whereas those in favour of women's emancipation tended to be members of the new upper middle class who were integrated into the Western sphere of influence, both economically and culturally, the opposition emanated from petit bourgeois intellectuals who felt marginalised and threatened by it.[12] In any case, the 'woman question' emerged as a hotly contested ideological terrain where women were used to symbolise the progressive aspirations of a secularist elite or a hankering for cultural authenticity expressed in Islamic terms. These fraught beginnings are often evoked to account both for the continuing centrality of Islam in debates concerning women and the family, and the ambivalence surrounding the issue itself in an ongoing search for identity in the Muslim world.

What is easily overlooked by a perspective that emphasises exogenous influences is that Muslim societies were also involved in distinct and varied processes of economic change, nation-building and secularisation. Sonn presents secularism both in the East and West as an integral part of the process of the breakdown of central, religiously legitimised empires and the emergence of geographically limited states attempting to achieve national unity around new notions of sovereignity and citizenship.[13] In a perspective that is particularly useful for our purposes, Anderson speaks of the transition from sacred communities and dynastic realms to the 'imagined community' of nation states.[14] These imagined communities are predicated upon both a consciousness of separateness and identity and a sense of communion and horizontal solidarity among their members. They require a different conception of time and space as well as the mobilisation of new images and symbols to 'think' the nation. In Muslim societies, as elsewhere, cultural nationalisms have flourished and generated their own symbolic universe. In the process of creation of modern nation states, cultural nationalisms have achieved a spectrum of distinct and shifting syntheses with Islam which are still a subject of contestation and redefinition. New ideologies have emerged to legitimise and support new forms of state power. The terms of the 'woman question' were forged in the process of this search for identity and legitimacy. Attention therefore needs to be paid to the nature of these formative experiences.

In Turkey (Ch. 2) where the process of secularisation went furthest, the shift from a multi-ethnic empire to an Anatolia-based nation state involved a progressive distancing between cultural nationalism and Islam and culminated in Kemalist republicanism. Mustafa Kemal Ataturk not only dismantled the central institutions of Ottoman Islam by abolishing the caliphate and secularising every sphere of life, but took measures to heighten Turkey's 'Turkish' national consciousness at the expense of a wider Islamic identification: the compulsory romanisation of the alphabet, the new dress code and an elaborate rereading of Turkish history stressing its pre-Islamic heritage were elements of the cultural mobilisation in the service of the new state. The secularisation of the family code and the enfranchisement of women were thus part of a broader struggle to liquidate the theocratic institutions of the Ottoman state and create a new legitimising state ideology.

In Iran, Reza Shah's nationalist-statist programme, despite its avowed similarity to the Kemalist project, fell short of radically transforming the organisation and structure of the Shi'a clergy which was, in any case, quite different from that of Ottoman Sunnism. Almost an adjunct of the state in the Ottoman case, the clergy retained its organisational and financial autonomy in Iran, with profound consequences for the shape of things to come. Najmabadi (Ch. 3) also notes that the distinction of Shi'ism from Sunni Islam made it possible for Iranian nationalists at the turn of the century to base their nationalism on an appropriation of pre-Islamic Iran, into which they could integrate the presumably distinct features of Shi'ite Islam. The fact that Reza Shah's power was consolidated not on the basis of a social movement but of a military coup, and that he put the army at the centre of his political project, provided a weak basis for legitimacy which was further eroded under the 'sultanic' rule of the last Pahlavi. The transition to the Islamic Republic led to a total 'moralisation' of the 'woman question' and a radical break with earlier discourses about progress and modernity.

In the Arab world, where cultural nationalism and Islam now appear as practically interchangeable terms,[15] there have also been shifting definitions of nationhood. Mernissi acknowledges that in Morocco opting for 'Arabness' was convenient in terms of finding a place and identity in the Arab world, just as the French colonisers found it expedient to stress the divisions between Arabs and Berbers for their own purposes.[16] Similar divisions exist in Algeria, also a former French colony. Egyptian national sentiment is also a complex amalgam, involving a dissociation from alien (albeit Muslim) Turkish rulers, pride in the pharaonic past and a connection to a broader Arab heritage crystallising around a common language and history, that of Islam itself.[17] Whatever the differing emphases of nationalist movements with respect to the links between Arabism and Islam, the former at the very least co-opted the latter, as is evident in the doctrine of Arab socialism in its Nasserite or Ba'thist versions.

Hijab notes the resistance of all Arab states to breaking with *Shari'ah* law in the case of the personal status codes, even when they have completely secular civil, commercial and penal codes.[18] She attributes this resistance to a total interpenetration between Islam and Arab cultural identity and the need to protect the latter from imperialist onslaughts. As a result, articles of personal status codes often conflict with the constitutions of Arab countries. While the latter guarantee equal rights for all their citizens, the former extend privileges to men in the family (in the areas of marriage, divorce and child custody) which are denied to women. This duality is illustrated by Badran's discussion of family legislation in Egypt (Ch. 8). Molyneux's analysis of family law reform in the People's Democratic Republic of Yemen (Ch. 9) also reveals the necessary concessions to Islamic codes and local customs in a context where the state attempted to use legislation as a tool of socialist transformation.

The tensions between religious affiliation and national identity are nowhere more apparent than in the South Asian sub-continent, where women have clearly borne the brunt of both their imperatives and contradictions. The juxtaposition of the studies on Pakistan, Bangladesh and India in this volume provide a stark demonstration of this statement.

In pre-partition India, Islam was a communally based religion which served as an 'ethnic marker'. In the case of Pakistan it became integral to nationhood itself. Despite the fact that the call for a separate Muslim state reflected the aspirations of many secular Indian Muslims, Islam was increasingly evoked as a legitimising, if tenuous, ideology for Pakistani unity and integrity. Jalal (Ch. 4) points out that it was no accident that Zia ul-Haq's 'Islamisation' package took women as its prime target. Establishing Islamic credentials through retrogressive legislation primarily affecting women was a logical step in a context where the control of women and of their appropriate conduct had long been used to demarcate the identity and boundaries of the Muslim community.

Bengali Muslim identity in Bangladesh has been more problematic. Kabeer (Ch. 5) notes that the quasi-colonial ties of dependence with Pakistan and the fact that the latter had appropriated the mantle of Islamic purity for itself enhanced the contradictions between Muslim and Bengali identity. Resistance to Pakistani cultural hegemony produced a rallying of nationalist forces around the symbols of a distinct Bengali identity. It is only within this highly charged context that we can appreciate the significance of Muslim Bengali women joining the independence movement. Protest marches just prior to independence from Pakistan witnessed these women dressed in their red and yellow traditional saris, wearing *bindis* on their foreheads (commonly the adornment of Hindu women in India) and singing Bengali nationalist songs. Kabeer analyses the tentative nature of current Islamisation policies in Bangladesh against this background of tension between Muslim and Bengali identities, and in the context of the country's increasing impoverishment and reliance on foreign aid.

Chhachhi (Ch. 6) explores the construction of communal identities in India and the particular implications for women of the minority status of Indian Muslims. She notes the uneasy tension in Indian nationalism from its inception between secularism and communalism. Although the Indian national movement was secular in its objectives, it capitalised upon Hindu communal sentiment and used the symbols and language of Hindu revivalism. Images of both Hindu and Muslim womanhood became central to the construction of not only distinct but antagonistic identities. The logic of communal politics thwarted any progressive attempts to redefine and expand Muslim women's rights, since this issue readily turned into a confrontation of majority and minority interests. This confrontation found its latest expression in the public outcry occasioned by the case of Shah Bano, a divorced Muslim woman who had pressed for her maintenance rights under the Indian Criminal Procedure Code, and resulted in a separate Muslim Women's Protection of the Right to Divorce Bill passed in 1986.

It should be quite clear from the foregoing that while the boundaries of Islam and the nation are indeterminate and their juxtapositions variable, the centrality of women in guaranteeing the integrity of both is not. The compelling association between women's appropriate place and conduct, however defined, and notions of cultural authenticity is a persistent theme which deserves further exploration.

WOMEN, ISLAM AND THE POLITICS OF AUTHENTICITY

There is a consensus among scholars that the age-old antagonism between Islam and Christendom, much of it a history of colonial domination and continuing ties of dependence with the West, created an area of cultural resistance around women and the family. These came to represent the ultimate and inviolable repository of Muslim identity.[19] Both colonial administrators and Christian missionaries attempted to reform the sexual mores and family traditions of Muslims as part of their 'civilising' mission. The interest in liberating oppressed Muslim women produced in the minds of many Muslims, a close association between feminism and cultural imperialism. Any attempt to change the position of women could henceforth be imputed to imperialist or neo-imperialist designs, the local collaborators of such a project being tainted with cultural inauthenticity, if not outright betrayal. A new set of terms evolved to indicate this alienation, among which were *alfranga* in Turkey, *M'Tournis* in Algeria and *gharbzadegi* in Iran. Although these carry different degrees of opprobrium, all denote a shameful aping of the West. Leila Ahmed voices the dilemma of feminists in the Middle East in poignant terms when she states: 'It is only when one considers that one's sexual identity alone (and some would not accept this) is more inextricably oneself than one's cultural identity, that one can perhaps appreciate how excruciating is the plight of the Middle Eastern feminist caught between these two opposing loyalties, forced almost to choose between betrayal and betrayal'.[20]

Although the West is frequently presented as the 'Other' in discourses on cultural authenticity, the problem is in fact a much broader one. The term representing the threatening and invasive Other can, in fact, take very different forms. Anti-imperialistic pronouncements about the West are often a thinly disguised metaphor to articulate disquiet about more proximate causes for disunity. These include the existence of indigenous social classes with different cultural orientations and conflicting interests, and the coexistence of religiously and ethnically diverse collectivities in the very bosom of the nation. Discourses on women's authenticity are therefore at the heart of a utopian populism which attempts to obliterate such divisions by demarcating the boundaries of the 'true' community and excluding the 'Other within'. This 'Other' may appear in different contexts as the Hindu, the Levantine, the Copt or the Jew, but it may just as readily refer to deviance among Muslims themselves. This aspect of populist ideology, then, serves above all as a mechanism of social control.

Islam has been a consistent vehicle for popular classes to express their alienation from 'Westernised' elites. It marks the great cultural divide between the beneficiaries and casualties of the changing socio-economic order, of comprador and upper-caste bureaucratic interests versus the traditional middle classes. In the populist discourse of the Khomeini regime, Islam represents the ideology of the 'people' confronting the corrupt, 'Western-struck' (*gharbzadeh*) elite of the Shah era. The deportment and dress of women became laden with great symbolic significance since they were explicitly singled out as the most dangerous bearers of moral decay (as the 'painted dolls of the Shah'). Precedents and parallels to this discourse abound, from depictions of the Western-aping elite of the post-*Tanzimat* novel in Turkey to the manifestos of the Muslim Brotherhood in Egypt. Islamic authenticity may therefore be evoked to articulate a wide array of worldly disaffections, from imperialist domination to class antagonism. This opens up the possibility of expressing such antagonisms in moral and cultural terms, with images of women's purity exercising a powerful mobilising influence.

The privileged place of women and the family in discourses about cultural authenticity may therefore be explained through a wide range of different factors converging to single out this area as a critical one. Despite important differences in the degrees of interference of colonial states, it often represents one of the few areas of relative autonomy left to societies whose ties of political and economic dependence severely restrict their choices in every other sphere. For intance, the history of Ottoman legal reforms (Ch. 2) starting with the *Tanzimat* (1839) illustrates the Turkish response to Western pressures, resulting in changes in every aspect of commercial life but not in the fields of personal status, family and inheritance laws. It is not surprising that the *ulema* (Muslim clergy), whose powers in Ottoman society were severely restricted by the *Tanzimat* reforms, claimed the sphere of personal status and family legislation as their own. More to the point, this was the only area where conservatism could create the broadest possible political consensus. The cold facts of Ottoman economic and political dependence decisively restricted the arena in which traditionalists could raise the banners of cultural integrity and relative autonomy.

In the contemporary Muslim world, where ties of external dependence have deepened and women have become much more visible in the public realm, the attractions of reasserting control in this sphere are ever present. The material bases of the traditional patriarchal controls to which women are subjected are being eroded by processes of socio-economic transformation, and existing authority thresholds are being tested by the exigencies of modern life.[21] Yet women continue to represent the 'privacy' of the group and the focal point of kinship-based primary solidarities as against a more abstract and problematic allegiance to the state. Herein lies the dilemma of the modern state, which must confront and to some extent eradicate these particularisms in order to create more universalistic loyalties and to liberate all the forces of development, including the labour potential of its female citizens. This brings us to a consideration of the incursions of the state into the private realm of the family and of its consequences and limitations.

WOMEN, FAMILY AND THE STATE

The process of subordination of the family to the state and state intervention through family legislation have been the subject of detailed analyses in both the capitalist West and in socialist states.[22] The object of such intervention is to expand the control of the state over the socialisation of its citizens and to free them from the shackles of social customs and practices which are deemed to impede social progress and development. This feature of state practice has received relatively little attention in the study of Muslim societies, despite its far reaching implications for family and gender relations.

A striking and uniform feature of early feminist tendencies in the Middle East is not merely that they tried to accommodate Islam but that their concern with women coincided with the search for a new family form which would produce a 'healthier' and more viable nation. A nationalist/feminist alliance of progressive men and women produced a new discourse on women and the family which was predominantly instrumental in tone. Women's illiteracy, seclusion and the practice of polygyny were not denounced merely because they so blatantly curtailed the individual human rights of one half of the population, but because they created ignorant mothers, shallow and scheming partners, unstable marital unions, and lazy and unproductive members of society. Women were increasingly presented as a wasted national resource. Jayawardena also links the demand for 'civilised housewives'[23] to the needs of the male reformers of the local bourgeoisie who wanted to enhance their own civilised image: the enlightened modern man was demanding his counterpart, the 'new woman'. The family form most suited to deliver this modernity was the nuclear family, based on stable monogamous unions, the free choice of spouses and companionate and egalitarian relationships among family members.

These ideas remained in the realm of polemic for a long time in societies with small urban populations, weak industrial bases and vast rural hinterlands with varying degrees of integration to markets. The limited outreach of the pre-modern state left many aspects of their citizens' lives untouched, especially the regulation of marriage and family life which remained firmly under local kin control. It is notable that customary law often accorded women even fewer rights than the *Shar'iah*, upholding the patriarchal privileges inherent in the latter whilst failing to honour their rights to inheritance under Muslim law. Neither the state nor the Muslim clergy acted to break the hold of local communities over the control of marriage alliances and women.

Joseph raises a number of important questions regarding the greater ability of Middle Eastern communities to resist the control of states than their European counterparts.[24] In her discussion of Goody's work on the development of marriage and the family in Europe,[25] she invokes the absence of strong centralising institutions such as the Catholic Church, competing for the control of alliances and family wealth. She also notes the greater interpenetration between the Muslim clergy and Islamic states which were themselves relatively unsuccessful in controlling their periphery. Zubaida's broader discussion of the 'externality' of pre-modern Middle Eastern states also illustrates their limited impact on local communities.[26] It is by and large as late as the nineteenth-century that we witness the first attempts at deeper penetration of society, which gained significant momentum after the emergence of modern nation states.

Tucker's work on nineteenth-century Egypt documents the expansion of state power under the rule of Muhammad Ali and examines its contradictory implications for women.[27] The destructuring of local communities and the loosening of traditional family forms occurred as unintended consequences of capitalist penetration into the countryside rather than the direct result of state policies. On the other hand, the interventionist policies of Muhammed Ali encouraged the recruitment of women into public works, state-run industries and into the expanding sectors of health and education, acting to remove them from total and exclusive control by their families. At the same time, the repressive apparatus of the state actually restricted the range of their more traditional activities and informal associations.

The first systematic but unsuccessful attempt at direct state intervention through family legislation took place in the Ottoman empire with the 1917 Family Code (Ch. 2). The Committee for Union and Progress (CUP) aimed to follow their political revolution of 1908, marking the transition to constitutionalism, with social reforms that would remould and renovate Ottoman society. This included the replacement of the traditional patriarchal Ottoman family by the nuclear, monogamous 'National Family' (*Milli Aile*). The 1917 Code could not abolish polygyny, since this would conflict with the *Sha'riah* law, but attempted to curb it by stipulating conditions which would make its practice more difficult. It also had separate sub-sections applying to Christian and Jewish subjects who were bound by their own religious laws. This attempt was met by pervasive resistance both from the traditional sections of the Muslim clergy and by the minorities, who considered state interference in this area as an intolerable curtailment of the autonomy of their own religious authorities. The struggling Ottoman state, which was soon to be overthrown, was unable to wrest control from religious and communal interests. The minorities were able to obtain a repeal of the clauses pertaining to non-Muslim marriages in 1919 under Allied occupation of the capital. The rural hinterland remained untouched by this Code. This was also the case, for a very long time, with the secular 1926 Civil Code of the Turkish Republic.

The attempts of post-independence states to absorb and transform kin-based communities in order to expand their control have, not surprisingly, had an important bearing on state policies relating to women and the family. Joseph's comparative analysis of Iraq and Lebanon (Ch. 7) illustrates the close connections between elite strategies for state-building and policies directed at women and the family. In Iraq, the Ba'th agenda for state construction required the mobilisation of female labour for economic development in a context of continuing labour shortages. The state-party also had an interest in wresting the allegiance of the population away from particularistic loyalties (to tribes and ethnic groups). Women were recruited into state-controlled agencies in an effort at resocialisation through rapid expansion of public schooling as well as more general vocational and political education. However, legislative reforms in personal status laws remained modest and attempts to undermine the allegiance of the population to traditional kin-based groups came up against the widespread mistrust of the state instilled by the pervasive climate of political repression, an important point to which we shall return. In Lebanon, where the state incorporated the religious/ethnic heterogeneity of society in its formal structure, the government relinquished matters of family and personal status to the religious authorities of the various communities. Subsidising private education was given preference over building a cohesive system of national education. This was consistent with a strategy by the ruling elite to maintain the balance of sectarian power in the state.

Molyneux's discussion of the People's Democratic Republic of Yemen (Ch. 9) illustrates a state project that stood apart in the Arab world in that its experience of socialist rule, unlike 'Arab socialism', made reference in its official doctrine to Marxism-Leninism rather than Islam. The socialist state used legal reforms as a vehicle of change, aiming to extend central legal authority into rural areas where religious, customary and tribal law prevailed. With repect to women, this meant a challenge to traditional kin control and the creation of new possibilities for their emergence as economic and political actors. The 1974 Family Law incorporates important provisions aimed at loosening traditional kin control over marriage and achieving greater equality in the marital contract. This legislation in fact made some concessions to Islamic law and local customs both in the formulation and in the application of the law. However radical the intent of the central authority might have been, accommodation to the relative strength of traditional communities, and the recognition of disparities between regions (in particular between rural and urban areas) appear to have proved necessary.

In a comparative analysis of Tunisia, Morocco and Algeria, Charrad argues that variations in the balance of power between the national state and locally-based communities during accession to independence are responsible for the significant differences in the family laws of the three countries.[28] Tunisia, which has achieved the most progressive family legislation with the 1957 Personal Status Law, is also the country where primordial communities appear to have had relatively less political autonomy and leverage and where the nationalist movement was led by a powerful party which was least reliant on them for political support.

The interventionist measures deployed by post-independence states, through direct family legislation or more general education, employment and population control policies, have been limited in their emancipatory potential for a variety of reasons. First, measures for the emancipation of women did not as a rule coincide with a drive for democratisation and the creation of a civil society where women's gender interests could be autonomously represented. On the contrary, these measures were mostly part of the general thrust of 'dirigiste' and frequently authoritian and repressive regimes. The same governments which granted women new rights proceeded to simultaneously abolish independent women's organisations where they existed, whilst setting up state-sponsored women's organisations which were generally docile auxiliaries of the ruling state-party. This tendency is well illustrated in Joseph's discussion of the General Federation of Iraqi Women and its links with the Ba'th Party. This was also evident during the single-party era in Turkey, under Reza Shah in Iran and under Nasser in Egypt, who immediately after granting women suffrage in 1956 moved to outlaw all feminist organisations. It is also significant that the only progressive attempt at family law reform in Pakistan with the 1961 Family Law Ordinance took place under the military rule of Ayub Khan. Authoritarian rulers might have ventured into territory where others feared to tread. However, although they might wish to harness women to economic development efforts or simply project a 'modern' image, they would be unlikely to risk affronting the patriarchal sensibilities of their constituents by radically tampering with male prerogatives in the family. It is ironic that such prerogatives were frequently justified with reference to Islam and respect for the *Shari'ah*, when in fact the customary laws regulating the lives of the vast majority of women were more notable by their breach rather than strict observance of Muslim law. This concern would, however, account for the resilience of customary laws and practices in the spheres of marriage and the family as well as the relative laxity in the enforcement of state laws if and when they confronted patriarchal interests.

Second, communal controls over women continued to flourish and were in some instances intensified. This took place in a context riddled with contradictions. On the one hand, processes of capitalist penetration frequently led to the destructuring of local communities, the aggravation of social inequalities and a weakening of kin solidarities. The 'protective net' which households were supposed to extend over their more vulnerable members – women, children and the elderly – grew increasingly threadbare as impoverishment and emigration forced all family members to fend for themselves. The material basis of traditional authority relations within the family between the young and the old and between genders was subjected to persistent assault. On the other hand, primary groups and particularistic allegiances assumed an increasingly prominent role in mediating citizens' access to resources such as jobs, credit, schooling, health and other social services. The failure of modern states to create and adequately redistribute resources intensified tensions and cleavages expressed in religious, ethnic and regional terms, and often stymied the secular pretensions of radical nationalist projects. As the state itself uses local patronage networks and sectional rivalries in its distributive system, citizens also turn to their primary solidarities both to protect themselves from potentially repressive states and to compensate for inefficient administration. This reinforces the stranglehold of communities over their women, whose roles as boundary markers become heightened. Chhachhi's analysis (Ch. 6) of the growing communalisation of politics and civil life in India illustrates this process well. Significantly, she notes that whereas the traditional exercise of patriarchal authority tended to rest with particular men – fathers, husbands and other male kin – the communalisation of politics, particularly when backed by state-sponsored religious fundamentalism, shifts the right of control to all men. Indeed, clergy and police in Pakistan or Iran may assume expanded functions of direct control over women's dress and deportment, elements of control more commonly exercised within the confines of the household and the immediate neighbourhood. Some have argued that the very erosion of the traditional structures of patriarchy has created a favourable climate for the emergence of a conservative backlash against the emancipation of women articulated in the idiom of religious fundamentalism.[29] While this may account for some of the popular appeal of conservative ideologies, it cannot fully explain their different degrees of incorporation into actual state policies.

Contemporary policies and ideologies relating to women are being formulated in an increasingly complex field of forces where governments respond to the contradictory pressures of different sections of their internal constituencies as well as to their international ties of economic and political dependence. The final section of this chapter will concentrate on an analysis of these cross-pressures.

WOMEN, THE STATE AND THE INTERNATIONAL NEXUS

Mernissi presents the progressive-regressive movements with respect to women's emancipation in Muslim societies as the expression of an insoluble impasse: 'Every political setback generates a new necessity to liberate all the forces of development in Islamic nations. But paradoxically, every political setback inflicted by infidels generates an antithetical necessity to reaffirm the traditional Islamic nature of these societies as well.'[30] We will argue in this section that neither the will to develop nor the reaffirmation of an Islamic identity can be understood without a consideration of the global context in which modern nation-states operate.

Although a discussion of the local forces promoting the rise of Islamisation policies remains outside the scope of this chapter,[31] two general points must be noted. First, cleavages between oil-rich and resource-poor states in the Middle East and South Asia have had an important effect on the flow of migration, aid and political influence in the region. Migrants have gone from poorer countries such as Egypt, Pakistan, Bangladesh and Turkey to the oil-rich countries of the Gulf, whilst a reverse flow of cash and political influence has left its imprint on their polities. This has served to strengthen the cultural and political prominence of local forces and parties representing Islamist platforms and prompted diverse accommodations with Islam in aid-dependent countries. Second, this influence was achieved through the medium of an internal constituency frequently nurtured by conservative governments as a bulwark against the radical left. The delicate tightrope act that some governments followed, oscillating between the suppression of all oppositional movements and ideologies, the judicious extension of patronage to some Islamist tendencies, and attempts at defusing the more radical Islamist groups by upstaging them and hijacking their platforms are illustrated in the case studies on Egypt (Ch. 8) and Bangladesh (Ch. 5).

At the same time, the international monitoring of local economies has reached unprecedented levels, from the structural adjustment packages of the World Bank to stabilisation measures advocated by the IMF and development projects sponsored by a wide variety of Western donor agencies. This has been accompanied in many instances by a drastic redefinition of priorities: departures from tight state control over the economy, extended access to private enterprise and foreign investment and an emphasis on export-led strategies of development. The gender effects of such state policies have been widely documented[32] and have been the subject of heated polemics on women and development which cannot be dealt with here. However, the international institutional framework within which these debates are carried out and its effects on government policies must be noted.

Since the International Women's Year in 1975 and the following United Nations Decade for Women, the women and development lobby has put pressure on national governments to recognise the role of women in combating poverty, illiteracy and high birth rates. Governments have also been invited to eliminate all forms of legal discrimination based on sex. In 1973, the Percy Amendment to the US Foreign Assistance Act required that US bilateral aid should pay particular attention to and promote projects integrating women into development efforts. Monitoring bureaucracies were set up within the US Agency for International Development and the foreign aid departments of all the main European and Scandinavian donor nations. Although these are still marginal to mainstream development funding, the growing vitality of women's movements in both industrialised and Third World countries put gender issues on the policy agenda. The 'official' feminist rhetoric which had been the exclusive province of post-independence states has now moved to supra-national monitoring bodies with seemingly contradictory consequences at the local level.

The case of Bangladesh (Ch. 5) is particularly instructive in this respect. The coup that brought Zia ur-Rahman to power coincided with the 1975 declaration of the United Nations Decade for Women. Zia-ur-Rahman built up considerable political capital by championing the causes of the women and development lobby. But he also needed the support of right-wing elements, including the army, to counter the opposition of the Awami League. Meanwhile, oil states like Saudi Arabia had joined the ranks of major aid donors and increased their political leverage considerably. Zia embarked on a progressive dismantling of state secularism and his successor, Ershad, finally declared Bangladesh an Islamic state in 1988. Both Zia's and later Ershad's strategies constituted a blatant balancing act between the conflicting gender ideologies implicit in different aid packages: thus the development projects encouraged women's participation in the labour force and the public sphere, while aid from richer Muslim countries strengthened the *madrassas* (religious schools) and those religious parties advocating stricter controls on women. The government now finances the Islamic Foundation – which published tracts condemning family planning – while supporting US-funded attempts at population control.

Jalal (Ch. 4) also notes that in Pakistan the establishment of a Women's Division as part of the Cabinet Secretariat to safeguard women's interests and promote development programmes coincided with the passage of the most discriminatory 'Islamisation' laws. The Hudood Ordinance of 1979 made no distinction between rape and adultery and made it practically impossible for women to press rape charges; the law of evidence passed in 1984 reduced the weight of women's evidence to half that of a man's; the law of *qisas* and *diyat* passed in the same year specifies compensation for bodily injury to a woman as half that for a man, and makes the testimony of Muslim women witnesses to a murder admissible for a lesser punishment than the testimony of Muslim men.

The creation of local machinery to channel development funds which are in principle designed to have empowering consequences for women and the increased presence of women in the workforce can often be seen to coexist with measures strengthening the patriarchal features of society. There is neither a contradiction nor a mechanical connection between these sets of events. The donor governments and agencies of the West act to harness women directly to their vision of a more effective, though not necessarily more equitable, international economic order. The very manner in which the recipients of aid are integrated into that order increases the likelihood of unstable and repressive regimes. Most are caught up in a corrosive cycle of foreign debt. The development policies they favour have by and large led to more visible disparities in wealth, which fuel widespread resentment and discontent, often in the absence of democratic channels of expression. The legitimacy crises engendered by these processes have favoured the rise of organised oppositional movements with Islamist platforms, as well as attempts at social control by governments emphasising their own commitment to orthodoxy. The arena in which these political projects can most easily be played out and achieve a measure of consensus is, for reasons already spelt out, the control of women.

It should be clear from our discussion that presenting the workings of world capitalism, individual states, the class system, sectarian communities and male-headed households as ultimately convergent on the grounds that they represent different facets of patriarchal domination would be a dangerous oversimplification. The case studies in this volume indicate that their operations can be antagonistic as well as collaborative. More importantly, women are neither homogeneous nor passive victims of patriarchal domination. They are full-fledged social actors, bearing the full set of contradictions implied by their class, racial and ethnic locations as well as their gender. This has important implications for women's movements, which are to a large extent determined by the wider social context of which they form a part.

In all the countries covered in this volume women have been active participants in nationalist movements and struggles for national independence. Their ability to organise and act in pursuit of broader goals which may not be directly related to their gender interests is therefore not in question. The more vexing issue of whether women have also been able to develop political platforms and movements to further and articulate their common gender interests[33] elicits varied evaluations from the authors. Jalal argues, for instance, that in the case of Pakistan the class accommodations of the predominantly urban and middle-class participants of women's movements, despite their undeniable achievements, have limited the radical potential of their demands. Kabeer suggests, on the other hand, that in Bangladesh women's groups were able to flourish

18   Introduction

in the spaces created by development projects and that women's NGOs
were able to initiate innovative forms of organisation and mobilisation. In
Iran, Iraq and the People's Democratic Republic of Yemen it is possible
to see the operations of 'official', state-sponsored women's organisations,
although these examples of state co-optation of women's movements are
by no means exceptional or isolated. In a wide-ranging discussion of Egypt,
Badran shows how women's organisations and movements have spanned
the whole political spectrum, from liberal nationalism and the communist
left to radical Islamist movements within a more pluralistic framework. She
contends, moreover, that autonomous feminist platforms have exhibited
both vigour and resilience in the Egyptian context. Her discussion of
Islamist women also suggests that women do not merely submit to the
strictures of religious fundamentalism as interpreted by men but are active
participants with their own versions of the ways in which Islam might
further their gender interests. Also commenting on the assertive element of
choice exercised by women taking up the veil in Egypt, el-Guindy states;
'Therefore, a woman in public has a choice between being secular, modern,
feminine and frustratingly passive (hence very vulnerable) or becoming
a *mitdayyinan* (religieuse), hence formidable, untouchable, and silently
threatening. The young women who are now in public and because of social
change will remain there, made the choice and it became a movement.'[34]

If some women's response to their vulnerability is a retreat into the
protective certainties of religious conservatism, others may be motivated to
struggle for a social order in which they no longer need the veil to legitimise
their public presence and to fend off male agression. Women will continue
to be divided over the definition of their gender interests, over the nature
of social arrangements which best serve them and over their visions of a
better society. It is important to remember that their various movements
are responses to similar sets of contradictions, and that their discourses
are circumscribed by the political cultures of their societies. Ultimately,
feminist movements in Muslim societies, as elsewhere, will take their place
alongside the social forces struggling for civil and democratic rights in their
respective countries.

NOTES

1. M. McIntosh, 'The state and the oppression of women' in A. Kuhn
   and A. Wolpe (eds), *Feminism and Materialism* (London: Routledge
   and Kegan Paul, 1978); E. Wilson, *Women and the Welfare State*
   (London: Tavistock Publications, 1977); A. Sassoon (ed.), *Women and*

the State (London: Hutchinson, 1987); N. Yuval-Davis and F. Anthias (eds) *Women-Nation-State* (London: Macmillan, 1989); C. Pateman, *The Sexual Contract* (Oxford: Polity Press, 1988).
2. B. F. Stowasser, 'Liberated Equal or Protected Dependent? Contemporary Religious Paradigms on Women's Status in Islam', *Arab Studies Quarterly*, 9 (1987) no. 2: pp. 260–3; Y. Z. Haddad, 'Traditional Affirmations concerning the Role of Women as found in Contemporary Arab Islamic Literature', in J. I. Smith (ed.), *Women in Contemporary Muslim Societies* (New Jersey: Associated University Presses, 1980).
3. N. al-Saadawi, 'Women and Islam' in A. al-Hibri (ed.), *Women and Islam* (Oxford: Pergamon Press, 1982); A. al-Hibri, 'A Study of Islamic Herstory' in *Women and Islam*; F. Hussain and K. Radwan, 'The Islamic Revolution and Women : Quest for the Quranic Model', in F. Hussain (ed.), *Muslim Women* (London: Croom Helm, 1984); F. Mernissi, *Le Harem Politique* (Paris: Albin Michel, 1987).
4. F. A. Sabbah, *Women in the Muslim Unconscious* (New York: Pergamon Press, 1984); M. Ghoussoub, 'Feminism – or the Eternal Masculine – in the Arab World', *New Left Review* 161 (January – February 1987): pp. 3–13.
5. E. Said, *Orientalism* (New York: Pantheon Books, 1978); B. Turner, *Marx and the End of Orientalism* (London: Ithaca Press, 1973). For a more specific discussion of the effects of orientalism on the history of women see, J. E. Tucker, 'Problems in the Historiography of Women in the Middle East: The Case of Nineteenth Century Egypt', *International Journal of Middle East Studies*, 15 (1983) pp. 321–6.
6. For an overview of the state of the art see UNESCO, *Social Science Research and Women in the Arab World* (London: Frances Pinter, 1984).
7. Anthropological monographs constitute an exception to this statement. Comparative attempts to tease out the specificity of Islam are very scarce. See: N. Youssef, *Women and Work in Developing Societies* (Berkeley: University of California Press, 1974); S. Joseph, 'Family, Religion and State: Middle Eastern Models', in R. Randolph, D. Schneider and M. Dias (eds), *Dialectics and Gender: Anthropological Approaches* (Boulder, Co.: Westview Press, 1988).
8. M. Barrett and M. Mckintosh, 'Ethnocentrism and Socialist-Feminist Theory', *Feminist Review* no. 20 (1985) pp. 23–48; D. Kandiyoti, 'Emancipated but Unliberated? Reflections on the Turkish Case', *Feminist Studies* 13 (1987) no. 2, pp. 317–38.
9. K. Jayawardena, *Feminism and Nationalism in the Third World* (London: Zed Press, 1988).
10. On the class background of reformers see: J. R. Cole, 'Feminism, Class and Islam in Turn-of-the-Century Egypt', *International Journal of Middle East Studies*, 13 (1981) pp. 387–407; P. R. Knauss, *The Persistence of Patriarchy: Class, Gender and Ideology in Twentieth Century Algeria* (New York: Praeger, 1984).

11. A. Hourani, *Arabic Thought in the Liberal Age 1798–1939* (London: Oxford University Press, 1962).
12. J. R. Cole, 'Feminism, Class and Islam'.
13. T. Sonn, 'Secularism and National Stability in Islam', *Arab Studies Quarterly*, 9 (1987) no. 3, pp. 284–305.
14. B. Anderson, *Imagined Communities* (London: Verso, 1983).
15. For a critique of this notion, see: A. al-Azmeh, 'Arab Nationalism and Islamism', *Review of Middle East Studies*, 4 (1988) pp. 33–51.
16. F. Mernissi, *Beyond the Veil* (London: Al Saqi Books, 1985).
17. L. Hamamsy, 'The Assertion of Egyptian Identity', in N. S. Hopkins and S. Ibrahim (eds), *Arab Society* (Cairo: The American University in Cairo Press, 1985).
18. N. Hijab, *Womanpower* (Cambridge: Cambridge University Press, 1988).
19. A. Boudhiba, *Sexuality in Islam* (London: Routledge and Kegan Paul, 1985); F. Mernissi, *Beyond the Veil*. L. Ahmed, 'Early Feminist Movements in Turkey and Egypt', in F. Hussain (ed.), *Muslim Women*, N. Hijab, *Womanpower*; M. Hatem, 'The Politics of Sexuality and Gender in Segregated Patriarchal Systems: The case of Eighteenth and Nineteenth Century Egypt', *Feminist Studies*, 12 (1986) no. 2, pp. 251–274.
20. L. Ahmed, 'Early Feminist Movements in Turkey and Egypt', p. 122.
21. D. Kandiyoti, 'Bargaining with Patriarchy', *Gender & Society*, 2 (1988) no. 3, pp. 274–290.
22. J. Donzelot, *The Policing of Families* (London: Hutchinson, 1982); M. Molyneux, 'Family Reform in Socialist States: The Hidden Agenda', *Feminist Review*, 21 (Winter 1985) pp. 47–64.
23. K. Jayawardena, *Feminism and Nationalism in the Third World*, p. 8.
24. S. Joseph, 'Family, Religion and the State: Middle Eastern Models'.
25. J. Goody, *The Development of Family and Marriage in Europe* (Cambridge: Cambridge University Press, 1983).
26. S. Zubaida, *Islam, the People and the State* (London: Routledge, 1988).
27. J. E. Tucker, *Women in Nineteenth Century Egypt* (Cambridge: Cambridge University Press, 1978).
28. M. Charrad, 'State Formation and Women's Rights: The Case of North Africa', paper presented at the conference on Family Law and Change in the Middle East, SSRC-ACLS Joint Committee on the Near and Middle East, Tuxedo, New York, October 1983.
29. F. Mernissi, 'Muslim Women and Fundamentalism', *MERIP Reports* no. 153 (July/August 1988) pp. 8–11; D. Kandiyoti, 'Islam and Patriarchy: A Comparative Perspective' in N. Keddie and B. Baron (eds), *Shifting Boundaries*, forthcoming.
30. F. Mernissi, *Beyond the Veil*, p. 11.
31. N. Keddie, 'Ideology, Society and the State in Post-Colonial Muslim Societies', in F. Halliday and H. Alavi (eds), *State and Ideology in the Middle East and Pakistan* (London: Macmillan, 1988).

32. B. Agarwal, *Structures of Patriarchy* (London: Zed Books, 1988);
    D. Kandiyoti, 'Women and Rural Development Policies: The Changing
    Agenda', *Development and Change*, 21 (1989) pp. 5–22; G. Sen and
    C. Grown, *Development, Crises and Alternative Visions* (New York:
    Monthly Review Press, 1987).

33. For a discussion and taxonomy of different types of women's movements
    see M. Molyneux, 'Female Collective Action, Socialist States and Revo-
    lution: South Yemen and Nicaragua', forthcoming in C. Sutton (ed.),
    Female Collective Action in Comparative Perspective.

34. F. El-Guindy, 'Veiling *Infitah* with Muslim Ethic: Egypt's Contemporary
    Islamic Movement', *Social Problems*, 8 (1981) pp. 465–85.

2 End of Empire: Islam, Nationalism and Women in Turkey

Deniz Kandiyoti

It is commonly conceded that among Muslim nations Turkey distinguishes herself by comprehensive, and as yet unparalleled, reforms with respect to the emancipation of women. These reforms, initiated by Mustafa Kemal Ataturk, the founder of the Turkish Republic, were part of a spate of legislation which amounted to a radical break with Ottoman Islam and its institutions. World War I had resulted in the dismemberment of the defeated empire and the occupation of the Anatolian provinces by the Allied powers. The active hostility of the last Ottoman Sultan-Caliph to Kemal's nationalist struggle in Anatolia, and his collaboration with the Allies, culminated in the abolition of the Sultanate by the Ankara government in 1922. The Turkish Republic was proclaimed on 29 October 1923. A few days earlier, on 24 October, the Istanbul head of police had taken an administrative decision desegregating public transport, so that men and women would no longer be separated by curtains or special compartments. Thereafter, a systematic onslaught on Ottoman institutions took place.

In a single day, on 3 March 1924, the Caliphate was abolished, education was made a monopoly of the state, and the *medrese* (religious education) system was terminated. Religious affairs and the administration of the *vakif* (pious foundations) were henceforth allocated to directorates attached to the office of the prime minister. This was followed by the elimination of religious courts in April of the same year. The *tarikats* (mystic religious orders) were banned in 1925. The constitutional provision accepting Islam as the religion of the state was finally abrogated in 1928.

It is against this background that the Turkish Civil Code, inspired by and almost identical to the Swiss Civil Code, was adopted in 1926. Unlike previous attempts at legislative reform which remained mindful of the provisions of the *Shar'iah*, this Code severed all links with it. Polygyny was outlawed and marriage partners were given equal rights to divorce and child custody. Although veiling was not legally banned, a vigorous propaganda campaign led by Ataturk himself exhorted women to adopt modern styles of dress, and dissenters were dealt with severely.[1] The enfranchisement of women followed in two steps: women were granted the vote at local elections in 1930 and at the national level in 1934. This meant that Turkey could present herself as a democratic nation electing women to parliament at a time when dictatorships held sway over some European states (namely Nazi Germany and Fascist Italy).[2]

Analyses of women's emancipation in Turkey have either tended to focus on the strategic aims of the first Turkish Republic, often stressing their radical break with the past, or to present the republican reforms as the logical culmination of earlier attempts at modernisation and westernisation, starting with the era of Ottoman reforms during the *Tanzimat* period (1839–76). These tendencies both reveal and obscure important aspects of a more complex picture. It is indeed after the *Tanzimat*, a period of intense encroachment by Western powers, that the 'woman question' appeared on the Ottoman political agenda, never to leave it again. The predominantly male polemicists on questions relating to women and the family used the condition of women to express deeper anxieties concerning the cultural integrity of the Ottoman/Muslim polity in the face of Western influence.[3] There have been some critical shifts in discourses on women between the *Tanzimat* and the Republic, however, prefiguring though not fully predictive of the eventual Kemalist position on this issue.

The transformation of the 'woman question' in Turkey between the latter half of the 19th century and the beginning of this century has involved a progressive distancing from Islam as the only form of legitimate discourse on women's emancipation, in favour of a cultural nationalism appropriating such emancipation as an indigenous pattern. The argument I will develop in this chapter is that the current parameters of the 'woman question' were shaped by the historically specific conditions of the rise of Turkish nationalism, starting with the Second Constitutional period (1908–19) and leading to the Kemalist republican regime. Although the tensions between Westernism, nationalism and Islam are by no means resolved and continue to occupy a prominent place in current political debate, I am suggesting that the specificity of the Turkish case with respect to the emancipation of women can be fully appreciated only through an examination of the process of her emergence from an empire based on the multi-ethnic *millet* (national and religious communities) system to the Anatolia-based secular nation-state.

THE REFORM ERA: TANZIMAT 'WESTERNISM' AND ITS CONSEQUENCES

The drive for Ottoman modernisation is commonly associated with the *Tanzimat* period (1839–76) despite earlier attempts at technical and administrative reform in the military sphere. The decline of the empire, signalled by two centuries of military defeat and territorial retreat, called for more radical and comprehensive measures. It is significant that the *Tanzimat* was officially announced on 3 November 1839, at a point when the Ottoman government was threatened by its Egyptian vassal, Mehmed Ali Pasha, whose own reforms made it possible to support a powerful modern army. Resit Pasha, then Minister of Foreign Affairs, saw the introduction of reforms as the only way of both matching Mehmed Ali's efficiency and winning British support against his claims. Capitalising upon Ottoman military misadventures to wrest trade concessions from them was in any case a well-established trend, as in the case of the Commercial Treaty of 1838 which opened up the vast Ottoman market to British manufactures by lifting trade restrictions and tariff walls. The *Tanzimat* edict, penned by Resit Pasha but supported and approved by the British, set the scene for extensive reforms with far-reaching consequences in the fields of administration, legislation and education.

The centralisation of power, which had already started under Mahmud II's reign (1808–39) with the abolition of the Janissary Corps, went further with the elimination of tax farming and the introduction of direct taxation in the context of a reformed provincial administration which limited the power of provincial landowners. The independent position of the *ulema* (the clergy) was undermined both by the introduction of state control of the *vakif*, the religious foundations which procured their most important income, and the inception of secular education in parallel to the *medrese* system. Power was increasingly concentrated in the hands of a new class of Ottoman imperial bureaucrats, who were relatively secure in their position within a secularised bureaucratic hierarchy. In the process of its modernisation the apparatus of the Ottoman state appeared to be more monolothic and authoritarian and more enmeshed in ties of dependence to the West than it had ever been.

The *Tanzimat* reforms have given rise to conflicting evaluations, denounced by some as total capitulation to the West and assumed by others to provide the foundation of all later developments in the creation of a secular state.[4] It seems beyond doubt that the Ottoman empire had suffered serious peripheralisation *vis-à-vis* European powers since the 16th century. It is thus not unreasonable to argue that the reforms had, among other things, the effect of creating a central bureaucracy which could become an instrument for the smooth integration of the Ottoman state into the world economy.[5] Indeed, the official document that ushered in the *Tanzimat*, the *Gulhane Hatt-i Humayunu* (Imperial Rescript of Gulhane) guaranteeing the life, honour and property of all Ottoman subjects regardless of their creed and religion, had as its net effect the extension of legal assurances to non-Muslim and non-Turkish mercantile groups affiliated to European commercial interests.

The new role that the *Tanzimat* bureaucracy had to assume meant that it had to adapt itself to the requirements of modernisation and to the expectations of Western powers in a manner that alienated the groups and classes which were excluded from the new 'modernised' structures (such as craftsmen, artisans, the urban lower middle class, petty civil servants and the lower ranks of the *ulema*). These classes were to become the focus of a resistance which often took Islamic forms. Thus the *Tanzimat* reforms were to create deep cleavages in Ottoman society, reflected both at the institutional level and at that of culture more generally.

The movement of the Young Ottomans, among whom were Şinasi, Ziya Pasha, Namik Kemal and Ali Suavi, emerged as a reaction to the authoritarianism, extreme Westernism and superficiality of *Tanzimat* policies. Their ideology involved a complex blend of Ottoman nationalism, Islamism and constitutionalism.[6] Influenced by European ideas of nationalism and liberalism, they were none the less conservatives attempting to achieve a synthesis between Western notions of 'progress' and a harmonious Islamic state. It is not uncommon, if slightly misleading, to find prominent Young Ottomans cited as the earliest advocates of women's emancipation, preparing the ground for later reforms. Şinasi's satirical play *Şair Evlenmesi* (The Poet's Wedding) written in 1859 is considered one of the earliest criticisms of the arranged marriage system. Namik Kemal was also vocal in his criticisms of the more oppressive and unjust aspects of marriage and family life, as well as women's overall position in society. He used the newpaper he edited, *Ibret*, to call for reforms in women's education and denounce the state of ignorance in which Ottoman women were kept. His novels *Intibah* (The Awakening) and *Zavalli Çocuk* (Poor Child) also offer critical commentaries on women's condition. It is worth noting that the most ardent reformists of women's condition were at the same time the most outspoken critics of *Tanzimat* 'Westernism'. Mardin suggests that the cultural tensions between a Western-oriented bureaucratic elite and popular classes committed to and protected by Ottoman communitarian conservatism were worked through in the post-*Tanzimat* novel, via biting satires of Western-struck upper-class males.[7] Those same authors, such as Ahmed Mithat Efendi, strongly advocated changes in women's position and denounced the practices of forced marriage, concubinage and polygamy as 'social ills'. Ahmet Mithat's works, *Diplomali Kiz* (The Girl with a Diploma), *Felsefe-i Zenan* (Women's Philosophy), *Teehhül* (Marriage) and *Eyvah* (Alas) touch upon a wide range of such concerns.

I have argued elsewhere[8] that the male reformers of the time found the plight of women a powerful vehicle for the expression of their own restiveness with social conventions they found particularly stultifying and archaic. 'Modern' men often felt alienated from Ottoman patriarchal structures which curtailed their own freedom considerably, even though women were the more obvious victims of the system.[9] They thus made a case for the emancipation of women in moralistic, sentimental and 'civisational' terms, whilst at the same time condemning and bemoaning the moral decay occasioned by Western influences in Ottoman society. However, as Mardin points out, the unity established with the masses of people against Western-struck male behaviour was undermined when women's independence was at stake. Conservatism in this area had long been a hallmark of popular resistance and figured prominently in all protests against innovation.[10] As will become clearer in the discussion of ideological currents during the Second Constitutional period (1908–19), later debates on women would both reveal and create bitter cleavages among the Ottoman elite itself, when the condition of women became more self-consciously identified as the touchstone of Ottoman cultural 'integrity' or 'backwardness', as the case might be.

The early reformers inscribed themselves on the one hand in a modernist Islamic perspective, arguing that their demands were compatible with the dictates of Islam, and on the other in an instrumentalist framework suggesting that changes in women's condition would benefit the 'health' of society as a whole. In contrast to the feminist-nationalist stance of later periods, Islam was the only legitimate terrain in which issues relating to women could be debated.

Fatma Aliye Hanim, the first Ottoman woman to engage in such debates, was the daughter of Cevdet Pasha, an enlightened member of the *ulema* and main author of the *Mecelle*, the Ottoman Civic Code. As a member of the upper class, she had benefited from private education and even taught herself French.[11] She distinguished herself through a polemic with the conservative Mahmud Esad Efendi who had published a series of articles in favour of polygyny, defending it both as a law of nature and as an article of the *Shar'iah*. She exposed her own views in a book entitled *Nisvan-i Islam* (Muslim Women) in 1891, which predates Qasim Amin's influential *Tahrir-i al Mara* (Liberation of Women) and foreshadows many of his arguments. It is also significant that the longest lived woman's weekly of the time, *Hanimlara Mahsus Gazete* (The Ladies' Own Gazette), to which Fatma Aliye Hanim was an important contributor, proclaimed on its title page that it served three principles: being a good mother, a good wife, and a good Muslim.

However, the very fact that conservatives of Mahmud Esad's persuasion had to adopt a defensive tone and rally around polygyny attested to the inroads made by new ideas in Ottoman society and to the growing strength of the constituency upholding them. In that sense, the *Tanzimat* may be said to have ushered in a painful and often bitter process of negotiation and compromise between the pressures of foreign powers, the requirements of modernity as perceived by different sections of the Ottoman elite, and the resistance of those most threatened by changes in the Ottoman order.

Ottoman legislative reforms are indicative of these tensions. The vizier Ali Pasha was in favour of the wholesale adoption of the 1804 French Civic Code. This initiative was blocked by the *ulema* and Cevdet Pasha used his scholarly authority to propose a modern Ottoman code based on the principles of the Hanefi school of Islamic law (*fiq' h*). A commission headed by Cevdet Pasha produced the *Mecelle-i Ahkami Adliyye*, a home-grown Ottoman Civic Code. However, a religious opposition headed by the *Sheyh-ul Islam* (chief canonical functionary of the empire) persuaded Abdulhamid II to disband the commission in 1888 once it had completed its work on commercial transactions, thereby blocking any further legislation in the fields of the family and inheritance. The religious authorities were claiming the sphere of personal status as their own, and were doing so in an environment where their overall influence had been shrinking. This led to a dual juridical system whereby secular courts (*mahkeme-i nizamiye*) operated under the aegis of the Ministry of Justice while religious courts (*mahkeme-i şer'iyye*) remained under the jurisdiction of the *Sheyh-ul Islam*. It was not until 1917 that a new Family Law would be put on the agenda and that the total monopoly of religious authorities in this area would be challenged. This coincided, as we shall later see, with a period when the Ottoman state was for the first time formulating a family policy in line with the nationalist, regenerative ideals of the Committee for Union and Progress.

For all the polemics around issues concerning women and the family, actual legislative advances had been relatively modest. The 1858 Land Law (*Arazi Kanunu*) extended and consolidated women's rights of inheritance. The imperial decrees banning female slavery (issued in 1854 for white slaves and 1857 for blacks) became effective with the ratification of international treaties in 1880 and 1890. Reforms in the educational

field were more significant. The Medical School started training local
midwives under the direction of European instructresses from 1842,
secondary schooling for girls (*[Kiz Rüştiyeleri*) started in 1858, a
girls' vocational school (*Kiz Sanayi Mektebi*) was opened in 1869 and
a women's teacher-training college (*Dar-ul Muallimat*) started operating
in 1870. Taşkiran in her evaluation of these initiatives comments on the
pressures resulting from the strict segregation of the sexes and the scarcity
of trained female teachers.[12] These constituted an important advance if
one considers that apart from private tutoring for upper-class women,
frequently involving foreign governesses, there were no provisions at all
for women's education beyond the barest rudiments of religious instruction
at the primary level.[13]

It is a matter of some debate whether the thirty-year absolutist rule of
Abdulhamit II and its Islamist backlash, following an abortive attempt at
constitutional monarchy (1876–8), actually held in check or reversed the
progress achieved. There was certainly a higher level of police interference
and surveillance over women's movements as well as attire (such as the
banning of the diaphanous *feradje* in favour of the black *charshaf*).[14]
Women's publications continued despite severe censorship (as in the case
of Fatma Aliye Hanim's book, *Nisvan-i Islam*, mentioned earlier) and so
did their education. However, some foreign observers commenting on the
sorry state of women's education under the Hamidian regime describe the
Dar-ul Muallimat (teachers' training college) in the following terms: 'It
was under the direction of a sleepy old Effendi who spent his time
lying on a divan in his office smoking a narghilé, and drinking coffee;
and classes were conducted when it was thought best, always with the
attempt not to place too great a strain on the nervous system and delicate
organisms of youth and beauty'.[15] This remark was a prelude to their
eulogy of state sponsored 'feminism' during the Second Constitutional
Period (1908–19).

WOMEN UNDER THE YOUNG TURKS: THE ERA OF PATRIOTIC
FEMINISM

The overthrow of Abdulhamit's autocratic regime in 1908 by the Young
Turks, members of the Committee of Union and Progress (hereafter
referred to as CUP) who had been fighting for a return to Constitutional
rule, was followed by a period of intense social upheaval and ideological
ferment. Women's rights issues were no exception. Impressed by the
changes she witnessed and by the policies of the CUP, a visiting

Englishwoman, Grace Ellison was to exclaim: 'A Turkish Feminist Government! To Western Europe this sounds strange.'[16] Tunaya lists no less than a dozen women's associations founded between 1908 and 1916, ranging from primarily philanthropic organisations to those more explicitly committed to struggle for women's rights.[17] Among these, *Teali-i Nisvan Cemiyeti* (The Society for the Elevation of Women) founded in 1908 by Halide Edib had links with the British suffragette movement (and required a knowledge of English from its members). The *Müdafaa-i Hukuk-i Nisvan Cemiyeti* (The Society for the Defence of Women's Rights) was the best known and most militant, fighting to secure women's access to paid professions.[18] New journals such as *Mahasin, Kadin* (Woman) and *Kadinlar Dünyasi* (Woman's World) played an active role in shaping public opinion.

It seems pertinent to reflect on the prominence of women's rights issues at this particular juncture. At least three sets of new influences appear to have been at work: the rise of Turkism as a dominant ideology among the intellectual currents of the Second Constitutional Period, the requirements of a war economy spanning the period from the Balkan War (1912) to the end of World War I, and their joint effects on the social and economic policies of the CUP.

The *Tanzimat* reforms which aimed at a consolidation of the empire signally failed to stem the tide of nationalism in the Christian Balkan provinces, whilst strengthening the hand of local Christian merchants who were the preferred trading partners of European powers in Ottoman lands. In Berkes' terms, the more Westernisation proceeded the more Turks felt excluded from it.[19] The Committee for Union and Progress who were the architects of the 1908 revolution did not delay in seeing that the Ottoman nationalism which united Muslim and non-Muslim subjects in a bid for 'freedom' during the overthrow of Abdulhamit's despotic rule would not arrest the progress of the secessionist movements in the ethnically heterogenous provinces. Toprak suggests that Turkish nationalism which was born from the liberal currents of 1908 also represented a reaction against such liberalism, especially against the economic liberalism which had cost the Muslim artisan so dear.[20]

The search for alternatives to liberalism produced a major shift in thinking about the economy and society. The dominant ideology in the CUP represented a blend of solidarism emanating from French corporatist thought and Ottoman guild traditions.[21] Throughout the war years the CUP consistently struggled to create a middle class consisting of Turkish-Muslim entrepreneurs, persistently stressing the ethnic dimension of the problem and favouring Muslim over non-Muslim. The same effort was apparent in the creation of trained local cadres. For instance, in 1916 a law was passed imposing Turkish as the language of correspondence on all foreign firms operating in the Ottoman empire. These firms, which had previously employed foreigners, now had the choice of either folding up or recruiting local employees. Meanwhile vocational evening classes, especially on commerce and banking, were started by CUP Clubs in an attempt to create skilled cadres that were competent in these fields. The University opened its doors to women in 1914 and the demand was such that the Ministry of Education instituted a women's section (*Inas Dar-ul-fununu*) which soon afterwards merged with the men's classes (producing irate reactions from traditionalist circles, in particular the *Sheyh-ul Islam* Mustafa Sabri). In this context, special business classes for women were also started when the Advanced School for Commerce opened a section for women, which was so popular that a second one soon had to be added.[22] The necessities of general mobilisation carved out a new space for women. Later, in the Republican period, women would be called upon to replenish the ranks of trained professional cadres.[23] In the Second Constitutional Period, it was primarily the war effort that drew them out into the workforce in unprecedented numbers.[24]

WOMEN AND WAR

Already during the Balkan War middle-class women were involved in social welfare activities, bringing relief to war orphans and attending to the wounded. The women's branch of the Red Crescent Society had started training Turkish nurses. Halide Edib's memoirs convey a powerful impression of the mood of shock and despondency that shook the nation as invalids and war refugees started flocking into Istanbul.[25] One also senses that women's 'patriotic' activities legitimised both their greater mobility and their visibility.

It was during World War I that the massive loss of male labour to the front created a demand for women's labour. The growth of female employment did not remain confined to white-collar jobs in post offices, banks, municipal services and hospitals but involved attempts at wider mobilisation throughout the Anatolian provinces. A law passed in 1915 by the Ministry of Trade instituted a form of mandatory employment which rapidly swelled the ranks of women workers.[26] Women volunteers were organised into workers' platoons to help the army with support services. In the agrarian sector, the Fourth Army (Syria and Palestine) formed Women Workers' Brigades. The Islamic Association for the Employment of Ottoman Women was founded in 1916 and aimed at promoting the employment of women under conditions that ensured them an 'honest' living. The first pro-natalist policies of the empire had the employees of the Association as their target. Marriage was made mandatory for women by the age of 21 and for men by 25, weddings were generously sponsored and financial incentives offered for the birth of each child.[27]

Whilst objective conditions may have stimulated an increased female presence in the labour force, it is clear that this was viewed with considerable ambivalence. Some accommodations had to be made, as evidenced by the imperial decree issued in 1915 allowing women to discard the veil during office hours. However, they were apparently often forced by the police to return home if their skirts were shorter than the officially prescribed length.[28] Indeed, the right to go out into the streets and to places of entertainment, and a limited right to work with freedom from police harassment were among the demands voiced by the women's press of the time, demands which were clearly very modest by later standards. There is little doubt that this period must have been fraught with confusion and contradictions. An announcement posted on Istanbul walls by the police in September 1917 gives us some indication of this:

In the last few months shameful fashions are being seen in the streets of the Capital. All Muslim women are called upon to lengthen their skirts, refrain from wearing corsets and wear a thick *charshaf*. A maximum of two days is allowed to abide by the orders of this proclamation.

This announcement was the subject of such indignation and furore that higher level administrators were forced to rebuke their over-zealous subordinates and retract the order. The new announcement read as follows:

The General Directorate regrets that old and retrograde women were able to induce a subaltern employee to publicise an announcement ordering Muslim women to go back to old fashions. We announce that the previous orders are null and void.[29]

One has to consider that the CUP itself was divided and that 1917 was the year when, in the midst of war, a committee was set up to discuss the suitable length for women's skirts. Enver Pasha, who held particularly conservative views, actually removed one of his commanders in the Dardanelles on the grounds that his daughters were seen sunning themselves on the Bosphorus.[30] The earlier progressive leanings of the

CUP were to prove short-lived, as they instituted their own autocracy. Significantly, a woman's periodical would proclaim on the fifth anniversary of the Constitution that it was 'Men's National Celebration Day', giving voice to women's dashed hopes.[31]

WOMEN AND THE IDEOLOGICAL CURRENTS OF THE SECOND CONSTITUTIONAL PERIOD

During the Second Constitutional Period, debates on women and the family became more tightly and self-consciously integrated into ideological positions representing different recipes for salvaging the floundering empire. These can be identified as the Islamist, Westernist and Turkist positions.

The Islamists, despite their internal differences, thought that the reasons for imperial decline had to be sought in the subversion and abandonment of Islamic institutions and laws.[32] They advocated a return to the unadulterated application of the *Shari'ah* and their political solution revolved around the idea of a pan-Islamic empire consolidated around the institution of the Caliphate. Although the adoption of Western technology and material progress were deemed to be inevitable, Western culture must on no account be allowed to contaminate the values of Islam. The position of women represented the touchstone of such contamination, and discussions on veiling, polygyny and divorce became bitterly political. The main proponents of conservative views on women among the *ulema* were Mustafa Sabri and Musa Kazim (both of whom held the office of *Sheyh-ul Islam*) who used the periodical *Beyan-ul Haq* as a platform. Musa Kazim exhorted the government to take punitive measures against the violators of the Islamic rules of veiling (*tesettur*). Mustafa Sabri emphatically rejected the views of apologists who maintained that women did not hold an inferior status in Islam:'Muslim religion does not need such lying and ignorant defenders . . . To distort the truth and attempt to reconcile the views of the adversary, and thereby approve such views, is not a service to Islam but treason'.[33] The initially more reformist Islamist periodical *Sirat-i Mustakim* hardened its position and reappeared under the name *Sebilürreşat*. The poet Mehmet Akif and Sait Halim Pasha were among the most prominent figures of this tendency. Mehmed Akif joined the polemic on women by translating Farid Wajdi's refutation of Qasim Amin's influential *Tahrir-al Mara*. This translation was first serialised in *Sirat-i Mustakim* and then published in book form under the title *Müslüman Kadini* (The Muslim Woman).[34] Akif's short preface makes his sympathy to Farid Wajdi quite clear. Sait Halim's views were equally uncompromising.

The Westernists were also heterogenous in their views, but united around certain major themes. Foremost among these was the conviction that the superiority of the West did not reside simply in its advanced technology but also in its rationalistic and positivistic outlook, which was free of the shackles of religious obscurantism and stifling superstitions. To varying degrees, they held Islam responsible for both obscurantism and what they saw as the debased condition of women, which they considered as one of the major symptoms of Ottoman backwardness. Of these, Celal Nuri Ileri, the author of *Kadinlarimiz* (Our Women) and Halil Hamit, author of *Islamiyette Feminizm* (Feminism in Islam) held moderate views, arguing that Islam was in no way inimical to the equality of women. Salahattin Asim's *Türk Kadinliğinin Tereddisi* (The Degeneration of Turkish Womanhood) takes a much more radical and uncompromising stance. Asim held religion directly responsible for what he considered as the progressive degeneration of Turkish womanhood into an abject state of subjection. He went as far as advocating a complete change in family laws. The poet Tevfik Fikret was equally radical in his denunciation of Islam and preached humanistic ideals. The combination of Western positivism, humanitarian ideals and respect for Islam finds one of its most contradictory expressions in the person of Abdullah Cevdet. His defence of women's rights was more indebted to biological materialism and the ideas of Ribot, a French disciple of Darwinism, than to humanitarian considerations. He took a frankly eugenistic position by claiming that, whatever the social extraction of their father, children born of enslaved women would in time lead to the degeneration of the race.[35] The rehabilitation of the mothers of the nation could thus be defended on 'scientific' grounds.

It is when the Turkists entered the fray, under their leading ideologue Ziya Gökalp, that the debates on women and the family really came to a head. Berkes comments that the Turkist theses raised such a tempest among the Islamists that 'their opposition to the Westernists assumed the appearance of a summer breeze'.[36] The Turkism of the Second Constitutional Period represented an attempt at recuperating a sense of national identity which did not rest solely on Islam. This was in many ways a fraught enterprise. As Berkes points out, the Turks were the last to achieve a sense of nationality in the whole Ottoman formation.[37] In the Ottoman context, Turkish nationalism could be perceived as divisive in a situation where other ethnic minorities were restive, and certainly found no favour among the Islamists, for whom the notion of a Turkish nation constituted a threat to the Islamic *umma*.[38]

The nationalism of the Turkish-Tatar intelligentsia in tsarist Russia provided the Turkist movement not only with ideas but also with its

cadres when its leading ideologues emigrated to the Ottoman empire.[39]
The earlier national awakening of Turks in Russia was both a reaction
to the rising oppression of nationalities due to pan-Slavic ideology, and a
reflection of the fact that the Turkish-Tatar bourgeoisie had matured to the
point of evolving its own nationalist ideals. Soon after the 1908 revolution,
Yusuf Akçura, Ahmet Ağaoğlu, Hüseyinzade Ali and others migrated to
the Ottoman capital. Taking advantage of the freedoms afforded by the
Constitution they set up their own organizations, the most important being
Türk Ocaği (the Turkish Hearth) officially established in 1912, with its
associated journal *Türk Yurdu* (Turkish Homeland). Among its prominent
members were Ziya Gökalp, Mehmet Emin Yurdakul and Halide Edib
Adivar. The nationalism of Ottoman Turkists in the nineteenth century had
remained confined to the cultural arena and had not yet challenged the state
ideologies of Ottomanism and pan-Islamism. By the turn of the century
these ideologies were no longer tenable. The Young Turks, who initially
were quite heterogenous politically, increasingly turned to Turkism as
successive military defeats threatened the empire further. After 1913, they
began to pursue the intensive policy of economic and cultural Turkification
referred to earlier. In time, cleavages were to develop between pan-turkist
nationalism and the non-irredentist Turkish nationalism which gave birth
to Kemalist ideology.[40]

The leading ideologue of this transition period was undoubtedly Ziya
Gökalp (1876–1924), the author of *The Principles of Turkism*. In his
extensive analysis of Gökalp's work and ideas, Parla suggests that Gökalp's
framework fixed the parameters within which mainstream political action
has been conducted in Turkey.[41] This has certainly been the case for the
politics of women's emancipation throughout the period of republican
reforms. Gökalp, who was deeply influenced by Durkheim's sociology,
replaced his notion of society with that of 'nation', emphasising the
national-cultural rather than Islamic sources of morality. His search for
national-cultural roots led him to an ecclectic examination of myths,
legends, archaeological and anthropological evidence of pre-Islamic
Turkic patterns, which he claimed were still alive in popular culture
despite the superimposition of alien civilisational influences, the latter
including those of Islam as well. In his *Principles of Turkism* he spells
out the programmatic implications of Turkism in the fields of language,
aesthetics, morality, law, religion, economy and philisophy.

Gökalp's views on 'moral Turkism', especially on the family and sexual
morality, represent a significant departure from earlier approaches to the
woman question. He suggested that family morality based on ancient
Turkish cultural values included norms such as communal ownership of

land, democracy in the 'parental' family as opposed to the autocracy of the patriarchal family, the equality of men and women, and monogamous marriage. He traces some of the origins of what he labels as 'Turkish feminism' (using these exact words) to the fact that Shamanistic religion and rituals were based on the sacred power vested in women. This made the sexes ritualistically equal, an equality which he thought permeated every aspect of life including the political sphere. The patrilineal and matrilineal principles were equally important, children belonged to both parents, women could control their own independent property, and interestingly, were excellent warriors (amazons, to use Gökalp's own words). This amounted to a pre-Islamic 'golden age' for women which was made much of by subsequent republican feminists. Gökalp was concerned that the Turks had lost their old morality under the impact of alien influences, most notably that of the Persians and Byzantines. The degradation of women's status was one of the symptoms of this loss. A return to cultural authenticity would automatically restore women their lost status and dignity:

When the ideal of Turkish culture was born was it not essential to remember and revitalise the beautiful rules of old Turkish lore? It is for this reason that as soon as the current of Turkism was born in our country the ideal of feminism was born with it. The reason why the Turkists are both populist and feminist is not simply because these ideals are valued in this century; the fact that democracy and feminism were the two main principles of ancient Turkish life is a major factor in this respect.[42]

This position was greeted with a certain amount of scepticism in some quarters. Mehmet Izzet, for instance, suggested that Gökalp's ideas might have been greatly influenced by pragmatic considerations:

At a time when Islamic law was being abolished, improvements in women's position sought and changes in family life along the Western model were being introduced, interpreting this movement as a return to ancient Turkish law and national identity would ensure greater goodwill and sympathy.[43]

Halide Edib is even more candid in her introduction to her book *Turkey Faces West*:

In the recent changes in Turkey, a great many intellectuals believe that there is a tendency to return to our origins. What is more important is that this belief is consciously propagated by a considerable number of intellectuals, partly for the sake of making these changes acceptable to the masses.[44]

On the subject of Gökalp, whom she praises for his feminist leanings, she adds: 'He probably stretched the point, to produce the necessary psychological effect in the minds of the people.'[45] Indeed, with respect to the position of women what might have been rather unpalatable in the form of Western influence gained a new legitimacy when it was recuperated by nationalist discourse.

Although Turkism may have provided a new ideological framework to debate these questions, Unionist family policies must ultimately be understood as an attempt to extend state control and intervention into the private realm of the family. Toprak suggests that this intervention was motivated by the necessity to follow up the political revolution of 1908 by a social revolution that would remould Ottoman society along more egalitarian and nationalistic lines. The Unionists attempted to hasten this transformation by adopting a new family model.[46] Their 'National Family' (*Milli Aile*) was nuclear and monogamous in contrast to the traditional Ottoman patriarchal family. It was not simply emulative of European ways, but rather grounded in the indigenous patterns referred to in our previous discussion of Gökalp. However, the encroachment of the state in this delicate realm was to prove extremely problematic. The compromises apparent in the 1917 Family Code are indicative of some of the difficulties. This law, which is the first written family code in the Muslim world, aimed at completing the task left unfinished by the *Mecelle* (the Ottoman Civic Code) by legislating aspects of personal status which had been totally abandoned to the rulings of religious authorities.[47] Apart from common clauses it had separate sub-sections applying to Muslim, Christian and Jewish subjects, who were still bound by their own religious laws. The intention to provide women with greater security in the conjugal contract was displayed by stipulating the presence of a specially empowered state employee alongside the two witnesses required by the *Shar'iah*, a clear step in the direction of secularisation. Marriages without consent were decreed illegal and divorce was made more difficult by the introduction of a conciliation procedure. However, not only was polygyny not abolished but it was actually legalised, although its practice was made more difficult by stipulating the consent of the first wife. Needless to say this law failed to satisfy either those who wanted to see fundamental changes in a family system considered to be in crisis, or those who saw these changes as clear-cut infractions of Koranic law. Minorities were also discontented with what they considered a curtailment of the power of their own religious authorities. In 1919, at the end of the war, they complained to the Allied forces then occupying Istanbul and obtained a repeal of the clauses pertaining to non-Muslim marriages. This law none the less remained in force until 1926 in Turkey, and until much later in the Ottoman periphery. It represented a timid move towards secularisation under precarious conditions in which a beleaguered central state was ultimately unable to wrest control from religious and communal interests. The secular project of the state, already incipient at this period, was to be realised under the Kemalist republic.

WOMEN AND KEMALISM: THE ADVENT OF CITIZENSHIP

At the end of World War I the Ottoman empire was defeated and the Anatolian provinces were occupied by the Allied powers. The landing of Greek forces in Izmir in May 1919 and the occupation of Istanbul by the British, French and Italian forces unleashed a wave of popular protest in which women took part, not merely as anonymous participants but as public speakers in open-air meetings where they made impassioned calls for the defence of the motherland.[48] One of the few first-hand chronicles of the different phases of the struggle for national liberation is to be found in the second volume of Halide Edib's memoirs, *The Turkish Ordeal*.[49] She was part of the small group who had joined the resistance movement in Anatolia, one of those facing a death sentence issued by the Istanbul government, and awarded the rank of corporal for her services by the Ankara government. Associations for Patriotic Defence started being formed in the Anatolian provinces. Women did not join those directly but set up their own parallel organisations. The Anatolian Women's Association for Patriotic Defence was founded in Sivas in November 1919. Studies of some branches of the Association suggest that the active members were the wives, daughters and sisters of local provincial notables and higher level state employees, who were the main supporters of the nationalist struggle, as well as some teachers and educational administrators. In other words, these were the women of the nascent local middle class which the Second Constitutional Period did so much to nurture.

During the global mobilisation occasioned by the War of National Liberation, peasant women in Anatolia also played critical roles which were celebrated and glorified in public monuments and patriotic rhetoric alike. Yet the coalition of nationalist forces which united behind Mustafa Kemal included men of religion who were going to remain totally inflexible on the question of women's emancipation. The First National Assembly which led the struggle for national independence was dominated by a conservative majority who systematically blocked any attempt to give women equal citizenship rights. More progressive deputies such as Tunali Hilmi Bey were repeatedly attacked and insulted for being 'feminist'. It is indicative that among the indictments directed at the then Minister of Education, Hamdullah Suphi, in 1921, and which led to his resignation, was the fact that he had conducted a mixed-sex teachers' congress.[50] The political opponents of Mustafa Kemal, the so-called Second Group of the First Assembly, were marginalised in the 1923 elections so that the Second Assembly consisted mainly of Kemalist loyalists. Nevertheless, there remained an important nucleus of resistance and procrastination on the question of women's rights. For instance, during the debate on the 1924 Constitution the clause concerning every Turk's right to vote was understood and interpreted by some deputies quite literally to denote every Turk of voting age, regardless of sex. However, the opposition was such that the clause had to be amended to specify 'every male Turk', and even some progressive deputies argued that the time was not ripe for such a drastic change.

An even clearer indication of the prevailing social conservatism can be found in the draft Family Law which was presented to the National Assembly on 27 November 1923 and went through several rounds of debates in 1923 and 1924. The commission in charge of formulating the new law actually cancelled some of the advances gained through the 1917 Code by endorsing polygyny, eliminating the need for consent by the first wife and lowering the legal marriage-age for girls to nine years. This proposal, which was subsequently rejected, was clearly part of the playing out of the opposition between religious and Kemalist forces, an opposition which was finally crushed by the abolition of the Caliphate and the abrogation of the *Shari'ah* in favour of secular codes and laws.[51] Berkes points out that this was also the first instance of a clear divergence between Gökalpist and Kemalist views manifesting itself in the field of legislation.[52] Indeed, while Gökalp had taken an accommodationist stance arguing for the mutual compatibility of Islam, Turkish culture and contemporary civilisation, Kemal had opted for a model that required the total privatisation of religion and the full secularisation of social life. There is little doubt that the woman question became one of the pawns in the Kemalist struggle to liquidate the theocratic remnants of the Ottoman state, a struggle in which male protagonists engaged each other while women by and large remained surprisingly passive onlookers.[53] Not only did women hardly participate in the debates on Family Law but the 'protest' reunion they were practically forced to stage was unable to generate any coherent suggestions. In fact, some progressive men went as far as using newspaper columns to take women to task over their acquiescent posture.[54] Despite other evidence of women's activism, especially later on the question of suffrage, this suggests that the process of mobilisation and co-optation of women into the ideological struggles of the Republic followed a path that was quite distinct from early feminist movements in the West. In the latter, the women's struggle took place against a background where legislation was lagging considerably behind the socio-economic realities of advancing industrialism and a growing labour movement. In Turkey, it was an ideological lever operating on a substantially unchanged economic base, at least as far as women's economic and familial options were concerned.

The decisive actions of Kemalism with respect to women's emancipation were the evacuation of Islam from the legislative and broader institutional sphere, and the inclusion of women into a new notion of 'citizenship' dictated by the transition from a monarchy to a populist republic. While it is by and large correct to suggest that the dominant legitimising discourse for women's emancipation in republican Turkey is a nationalism which has its roots in the Turkism of the Second Constitutional Period, it is also important to acknowledge the ideological break represented by Kemalism. Indeed, Mustafa Kemal was to distance himself from Islam to a much greater extent than Gökalp and other Turkists could ever have envisaged. This was partly possible due to the specific historical circumstances of the struggle for national independence. Although initially most of the Associations for Patriotic Defence had a clearly Islamic outlook and couched the defence of the motherland in religious terms (as a *jihad* or holy war against the infidel), the Istanbul government headed by the Sultan-Caliph had reached an agreement with the occupying powers to stamp out Kemalist resistance. In April 1920 the *Sheyh-ul Islam* issued a *fetva* (canonical proclamation) declaring a holy war against the 'Ankara rebels'. A military court condemned Ataturk and a group of his supporters to death *in absentia*. Civil war and the defection of his forces to the Army of the Caliphate were only averted after the outrage created by the humiliating treaty of Sèvres. Henceforth religious reaction (*irtica*) was to be identified as one of the main enemies of Kemalist nationalism. Moreover, it was not merely the official Islam of the centre, which was seen to have acted treasonably by abetting imperialist designs on Turkey, that Mustafa Kemal condemned. He also took an uncompromising stand on popular Islam. This was the Islam practised by the diverse religious sects, the *tarikats*, which he considered to be centres of obscurantism, superstition, passivity and laziness; in short, representatives of a world-view totally incompatible with his Enlightenment vision of progress, with its twin components of rationalism and positivism. The fact that they were also the focuses of local allegiances and particularisms which the central bureaucracy sought to eliminate in favour of more universalistic principles of association was clearly relevant. Thus, whatever the politically strategic motives informing the timing and content of Kemal's emancipatory reforms, it must be recognised that they fitted in well with his conception of 'civilisation' and with republican notions of citizenship.

It would be a serious misrepresentation, however, to suggest that these were merely the culmination of earlier attempts at Westernisation. In fact, Kemal's attitude to nineteenth century Ottoman statesmen was dismissive if not outright hostile, since he considered them as 'the gendarmes of foreign capital'[55], and their brand of Westernism as a shameful capitulation. He sought to break away from the fetters of an Ottoman past he considered as decadent and to forge a radically new sense of nationhood.

This attempt is nowhere more apparent than in the 'Turkish History Thesis' which was launched in the 1930s. It was Afet Inan, Mustafa Kemal's adoptive daughter, who was entrusted with the task of setting the historical record right on the question of the origins of Anatolian civilisations and of the role of Turks within them. This thesis stated that the Turks' contribution to civilisation had started long before their incorporation into the Ottoman empire and their conversion to Islam. They originated from an urban civilisation in Central Asia from which many subsequent civilisations of Asia Minor and Mesopotamia had sprung. As such, they were the true heirs of their Anatolian homeland and could claim their rightful place in the development of world civilisations. Berktay suggests that the history thesis had an orientation to the Ottoman past which is reminiscent of that of the French revolution to its *ancien régime*.[56] It constituted a break from the 'sacred' histories of Ottoman chroniclers, who presented the empire as a glorious chapter in the history of Islam, and resulted in a 'laicisation' of Turkish history through its integration into the mainstream of world civilisations. It seems quite clear that the early 'romantic phase' of Turkish nationalism was inspired at least in part by a reaction to the extremely negative and ethnocentric views of European historians. Assumptions about the elevated position of women in Central Asiatic societies can be seen to emanate from this 'romantic phase', and have continued to influence republican rhetoric on Turkish women. A case in point is Afet Inan's classic book, *The Emancipation of the Turkish Woman*, in which she devotes an important section to the status of women before the advent of Islam.[57] She suggests that the transition to Islam brought about a decline in the status of Turkish women, although she puts this down to the social customs of Arabs and Persians rather than to Islam *per se*. Thus, the 'new woman' of the republic had ancient and respectable antecedents to invoke.

The 'new woman' of the Kemalist era became an explicit symbol of the break with the past, a symbolism which Mustafa Kemal himself did much to promote. He did so personally through the inclusion of Latife Hanim, his wife, in his public tours, through his relations with his adoptive daughters, one of whom, Afet Inan, became a public figure in her own right, and through his broader endorsement of women's visibility, attested to by photographs of the period ranging from ballroom dancing to official ceremonies. This has had a decisive influence on the socialisation of a whole generation of women who internalised the Kemalist message and forged new identities as professionals as well as patriots.[58]

The extent to which the paternalistic benevolence of the Kemalist era actually fostered or hindered women's political initiatives has never really been explicitly addressed. On the one hand, it is during the first republic that women achieved their highest level of representation in parliament. In the 1937 general election, following the enfranchisement of women in 1934, 18 women deputies were elected, making up 4.5% of the National Assembly. This was an all-time high, never to be equalled again. This level of representation slipped steadily back, especially from 1946 onwards after the transition to a multi-party democracy when the quasi-automatic election of women by an 'enlightened' party vanguard could no longer operate.

On the other hand, there is evidence that women's autonomous political initiatives were actively discouraged. The first such instance was the refusal to authorise the Women's People's Party founded in June 1923. This coincided with the preparations for the foundation of the Republican People's Party and was therefore considered untimely and divisive. Despite women's subsequent appointment of a male figurehead as their party leader, Ankara withheld its consent and advised women to found an association.[59] This led to the creation of the Turkish Women's Federation in 1924, which was disbanded in 1935, a fortnight after it had hosted the 12th Congress of the International Federation of Women. The choice of Istanbul as a venue for the Congress was clearly inspired by the advent of women's suffrage in Turkey and was meant to be an international display and celebration of this momentous event. Indeed, all the foreign delegates, including Huda Sharawi of Egypt, were expressing their gratitude to Atatürk on behalf of world womanhood. How is it possible to explain the self-elimination of the Federation, under directives from Ankara, so soon after this obvious success? Toprak points out that one of the prominent themes of the Congress was peace, and that the Turkish delegates were swayed by the pacifist appeals of the British, American and French delegates who dominated the Congress. (Germany and Italy did not participate.) Turkey had unwittingly been made a tool of allied propaganda through the feminist platform of the Congress. On the eve of a major conflagration in Europe and at a time when defence spending was increasing its share of the national budget, Turkish feminists' stand on disarmament was inopportune, to say the least.[60] The public rationale offered by its president, Latife Bekir, for the closure of the Federation and the dispersal of its assets is none the less quite telling. She claimed that Turkish women had achieved complete equality with full constitutional guarantees, and that the goals of the Federation having thus been totally fulfilled there was no further justification for its continued existence. This ended the brief career of women's sole attempt at political organisation during the single-party era.

Thus, the republican regime opened up an arena for state-sponsored 'feminism', but at one and the same time circumscribed and defined its parameters. It would be quite erroneous to single out the women's movement as a privileged target of state control, since workers' associations and cultural clubs (such as the influential Turkish Hearths referred to earlier) were similarly abolished. This accorded well with the corporatist populism of the single-party era, which negated the existence of class and other sectional interests in the body politic, and saw the party as the representative of the whole nation. This is in no way specific to Turkey, but quite typical of many post-independence and post-revolutionary Third World states. What singles out the Turkish case, especially in the broader context of the Muslim Middle East, is a particular positioning of Islam *vis-à-vis* nationalism, and the important implications deriving from it. This positioning cannot be understood without considering the nature of the Ottoman state and the 'secular' tendencies of Ottoman Islam itself,[61] nor without taking account of the specific characteristics of Turkish republican ideology. Despite the dramatic changes and realignments currently taking place in state and society, the imprint of this formative moment has to be reckoned with.

CONCLUSION

This chapter traces some of the critical transformations that Turkey underwent in the transition from a multi-ethnic empire to a secular nation state. I have attempted to show how the appearance of women, first as objects of political discourse and later as political actors and citizens, was intimately bound up with the changing nature of the Ottoman/Turkish polity.

It is no accident that issues relating to women first became 'ideologised' during the *Tanzimat* period, when pressures to Westernise created a climate of enhanced self-awareness and soul-searching among the Ottoman elite. It is noteworthy that at this stage both progressives and traditionalists invoked Islam as the sole paradigm within which issues pertaining to the position of women could be debated, against a more distant background of Western notions of 'progress'. Few women actually participated in these debates. The first outspoken would-be reformers of women's condition were not the *Tanzimat* Westernists, but the Young Ottomans, whose position could best be defined as a modernist Islamism, indicating an early link between nationalist discourse and concerns over the condition of Turkish womanhood.

It is after the 1908 revolution, which brought the Young Turks to power, that women emerged as activists, forming their own associations and expanding the volume of their publications. Among the complex set of influences at work, I singled out rising Turkish nationalism in the threatened empire, and more specifically the effects of Turkist ideology and CUP's drive to create a national bourgeoisie. Women first demanded their rights under the banner of patriotism, as participants in the war effort and the broader goals of national mobilisation. Turkism as a legitimising ideology of women's emancipation created a discursive space in which nationhood could be invoked alongside Islam. However, the position of women was so closely identified with Ottoman cultural integrity that it continued to elicit conservative reflexes which united men, sometimes across political persuasions, well into the republican period. Indeed, the vagaries of successive legislative exercises with respect to personal status and the family attest to the difficulties of reformative action in this domain until Atatürk severed the gordian knot of the *Sha'riah*.

Women's emancipation under Kemalism was part of a broader political project of nation-building and secularisation. It was a central component of both the liquidation of the 'theocratic remnants' of the Ottoman state and of the establishment of a republican notion of citizenship. It was also the product of a Western cultural orientation, which despite its anti-imperialist rhetoric, inscribed Kemalism within an Enlightenment perspective on progress and civilisation. However, the authoritarian nature of the single-party state and its attempt to harness the 'new woman' to the creation and reproduction of a uniform citizenry aborted the possibility for autonomous women's movements.

A separate history of Turkish women's movements still remains to be written. Establishing the extent to which women of different social extraction colluded with patriarchal definitions of their place in society

(Jalal, this volume), or were able to carve out a relatively autonomous political project (Badran, this volume) would require further meticulous investigation. The more limited objective of this chapter has been to capture, at a time when the Kemalist legacy is being actively contested and reappropriated by different political tendencies, some of the basic ingredients of Turkey's specificity and to promote a better understanding of the baseline from which future women's movements have to operate.

NOTES

1. Caporal mentions trials and short prison sentences for those spreading counterpropoganda. B. Caporal, *Kemalizm ve Kemalızm Sonrasinda Türk Kadını* (Ankara: Türkiye İş Bankası Kültür Yayınları, 1982), p. 649.
2. Tekeli argues that this was one of the strategic goals sought by the Kemalist regime in enfranchising women. S. Tekeli, 'Women in Turkish Politics' in N. Abadan-Unat (ed.), *Women in Turkish Society* (Leiden: E. J. Brill, 1981) pp. 293–310.
3. D. Kandiyoti, 'Women and the Turkish State: Political Actors or Symbolic Pawns?' in N. Yuval-Davis and F. Anthias (eds), *Woman – Nation – State* (London: Macmillan, 1989).
4. N. Berkes, *The Development of Secularism in Turkey* (Toronto: McGill University Press, 1964); S. J. Shaw and E. K. Shaw, *History of the Ottoman Empire and Modern Turkey* (Cambridge: Cambridge University Press, 1977) Vol. 2; B. Lewis, *The Emergence of Modern Turkey* (London: Oxford University Press, 1961); T. Timur, *Türk Devrimi: Anlamı ve Felsefi Temeli* (Ankara: Sevinç Matbaası, 1968); I. Ortaylı, *Imparatorluğun En Uzun Yüzyılı* (Istanbul: Hil Yayın, 1983).
5. H. Inan, 'Osmanli Tarihi ve Dünya Sistemi: Bir Değerlendirme,' *Toplum ve Bilim*, 23 (1983) pp. 9–39. For a broader discussion of the different phases of the articulation between state, bureaucracy and society see Ç. Keyder, 'Class and State in the Transformation of Modern Turkey' in F. Halliday and H. Allavi (eds), *State and Ideology in the Middle East and Pakistan* (London: Macmillan, 1988).
6. Ş. Mardin, *The Genesis of Young Ottoman Thought* (Princeton: Princeton University Press, 1962).
7. Ş. Mardin, 'Superwesternization in Urban Life in the Ottoman Empire in the last quarter of the 19th century' in P. Benedict and E. Tumertekin (eds), *Turkey: Geographical and Social Perspectives* (Leiden: E. J. Brill, 1974).
8. D. Kandiyoti, 'Slave girls, Temptresses and Comrades: Images of Women in the Turkish Novel', *Feminist Issues*, 8 (1988) no. 1, pp. 33–50.
9. This alienation appears as a persistent theme in literary works. It is expressed eloquently by Ömer Seyfettin who ridicules the tight controls

imposed on the younger generation and bemoans the absence of female companionship and romantic love in Turkish men's lives: 'Here in our surroundings, the surroundings of the Turks, love is strictly forbidden. It is as forbidden as an infernal machine, a bomb, a box of dynamite . . . ' *Aşk Dalgası* (Istanbul: Bilgi Yayınevi, 1964), p. 52.

10. Ş. Mardin, 'Superwesternisation in Urban Life . . . ', p. 442.
11. E. Işın, 'Tanzimat, Kadın ve Gündelik Hayat', *Tarih ve Toplum*, 51 (1988) pp. 150–55.
12. T. Taşkıran, *Cumhuriyetin 50. Yılında Türk Kadın Haklari* (Ankara: Başbakanlık Basimevı, 1973).
13. For further details on women's education see F. Davis, *The Ottoman Lady: A Social History 1718–1918* (London: Greenwood Press, 1986).
14. On state control over Ottoman women's attire see N. Seni, 'Ville Ottomane et Représentation du Corps Feminin', *Les Temps Modernes* no. 456–7 (1984) pp. 66–95.
15. E. D. Ellis and F. Palmer, 'The Feminist Movement in Turkey' *Contemporary Review*, 105 (January–June 1914) p. 859.
16. G. Ellison, *An Englishwoman in a Turkish Harem* (London: Methuen, 1915) p. 81.
17. T. Z. Tunaya, *Türkiyede Siyasi Partiler*, vol. 1 (Istanbul: Hürriyet Vakfı Yayınları, 1984).
18. As in the case of Bedriye Osman, who applied to become an employee of the Telephone Company but was not hired. This was made a matter of public debate by the Society and led to the backing down of the Company, which from then on had to employ women. T. Z. Tunaya, *Türkiyede Siyasi Partiler*, p. 482.
19. N. Berkes, *Batıcılık, Ulusçuluk ve Toplumsal Devrimler* (Istanbul: Yön Yayınları, 1965).
20. Z. Toprak, *Türkiyede Milli Iktisat (1908–1918)* (Ankara: Yurt Yayınları, 1982).
21. Z. Toprak, 'Türkiyede Korporatizmin Doğusu', *Toplum ve Bilim*, 12 (1980) pp. 41–9.
22. Z. Toprak, *Türkiyede Milli Iktisat*, p. 83.
23. A. Öncü, 'Turkish Women in the Professions: Why so Many?' in *Women in Turkish Society*, pp. 81–193.
24. S. Tekeli, *Kadınlar ve Siyasal Toplumsal Hayat* (Istanbul: Birikim Yayınları, 1982), p. 198; N. Abadan-Unat, 'Social Change and Turkish Women' in *Women in Turkish Society*, p. 8.
25. H. Edib, *The Memoirs of Halide Edib* (London: John Murray, 1926).
26. A new stocking factory set up in Urfa employed 1000 women. In the Izmir, Ankara, Sivas and Konya provinces, 4780 women were employed in carpet production. In Aydin 11 000 and in Kütahya, Eskisehir and Karahisar 1550 were employed in textile manufacture. In Diyarbakir they replaced men at 1000 looms.
27. Z. Toprak, *Türkiyede Milli Iktisat*, 317–18; Z. Toprak, 'Osmanlı

Kadınları Çaliştırma Cemiyeti, Kadın Askerler ve Milli Aile', *Tarih ve Toplum*, 51 (March 1988) pp. 162–6.

28. E. Yener, 'Eski Anakara Kıyafetleri ve Eski Giyiniş Tarzları', *Dil, Tarih ve Coğrafya Fakültesi Dergisi* 3 (1955) no. 13, pp. 123–9.
29. J. Melia, *Mustafa Kemal ou la Rénovation de la Turquie* (Paris), 1929, quoted in B. Caporal *Kemalizmde ve Kemalizm Sonrasinda Türk Kadini*, pp. 147–8.
30. F. Rifki Atay, *Bariş Yılları* quoted in Ş. Mardin, 'Superwesternization in Urban Life', pp. 433–4.
31. T. Taşkıran, *Cumhuriyetin 50. Yılında*, p. 38.
32. T. Z. Tunaya, *Islamcılık Cereyanı* (Istanbul: Baha Matbaası, 1962).
33. Mustafa Sabri, *Mes'eleler* (Istanbul: Sebil Yayınevi, 1984; 2nd edition), p. 95.
34. It has gone into several printings in modern Turkish. See M. F. Vecdi (translator Mehmet Akif Ersoy), *Müslüman Kadını* (Istanbul: Sinan Yayınevı, 1982; 3rd edition, first published in 1909).
35. M. S. Hanioğlu, *Doktor Abdullah Cevdet ve Dönemi* (Istanbul: Üçdal Neşriyat, 1981).
36. N. Berkes, *The Development of Secularism*, p. 390.
37. N. Berkes, *Batıcılık, Ulusçuluk ve Toplumsal Devrimler*, pp. 52–3. Also on this question see W. H. Hadded 'Nationalism in the Ottoman Empire' in W. H. Haddad and W. L. Ochsenwald (eds), *Nationalism in a non-National State: The Dissolution of the Ottoman Empire* (Columbus: Ohio State University Press, 1977).
38. For a discussion of the tensions between Islamism and nationalism see T. Z. Tunaya, *Islamcılık Cereyani*, pp. 77–86.
39. For details see F. Georgeon, *Aux Origines du Nationalisme Turc: Yusuf Akçura (1876–1935)* (Paris: Editions ADPF, 1980); D. Kushner, *The Rise of Turkish Nationalism (1876–1908)* (London: Frank Cass & Co. Ltd., 1977); T. Timur, 'The Ottoman Heritage' in I. C. Schick and E. A. Tonak (eds), *Turkey in Transition: New Perspectives* (New York, Oxford: Oxford University Press, 1987).
40. J. Landau, *Pan-Turkism in Turkey: A Study in Irredentism* (London: Hurst & Co. Ltd., 1981).
41. T. Parla, *The Social and Political Thought of Ziya Gökalp 1876–1924* (Leiden: E. J. Brill, 1985).
42. Z. Gökalp, *Türkçülüğün Esasları* (Istanbul: Inkilap ve Aka Kitabevleri, 1978), p. 148.
43. Mehmet Izzet quoted in M. Eröz, *Türk Ailesi* (Istanbul: Milli Eğitim Basımevi, 1977), p. 13.
44. Halide Edib, *Turkey Faces West* (New Haven: Yale University Press, 1930).
45. Ibid., p. 213.
46. Z. Toprak, 'The Family, Feminism and the State during the Young Turk period, 1908–1918', Paper presented at the 'Workshop on Turkish Family and Domestic Organisation', New York, 23–35 April 1986.

47. Z. F. Fındıkoğlu, *Essai sur la Transformation du Code Familial en Turquie* (Paris: Editions Berger-Levrault, 1936).
48. T. Taşkıran, *Cumhuriyetin 50. Yılında*, pp. 68–73.
49. Halide Edib, *The Turkish Ordeal* (London: John Murray, 1928) was first published in English while she was in political exile. It was not translated into Turkish until much later, since it was at variance on many points with the 'official' account of this period which is mainly based on Mustafa Kemal's own memoirs and speeches. It was first serialised in a periodical in 1959–60, and published in book form in 1962.
50. T. Taşkıran, *Cumhuriyetin 50. Yılında*, pp. 91–100.
51. P. Benedict, 'Başlik Parası ve Mehr' in A. Güriz and P. Benedict (eds), *Türk Hukuku ve Toplumu Üzerinde İncelemeler* (Ankara: Sevinç Matbaası, 1974), p. 19.
52. N. Berkes, *Türkiyede Cağdaşlaşma* (Istanbul: Doğu-Bati Yayinlari, 1978), p. 519.
53. T. Taşkıran, *Cumhuriyetin 50. Yılında*, pp. 106–109.
54. Such as Necmettin Sadak, 'Hanımlarimiz ve Aile Hukuku Karanamesi', *Akşam* 21 January 1924, quoted in Taşkıran, *Cumhuriyetin 50. Yılında*, p. 109. Sadak wrote an inflammatory article suggesting that the republic was insulting women with its laws while they were being incomprehensibly passive.
55. G. Ökçün, *Türkiye İktisat Kongresi – 1923 Izmiri: Haberler, Belgeler, Yorumlar* (Ankara: Ankara Universitesi Siyasal Bilgiler Fakültesi Yayınlari, 1968).
56. H. Berktay, *Cumhuriyet İdeolojisi ve Fuat Köprülü* (Istanbul: Kaynak Yayınlari, 1983).
57. Afet Inan, *The Emancipation of the Turkish Woman* (Paris: UNESCO, 1962).
58. A. Durakbaşa, *The Formation of 'Kemalist Female Identity': A Historical-Cultural Perspective*, unpublished M. A. thesis, Istanbul: Bogazici University, 1987.
59. Z. Toprak, 'Halk Firkasindan Önce Kurulan Parti: Kadınlar Halk Fırkası', *Tarih ve Toplum* 51 (March 1988) pp. 30–31.
60. Z. Toprak, '1935 Istanbul Uluslararası 'Feminizm Kongresi' ve Barış', *Düşün* (March 1986) pp. 24–9.
61. Ş. Mardin, 'Turkey: Islam and Westernization' in C. Caldarola (ed.), *Religion and Societies* (Berlin: Mouton, 1982).

3 Hazards of Modernity and Morality: Women, State and Ideology in Contemporary Iran

Afsaneh Najmabadi

INTRODUCTION

There are two periods in modern Iranian history in which the terms of the 'woman question' *(mas'ale-ye zan)* have been shaped as a central part of an emerging climate of political ideas and social concerns. The first, in the late-nineteenth/early-twentieth century, ushered in the era of 'modernity' and 'progress', an era during which, despite an underlying animosity towards European intrusion, Europe's social and political achievements provided the model for modernity and progress. It was generally thought the intrusion itself could be resisted through becoming like the European Other. The 'woman question', meaning the now problematic place of women in a modern society, was for the first time posed in that context. The second period, from the mid-1960s to the present time, marks the rejection of the previous paradigm and the creation, reappropriation, and redefinition of a new Islamic political alternative.[1]

During the transition between these two powerful paradigms, Iran went through two important phases of societal change: Reza Shah's state-building years (1926–41) and Mohammad Reza Shah's transformative years (1963–78).

In order to understand the changing situation of women in twentieth-century Iran, we need to investigate the nature of the ideas that went into the making of each of the two political paradigms, on the one hand, and of the transition period, on the other, to concentrate on what kind of state and society was being built under the rule of each Pahlavi shah. Post-1979 Iran is experiencing a unique situation in which a very strong social transformative experiment has been ushered in by a revolution that above all embodied the new Islamic paradigm. It, therefore, has witnessed a dynamic interaction between the exigencies of the two.

The above proposition does not deny elements of continuity between the two periods. Indeed without important elements of continuity and common boundaries such a colossal shift would be impossible for any society. To anticipate a future argument, the shift in the image of the ideal woman from 'modern-yet-modest' at the turn of this century to 'Islamic-thus-modest' within the present paradigm could only take place because a crucial shared social boundary regarding modesty was retained between the two. Yet in order to understand the workings of that common boundary, we need to differentiate and investigate the significance of each paradigm.

Nor does the proposition imply that the Pahlavi period was void of any new ideas. The present essay, as it is devoted to the state-building and transformative periods, will investigate the nature of ideas and models that provided the guidelines for these periods of change. None the less, it is important to pull out of the complexities of social change in each period those elements that proved to be more decisively formative in the experience of Iranian society.

Over the past decade a rapidly expanding body of literature on women in the Middle East has appeared. The massive participation of women in the 1979 Islamic revolution in Iran, the 'prized' place of the 'woman question' within the new Islamic politics, and the general expansion of women's studies have provided a climate of ideas conducive to such focused attention. Within this context, contradictory evaluations of the changes in the status of Middle Eastern women have become commonplace.

In the case of Iran, pro-Pahlavi sources invoke the legislation drawn up under both Pahlavi shahs that expanded women's participation in the social, economic and educational life of the country. They point to the growing participation of women in the workforce, to the increasing rate of literacy and the more prominent profile of women with higher education or in professional careers. They point to the increasing integration of women into political life, evidenced by the granting of female suffrage by the shah in 1963, election of women to the *Majlis* (parliament) and the Senate, their appointment as judges and members of the cabinet. They point to the family reform legislation of the 1960s and 1970s that modified existing laws in favour of women.[2] They point to the appointment of the first Minister of State for Women's Affairs in 1976.[3] They refer to 8 January, 1936 (when Reza Shah decreed compulsory unveiling of women in all public places) as the day of women's liberation in Iran, as a feminist holiday.[4]

The secular critics of the Pahlavis emphasise the limited nature of these reforms, the continued legal, economic and social inequalities of women under the Pahlavis. They argue that these reforms were more cosmetic than substantive, and that the overall economic and social changes under the Pahlavis intensified women's oppression in Iran, except possibly for a small minority of upper-class women. Moreover, they share with the Islamic critics a deep concern over women's 'moral corruption' and the commoditisation of women's sexuality in Pahlavi Iran.[5]

The Islamic critics of the old regime consider the changes under the Pahlavis completely undesirable, and responsible for moral corruption and the subordination of an Islamic society to neo-colonialist powers. They refer to 8 January, 1936 as the day of shame, symbolising the assault of corrupt Western culture upon Islamic values, whose effect has been the undermining of public morality.[6]

Writers critical of the Islamic regime in post-revolutionary Iran are similarly not short of documentary evidence to support their view that the new regime has made a wholesale attack on women's rights. Compulsory veiling, barring women from the judiciary, segregation in transport, sports and many public places, and the introduction or reimposition of discriminatory laws lead to such conclusions as, 'The Islamic Republic in Iran has created two classes of citizens; the male . . . , and the female', and that women have become second-class citizens 'who have no place in the public arena and no security in the domestic sphere'.[7]

Writers sympathetic to the Islamic Republic argue that what is upheld as equality of rights in Western societies is in fact similarity of rights, and that women's quest for such similarity of rights is both immoral and unjust, running contrary to the divine plan as well as the natural disposition of women. In their view, women and men are created differently and are suitable for different roles in their social and private lives.[8] Given such differences, equality between the sexes becomes injustice. More significantly, they point to the roles in which women have found a new identity under the Islamic regime. They argue that the Islamic regime, by purifying the social atmosphere of the old corrupt practices, has for the first time made it possible for the majority of Iranian women to find meaningful social involvement without demeaning themselves by becoming exposed to non-Muslim practices.

Clearly all such evaluations, explicitly or implicitly, move from a set of notions concerning what is desirable for Iranian society in general and for women in particular. Such desirability may have been defined in terms of the ideals of progress, the requirements of civilisation, the needs of the modern state and the duties of the modern citizen, the objective laws of historical development, or the harmonious projections of divine wisdom. Since the mid-nineteenth century, the 'woman question' has been central to notions of progress, civilisation, the developmental march of history, 'westoxication' *(gharbzadegi)* and its current antidote 'westeradication' *(gharbzeda'i)*. In turn, the terms of the 'woman question' have been defined and redefined by these ideas. In the earliest formulations, in the mid-nineteenth century, 'the traditional woman' became the most visible symbol of backwardness. Correspondingly the journey into modernity was defined as one of educating and unveiling this backward subject. Yet by the 1970s it was this very subject, now designated as 'superwesternised', who had become the site of all social ills. This transformation was separated by a period in which, on the one hand, the modern state appropriated the 'woman question', much as it took over many other corners of societal space, and harnessed it to its project of propelling Iran into the era of a 'Great Civilisation'. On the other hand, the opposition to the Pahlavi state, secular or Islamic, absorbed this question into their respective programmes for revolutionary transformation.[9]

The present chapter focuses on the appropriation of the 'woman question' by the Pahlavi state, the interaction between the transformation of the state and the redefinition of the 'woman question', leading to the paradigmatic shift into Islamic politics with its own concepts regarding womanhood in a revolutionary Islamic state.

The most striking feature of the Pahlavi period is the establishment of a modern centralised state and the state's attempts at transforming the society. The earlier part of the Pahlavi period, corresponding to Reza Shah's reign, was a period of state-building. The later part, in the 1960s and 1970s, after Mohammad Reza Shah consolidated his power in the 1950s, was a period in which the state took aggressive steps in remoulding the economic and social structure of Iran.

REZA SHAH: CITIZENS AS SERVANTS OF THE STATE

Reza Shah took power in a military coup in February 1921 and by December 1925 he had a constituent assembly deposing the last Qajar Shah and declaring him the shah of a new dynasty. He rose to power in an atmosphere of political demoralisation. Despite the military victory of the constitutionalist forces over the absolutist monarch Mohammad Ali Shah in July 1909, the following decade witnessed such a deep disillusionment with constitutionalism that by the 1920s Iranian reformers were talking of the necessity for a 'revolutionary dictator'.[10]

Most accounts attribute the impotence of the early constitutional governments (1909–20) to foreign intervention. Indeed, there were foreign pressures and military threats and interventions by both Russia and Britain.

But more than foreign pressure went into the failure of the constitutional experiment.

The Constitutional Movement eliminated the monarch as the effective head of the state. It created a strong legislative body, by transferring much of the royal prerogatives to the *Majlis*, but had no plan for building a functioning executive power. Formally the monarch, and through him the prime minister, headed the government. But in fact by destroying the old authority of the Crown, there seemed to be no executive power left in the country. *Majlis* proceedings increasingly looked like endless pointless squabbles, a waste of time that got the country nowhere. While the country was burning, it seemed that the *Majlis* was playing second fiddle to the parliaments of Europe.

A series of cabinet crises led to demoralisation. The provinces, impatient with central government, began to form their own local administrations. Eventually localist movements surfaced in several important provinces. By 1914, the British Minister in his Annual Report to the Foreign Office would write that the central government had ceased to exist outside the capital.[11] The weakness of central government came to be seen as responsible for all ills. By the early 1920s, important constitutionalists became advocates of a strong state.[12] In 1921, a prominent constitutionalist statesman, Moshir od-Dowleh, put it in these terms; 'I want the Constitution for the country, not the country for the Constitution. If the good of the country requires it, I would trample upon the Constitution'.[13]

The first generation of Iranian reformers had been primarily attracted to the constitutional monarchies of Europe. Now, a new generation increasingly found Italy and Germany more suitable models for Iran to follow: '[O]ur only hope is a Mussolini who can break the influence of the traditional authorities, and thus create a modern outlook, a modern people, and a modern nation', wrote one influential journal in 1924.[14] The terms of political discourse had drastically changed. While the early generation of reformers saw progress as possible only through a constitutional regime, the reformers of the 1920s began to see democracy as an impediment to progress.

This apparent contradiction between democracy and progress haunted the country for the next half a century. Reza Shah took power in an atmosphere of craving for a strong central state, for statist policies, for law and order, for a regime that got something done, almost regardless of how it got it done. It is this political atmosphere that made it acceptable to see the army as the agent of progress: perhaps the army could succeed where administrative, educational, and constitutional civil reformers had failed. In other words, Reza Shah's vision of the centrality of building the army to building the country coincided with the new orientation of a whole stratum of statesmen and intellectuals.

For Reza Shah the new state consisted above all of a modern army. He repeatedly emphasised that 'the greatness of the country depends on the progress and strength of its army, weakness and decay of the country results from the incapacity and degradation of its military forces'.[15] This did not simply mean a high priority for building a strong army ('An army before and above everything. Everything first for the army, and again for the army').[16] But more importantly, for Reza Shah the army was a model for the construction of a nation-state. His ideal was to create a nation of disciplined, obedient, efficient citizens. His remarks about the reasons for Ataturk's success are indicative: the Turks are more submissive and easier to lead. The Iranians are more capable, but undisciplined.[17] He hoped to introduce military discipline into all other branches of government and upheld the soldier as a model for citizenship. At a ceremony in 1933, at the newly established National Bank of Iran, he demanded of the Bank employees to 'act as soldiers. A soldier gives his life for his country on the battlefield. You should do the same thing. You must sacrifice yourselves for the prestige of your country'.[18] It is symbolic of the importance of the army in Reza Shah's mind that he appeared on all public occasions in military uniform.[19] This vision of the army-as-model implied a strong drive towards the creation of uniformities. The dress code for civilians (men and women) was just one aspect. So was the abolition of traditional aristocratic titles and the requirement for registering under a surname. The imposition of the dress code has often been simply regarded as the emulation of European gear. But for Reza Shah, it was more than that. Introducing a uniform into the army had been an important measure in constructing a modern army based on conscription, instead of the hodge-podge of tribal levies and various military units. In a similar vein, the introduction of 'civilian uniforms' was not simply a discarding of traditional garb and imitation of everything European. It signified a step towards the creation of the citizen-soldier, those 'instruments' with which he intended to realise his vision of Iran, 'the bones and muscles of the reconstruction' for which 'he was its mind'.[20] For Reza Shah it was a duty as well as a privilege for a citizen to serve the state. More concretely, citizens were expected to contribute to the building of a new society by becoming part of the growing state bureaucracy. An attitude was cultivated that looked down upon those not inside the state apparatus, as if working for the state were now the ultimate expression or test of good citizenship.

The role of women in Reza Shah's vision can be situated within this larger project of state-building. Like men, women were expected to contribute to the building of the new society through hard work and participation in state-building. Here is how he put it when addressing a group of teachers and female students on 8 January 1936:

> Women in this country [prior to this day of unveiling] could not demonstrate their aptitude and inherent qualities because they remained outside of society, they could not make their proper contribution to the country and make appropriate sacrifices and render their services. Now they can proceed and enjoy other advantages of society in addition to the remarkable task of motherhood . . . I believe that for the progress and happiness of this country we all must work sincerely, there will be progress if government employees work, the country needs effort and work . . . Now that you, my daughters and sisters, have entered the social arena . . . you must know that it is your duty to work for your country. Future prosperity is in your hands. You train the future generation. You can be good teachers and good people can emerge from your training. I expect of you, learned ladies, now that you are going out in the world to learn about your rights and duties and to perform services to your country, you should be wise and work, become accustomed to frugality and avoid luxuries and overspending.[21]

This is not the same as encouraging women to join the labour force because of the need of an emerging capitalist economy for an expanded labour force, as has sometimes been argued.[22] Women were urged to go to universities, become teachers, join the expanding ministries, that is to participate in the building of a newly forming state bureaucracy, rather than become part of the labour force in factories. The development of a market economy as such was marginal to Reza Shah's project.[23] This limited the project from the start to certain sections of upper and middle class urban women. The new state, moreover, was to be a modern one, eliminating whatever was seen as vestiges of backwardness such as the veil.[24] The model of a modern state was ultimately a European one, but this was in great part mediated for Iran through the model of the emerging Turkish state under Ataturk. In fact from the early nineteenth century, Ottoman reforms and reformist literature had provided aspiring Iranian reformers and intellectuals not only with a model but also a certain legitimacy: that another Islamic state had already adopted administrative, military and legal reforms to buttress its stand against European encroachment made the argument for the compatibility of reform with Islamic requirements more convincing. Not only were Qajar reforms largely modelled after their Ottoman counterparts, which sometimes had preceded them by several decades, much of Persian reform vocabulary was borrowed from the Ottomans.

Despite the profound influences of the Turkish model on Reza Shah's reforms, however, there were important differences between the two states. The Iranian reforms remained more limited in content but were carried out more brutally. To begin with, state initiated or privately backed reforms had a much longer history, scope, and cumulative effect in the nineteenth century Ottoman Empire compared with the few, short-lived, and limited measures at reform in Qajar Iran. A few comparative dates relating to women's lives give an indication of the scale of this time gap. The first modern school for girls was established in Istanbul in 1858, in Tehran not until 1907. A Teachers' Training College for women was opened in 1863 in Istanbul, in 1918 in Tehran (both were called, by the way, *dar al-mo'allemat*). The first women's magazines appeared in Turkish in 1869, in Persian in 1911. Women gained access to university education in 1914 in Istanbul, but only in 1936 in Tehran.

Moreover, and perhaps more importantly, the Turkish state was founded on the ruins of the Ottoman Caliphate. As such, it defined itself in contra-distinction to the old state as a secular state, and indeed remains the only secular state in the Middle East. There was a conscious attempt to make a new ethnic and territorial nationalism the ideological foundation of the new Republic.[25] This accounts for the more thorough break of Ataturk's reforms from Islamic laws and traditions. Ataturk's project, moreover, was to build a state resting on a political movement, despite his own background as a military man. By contrast, Reza Shah put the army at the centre of his project and chose to fall back on Islam as an anchor of legitimacy.[26] This difference proved crucial with respect to the changes in the social and legal status of women in the two states. In Iran, although in the process of modern state-building many prerogatives of the clerical establishment were curtailed or eliminated, the break with Islam remained partial and tenuous. For instance, a new criminal code was drafted largely on the basis of European codes, while the civil code (which included family laws, inheritance, etc.) remained Islamic.

The reasons for this contrast should be sought in the different processes that gave birth to the two states. The new Turkish state was established after a War of Liberation, during which a political movement and a central army were built in close association with each other. The clerical forces had compromised themselves by backing occupying powers, while the whole period of the Young Turks had created wide acceptance of a new concept of Turkish nationhood, based partially on non-Islamic definitions and affiliations. By the time the Turkish Republic was declared, it had become possible, legitimate, and desirable to abolish not only the Sultanate but also the Caliphate.

In Iran, on the contrary, a significant part of the Shi'ite clergy had supported the Constitutional Movement, and despite periods of alienation from the secular constitutionalists, it continued to keep its traditional legitimacy as the voice of the people. The distinction of Shi'ism from Sunni Islam made it possible for Iranian nationalists, at the turn of this century, to base their nationalism on the appropriation of pre-Islamic Iran and to integrate the presumably distinct Shi'ite Islam into that nationalism, proving the superiority of Iranians over their Arab and Turkish brothers. Shi'ism came to be projected as Iran's 'nationalisation' of Islam.[27]

The specific circumstances of Reza Shah's rise to power further accentuated this uneasy alliance between Iranian nationalism and Shi'ite particularism. Unlike Ataturk, Reza Shah came to power through a military coup. His new power was not consolidated on the basis of a social movement or a social class, but by building a modern army. While building the army, militarily and in terms of the legitimacy of its authority, through various campaigns to suppress provincial movements and tribal unruliness, he astutely manoeuvred himself into the space created by the mutual hostility and suspicion of two major political forces: secular democrats craving for a strong modern leader to eradicate clerical influence and save the masses and the country, and the Shi'ite clergy, threatened by the rising influence of secular anti-clerical intellectuals and politicians, who were deeply worried by the developments in Turkey. He used the former to push through such laws as the conscription act, against the protests of the clergy, and used the latter's support to dethrone Ahmad Shah and clamp down on the unruly press and political debates.[28]

Under Reza Shah reformers of the constitutional era faced a dilemma: many of their projected reforms were possible to achieve, not through their original vision of a parliamentary system, but through the construction of a corporatist state, that would not tolerate any independent citizens' initiatives. For example, by the mid-1930s all independent women's societies and journals were closed down at the same time that the state took over the implementation of their specific reforms, such as opening up schools for girls, encouraging higher education for women, female employment in state bureaucracy, opening some public arenas to women's participation, and requiring the discarding of the veil.[29] We know from existing historical accounts that many of the male reformers and intellectuals faced a bitter dilemma. When for a brief period Reza Khan launched a campaign for abolishing the monarchy and establishing himself at the head of a republic, many republican intellectuals campaigned against a republic to stop his rise to power.[30] (With historical hindsight, the wisdom of this countercampaign is debatable, since Reza Khan established himself as a dictator in any case, but as a dictatorial shah rather than a president.) Other reformers soon decided that opposition to Reza Shah was fatal and futile, and resigned from active politics. Yet others felt whatever reforms could be achieved through serving a corporatist state were crucial for the revitalisation of Iranian society; indeed some identified the very construction of a strong centralised corporatist state as the embodiment of new Iranian nationhood.

Did women reformers of the same period experience similar dilemmas and face similar choices? So far, we have virtually no accounts of women resisting the closure of their associations and journals. Most current accounts of this period lay heavy emphasis on repression, when discussing the decline of independent women's groups and activities under Reza Shah. Sanasarian, for instance, considers 'the first and the most obvious reason' to be 'the presence of an absolute ruler willing to use force. Reza Shah was well-known for his stern punishment of resisters'.[31] Without denying the impact of Reza Shah's pervasive brutality, we cannot but observe that there were very few resisters among women's rights activists to the disbanding of their societies and curtailment of their publications. More importantly, as Sanasarian explains, many 'welcomed the new regime's interest in women's issues. They had worked alone, with no support, for too long. It was a relief to be part of a government that possessed enforcement power . . . Feminists such as Zandokht Shirazi were fond of Reza Shah and had high hopes for his contribution to the women's cause. Many of these women did not hesitate to join the new administration'.[32] It would be all too easy to dismiss these women as bourgeois betrayers of the feminist cause. In a sense these women had gone through a double disillusionment with constitutionalism. Not only were they influenced by the general political mood away from the parliamentary experiment toward 'the revolutionary dictator', they had been particularly disappointed by the constitutionalists themselves. First, the constitutionalists had rejected female suffrage. Second, while the constitutionalists had been prepared to break from Islamic tradition and law on a whole series of issues, such as the setting up of a secular judiciary, when it came to women's issues they went out of their way to defend the faith. When the issue of the legitimacy of women's associations was debated in the *Majlis*, there was virtual unanimity that such societies were un-Islamic, dangerous to and seditious of public morality.[33] This double disillusionment could in part explain the initial flourishing of women's societies and publications *after* the defeat and dissipation of constitutionalism. It may have also made it that much easier and more plausible to look for a 'modern leader', where the modern movement had failed.

The radical consequences of Reza Shah's state-building period in redefining the terms of the 'woman question' hecame evident after his abdication in 1941. The rise and consolidation of a corporatist state found its oppositional political reflection in totalising party political platforms. In the open political turmoil, public debates and political recomposition of 1941–53, Iranian politics was moulded around party political platforms and organizations such as the Tudeh Party, the Democratic Party, and the National Front. Correspondingly, the 'woman question' became part of broad political utopias, with packages for social change, rather than issue-centered, for instance, around female education and family laws, as had been the case during the constitutional period. More significantly, from this period onwards, women's organisations tended to become formed largely as de-facto auxiliaries of political parties. This implied a clear hierarchy of priorities. Subordination and absorption of the 'woman question' into the cause of state-building under Reza Shah now found its oppositional echo in its subordination to higher political causes. This redefinition and hierarchisation was only partial in this period. In the subsequent consolidation of the state under Mohammad Reza Shah, it became total.

MOHAMMAD REZA SHAH: CITIZENS AS GRATEFUL BENEFICIARIES OF THE STATE

There were important changes in the character of the Pahlavi state under Mohammad Reza Shah, once he consolidated his hold on power in the 1950s. The post-1953 regime in Iran is often treated as a twenty-five–year black box of repression and/or modernization, which we have only just begun to scrutinize. On closer examination it is becoming evident that the 1959–63 period was politically crucial for the Iranian state, as well as for politics and society in Iran.

On the level of the state, there was a significant change in the character of the shah's rule; in the words of one scholar, from a traditional monarchy to a sultanistic state.[34] What made this shift possible was inceasing oil revenues, allowing the state to become progressively more autonomous from civil society. No longer dependent on internal taxation for revenues, or even on internal production for survival, the limited level of political participation of the elite in politics diminished drastically, eventually reducing the politically relevant body of decision makers to the person of the shah.[35] There were significant differences, for instance, between the *Majlis* elections of the 1950s and those of the mid-1960s onwards. In the 1950s, the *Majlis* was dominated by landlords and notables who could, as local patrons, muster an electoral following to whom they in turn felt some patriarchal sense of obligation.

From 1965 onwards, with the election of the 21st *Majlis*, this 'organic' tie ceased to exist. All candidates were selected by the Ministry of the Interior, vetted and approved by the shah personally. If one wanted to be elected as a parliamentary deputy, it was no longer the local landlord with whom one had to curry favours but with the shah himself.[36] In return, the deputies owed allegiance only to him. The old political elite ceased to be decision makers in any sense. A new layer of co-opted technocrats were appointed by the shah. The former became de-politicised, the latter were apolitical.[37] The shah, in turn, came to view himself not as the head, or even as the embodiment, of the state (as his father had projected himself), but as the state itself.[38] A reading of his writings makes this very clear. While Reza Shah would typically use such phrases as 'I expect my government carry out this reform', his son would say 'I shall carry out this reform'.[39] Eventually, he came to see himself not only as the sole decision maker, but as the architect of the society, as the omnipotent source of benevolence from whom all progress emanated. The point is that he not only wanted to see Iran progress to 'a Great Civilisation', but that this progress had to be totally of his making: 'There should not even arise a case that We have not foreseen and about which We have not made the necessary decisions'.[40] In the words of Goodell, 'modernization was non-negotiable'.[41] The Shah's 'rigid benevolence' prescribed the 'boundaries of freedom, initiative, and control'[42]; the society was to be uplifted according to a Grand Plan, which should never spawn expectations, confidence, or initiative – 'a control far more subtle than "oppression"'.[43]

Correspondingly, citizens were no longer expected to contribute to the building of the state, to be at its service, but to be its grateful beneficiaries.[44] Loyalty to the person of the shah, the Great Benefactor, replaced loyalty to the state as the test of citizenship. The population itself became complacent in abiding by the rules of gratitude, for some time, before it became convinced that the Great Benefactor was unjust and must thus be overthrown.

A second important change in this period concerns the fate of secular political organisations such as the National Front and the Tudeh Party. The shah opted for a programme of socio-economic reforms, known as the White Revolution. The Tudeh Party, with its virtual support of this programme, further lost its political legitimacy as an oppositional force.

As for the National Front, it lost all political *raison d'être*. In 1953 it had been defeated by force. In 1962–63, it became politically redundant; the shah's reform programme was much bolder and radical than anything the National Front had ever projected. Its political demise was sealed in this period, not in 1978–79.

A third important shift was the emergence of Islamic politics as a new political paradigm in Iran. Here again the confluence of two trends occurred: the politicisation of an important sector of the Islamic clergy under Khomeni's leadership, and the Islamisation of previously secular politics, as seen in the emergence of such organisations as the Liberation Movement of Iran (*Nehzat-e azadi*, led by Bazargan), and the popularity and prominence of such intellectuals as Al-e Ahmad and Shari'ati.[45]

With these shifts, the 'woman question' underwent an important change. With the demise of secular politics, discourses on women within opposition politics became progressively moralised, and eventually Islamicised. The autonomous space of the 'woman question' in upper-class politics – whence important initiatives had often originated – was eliminated altogether and replaced totally by the initiatives of the state, or rather the initiatives of the shah.

The shah's attitude towards women's rights was indicative of his new outlook on the nature of his own rule: women's rights were to be royal grants.[46] All women's initiatives, even of a charitable nature, had to be absorbed and controlled centrally by the state – the sole authority to decide the timing of each initiative. Put in this context, there is little contradiction between the shah's traditionalist views on the role of women as expressed in his early writings,[47] his contempt for women as expressed in his later interview with Fallaci[48] on the one hand, and his reforms for and on behalf of women on the other. As in the case of society at large, it was he who was doing the uplifting, the timing was his, the limits were prescribed by him.

To begin with, women's organisations that had been formed in the 1940s and escaped the repression of the 1950s were gradually absorbed into a central organization under the tutelage of Ashraf Pahlavi, the shah's sister. Initially, in 1956, a loose organisation for co-ordinating activities was formed by fourteen women's societies. Some of these belonged to religious minorities, such as the Society of Zoroastrian Women, the Society of Jewish Women, and the Society of Armenian Women. Others belonged to the Graduates of the American College, or were more broadly defined, such as the Society of the New Path (*Rah-e Now*).[49] Within two years, this co-ordinating body was dissolved into a state-sponsored body, the High Council of Women's Organisations, presided over by Ashraf Pahlavi. The significance of this change was not missed by the women involved:

'I think the bureaucracy *(tashkilat)* began to think that if they put Her Highness Ashraf, an intelligent and capable person, at the head of women's organisations, they would help these organisations and bring them under their own control, under the control of the system *(dastgah)* so that things did'nt get out of hand'.[50] With the increasing centralisation and take-over by the state of all public life in the 1960s, the High Council was dissolved and replaced by a single organisation, the Women's Organisation of Iran. Some of the old societies kept an informal life of their own, but now instead of being one amongst several roughly equal societies, they were faced with a single all-powerful organisation, with a significant power and budget.[51] Though resentful of losing their own little autonomous domains, women activists of these societies soon learned to adapt their cause to suit the initiatives of the shah. Moreover, the upper-class women activists of the 1940s and 1950s were joined, outnumbered and in part displaced by a new group of women that was itself created by the changes of the late 1950s and the 1960s. Prior to the 1950s, women from upper-class circles did not work in the state bureaucracy, but only engaged in voluntary charitable activities. As far as they were concerned, only women of lower classes would work for wages. By the late 1960s, this was no longer the case. A whole stratum of women, from the upper and middle classes, were working, not only as highly skilled professionals (such as doctors, engineers, architects, pharmacists, university professors, judges), but also throughout the various levels of governmental bureaucracy. Paid work had become respectable.[52] It was this new category of women that later provided the activists and leaders of the Women's Organisation of Iran.

There were significant differences between these two generations. The earlier generation had come from more aristocratic families, had mostly engaged in voluntary charitable work and drew satisfaction from the personal prestige such work brought with it. Centralisation of all women's activities, including charities, into the WOI and other state institutions, robbed such work of its personal prestige and made it anonymous, the glory going to the state (and increasingly to the shah). Although many of these women became prominent figures in the upper echelons of the state and served as parliamentary deputies, senators, ministers, and ambassadors, they resented this loss of personal recognition and control. Moreover, they belonged to a generation of the aristocracy and upper-class Iranians that had a political culture of its own and resented its loss. They did not share the same identity with the state institutions that the new apolitical layer of state technocrats, and their counterparts in the WOI felt. For the new generation of women in the WOI, however, the concern was to get things done efficiently. They were the products of the process of depoliticisation of the state in the 1960s; they were 'born' into the new apolitical state.

Within the new order, they 'knew' they had to depend on royal patronage to get anything done:

> 'One phase of legal action always involved convincing the Monarch – whose national role was the essence and symbol of patriarchy. Since he was regularly briefed by the Queen and Princess Ashraf (both intelligent, active, professional women), constantly exposed to international opinion and attitudes, and possessed by a vision of Iran as a 'progressive' nation, it would sometimes suffice to demonstrate to him the importance of the proposal to national development.[53]

The WOI became an important vehicle for projecting the shah's image internationally as a champion of women's rights in Iran. Internally, the organisation channelled some of the women activists' energies into local projects, while some prominent women's rights' activists felt that, in exchange for giving their monarch the image he wanted, they could, and did, accomplish some reforms.

However, no reform was allowed even to be perceived to have resulted from women's own initiatives. When, in the early 1960s, the government began discussing reform of the election laws, a group of women from the High Council of Women's Organisations were dissuaded from lobbying by prominent members of the shah's entourage.[54] Once the shah decided to grant the vote, however, women were required to express their gratitude by voting in the national referendum of 1963. This pattern of the state determining the pace and details of reforms for women became quite established. What determined the timing was in part the international image of the state. For instance, Dolatshahi recalls that up to 1963, the only two countries which were represented by men in the Women's Affairs Committee of the United Nations were Iran and Saudi Arabia. In that year the government decided that this state of affairs was embarrassing and that from now on a woman should be sent.[55] Similarly, she traces the idea of forming the WOI to Ashraf Pahlavi's concern that many other countries had women's organisations whose membership numbered in the millions while Iran did not.[56] Her own appointment as Iran's first female ambassador (to Denmark) in 1976, she attributes to the government's decision that it was time to have a female ambassador.[57] This is not to deny that a whole section of women, through WOI and outside it, were active in pushing for reforms. This was particularly true for reforming family laws.[58] But what determined when and how a law was reformed was not of their making. If a given reform, for whatever reason, was not on the government agenda, it would have no effect. In the mid-1970s, for instance, a woman senator and well-known lawyer, Manuchehrian, proposed that the requirement of the husband's permission for a married woman to obtain a passport be eliminated.[59] The government rejected this for no obvious reason, except that it was not of its making and timing, causing Manuchehrian to resign her seat. Reading the reminiscences of many of these women, one is struck by a consistent pattern: not a single instance is recorded in which they felt reforms for women were being held back by the traditionalism of the population, while repeatedly they complain about the tokenism of the government on women's issues and refer to the system *(dastgah)* as the single most important obstacle to getting things done.

Not only did the opposition view the changes in women's status under the shah as meaningless tokenism, but prominent statesmen from the old regime viewed, and continue to view, them in such terms:

> These privileges that were granted [to women], it was not as if this class had felt deprivation and then had engaged in any struggles to remove that deprivation; there had been no dialogue. The Shah just decided that Iranian society should make use of the luxury of male-female equality as much as other countries; this was a luxury for our society . . . In Iran they [women] were granted these on a platter; they were given too many rights.[60]

Between the two periods of state-building, the 1930s versus the 1970s, an important shift occurred in the symbolic significance of the women's rights' issue in Iran. In the first period, women's status was seen as a symbol of modernity of the new nation and the new state. In the second period, it became the symbol of the modernity of the monarch and his progressive benevolence toward women.

MORALISATION OF THE WOMAN QUESTION AND THE RISE OF ISLAMIC POLITICS

Women have acquired a very prominent position in the ideology as well as practice of the Islamic Revolution and the Islamic Republic. In the literature on Islam and Islamic positions on women, in sources both sympathetic and hostile, including some of my own earlier writings,[61] there is a tendency toward an essentialist conception of Islam, reducing Islam to a given set of doctrines, with a given set of edicts on women, and attributing the current

practices and ideology of Islamic movements to the implementation of
these doctrines.[62] From the outset this outlook was open to two kinds of
criticism: if the current state of Islamic politics and its impact on women
derive from some essential doctrines within Islam, why is it happening
now? Why were they not operative decades ago, when societies were
more traditional and more observant of religious norms? Here sociological
observations offer a somewhat unsatisfactory explanation: urbanisation has
brought millions of previously land-based peasants into the cities. These
recent migrants are more religious and more traditional. There is, therefore,
a new impetus for a religious revival. Sociologically, however, the recent
Islamic movements are not peasant-based but urban middle and lower
middle class in composition. In the case of women, for instance, the most
militant advocates of Islamisation are among the highly educated graduates
of universities. The second problem with such essentialist tendencies is the
multiplicity of Islamic politics, ranging from fundamentalist positions all
the way to modernist reformism. Each with equal justification claims its
Islam to be the true Islam. With such a diversity of 'essential Islams',
how does one arrive at the dominance of one on the basis of its doctrinal
positions?

To overcome this problem, we need to come to terms with the rise of
the Islamic movements as a political phenomenon, rather than as religious
revival, as a conscious political rejection of the West and the political
models associated with it (be they nationalism, socialism, parliamentary
democracy, etc.) in favour of the construction of an Islamic order, as a
shift from modernisation as the central project and concern of society to
moral purification and ideological reconstruction.[63]

Post-1953 Iran witnessed not only consolidation of a new state, but also
a thorough reshaping of oppositional politics. This reshaping eventually
encompassed the whole experience of the country over the previous century, proclaimed its rejection, and declared a shift to a new type of politics,
which was eventually embodied in the Islamic Revolution of 1979. Central
to the new politics became the concept of *gharbzadegi* – westoxication or
weststruckness – popularised by Jalal Al-e Ahmad. It is important at the
outset to emphasise two points. First, the concept was accepted by a whole
generation of Iranian radical youth in the 1960s and 1970s, regardless of
secular or Islamic sympathies. Al-e Ahmad's book, with the same title, was
read and acclaimed by every oppositionist.[64]

The second point is that the concept and the sentiment to which it gave
such powerful expression involved a thorough break with past politics of
whatever colour. It was not posed, from the start, as a critique of 'excesses
of modernisation', but of the whole project. It did not oppose just the rise

of the 'authoritarian benevolence' of the shah, but viewed the political experience of the country from the Constitutional Movement itself, through the experience of the National Front and the Tudeh Party, as politics of alienation and subjugation. In other words, it became a rejection of not only the politics and policies of the Pahlavi state, but also of oppositional and reform politics of the whole previous century.

Perhaps nowhere has this total rejection touched popular as well as intellectual imagination more acutely than in its rejection of the *gharbzadeh* woman. The *gharbzadeh* woman came to embody at once all social ills: she was a super-consumer of imperialist/dependent-capitalist/foreign goods; she was a propagator of the corrupt culture of the West; she was undermining the moral fabric of society; she was a parasite, beyond any type of redemption.

Who was a *gharbzadeh* woman? In its crudest form, she was identified with a woman who wore 'too much' make-up, 'too short' a skirt, 'too tight' a pair of pants, 'too low-cut' a shirt, who was 'too loose' in her relations with men, who laughed 'too loudly', who smoked in public. Clearly, it signified a subjective judgement; at least to some extent it was defined in the eyes of the beholder. While an Islamic militant would consider any unveiled woman as *gharbzadeh*, a secular radical would perhaps limit the concept to what became known as 'the painted dolls of the Pahlavi regime'. Yet both felt comfortable in denouncing *gharbzadegi* and the *gharbzadeh woman* in a single voice. What was, then, the common thread unifying such diversity of prejudice? Discussing what had become a common type of over-Westernised man in late nineteenth century Ottoman literature, Şerif Mardin argues that what 'appears as a critique of over-Westernization at its deepest level is simply social control applied against those who transgress the norms of the community'.[65] *Gharbzadegi* as a social and political critique in Iranian society of the 1960s was also concerned with social control above anything else. The 'norms of the community' were different for Islamic traditionalists and the radical secular left. But there was some common ground. First and possibly most important, was the common acceptance of the legitimacy of the community's prerogative to set the limits of individual moral behaviour. Second, although the actual limits were vastly different between the two extremes of political opposition, there was a connecting thread that made sense of the common denunciations of the *gharbzadeh* woman: the preservation of 'modesty' as a desirable characteristic of a woman. Here we need to go back to the turn of the century to look at the tension between modernity and modesty that has devastated Iranian women since then.

I have already referred to the image of the woman within the new discourse of modernity at the turn of this century as 'modern-yet-modest'. This duality became, and continues to remain, a source of cultural, moral, social, and political 'schizophrenia' for non-traditional Iranian women.[66] The boundary between modernity and modesty is of necessity a socially defined and fluid one, that leaves the woman herself in a perpetual state of uncertainty. The boundary becomes clear only in its transgression, which renders the transgressor an outcast. Perhaps a few examples would demonstrate the point. Let us look more closely at the pair of concepts, *ommol* (too traditional) and *jelf* (too loose), presumably the very negations of modernity on the one hand and modesty on the other. Where was one to draw the line? Wearing make-up for an unmarried girl in traditional families was already beyond 'the norms of the community'. In such circles, if a girl plucked her eyebrows prior to the marriage ceremony, she was considered to have been corrupted. For others, it was a requirement for being accepted as modern; otherwise, one would be considered *ommol*. And of course 'how much make-up' was an even more hazardous terrain to tread.

Similar problems were raised by the 'dress code'. In the late 1960s, when miniskirts became the fashion, the exact length of one's skirt posed the same 'boundary' problem: too long a skirt indicated an outmoded outlook; too short a skirt was unacceptable sexual invitation. How would any young girl know how many inches was the socially perfect – modern-yet-modest – skirt length? The socially acceptable length became all too evident in its transgression: one young woman, with 'too short' a skirt was raped in public, in front of a circle of spectators, whose unanimous opinion was that she had asked for it.

Possibly the most dangerous domain was that of male-female sexual relations. A woman such as Forugh Farrokhzad, who dared not only to transgress socially legitimate boundaries of male-female sexual relations, but to celebrate her sexuality openly in her poetry became an outcast, even among the most enlightened Iranian intellectuals of her time. Only after her death, when such transgressions were of the past and only remained in her poems, did she become safe to embrace as a great poet.

But such breaks with the notion of the desirability of social control of individual moral behaviour remained on the cultural margins of social life in Iran. Indeed, only in the post-1979 period have discussions emerged that pose the dilemma faced by some women as one of individual choice versus social control. In the 1960s and 1970s projection of any such discussion would have been seen as the apogee of *gharbzadegi*.

Within this context, the attraction of the newly rising Islamic politics for a whole section of Iranian women, torn by such tensions, becomes clear. The active Islamic militant woman, simultaneously a Fatemeh and a Zeynab,[67] became the symbolic resolution of this tension.

In the new Islamic paradigm, the 'woman question' came to acquire tremendous weight for two important reasons. First, in this new thinking, similar to some secular Third World conceptions, the imperialist domination of Muslim (Third World) societies is seen to have been achieved through the undermining of religion and culture, not through military or economic domination as the earlier generations of nationalists and socialists had argued. Moral corruption is viewed as the lynch-pin of imperialist designs. Within such an outlook women as mothers and wives are seen to bear a heavy responsibility for the moral health and therefore the political fate of the country. Second, women's sexuality is accorded tremendous power over men and provides the basis for all the arguments for segregation and veiling of women.

This new vision is amply expressed in an editorial that appeared in the 7 April 1984 issue of *Zan-e Ruz*, a weekly women's journal published in Tehran. In this editorial many of the important tenets of the new ideology are formulated in an interconnected manner. It begins by reiterating that the 'hegemonic aims' of colonial powers in our time were achieved not through force, but in the first instance through subversion of culture. Women's liberation is presented as one such instance:

> Colonialism was fully aware of the sensitive and vital role of woman in the formation of the individual and of human society. They considered her the best tool for subjugation of the nations. Therefore, under such pretexts as social activity, the arts, freedom, etc., they pushed her to degeneracy and degradation and made of her a doll who not only forgot her human role, but became the best tool for emptying others of their humanity . . . In Western societies where capitalism is dominant . . . women's liberation is nothing but the liberty to be naked, to prostitute oneself . . . In the underdeveloped countries . . . women serve as the unconscious accomplices of the powers-that-be in the destruction of indigenous culture. So long as indigenous culture persists in the personality and thought of people in a society, it is not easy to find a political, military, economic or social presence in that society . . . And woman is the best means of destroying the indigenous culture to the benefit of imperialists.

It is important to pause here and note that there is little in the editorial so far that many radical secular critics of the Islamic Republic would object to, apart, perhaps, from the tone. Such identity of vision between the current regime and its critics should makes us realise what power the new ideas exerted over oppositional social and political discourse in the last years of the shah's rule – a power that remains largely unchallenged even after the unity-in-opposition has broken down in the post-revolutionary decade. We need to ask ourselves what made such a powerful identity of vision possible in the first place.

The editorial then continues by discussing the specificities of Islamic societies in these words:

> In Islamic countries the role of woman is even more sensitive. Islamic belief and culture provides people of these societies with faith and ideals . . . Woman in these societies is armed with a shield that protects her against the conspiracies aimed at her humanity, honour and chastity. This shield is verily her veil. For this reason . . . the most immediate and urgent task was seen to be unveiling . . . Then she became the target of poisonous arrows of corruption, prostitution, nakedness, looseness, and trivialities. After this, she was used to disfigure the Islamic culture of the society, to erase people's faith and drag society in her wake toward corruption, decay and degradation.

After detailing the 'political, cultural, economic and social dimensions' of the impact of women on Iranian society during the reign of the Pahlavis, the editorial turns to the significance of the Islamic Revolution:

> It is here that we realise the glory and depth of Iran's Islamic Revolution . . . Today the Muslim woman has well understood . . . that the only way for her social presence to be healthy and constructive is to use Islamic veil and clothes . . .

The Islamic Revolution is described as a miracle, for which Muslim women must offer thanks to God, not just in the form of uttering the words, but by 'using all their God-given possibilities and resources to consolidate the Islamic Republic'. To make this offering of thanks possible, the editorial, obliquely, turns to the authorities and demands of them to make the social involvement of women in the consolidation of this miracle possible:

> It is clear that an active and effective presence of women . . . in many positions such as education, medical professions, higher education is indispensible. So those in authority should prepare the grounds for women's participation in society. Faithful and committed women should

expand their abilities in order to be prepared to carry out important social tasks and responsibilities that the Islamic Revolution has placed on their shoulders.

In this editorial, we also find an ideological exposition of the various phases that the policies of the Islamic Republic toward women have gone through.[68]

There have been two distinct phases in these policies, separated by an interregnum. In the first phase, in the immediate aftermath of coming to power, policies towards women were marked by the intent to destroy what was seen to be the corrupt legacy of the past. This included annulment of many laws seen as un-Islamic, elimination of women from the judiciary, segregation of women in public places, such as buses, sports grounds, beaches, and the campaign to impose the veil. The importance given to the imposition of the veil and a proper dress code can be seen from the above editorial, where the veil is described as the crucial shield without which the woman turns into the corrupt creature that opens the society at all levels to colonial domination. The central theme of this phase was the purification of society and of women. It was because this purification meant an all-out attack against all that had been gained by sectors of urban women over the previous fifty years that it looked as if the new regime wanted women pushed back to the domestic sphere, as exemplified by the role assigned to women in the construction of the new order in the Islamic Constitution passed in December 1979.

After this initial phase, there were debates over the role of women in the construction of the new order. The debates basically revolved around how to resolve the tensions between women's domestic role and their social responsibilities in an Islamic order. What eventually decided the outcome of the debate was not theoretical supremacy of one side over the other, but the exigencies of the Iran-Iraq war, with its enormous toll on male lives in Iran. Women became mobilised in a whole series of activities: they staffed the mass laundries and kitchens servicing the war front, they served as nurses in the military hospitals. They were also given a more pronounced civilian profile in many government offices. Contrary to the initial assault against day-care, for instance, as an imperialist plot to separate mothers from children, good child-care centres were now projected as a social necessity so that the mother could perform her services with peace of mind.

One might have expected that if the Islamic regime was in need of absorbing more women into the work force, government offices, war-support activities, it would relax its regulations on the veil and its strictures on the moral codes of public behaviour. The contrary has been the pattern. The more women have become involved in social life, the more necessary it has become to enforce the moral codes to ensure that such increased contact between men and women does not unwittingly undermine the moral fabric of the Islamic community and open it up to alien penetration. Thus over the past several years we have witnessed both numerous campaigns to root out the smallest manifestations of breaking the moral codes, while at the same time prominent spokesmen and politicians of the regime, such as Rafsanjani and Khamene'i, have expounded the necessity of women's involvement in social tasks, within limits such as not to damage their roles as mothers and wives.

In the words and deeds of the Islamic Republic, we witness the ultimate ideologisation and instrumentalisation of the 'woman question'. Since its inception in the mid-nineteenth century, this question in Iran (and the rest of the Middle East) has become forcefully shaped on the terrain of the contest between emerging modern ideologies and states and pre-modern loyalties and social hierarchies. The conflict-ridden concept of a modern-yet-modest woman was born out of the modern man's desire for a modern female counterpart. The traditional woman, for the progressive man of the nineteenth century, became the symbolic location of social backwardness. Yet the boundaries of the new were shaped in tension with another set of symbols: women simultaneously became the symbolic location of social morality and cultural conservatism. To break out of backwardness without transgressing the boundaries of social morality, without betraying the national/Islamic culture within which the modern ideologies were shaped, became the impossible task of becoming modern yet remaining modest and authentic.

Moreover, with the consolidation of the Pahlavi state, women became objects of contestation of loyalty, as they became crucial to the state's project of social transformation, while remaining central to the Islamic claims of a moral community. This contest between the modern State and the traditional God determined the narrow confines within which women have attempted to appropriate the 'woman question'.

Nowhere has this space been so narrowed, to the extent of virtual elimination, as in the Islamic Republic with the total identity of God and State. The existential passion with which many Iranian women have now turned to feminism in order to carve a social space of their own has its counterpart in the passion with which the Islamic state has set itself to mould women in its godly image. To have a room of her own, the Iranian woman is now faced with subverting God and State.

ACKNOWLEDGEMENTS

The first draft of this paper was presented to a seminar on 'Women, State, and Islam', organised by Deniz Kandyioti, in London, 15–16 May, 1987. I benefited enormously from the discussions and comments of all participants in that seminar, particularly those of Nahid Yeganeh, Florida Safiri, Roxan Zand, and Michael Gilsenan. Nilufer Cagatay and Farzaneh Milani made extensive comments on that draft for which I am very grateful. Milani's comments on that draft and on a later one transformed many sections of this paper. Aside from her critical intellectual support, the gift of her friendship saw me through the vicissitudes of writing this paper during a difficult time of my life. My thanks also to Deniz Kandyioti who, as the editor of this collection, had the thankless task of reading and commenting on every draft I produced. I would also like to thank Kanan Makiya, Malmaz Afkhami and Ramine Rouhani for comments on a later draft, and Habib Ladjevardi and Malmaz Afkhami for making the archives of the oral history projects at Harvard University and at the Foundation for Iranian Studies (respectively) available for my work. The final work on this paper was carried out while I was a research fellow at the Women's Studies in Religion Program at Harvard Divinity School and at the Pembroke Center for Teaching and Research on Women. Both occasions provided me not only with financial support, but more importantly with an invaluable atmosphere for exchange of ideas.

NOTES

1. For a discussion of this paradigm shift in Iranian politics, see my paper, 'Iran's Turn to Islam: From Modernism to a Moral Order', *The Middle East Journal*, vol. 41 (1987) no. 2, pp. 202–17.
2. For a survey of these changes see B. Pakizegi, 'Legal and Social Positions of Iranian Women', in L. Beck and N. Keddie (eds), *Women in the Muslim World* (Cambridge, Mass.: Harvard University Press, 1978); Gh. Vatandoust, 'The Status of Iranian Women during the Pahlavi Regime', in A. Fathi (ed.), *Women and the Family in Iran* (Leiden: E. J. Brill, 1985).
3. See Mahnat Afkhami, 'A Future in the Past – The 'pre-revolutionary' Women's Movement', in R. Morgan (ed.), *Sisterhood is Global* (Garden City: Anchor Books, 1984).
4. L. P. Elwell-Sutton, 'Reza Shah the Great: Founder of the Pahlavi Dynasty', in G. Lenczowski (ed.), *Iran Under the Pahlavis* (Stanford: Hoover Institution Press, 1978) p. 34.
5. See, for instance, 'Struggle for Women's Liberation in Iran', in Persian, published by the Committee for Women's Liberation in Iran, London, 1978; and editor's preface in 'The Marxists and Woman Question', in Persian, published by Edition Mazdak, n.p., 1975. More moralistic

and extreme formulations appear in many articles that appeared in the 1970s in publications of secular left organizations, such as the Tudeh Party, the Revolutionary Organization of the Tudeh Party, Peykar, and the Fada'iyan.

6. See S. Vahed, *Goharshad Uprising*, in Persian (Tehran: Ministry of Islamic Guidance, 1982).
7. H. Afshar, 'Women, State and Ideology in Iran', in *Third World Quarterly*, vol. 7 (1985) no. 2, pp. 256–78.
8. See N. Yeganeh, 'Women's Struggles in the Islamic Republic of Iran', in A. Tabari, A. and N. Yeganeh (eds), *In the Shadow of Islam: The Women's Movement in Iran* (London: Zed Press, 1982).
9. For a fuller discussion of this topic, see the text of my 6 April 1989 talk at Harvard Divinity School.
10. E. Abrahamian, *Iran Between Two Revolutions* (Princeton: Princeton University Press, 1982), pp. 124–5.
11. Ibid, p. 103.
12. M. T. Bahar, *A Brief History of Iran's Political Parties*, in Persian, (Tehran: Jibi Publications, 3rd edn 1978 [1942]) pp. viii–xi.
13. Quoted by Bahar, ibid., p. 306.
14. Abrahamian, *Iran*, p. 124.
15. A. R. Sadeqipur (ed.), *Collection of Speeches by the Late Majesty Reza Shah the Great*, in Persian (Tehran: Javidan Publishers, 1968) p. 41.
16. Quoted in D. N. Wilber, *Reza Shah Pahlavi* (Hicksville, NY: Exposition Press, 1975), p. 49.
17. Ibid, p. 159.
18. Ibid, p. 154.
19. Abrahamian, *Iran*, p. 136.
20. Wilber, *Reza Shah*, p. 238.
21. Sadeqipur, *Collection* of *Speeches*, pp. 137–9.
22. See, for instance, 'An Analysis of the Socio-Economic Situation of Women in Iran', by National Union of Women, which gives 'utilization of the cheap labour of women for the labour market of colonialist and dependent capitalism' as one of the reasons for measures taken by Reza Shah (Tabari and Yeganeh, *In the Shadow*, p. 147).
23. Sh. Akhavi, 'State Formation and Consolidation in Twentieth-Century Iran: The Reza Shah Period and the Islamic Republic', in A. Banuazizi, and M. Weiner (eds), *The State, Religion and Ethnic Politics: Afghanistan, Iran, and Pakistan* (Syracuse: Syracuse University Press, 1986).
24. It is indicative of Reza Shah's subordination of everything, including his own personal beliefs, to state-building that he issued the decree on compulsory unveiling of women. Some time before the decree he is quoted as saying, 'Well, if it is really necessary to introduce this change, one cannot stop the progress of the country. But in that case, I think I would first divorce both my wives'. Quoted in Mehrangiz Dolatshahi, tape no. 5, page 22, interviewed by Shahrokh Meskoob, Paris, 18 May, 1984, for Iranian Oral History Project [hereafter referred to

Women, Islam and the State

as IOHP], Harvard University. A somewhat different account is given by another interviewee of IOHP, Mohammad Baheri, interviewed by Habib Ladjevardi, Cannes (France), 8 August, 1982, who quotes Reza Shah's wife (Mohammad Reza Shah's mother) as saying that when Reza Shah on the 8 January 1936 came to take her unveiled to the public ceremony, he told her, 'It is easier for me to die than to take my wife unveiled amidst strangers, but I have no choice. The country's progress requires that women must be set free, and I must be the first person to do this.' See tape no. 9, page 11.

25. See chapter 2 of the present volume for fuller discussion of Turkey.
26. See, for instance, his coronation speech on 25 April, 1926, in Wilber, *Reza Shah*, p. 115.
27. For further discussion of the contrast between Turkey and Iran see C. F. Gallagher, *Contemporary Islam: The Plateau of Particularism, Problems of Religion and Nationalism in Iran* (New York: American Universities Field Staff Reports, 1966) and *Contemporary Islam: The Straits of Secularism: Power, Politics, and* piety *in Republican Turkey*, Southwest Asia Series, vol. XV, no. 3 (Turkey) (New York: American Universities Field Staff, 1966). See also R. Pfaff, 'Disengagement From Traditionalism in Turkey and Iran', in *Western Political Quarterly*, vol. 16 (March 1963) pp. 79–98, and B. Lewis, *The Emergence of Modern Turkey* (Oxford: Oxford University Press, 1961).
28. For a full discussion of these skilful manoeuvres, see Abrahamian, *Iran*, pp. 118–9.
29. For a full discussion of women's societies and journals of this period, see chapter 3 of E. Sanasarian, *The Women's Rights Movement in Iran* (New York: Praeger, 1982).
30. See, for instance, 'Eshqi's famous poems against Reza Khan's republican claims, M. 'Eshqi, *Collected Works*, ed. A. Moshir Salimi, in Persian (Tehran: Amir Kabir, 1971) pp. 277–99.
31. Sanasarian, *The Women's Rights Movement*, p. 69.
32. Ibid, p. 71.
33. F. Adamiyat, *The Ideology of Iran's Constitutional Movement*, in Persian (Tehran: Payam Publishers, 1976) pp. 426–429.
34. See H. E. Chehabi 'Modernist Shi'ism and Politics: The Liberation Movement of Iran'. Ph. D. dissertation, Yale University, 1986.
35. See A. Najmabadi, 'Depoliticisation of a Rentier State: The Case of Pahlavi Iran' in H. Beblawi, and G. Luciani (eds), *The Rentier State* (London: Croom Helm, 1987).
36. See, for instance, M. Dolatshahi's account in IOHP tape no. 6, pp. 3–4, where she explains how in 1963 once she decided to run for the *Majlis*, she wrote a letter of appeal (*'arizeh*) to the Shah, asking his permission to stand as a candidate from Tehran or Kermanshah.
37. See Gh. R. Afkhami, *The Iranian Revolution: Thanatos on a National Scale* (Washington, D.C.: The Middle East Institute, 1985) pp. 76–77.
38. This transformation of his role and his self-image began after the 1953

coup. Bayne *(Persian Kingship in Transition,* New York: American Universities Field Staff, 1968, p. 105) refers to conversations with the shah around 1955 in which he would emphasise that 'I will rule'. One of the older generation statesmen, Jamal Emami, is quoted as having once retorted, 'Your Imperial Majesty, I don't understand why you insist on becoming a prime minister!' (IOHP, Hossein Azmoudeh, interviewed by Zia Sedghi, Paris, France, 24 March 1984. Tape no. 2, p. 9). Bayne (p. 188) in fact refers to 'the shah's desire to be his own Prime Minister' in the mid-1960s.

39. See, for instance, M. R. Pahlavi *Answer to History* (New York: Stein and Day, 1980).
40. M. R. Pahlavi *Towards the Great Civilization,* in Persian (Tehran: Pahlavi Library Publication, 1978) p. 89.
41. G. E. Goodell,*The Elementary Structures of Political Life: Rural Development in Pahlavi Iran* (New York and Oxford: Oxford University Press, 1986) p. 182.
42. Ibid., p. 181.
43. Ibid., p. 183.
44. In this process, the old attitude of the citizen towards the state, one of 'avoidance', became replaced by one of total dependency on the state. Neither attitude is conducive to the creation of a public arena, of open politics, of dialogue and reform. The state, 'like Allah', is viewed 'independent of the world of men' (Goodell, p. 153). One can totally reject it (and overthrow it), but cannot reform it, or negotiate with it. This is why even when the Shah was engaged in initiating reforms that oppositionists themselves had projected, such as land reform, women's vote, reform of family laws, the oppositionists could not view these initiatives as reforms. To do so would have moved them from the domain of rejection of the state to the domain of total dependency on and legitimation of the state; there was no political space in-between the two.
45. See, A. Najmabadi 'Iran's Turn to Islam: From Modernism to a Moral Order', *The Middle East Journal,* vol. 41 (1987) no. 2, pp. 202–17.
46. See M. R. Pahlavi, *The White Revolution,* in Persian (Tehran, 1967) and *Answer to History.*
47. See, for instance, M. R. Pahlavi, *Mission for My Country,* in Persian, (Tehran, 1960) pp. 474–480.
48. O. Fallaci, *Interview with History* (New York: Liveright 1976)
49. For a description of some of these organisations see 'The Reminiscences of Farangis Yeganegi' (interviewed by Mahnaz Afkhami, Los Angeles, November 1983), pp. 12–20, in the Oral History of Iran Collection of the Foundation for Iranian Studies, Bethesda, Maryland. See also Mehrangiz Dolatshahi, interviewed by Shahrokh Meskoob, May 1984, Paris, France, IOHP.
50. IOHP, Dolatshahi, tape no. 4, p. 15.
51. Ibid, p. 25.

52. Dolatshahi traces this change in occupational pattern and in upper-class women's attitudes towards government employment to the activities of Point IV – a development aid programme launched by the United States in 1949 – in Iran, which began in the early 1950s. According to her account, Point IV needed women who were fluent in English. They apparently recruited women from the upper classes, sent them for training to the United States, and employed them in highly skilled positions upon return. This process transformed both the job categories in which women were employed and the women's image of such work (Dolatshahi, IOHP, tape no. 3, p. 14).
53. Afkhami, 'A Future . . . ', p. 333.
54. See 'The Reminiscences of Farangis Yeganegi', pp. 21–22.
55. IOHP, tape no. 5, p. 3.
56. IOHP, tape no. 4, p. 22.
57. IOHP, tape no. 8.
58. For a survey of changes in family laws in the 1960s and 1970s, see B. Pakizegi and Gh. Vatandoust, as in note 2 above.
59. See 'The Reminiscences of Malmaz Afkhami', interviewed by Fereshteh Nura'i, Washington, D.C., September 1982, in the Oral History of Iran Collection of the Foundation for Iranian Studies, Bethesda, Maryland.
60. IOHP, Mohammad Bahen, interviewed by Habib Ladjevardi, August 1982, Cannes, France, tape no. 9, p. 13. For similar remarks, see IOHP, Hossein Azmoudeh, interviewed by Zia Sedghi, Paris, France, March 1984, tape no. 2, pp. 8–9.
61. A. Tabari, 'Islam and the Struggle for Emancipation of Iranian Women', in A. Tabari, and N. Yeganeh (eds), *In the Shadow*.
62. For a discussion of these points, see Yeganeh, 'Women's Struggles . . . '.
63. For a discussion of these political shifts in the broader Middle Eastern context, see S. Amir Arjomand (ed.), *From Nationalism to Revolutionary Islam* (Albany: State University of New York, 1984); for Iran, see Najmabadi, 'Iran's Turn . . . '.
64. Since the appropriation of the concept by the Islamic Republic, many critics of the new regime have distanced themselves from it. In fact Al-e Ahmad is in the unfortunate situation of metamorphosing from the indigenous intellectual hero into a demon held responsible for the rise and consolidation of Islamic theocracy in Iran.
65. S. Mardin, 'Super Westernization in Urban Life in the Ottoman Empire in the Last Quarter of the Nineteenth Century', in P. Benedict, E. Tumertekin and F. Mansur (eds), *Turkey: Geographic and Social Perspectives* (Leiden: E. J. Brill, 1974) p. 415.
66. See F. San'atkar, 'Political Marriages of Mojahedin-e Khalq', in Persian, in *Nimeye Digar*, nos. 3–4 (Winter 1986), pp. 10–33, and 'Feminism and Women Intellectuals', in Persian, in *Nazm-e Novin*, vol. 8 (Summer 1987), pp. 56–85.
67. Fatemeh, the dughter of the Prophet and wife of Ali, and Zeynab, wife of the martyred Hussain, grandson of the Prophet, are held out to the

women of Iran as paragons of Islamic purity and militancy and a models to emulate.

68. For a fuller discussion of post-revolutionary changes for women in Iran, see my paper, 'Power, Morality, and the New Muslim Womanhood,' presented at the workshop on 'Women and the State in Afghanistan, Iran and Pakistan', 20 March, 1989, Massachusetts Institute of Technology, Center for International Studies.

4 The Convenience of Subservience: Women and the State of Pakistan

Ayesha Jalal

The relationship between women and the state in Pakistan has been both compelling and paradoxical. After nearly a decade of state-sponsored attempts at stifling women's voices in the public arenas and pushing back the boundaries of their social visibility, Pakistan has become the first state in the Islamic world to have a woman prime minister. A state media which until yesterday poured scorn upon articulate and assertive women is today faithfully and respectfully projecting the voice and person of Benazir Bhutto. In so far as the role of women in Muslim societies has symbolic connotations, it is tempting to see Benazir Bhutto's advent as something of a psychological 'revolution'. A Western cartoonist hinted as much while portraying her in an impish mood asking a line of attendants veiled from head to toe: 'How do you like your new outfits, Gentlemen?'[1]

But where humour elates, reality deflates. Despite the apparent shift in the psychological balance between the genders wrought by developments in the electoral arena, women's relationship with the state in the Islamic social setting of Pakistan remains substantially unchanged, economically, legally and politically. Over 75 per cent live in the rural areas, not infrequently in conditions of abject poverty; an overwhelming majority have little knowledge of doctrinal Islam, much less of their rights as citizens of the Pakistani state. In the stirring language of a report by the government-sponsored Commission on the Status of Women: 'the average rural women of Pakistan is born in near slavery, leads a life of drudgery and dies invariably in oblivion'.[2] A mere 16 per cent of the total female population qualify as literate, and that too just barely. And however much one might inveigh against the faulty methodology employed to compute the absolute figure, it is nevertheless significant that Pakistan has one of the lowest rates in the world of female participation in the labour force.[3]

So why allude to women's subservience as a form of social convenience when the notion flies in the face of the social and economic injustices forced upon the vast majority of them in Pakistan? But then Pakistani women are not of a piece. As in other parts of the world, rural-urban differences, not to mention social, economic and regional disparities divide women quite as much as the weight of religious precepts and local customs separate them from men. Indeed to speak of Pakistani women without qualification is to lump them into a category defined by legal aggregation rather than socio-logical fact. In any case, subservience owes as much to objective conditions as to subjective perceptions of them. No doubt most women in Pakistan have small choice except to submit to a subservience decreed by a highly inequitable socio-economic order, buttressed by a thin veneer of ostensibly Islamic morality. It may well be that a closer investigation of the mental worlds of these poor, unlettered women – yet to be undertaken – will reveal that their submission is not entirely unqualified. But if the lives of these women are speckled by everyday forms of resistance, these have been muted in effect.

As for those Pakistani women who are neither poor nor unlettered, submission can be socially rewarding. So long as they do not transgress social norms, women from the middle and upper strata in rural and urban areas alike are accorded respect as well as a modicum of privileges within the sphere of the family and, depending upon their generational and marital status, also in wider social networks. A striking proportion of lower middle, middle and upper class women, those belonging to commercial and business groups in particular, actually endorse the state's Islamisation policies. In fact with a few notable exceptions of symbolic dissent – for instance a refusal to accept the institution of arranged marriage or the defiant pursuit of a professional career – most women drawn from these social segments have chosen the path of least resistance, perhaps because so far the most retrogressive 'Islamic' laws have not affected them in any appreciable manner. Simply put, women belonging to the relatively better-off Pakistani families are not quite the hapless and unsuspecting victims of 'Islamic' chauvinism which certain secular critics and especially the 'feminists' among them would like to believe.

This is not to say that the constraints of convention, which for so long have militated against their mobility and self-fulfillment, are any less real for Pakistani women. Nor does it suggest that no Pakistani woman is irritated by anachronistic social conventions. But there is a gap between individual awareness and collective action. This is precisely why the role of relatively economically privileged and educated women in the reproduction of the gender biases underpinning their subservience has to be plainly acknowledged. Refusing to accept an element of complicity on the part of women, as indeed of their counterparts elsewhere in the world, is tantamount to viewing them as passive victims acted upon by social forces over which they have no control. Holding them responsible, might serve as a goad for some and confirmation for others to undertake the critical self-evaluation that is so essential if they are to realise their potential as active agents with choices in shaping the processes of social change.

In Pakistan, as in other parts of the world, the class origins of those who have formed the vanguard of the 'feminist' movement have been the decisive factor in the articulation of women's issues at the level of the state. Educated urban middle and upper class in the main, these women have toyed with notions of emancipation but carefully resisted challenging their prescribed roles in society. Such deference is merely the outward expression of a deeper and largely subjective consideration: the stability of the family unit and by implication of the social order itself. As beneficiaries of social accommodations worked out over long periods of history, middle and upper class women everywhere have a stake in preserving the existing structures of authority, and with it the convenience of a subservience that denies them equality in the public realm but also affords privileges not available to women lower down the rungs of the social hierarchy. This is why the seemingly curious notion of the 'convenience of subservience' provided the inspiration for this essay on the triumvirate of Islam, women and the state in Pakistan. At each step it served as a sobering reminder that insofar as Pakistani women share a common fate, subservience has been relatively more convenient for some than for others.

An historical overview of the dynamics shaping the relationship between women and the Pakistani state can bring these conceptual generalisations into sharper relief. By placing the state at the centre of analysis and tracing the evolution of its insecurities – or more politely, its security complex – it is possible both to understand the significance of Islam's legitimising role in Pakistani society and the political uses made of it to effect changes, whether progressive or retrogressive, in the position of women. Such an approach must necessarily take into account the years preceding the creation of Pakistan in 1947– the period of nationalist ferment – followed by an investigation of the turbulent four decades after independence.

SYMBOLS OF MUSLIM IDENTITY: WOMEN IN SOUTH ASIAN ISLAM

Relatively little has been written about women in the history of Islam in South Asia. While true of the historiography of the Muslim world in general, the lacuna poses special problems in a context where Islam has been the religion of a geographically dispersed, linguistically diverse and culturally diffuse minority. Yet despite local and class variations in their status, women have been the pillars of Muslim social structure, wherever and however adopted. So in spite of the fragmentary nature of the empirical evidence on Muslim women in the annals of South Asia, it is still possible to draw upon some of the more obvious results of Islam's efforts to adapt itself to its Indian environment.

Even before the challenge of Western colonialism, when state power was in the hands of Muslim dynasties, the Faithful had to seek accommodations with peoples of religious convictions other than their own. To win the allegiance of an overwhelmingly non-Muslim population, Muslim dynasts had often to underplay the specifically Islamic concerns of their co-religionists. But if the terms of co-existence militated against the state's defining its policies in the idiom favoured by the religious guardians, it was dicier still to invite charges of irreligiosity. The stability of Muslim rule from the days of the Delhi Sultanate to the twilight of the Mughal empire rested on a careful apportioning of patronage: non-Muslims were pressed into the service of the state and the quiescence of Muslim religious leaders was secured through material and other royal nostrums.

It was a delicate tight-rope walk none the less. The compromise touched a raw nerve in the Muslim conscience, among the *ashraf* (the upper classes) rather more so than the *ajlaf* (the lower classes): the fear of losing their religious identity in a sea of infidels. But there was consolation in the knowledge that the real strength of the Islamic social order lay in the continued stability of the family unit, and more specifically the social control of women. By fiercely clinging to these two seemingly immutable symbols of the Islamic way of life, Muslims could hope to preserve their separate religious identity without putting at risk those social and political accommodations so painfully worked out by successive generations of empire-builders.

The two-pronged approach adopted by the forefathers of contemporary Muslim society in the subcontinent – the dialectic of accommodations with members of other religious communities on the one hand, and a continuing social convervatism in the domestic sphere on the other – was reinforced further with the imposition of the British Raj. Now more than ever, it was necessary to raise the shield of Muslim cultural resistance: the Faithful were not merely hopelessly outnumbered but state power had slipped out of the hands of their co-religionists.

In fashioning the Muslim response to Western colonialism, late nineteenth century social reformers – Sayyid Ahmad Khan in particular –

avoided broaching issues that involved fundamental changes in the Islamic world view nurtured and sustained by the domestic structures of Muslim society. Political accommodation with the colonial masters was acceptable, indeed desirable, but only so long as it did not entail adjustments in the established status quo of the private domain.

So while urging Muslim men to secure Western education and jobs in the colonial government, Sayyid Ahmad Khan remained adamantly opposed to women's education outside the religious mode. Just as there was no question of allowing the colonial state to tinker with the *Shari'ah*, particularly as it affected the structure of the family, education for women had to begin and end within the secure walls of the domestic arena. In 1882, Sayyid Ahmad confessed that the 'general state of female education among Muhammadans . . . [was] far from satisfactory'; but there could be no question of the government's 'adopting any practical measure by which . . . respectable Muhammadans may be induced to send their daughters to Government schools for education'. According to this great Muslim social reformer, 'there could be no satisfactory education . . . for Muhammadan females until a large number of Muhammadan males [had] receive[d] a sound education'.[4]

These opinions were consistent with Sayyid Ahmad's opposition to bringing women out of *purdah*, a loose term for their institutionalised seclusion[5], an integral feature of Muslim society. Quite as much as the *Shari'ah*, the *purdah* symbolised the Indian Muslim's identity and the integrity of the community as a whole. Confining women's education to household chores and religious teachings insulated them from the corrupting influences of the public realm. Above all, it confirmed Muslim cultural resistance against colonialism and Hinduism alike. Maulana Ashraf Ali Thanawi's *Bihishti Zewar* (Heavenly Ornaments) is a classic example of attempts at controlling and in the process conditioning women's own perceptions of the role ordained for them by Islam.[6] Deemed by many to be a mandatory part of the *jehaz* (dowry), it details in meticulous and almost embarrassingly explicit fashion how a good Muslim woman should address and serve her husband, behave towards her in-laws, the mother-in-law in particular, as well as her own kith and kin. Delineating a rigorous set of rules for the most amazingly mundane activities, including how to write letters to the husband, bathe, dress, walk, speak, look, pray, it is a veritable gold-mine for teasing out the inner recesses of the conservative Muslim psyche.

Throughout the early part of the twentieth century, middle and upper class Muslim women fed on religious scriptures and household wisdom rarely, if ever, staked a claim for a role in public affairs. In 1924, a mere 137800 qualified as literate; of these some 3940 had been touched by

Western learning.[7] Lagging behind men in education and conscious of the minority status of their community, Muslim women when forced to assume functions outside the domestic sphere did so 'as extensions of their familial roles', not merely in 'deference to male opinion' but 'because they felt more comfortable defining their public ventures in such terms'.[8] Women's need for social acceptability was too deeply ingrained for them to risk being anything other than the docile appendages of their families.

It was only in response to the 'growing desire of educated Muslims to find educated wives' that women were allowed to receive schooling outside their homes.[9] For some this marked a break with *purdah* in its extreme physical form. But though the educational institutes were strictly segregated, in the eyes of the majority of other students who continued to demonstrate their seclusion by donning the *burqa* – a tent-like garment covering them up to the ankles – these were the 'fallen' women, traitors to the Islamic cause.

In traditional Muslim mentality, education was not a prelude to female emancipation. The establishment of educational institutes for Muslim women was intended to counter the mushrooming of Christian missionary schools and to mitigate the effects of Hindu revivalist activities. In the Punjab certainly, it was the *Anjuman-e-Hamayat-e-Islam* (Organisation for the Defence of Islam) that was instrumental in setting up women's schools and colleges.[10] Few Muslim families were prepared to send their daughters to missionary institutes. Michelle Maskiell notes that the government-sponsored Lahore College attracted more Muslim women than Kinnaird, its Christian missionary equivalent. According to her findings, in 1931 nearly 30 per cent of the students in Lahore College consisted of Muslim women. On the other hand, between 1913–32 and 1933–47, Muslim women formed a mere 8 per cent and 16 per cent of Kinnaird's students.[11]

After the late 1920s, upper and middle class urban Muslim women in their hundreds, if not yet in their thousands, were attending English-medium schools and colleges. For the unlettered millions, whose ranks continued to swell, little changed and that too only for the worse. The social stigma attached to women acquiring an education, let alone one wholly in the Western mould, remained formidable. The small number of Muslim families that could shake its psychological hold took care to provide their daughters with religious training at home. So far from diminishing the role of the family in shaping the social outlook of Muslim women, the new educational trends heightened it further still. Even the most enlightened of Muslim families conceded that education for women was a worthwhile pursuit only if it enhanced their roles within the natal and the marital family. The great poet-philosopher of Pakistan, Muhammad Iqbal, found women pursuing careers other than those of wives and mothers abhorrent. European suffragettes in his opinion were 'superfluous women . . . compelled to "conceive" ideas instead of children'. The demand for the vote was in fact a plea for husbands and polygamy was the solution to this 'riot of the unemployed'.[12]

The political activities of Muslim women – limited though they were both in time and scale – were naturally accommodated within a framework defined by the dominant values and political preoccupations of Muslim men. If the All-India Muslim League's objective was to spot the blot in the Indian National Congress's claim to be representative of all India, the *Anjuman-e-Khawatin-e-Islam* or the All-India Muslim Ladies' Conference checkmated the pretensions of organisations claiming to speak for all Indian women. Founded in Aligarh in March 1914, the *Anjuman-e-Khawatin* claimed to represent the interests of all Muslim women; the reality eluded it quite as much as it did the Muslim League. Besides working for the social and educational uplift of Muslim women, the Anjuman's main contribution was to popularise a new style of *burqa* patterned on the Turkish model.[13] Its provincial branches, limited to key urban centres, soon became bases from which to launch an assault against the small group of Aligarh women who dominated the *Anjuman*. In their politics, Muslim women were understandably enough no more united than their men.

By the early 1930s, the *Anjuman* had practically faded into oblivion, a victim of internal dissension and ideological bankruptcy. The Muslim League at the time was also storming in the doldrums for many of the same reasons. In June 1932, however, the League passed a resolution favouring suffrage, adequate representation and equality for women.[14] This was a product of political calculations, not a sign of a sea-change in its attitudes towards women. Constitutional reforms were on the anvil and the Franchise Commission had on this occasion met with representatives of women's organisations like the All-India Women's Conference. As anticipated, the Government of India Act of 1935, though it fell short of the demands put forward by the All-India Women's Conference, did grant women a limited franchise; they were to have 6 out of a total of 150 seats in the council of state and 9 out of 250 seats in the federal assembly. So for the first time in the history of British India, women with the requisite property and educational qualifications could exercise the right of political choice and take their places alongside men in provincial as well as the federal assemblies.

The resuscitation of the Muslim League in the mid-1930s under the leadership of Mohammad Ali Jinnah opened a fresh chapter in the politics of Muslim India. Women were now encouraged to partake of public life, not as claimants of their rights so much as symbols of a special Muslim identity. On the grounds that there was a disjunction between Islamic strictures and Muslim customs, women from the more enlightened political families seized the opportunity to raise objections to polygamy, purdah and the denial of inheritance rights granted to them under the *Shari'ah*. Encouraged by Jinnah's 'modernist' intepretations of Islam, not to mention the outright opposition to the Pakistan demand by some of the most notable orthodox and fundamentalist of the religious guardians, Muslim women saw no contradiction between their gender interests and their role as symbols of the Muslim 'nation'.[15] After December 1938, there was an All-India Muslim Women's League with branches in the different provinces of British India. In March 1940 when the All-India Muslim League formally orchestrated the demand for a Pakistan, one of the more remarkable features of the session was the presence of a 'large number of Muslim women'.[16]

Undeniably many, though obviously not all, Muslim women played a part in the League's movement for Pakistan. The League's resounding success in the crucial 1945–46 elections owed much to enthusiastic campaigning by its women's wing and, above all, to those thousands of *burqa*-clad Muslim women who stepped out of the four walls for the first time in their lives to cast votes in the urban constituencies. The Muslim Women's League went to much greater lengths to get women to the polling stations in constituencies where the League's electoral prospects were uncertain – a true measure of the significance of the women's vote for the success of the League's movement for Pakistan. But the symbolism used in the elections – a vote for the Muslim League was presented as a religious duty – was potentially fraught with contradictions not only for the League's secular leadership but also for women's relationship with the future state of Pakistan. For the League leadership because the demand for a Pakistan was a political struggle against perceived Hindu domination in an independent India, not a movement to create a religious theocracy. And for women because the political use of religion and references by League leaders to the 'Islamic ideology' of the Pakistani state exposed them to orthodox and fundamentalist interpretations of an 'Islamic state'.

Although women were apparently welcomed into the public domain as participants in the Pakistan movement, most of them did so not as autonomous actors but as appendages of their men. The most prominent members of the Muslim Women's League were almost invariably the mothers, wives, daughters or sisters of influential Muslim politicians – a well-known phenomenon in South Asian politics be they Muslim, Hindu or Sikh. Fatima Jinnah and Begum Rana Liaquat Ali Khan are among the best known personalities of the period; the former was Mohammad Ali

Jinnah's sister and the latter the wife of Pakistan's first prime minister. Even the two women who have written about their personal experiences in the Pakistan movement, Begum Jahan Ara Shahnawaz and Begum Shaista Ikramullah, were members of important political families. Both go to some length to downplay any contradictions between their gender and national interests.[17]

For women who had neither the advantages of a privileged background nor the political connections of a Fatima Jinnah or a Rana Liaquat Ali, participation in the nationalist struggle may have been something of a liberating experience. But it was too brief to bring about a qualitative change in their lives. The mobilisation of women in a political movement claiming an ideological orientation based on the distinctive cultural identity of Indian Muslims instead of undermining conventional attitudes had, albeit imperceptibly, reasserted them with a fresh vengeance.

THE INSECURITIES OF FREEDOM

The creation of Pakistan did not solve the problem of a Muslim identity. Of the ninety-five million Muslims in British India at the time of partition, only sixty million became citizens of Pakistan. This, together with a communal holocaust and one of the largest movements of peoples in recorded history, not to mention the initiation of hostilities with India and chronic internal political instability, were all classic ingredients for an insecurity complex, one that was reflected in the state's policies as well as in the attitudes of the upper echelons of society.

These frenzied insecurities had predictable effects on social perceptions of women. The communal disorders had underlined the vulnerability of women deprived of the protection of male family members. It was irrelevant whether the victims of the horrors were primarily women belonging to the least privileged strata of society. The mere presence on Pakistani soil of tens of thousands of women who had been abducted and raped was an ignominious blot on the conscience of a social order that made a fetish of safeguarding female honour.

In the aftermath of independence in 1947, the emphasis on women's security was, in many respects, a sublimation of the broader concerns about the security of the state. The analogy is of some value in understanding the difference in the relationship between women and the state in the colonial and post-colonial periods. So long as the British remained at the helm, political accommodations aimed at circumscribing state intervention in the domestic arena. With the departure of the colonial rulers, the state was the ultimate guarantor of the social order whose moral underpinnings were symbolised by women. The legitimacy of the state depended on its ability to play this role to the satisfaction of most, if not all, its citizens.

This is where Islam proved to have its uses; but only to a point. Asserting that Islam was the ideological basis for Pakistan could give the state a veneer of legitimacy without necessarily squaring the circle of conflicting social interests. But paying lip service to the ideal of an 'Islamic state' they could barely define, much less give expression to in their policies, soon exposed Pakistan's early managers to a chorus of charges from the religious lobby.[18] A common note, and one with the loudest ring of truth, was that they had no intention of translating their Islamic rhetoric into actual policy. So political leaders and state officials – otherwise given to uttering 'progressive' views about Pakistan's future – peppered their denials by reasserting their commitment to Islam or by skating around issues which could give their religious opponents an opportunity to exploit popular sensibilities.

Nothing could disturb the precarious balance between state and society more than the issue of women. This was why the managers of the state decidedly followed a policy of non-action. Put unequivocally, the legitimacy of the new state rested in large part on avoiding policies that gave women rights above and beyond those granted to them by Pakistan's regionally diverse social orders. It was only when Islam gave women more rights than the existing social customs that the state could expect to intervene on their behalf with a degree of impunity.

Inheritance rights was one of the rare cases where Muslim women had something to gain by switching from customary to Islamic law. Under Islamic law women's right to inherit property, including agricultural land, was restricted to half that of their male siblings. But under the customary law in operation in various provinces of British India – most notably in the Punjab – women were denied all rights of inheritance. This was a convenient way of avoiding the fragmentation of family property and caused few pangs of conscience, since it was customary to compensate daughters with elaborate dowries at the time of marriage. The demand for women's right of inheritance had been taken up by the *Anjuman-e-Khawatin*, but to no avail. In 1937, although Jinnah forced the Muslim Shariat Application Act through the central assembly, which gave women some inheritance rights, he did so only after omitting agricultural land from the category of property families could pass on to their daughters.[19] The resistance of the landed notables of the Punjab had proven to be overwhelming.

The establishment of Pakistan revived hopes of extending women's inheritance rights to landed property. By January 1948, the West Punjab provincial assembly was desperately manoeuvering to resist pressures for a blanket adoption of Muslim inheritance laws. Given the inequality enshrined in these laws, clamouring for women's inheritance rights under the Islamic umbrella amounted to legalising their inferior status in relation to men. But as far as the urban educated women were concerned, a successful battle for property rights would grant them recognition as independent legal entities in a social order where they were consigned to being wholly dependent on men from birth until death.

For the members of a landlord dominated assembly, it was the implications and not the principles underlying the West Punjab Muslim Shariat Application Act of 1948 that mattered. Though the majority were by now cheerfully waving the Muslim League flag, they were by no means ready to sacrifice their interests at the altar of religious rectitude. So there were the inevitable snags and delays. Stonewalling by some members postponed the discussion on the West Punjab Muslim Shariat Application Act. In what was the first time ever in the history of the new state, a few hundred women gathered outside the assembly chambers to demonstrate their disgust at these delaying tactics. This public display of anger by urban educated women, many of whom were in *purdah*, suggests that for them unequal rights under Islam were better than no rights at all. It was not simply that some women were now turning their limited experience in political agitation gained during the Pakistan movement towards new directions. This display of protest had the added advantage of being able to invoke Islam on its side.

In the event, the Punjab assembly did pass the Act. But the force of the opposition continued unabated. Mindful of the risks involved in upsetting the local apple-cart in the Punjab, Jinnah as Governor-General withheld consent from the bill, proving yet again that 'progressive' ideas were no substitute for the attractions of political expediency. A state still in the process of assembling its central apparatus was in no position to alienate the dominant social classes on the question of gender. Even after it had been placed on the statute books, the provisions of the West Punjab Muslim Shariat Application Act were by no means binding. The state had willy-nilly to allow families the right of personal discretion. Those who refused to give their daughters a piece of the family pie could confidently appeal in a local court, since the Shariat Application Act was intended to supplement rather than supplant existing customary laws.[20]

Clearly then, unless willing and able to bridge the gap between law and its practice, the state's receptivity to women's causes cannot be measured in terms of legal enactments alone. By far the more revealing indicators of the state's attitudes towards women are the stray instances which tend to escape the eye of the most discerning analysts. The Pakistani state's stance on the rehabilitation of women abducted during the partition riots is a fine example. Sadat Hassan Manto – a well-known writer of Urdu short stories – was prosecuted twice for his hair-raising accounts of women's traumatic experiences in the partition disorders. The two stories – 'Khul Do' and 'Thanda Ghosht' – were banned on the novel grounds that too explicit a statement of the tragedy of women subjected to abduction and rape bordered on obscenity.

The real point, however, was that murmuring the truths of human deprav- ity in narrative form would make families hesitate before taking back women relatives. So on the face of it, a noble enough stance; one consistent with the state's duty to uphold the norms of Islamic morality. Yet despite the hue and cry about retrieving abducted women, the authorities showed few actual signs of springing into action. It was only after being lambasted by the Indian government for its dilatory policy[21] and, more decisively, due to extreme pressure from women's social welfare groups hurriedly organised in the aftermath of partition that the state managed to gear itself to the unwholesome task of rehabilitating dishonoured women. By April 1949, although some 50 000 had been retrieved,[22] the social barriers to their resettlement had still to be surmounted. The state's initial disinclination to aid and abet the rehabilition of abducted women may have been an inversion of Islamic morality, but given the rigidities of society it was not entirely surprising.

The plight of 'fallen' Muslim women is, admittedly, an extreme illustration of the constraining influence of social values on state action. Yet even where the state could plausibly exercise autonomy of judgement, its record on women is remarkably threadbare. Social conditioning, and not state initiative, was the more pronounced factor shaping attitudes towards women. While women could certainly voice their opinions, public platforms remained the preserve of the wives, daughters or sisters of eminent personalities; not the most convincing proof of an increase in the visibility of women. *Purdah* may have been on the decline, but the boundaries of mobility for the majority of women continued to be defined by domestic arena. Mixed gatherings were exceptions to the rule: a privilege of liberal urban upper and middle class families that was to be deplored, not imitated.

Western observers of Pakistan are often struck by the strange anomaly of highly articulate and accomplished women in a society tarred with repeated brush strokes of conservatism. The reason for these women's survival may be among the better kept secrets of Pakistani society. Yet it has to be disclosed if only to appreciate the peculiarity of the accommodation worked out between state and society within years of independence. According to the terms, the state's social pronouncements would always be dipped in the Islamic idiom. But it would not neglect to protect the right of its liberal citizens to deviate from the literal interpretations of the Islamic way of life. In sum, the state would tolerate all variants of Muslims, even the occasional emancipated women, only so long as its own Islamic credentials – intrinsic to its claims to be legitimate – were not put to the test.

This is why women of grit and mirth can be found in every phase of Pakistan's history, a tribute to the resilience of families that deride but never challenge the laws of social oppression, much less of state repression. It also explains the relative isolation of enlightened Pakistani families in a society whose values are shot through with an unrelenting, though by no means monolothic, conservatism. Above all, it suggests why educated Pakistani women, while they might complain about the lack of employment opportunities, are wont to opt for certain and not so certain comforts of their homes.[23]

This curious phenomenon, which is part and parcel of the accommodation between the dominant classes and the state, has had large implications for Pakstani women in general. Women who concerned themselves with extracting concessions from the state belonged mostly to the dominant classes. While airing demands on behalf of all women, they generally avoided overstepping the terms of their class accommodations with the state. By the same token, these proponents of women's rights had to respect the limits within which the state could formulate policies. These limits, once again, were defined by the state's readiness to counter the forces of reaction without exposing the chinks in the conservative posture it had to maintain to fit the sensibilities of broader sections of society. So the relationship between women and the state had necessarily to develop along a spectrum whose two extremes can only be defined as a conservatism of reaction and a conservatism of liberalism.

The ground-rules of social conservatism and the shaky foundations of its own project of construction and consolidation debarred the state from intervening openly on the side of women. In February 1949, when at its very first session the All-Pakistan Muslim League's Council summarily refused to consider electing a woman candidate for the office of Joint Secretary, no official rebuke was issued. But the dramatic walk-out by all the women members of the League could not be treated lightly. The state had to come forward to cajole and console, not least because the band of infuriated women was led by the prime minister's wife, Begum Rana Liaquat Ali Khan.

Within days of the incident, Begum Liaquat Ali Khan laid the foundation-stone of the All-Pakistan Women's Association.[24] Described as a 'non-political' organisation of women, irrespective of caste, creed or colour, it was seen to be the 'clearest indication' thus far by the Pakistan government to 'adopt a progressive attitude towards female emancipation'.[25] The extensive official publicity given to APWA is an indication of the state's eagerness to support women's rights activists willing to work within prescribed limits.

Extending patronage to organisations like APWA was more in the form of a political calculation than a commitment to female emancipation. APWA might preempt the growth of women's pressure groups over whom the state had no influence.[26] Moreoever, the class origins of its leading lights was the best insurance that women's demands on the state would not be radical or embarrassing. The prospect of groups dominated by working class women, however distant and remote, was enough to persuade the state to support APWA's preoccupations with social welfare and educational activities. Accounting for the interests of the small number of women who were being pushed into the labour market by material necessities, or the woeful condition of the rural multitudes facing economic deprivation and the sexual tyranny of local bigwigs, would have placed the state in an impossible quandary. So it had every reason to choose to view women's rights in terms defined by the representatives of the dominant classes, especially if these were voiced from the safety of officially subsidised public platforms.

The demands voiced by a woman government employee before Pakistan's first Pay Commission makes the point fairly and squarely. It was the opinion of Ms S. J. Begum that women in government service should be given 50 per cent more in wages than men due to their appreciably higher cost of living. For instance, transportation alone cost women four times as much as men.[27] What she was really angling for was a higher minimum and a lower maximum wage, since under government rules, which also restricted them to mainly clerical jobs in the accounts or the medical departments, women could not remain in service after marriage. These arguments were rejected out of hand on the grounds that men and women had to enjoy equality of employment. The members of the Pay Commission, true to the double standards of their society, had no trouble reconciling this view with their continued support for rules that not only denied women equal employment opportunities but forced them to resign from sevice upon contracting marriage. As a minister in the central cabinet put it plainly, women could not enter certain services because of their 'physical disabilities' which it was 'not in the power of any Government to remove'.[28]

Seeking refuge in the laws of nature was the perfect defence for a government culpable of sexual discrimination. Making hypocrisy a state policy was another. The interim report of the constitutional committee on fundamental rights had taken special care to incorporate sweeteners for women affiliated with APWA. Pakistani women were to have 'equality of status, equality of opportunity and equal pay for equal work'.[29] In the opinion of Begum Jahan Ara Shahnawaz, a member of parliament, the interim report was a 'golden hour' in the 'history of the women's movement in this country', especially for those 'whose families ha[d] been working for the acceptance of [the] basic principles of Islam for the women of Pakistan for generations . . . '[30]

Such unbridled emthusiasm was not easy to either promote or sustain. The women's question was not a priority for the constitution-makers; the whole exercise was floundering badly because of interminable quibbling among the provinces and between them and the centre. The truths about women's less than sweet predicament in the affairs of the state were, however, too glaring not to occasionally penetrate through the well-insulated walls of parliament. But even this was acceptable, and certainly less likely to arouse controversy than the sight of determined women marching in tandem through the bazaars and mohallas of Pakistan.

So no one flinched when Begum Shaista Ikramullah tried to draw parliament's attention to the government's 'retrograde and . . . reactionary policy' towards women on the educational as well as the employment fronts. Not only was government slashing allocations for their higher education, but was 'definitely taking steps to discourage and prevent women from taking their fair share in the Government of the country'.[31] Women were beginning to secure better grades than men in most qualifying examinations. Yet they could not look forward to careers in a range of government departments, including the prestigious foreign service. To add insult to injury, those persuaded or coerced into liking marriage had to do so by lumping their jobs in government. The Begum was heard with the respect due to women of her class. But at the end of it all, the government rebuttal was patronising enough to sound almost insolent. A passing remark about men being allowed to take second and fourth wives was picked up by the government spokesman to query Begum Ikramullah whether she favoured similar rights for women. Her response splendidly sums up the dialogue between women and the state: 'I mean their rights to an equal share in the country's government, in the country's legislature and in every other sphere of work . . . The fault lies in your *own nasty minds*. I cannot help that'.[32]

With the Islamic dagger lying so close to the heart of women's case for a better and fairer deal, it is not surprising that so few of their self-professed representatives could argue for rights without first asserting their religious convictions. A popular theme, expressed from every public platform open to them, was that Islam had given women more rights than any other religion; there was nothing fundamentally wrong with Quranic prescriptions for women, the problem lay in their never having been applied properly. These were the women apologists of Islam. Others more squarely identified with religious organisations like the fundamentalist *Jamat-i-Islami* went a step further, demanding a blanket adoption of the Shari'ah as a way of regulating women's lives.

Those less enthused by Islamic tenets on the relationship between the sexes, justified their claims to operate outside the domestic frontiers by emphasising social welfare activities. Almost all the women's organisations formed during this period were concerned with issues of motherhood and child-rearing or with goals so specific as to make them wholly marginal or at best the extension of APWA. Some of the examples include the Family Planning Association of Pakistan, the Pakistan Child Welfare Council, the Pakistan Red Cross, the Pakistan Nurses' Foundation, the Housewives' Association, the Federation of University Women and the Karachi Business and Professional Women's Club.[33] Begum Rana Liaquat Ali Khan, the President of APWA, went so far as to assert that social welfare was the 'bed rock on which the whole structure of our national life can be raised'. This was also the one field where women could make the 'greatest contribution'.[34] She was right. And while taking nothing away from the contributions made by APWA and other women's organisations towards the social betterment of some women, the marginality of these activities in a context where millions needed a helping hand cannot be over-emphasised.

So long as the façade of parliamentary government remained intact, APWA's other main contribution was to toe the government's line on most political issues. Even organisations formed with the expressed objective of raising women's political consciousness – the left-leaning Democratic Women's Association and the more eclectic United Front for Women's Rights for instance – continued nevertheless to operate within the same broad parameters as APWA. The overlapping membership of these women's organisations tended to limit the range of serious ideological disagreements among them. Belonging to the urban educated middle and upper class strata of society, these women limited their forays into the political arena to demanding a few more seats for themselves here or there or, more frequently, to buffeting the government's position vis-à-vis the religious ideologies, for whom the only acceptable face of Islam was that of uncompromising reaction. However, by their consistently fierce opposition to the Islamic world-view propagated by the religious leaders – whether the low-lying *mullahs* or the high-flying *ulema* – these women's organisations, and APWA in particular, can claim to have justified their existence.

An undoubtedly positive result of pressures by the United Front for Women's Rights and APWA's collaboration with the state was the setting up in June 1955 of a Commission on Marriage and Family Laws. Among its members were the Chief Justice of the Supreme Court, Justice Abdur Rahman; leading intellectuals like Dr Khalifa Shujauddin and Dr Khalifa Abdul Hakim; a representative of the religious lobby, Maulana Ihtshamul Huq Thanvi and Begum Jahanara Shahnawaz, Begum Anwar G. Ahmed and Begum Shamsunihar Mahmood. The Commission's brief was to find ways of restricting polygyny and giving women more rights of divorce than had been granted under the Muslim Marriage Dissolution Act of 1939. Its report, which included a long-winded note of dissent from Maulana Ihtshamul Huq Thanvi, was made public six months later. But as late as July 1958, APWA in conjunction with other women's organisations was holding a 'Women's Demands Day' to coax the government to implement the Commission's recommendations and introduce reforms in family law.[35]

The reasons for the prevarication are not difficult to discern. The Commission's report had caught the state seriously off balance. By 1958, political wranglings among its constituent units, a veritable crisis of the economy and, the result, mounting social tensions, had all served to heighten the state's insecurities. A concerted assault by the forces of religious orthodoxy against the Commission's 'progressive' and, therefore, 'unIslamic' recommendations was the last straw. Unless and until the state could claw back a sense of security, so fleetingly glimpsed during the first decade of its creation, there was no question of gambling away that Islamic card which gave it such legitimacy as it possessed. So the women who could expect to do well out of the reforms in family law had no alternative except to take the back seat while the state found a way out of the quagmire and embarked upon the stony road to consolidation.

TOWARDS STATE CONSOLIDATION AND FAMILY REFORMS

In October 1958 a military *coup d'état* led by General Ayub Khan sounded the death knell for Pakistan's muddled experiment with parliamentary government. With politicians and parties reduced to watching from the sidelines, senior bureaucratic and military officials could look forward to consolidating the authority of the Pakistani state. But to do so successfully they had still to maintain a semblance of a balance between their own frequently conflicting interests and those of the dominant provincial interest groups – the landlords and the business groups in particular – without at the same time exposing the state to the fatal charge of neglecting its duty as the ultimate guarantor of an Islamic society.

Just how easily such a charge could derail the consolidation drive can be seen in the fierce battle of wits between orthodox and liberal opinion following the state's one attempt, and a bold one at that, to give women and children rights hitherto denied by the existing social order. The provisions of the Family Law Ordinance of 1961, based on the considered recommendations of the Commission on Marriage and Family Laws, gave the forces of religious orthodoxy and the political opposition an opportunity to lash out against the regime's Islamic pretensions.

The provisions of the Ordinance were hardly revolutionary. All marriages now had to be registered with the local councils. The real cut for those who saw unfettered male supremacy as an immutable part of the Islamic way of life were the measured steps to curb polygyny. In concert with Quranic law, the Ordinance did not abolish a man's right to marry more than one woman at a time; it merely stipulated that he first obtain the permission of his existing wife. Since even this could be construed as too stringent a restriction on the prerogatives of the Muslim male, the Ordinance inserted a convenient loop-hole. In the event that a wife was unable or unwilling to give her husband permission, he could file an application at the local council whose chairman would set up an arbitration board to decide whether the man's reasons for taking another wife were 'necessary and just'.[36]

It is difficult to imagine how a handful of mortals could determine what was just or necessary for a Muslim man who until now had divine sanction to contract as many as four marriages. But if this were the poisoned arrow in the Ordinance's onslaught against diehard male chauvinism, its other provisions were no less biting. Men lured by the joys of polygyny had to maintain each of their wives 'adequately',[37] while those preferring the simplicity of divorce had to pay the dower agreed upon at the time of marriage. From the point of view of women, the Ordinance was an improvement on the Muslim Marriage Dissolution Act of 1939, which had already given them the right to initiate divorce proceedings, and a better insurance for claiming the custody of their children. The Ordinance also provided security for children whose parents were dead by legalising their right to inherit the property of their grandparents. In addition, it amended the Child Marriage Restraint Act of 1929, raising the legal age from fourteen to sixteen for females and from eighteen to twenty-one for males.[38]

So all in all women, or rather those who could understand the implications of the Ordinance, had cause to rejoice. If it had not been for General Ayub's personal interest in the matter and extremely effective lobbying by APWA as well as other women's groups, the Family Ordinance would have been nipped in the bud.[39] Whatever its limitations, the Ordinance did go some way towards giving women a basis from which to assert their rights without being laughed out of court. Scenes of women in their hundreds demonstrating outside the President's residence and the national assembly building is a poignant comment on the importance they attached to the Ordinance. For the informed Pakistani women, the 1961 Ordinance has remained the symbol of her legal rights, and has come to be seen as a high point in the state's relationship with women. But it is only by placing that relationship in the wider context of the state's development and overall objectives that it is possible to appreciate the reasons for issuing the Ordinance and the changes it actually wrought in the lives of Pakistani women. An Ordinance purporting to reform the family, a measure that was almost inconceivable due to the uncertainties of the first decade after independence, was more in the way of a symbolic attempt to demonstrate the state's newly forged sense of self-confidence than a realistic statement of its capacity to delve into the minefield of social reform policies.

The Family Law Ordinance of 1961 was the first, and so far the only, attempt by the state to assert its autonomy of action from those upholding the strictures of the social order, even if it meant impinging on the hitherto sacrosanct domain of the family.[40] On the face of it, it was proof that the consolidation of state authority had proceeded satisfactorily enough to imbue decision-makers with the confidence needed to dabble in such explosive matters as Muslim marriage and divorce laws. But the obstacles to implementing the Ordinance and, more emphatically, its visible failure to effect a substantial change in attitudes beyond a small section of society, points to quite a different set of conclusions. The implementation of the Ordinance depended on the success of the local councils set up under Ayub's system of Basic Democracies, which aimed at extending bureaucratic control over the political process at all levels of Pakistani society. Yet the essentially undemocratic nature of the system was one of the main targets of opposition to the General's rule and, consequently, the Family Law reforms suffered in no uncertain manner from its unpopularity. The almost universal disdain for controlled 'democracy', together with the inherent weaknesses of its internal structure, exposed the state to a conservative backlash long before it had mustered up the courage to begin implementing its 'progressive' policy initiative to bring about any significant change in the status of the vast majority of Pakistani women.

The proposed reforms were an expression of the self-assurance of a military ruler eager to be seen in the role of 'moderniser' not only by his Western patrons but also by a small yet vocal 'modernist' constituency in Pakistan. But to this day the Ordinance has remained vulnerable to the same slings and arrows that have so often shaken the Pakistani state's resolve to adopt policies which can even remotely be seen as diverging from the tenets of Islam as interpreted by those of orthodox, if not fundamentalist, persuasions. In so far as the Ordinance was an early target of orthodox and fundamentalist groups, it has served as a sharp reminder to the 'modernist' constituency both within and outside the state apparatus that the disadvantages of venturing into the realm of social policy outweigh the advantages. The fact that the main thrust of the women's movement in Pakistan has been to dissuade the state from repealing the Ordinance suggests the extent to which reaction and regression have formed the main currents ever since its adoption.

As late as 1965, members of the provincial and national assemblies – egged on by the religious leaders – continued toying with the idea of repealing the Ordinance.[41] If it had not been for the crusade launched by women's organisations like APWA, it may well have been impossible for General Ayub's government, by now reaping the whirlwind of unintended consequences of controlled politics and economic policies promoting growth at the expense of redistribution, to save the Ordinance from the sharpening jaws of the religious opposition. The more so since opponents of the Ordinance were not just responding to the state's one 'progressive' social policy initiative but reacting to the potentially, if still not as yet noticeably, destabilising effects of its economic policies on relationships within the family.

Among the many unforeseen consequences of the state's ambitious policies for economic development was an increase in the participation of women in the labour market. In 1951, women constituted a mere 3.1 per cent of the total civilian labour force; by the time of the 1961 census the figure had gone up to 9.3 per cent.[42] Economic hardship rather than any sense of awareness – some 7.6 per cent of the total female population was literate[43] – had begun forcing women to take up employment outside their homes. And while the vast majority (89.12 per cent) were engaged in agricultural activities, between 1961 and 1964 the number of women employed in the non-agricultural sectors of the economy increased by approximately 250 000.[44] Though the total number of women gainfully employed outside the home was not large – in 1961 as many as 48 per cent still classified as housewives[45] – the trend along with an increase in the female population attending university came to be widely viewed as a scarcely veiled threat to the established value structures of a self-consciously Muslim society. Denied access to the state-controlled media, orthodox and fundamentalist defenders of the faith expressed their outrage at faltering moral standards through all available means: Friday sermons, pamphleteering and simple word of mouth.

But for the social tensions generated by the state's political and economic policies, conservative sniping at the Ayub regime alone could not have triggered off the mass urban uprisings that resulted in its downfall. By March 1969, General Yahya Khan, the Commander-in-Chief of the Pakistan army, had taken over the reins of power to make a last ditch attempt at putting the state back on the rails. The army action to quell the movement for autonomy in East Pakistan reveals the double paradox of a state disintegrating after a decade of efforts at consolidation and, more tragically, of a military regime which in the first flush of confidence granted concessional reforms to Pakistani women but ended up exploding the myth of its commitment to them or the Islamic morality they symbolised by perpetrating a campaign of repression and rape, in which countless Bengali women were brutalised.[46]

WOMEN AND THE PARANOIAS OF 'POPULISM'

The breakaway of East Pakistan following the army's ignominious defeat at the hands of its Indian counterpart lent urgency to old uncertainties about the state's capacity to survive. Yet the context had been altered dramatically by the massive socio-economic transformations which occurred during the much vaunted decade of 'development' and consolidation.

The insecurities of the Pakistani state had always been an effective foil to its pronouncing 'progressive' social policies for women. The period of Zulfiqar Ali Bhutto's 'populist' and 'progressive' Pakistan People's Party regime was no exception. The politicisation of such socially marginalised groups as industrial labour or the growing armies of umemployed rural-urban migrants, and their tendency to violent outbursts, had enhanced the collective paranoias of state managers and the dominant classes alike. This in itself was sufficient to foreclose the possibility of the state adopting too 'progressive' a posture towards women. The strength of the religious opposition to Bhutto's 'secular' social and political style and, therefore, 'unIslamic' rule was an even bigger hurdle.[47] The claim that it was not the ineffectiveness of religion to weld together Pakistan's diverse constituent units but the state's lack of Islamic morality which had led to the disintegration of the country touched a sympathetic chord across broad sections of society. It provided consolation for the more religious lower middle classes – the small shopkeepers and petty merchants, teachers, the semi-professional and educated unemployed.[48] Exhortations about an 'Islamic revival' also held out attractions for those in the higher echelons of society frightened by the implications of the PPP's 'populism'.[49] Islam in the Pakistani context, after all, was a proven bulwark against left-leaning tendencies. With his regime's Islamic credentials under challenge, Bhutto was not about to risk his political survival by harping on peripheral issues such as women's emancipation.

Yet despite the renewed social emphasis on Islam, the 1970s continued to see more and more women taking their place alongside men in the public domain.[50] If better access to education and the overall direction of socio-economic change were inducing women to abandon the security of the domestic arena, the Bhutto regime's apparent liberal leanings were reassuring. The public visibility and outspokenness of Mrs Bhutto was quite a contrast to the observance of *purdah* by Mrs Ayub Khan. Even more symbolic than the role of the first ladies was the increasing regularity with which unveiled women from different walks of life appeared on television during the Bhutto era.

The direct relationship between the PPP's 'populism' and women's growing social and political awareness was more dubious. The 'populism' of the Bhutto period amounted to reformist postures in favour of smallholding peasants, sharecroppers and industrial labour as well as the millenial expectations aroused by the slogan *Roti, Kapra aur Makan* (Food, Clothing and Shelter). There was admittedly something here for women from the lower stratas of society. But the Pakistani state's policy under Bhutto was based, as it always had been, on issues of class rather than of gender. So it was the peculiarities of their class situations, and the particular ideological orientations of their families, that determined the extent to which women were able, if at all, to take advantage of state 'populism' and extricate themselves from some of the more oppressive moorings of Pakistani society. A 1974 survey of a cross-section of lower, middle and upper class women – housewives as well as those with paid jobs – showed 98 per cent of the respondents 'brand[ing] themselves as adherents to traditional values'. The vast majority still regarded women's primary role to be in the domestic arena; 72 per cent of the domesticated and 46 per cent of the career women accepted the cultural dominance of men.[51] So irrespective of an increase in the number of women's groups during the Bhutto era,[52] Pakistani women did not wrest half as many benefits as might otherwise have been expected in a period of 'populism'.

In 1973, as part of Bhutto's administrative reforms, women at long last became eligible to join the superior civil services. The Constitution, drafted in the same year, defined equality for all citizens as one of the basic principles of its Fundamental Rights policy; there was to be 'no discrimination on the basis of sex alone'.[53] The state also undertook to make 'special provisions for the protection of women and children',[54] and assumed the responsibility to 'ensure full participation of women in all spheres of national life'.[55] Another article of the Constitution promised maternity benefits to employed women.[56]

Those who hailed these polite nods to women as a milestone in the Pakistani state's efforts to safeguard their interests[57] could not have guessed that the 1973 Constitution, like its predecessors, would be honoured more in the breach than in the observance. A far better measure of the lack of advances made by Pakistani women both before and during the Bhutto years was the reservation of ten seats for women by constitutional provision for a period of ten years. This was necessary because in spite of equal rights to vote and better access to education and ensured entry into both the national and provincial assemblies, only five women had actually managed to get themselves elected in the 1970 elections. So although nearly half of the total population, ten women were nominated to the assembly; a good indicator of the persistence of cultural barriers to their participation in politics.

In 1975, the 'people's government' did make the right noises about the unsatisfactory condition of women in Pakistan. Not because it had been seized by an urge to do something, but because 1975 happened to be designated by the United Nations as the 'International Women's Year'. So the PPP-dominated national assembly adopted a declaration on women's rights with a view to improving their social, economic and legal status.[58] Since Pakistan was a signatory to the objectives declaration of the International Women's Year, the Bhutto government appointed a special Commission on Women's Rights. Set up in January 1976, the Commission presented its first report by the summer of the same year.[59] The recommendations, predictably ambitious in conception, reveal just how much ground remained to be covered before the Pakistani state could plausibly claim to have rooted out the evils of sexual discrimination. The members of the Commission, ten women and five men, regretted the lack of success in the actual implementation of the Family Law Ordinance of 1961, suggested how the obstacles might be overcome and proposed a series of changes in its existing provisions. They made a great deal of the desirability of associating women with all aspects of national life, especially public office; proposed better facilities for family planning; suggested raising the legal age of marriage for men from eighteen to twenty-one; requested an amendment of the Political Parties Act which would require any party setting up more than ten electoral candidates to give 10 per cent of the tickets to women and, finally, urged the government to appoint a permanent Commission on Women.

If the bottles of ink spilt on women's issues during 1976 alone are taken as the gauge, Pakistan under Bhutto certainly did not lag behind other states in affirming the United Nation's stance on equality between the sexes. But symbolic gestures, unless backed by concerted policy measures to effect a change in social attitudes, cannot overcome the force of cultural resistance to dealing with women on terms other than those defined by the marriage of convenience between local customs and the great traditions of Islam. This is partly borne out by some of the underlying effects of 'populism' on Pakistani women. Those who are able to think dispassionately about the Bhutto years, and there are not many, agree that for all the talk about democratic freedoms, socialism and sporadic statements about women's rights, this was also the period which saw the state resorting to political intimidation. Terrifying political opponents with threats to the security of their female relatives – a security held to be synonymous with male honour – was not uncommon. Horror stories of women with meagre resources living outside the protected walls of the traditional Muslim family being forced into prostitution in the oil-rich Gulf states were among the most widely read news items of the time.

The easy convergence of socio-economic and political discontents with religious sensibilities, so well manifested in the Pakistan National Alliance's[60] campaign against Bhutto's alleged rigging of the 1977 elections, suggests just how barren the PPP's 'populism' had proven to be. As for women, their involvement in activities outside the bounds of the family appears to have resulted in a perversion of traditional norms of honour and protection. Returning women to the sanctity of the *chardivari* (literally, 'the four walls of the home') was among the many demands of the movement for a *Nizam-e-Mustafa* (the system of the Prophet Mohammad), which brought down Bhutto's government, leading the way for the extreme backlash of social conservatism in the 1980s. This gave the Pakistan army a chance to make a comeback to the political arena with aplomb, since it was now under a general claiming to hold a direct brief from Allah.

WOMEN ON THE 'ISLAMIC' ANVIL

General Zia-ul-Huq, Pakistan's new military ruler, had some rather rigid notions about the state's role in society. A devout Muslim, Zia proclaimed himself divinely ordained to steer Pakistani society back to the moral purity of early Islam. Pakistan and Islam, he argued, were inextricably linked, and the preservation of both had been enjoined upon the military establishment. In case the equation between Pakistan, Islam and the military failed to register, Zia appropriated the call for a *Nizam-e-Mustafa* – that umbrella term dignifying an ideologically and economically fragmented opposition – and tried turning it into a personal mandate from the people.

Realising that very few had been persuaded, the General, a wily social tactician, calculated that playing the women's card could confirm his regime's commitment to Islam and, by extention, its legitimacy. It was a brilliant ploy. Making women the focal point of his 'Islamisation' programme would win him a round of applause from the religious parties as well as the muted approval of broad sections of society. His promises to protect the sanctity of the *chador* (or the veil) and the *chardivari* (or the home) – those well-known symbols of women's honour and the security of the traditional family – according to one analyst, 'touched the vital chord in the priority structure of middle and lower middle class values'.[61] It did more than that. With memories of 'populism' still fresh in their minds, specifically the glimpses it had given of the very real potential for anarchy among a poor and illiterate populace, even upper-class liberals were not about to challenge a return to moral decency if it meant more security and protection for women.

Zia had found the elements of a consensus, albeit by default. On 10 February 1979, when he injected Pakistan with the first dose of his Islamic laws, people were neither exhilarated nor outraged. Apathy and resignation were almost all-pervasive. The disgruntled gave vent to their anger in private. But the General was not concerned, and never was to be, about what people said in the privacy of their homes, since the terms of his one-man 'social contract' demanded that he resort to the sledgehammer only if whispers turned into wails. Until then he could depend on some of his lay friends to laud the reforms as a first real step towards giving substance to the Islamic ideology which, as they had always maintained, was the *raison d'être* of Pakistan.

These are precisely the sorts of claims which make Zia's Hudood Ordinance of 1979 – with its single-minded emphasis on the Islamic appetite for punishment rather than justice – seem so insidious from the perspective of Paksitani women. The provisions of the Ordinance deal with a variety of offences, including the security of property, by prescribing such medieval punishments as amputating the fingers and hands of the accused, as well as the number of public lashings appropriate for a particular crime.[62] But the parts most affecting women relate to *zina* (extra-marital sex) and *zina-bil-jabr* (rape).[63] Under the provisions of the Ordinance, men and women accused of *zina* are to be meted equally stringent sentences, namely death by stoning or a hundred lashes.[64] Self-confession or the testimony of four Muslim males of known moral repute is sufficient for establishing the guilt of the suspects. But here is the twist. By applying the same set of principles to cases of *zina-bil-jabr*, the Ordinance effectively blurred the distinction between rape and adultery. In other words, failing a confession by the rapist, the presence of four morally upright Muslim men at the scene of the crime is necessary to establish guilt! Of course, the Ordinance did not explain how four good, and one would assume sturdy, Muslim men could allow the rape to take place in the first place. In another convenient oversight, the Ordinance did not address itself to the problem of an unmarried woman subjected to rape, but whose pregnancy could incriminate her of adultery.

That the Ordinance was giving legal sanction to sexual discrimination against women hardly needs to be stressed. What does need pointing out, however, is that its main victims without exception have been women belonging to the poorest strata of Pakistani society. The cases of Safia Bibi and Lal Mai illustrate the subtle but sure class bias underlying the enforcement of General Zia's Islamic laws. A practically blind domestic servant, Safia became pregnant after being subjected to multiple rape by her landlord employer and his son. She was charged with adultery and awarded fifteen lashes, three years imprisonment and a fine of Rs. 1000. The father and son responsible for the crime were let off the hook by the local Sessions Judge on the lame pretext of insufficient evidence. It took a concerted campaign by educated urban middle and upper-class women, naturally alarmed by the implications of the ruling, for the Federal Shariat court to repeal the decision. Lal Mai suffered the same fate as Safia Bibi, but ended up being accused of adultery. A crowd of eight thousand watched her receiving fifteen lashes from a man. Yet another victim of 'Islamic justice' was a woman from a relatively poor family in Swat; she was sentenced to eighty lashes. The men in each instance got off scot free.[65]

Clearly then, the effect of laws based on gender discrimination in Paksitan are better grasped by differentiating between women according to class. While the Hudood Ordinance is in principle a threat to all Pakistani women, those belonging to middle and upper class families are less likely to suffer its consequences, except of course indirectly. The high premium placed on *izzat* (honour) by economically and socially privileged families demands that the state turn a blind eye on their sexual transgressions, including those of their women. Simply put, Zia was not in a position to push his campaign for Islamisation to the point of questioning the honour of middle- and upper-class women. To do so would have meant eroding the very basis of the social accommodations which for so long had underpinned relations between the state and middle- and upper-class families in Pakistani society.

General Zia in any case liked taking with one hand and giving back something with the other. From the very outset, his regime's plans to enforce Islamic norms of behaviour on women extended beyond the legal realm to the two areas where they were slowly but surely making their presence felt: education and the labour market. So in order to forestall domestic and international criticism of his future policies towards women, Zia set up a Women's Division as part of the Cabinet Secretariat a month before the Hudood Ordinance.[66] Its explicit purpose was to safeguard the needs and interests of women in the policies and programmes of governmental and non-governmental agencies. But for all the fanfare about its activities and the allocation of national resources to improve knowledge about as well as the condition of the female population, the Division's impact on women's rights and development-related activites has been nominal. Ironically, the most discriminatory 'Islamisation' laws were all passed while the Division was pushing for the rapid implementation of women's programmes within the state apparatus.[67]

In 1980, the *Qisas* (retaliation) and *Diyat* (blood-money) Ordinance tried to put the coping stone on legal inequality between men and women. Under its provisions, which failed to make it to the statute books, the compensation for a woman, if bodily harmed or murdered, was to be only half that for a man. Yet if found guilty of murder, a woman was to receive the same sentence as a man.[68] However, it was the Council on Islamic ideology's recommended Law of Evidence that generated the most controversy, pitting a small but vocal group of urban middle- and upper-class women against the regime. By appearing to go along with the proposed Law of Evidence, which aimed at reducing the weight of a female witness's evidence to half that of a man, General Zia provided fresh impetus to the women's movement in Pakistan.

The paradox is all the greater since, private mutterings aside, women's organisations – estimated to be around a hundred[69] – did not gear for action until the implications of certain 'Islamic laws' began to be felt. In September 1981, a group of educated urban middle- and upper-class women formed the Women's Action Forum (WAF) in Karachi, after a military court charged a fifteen-year-old girl for adultery; she had flouted parental authority in order to marry a man of working-class origins and, in accordance with the *Zina* Ordinance, was sentenced to flogging.[70] In registering their protest publicly, the members of WAF were doing much more than challenging a court decision. Even though the initiative was confined to a very small section of urban, educated Pakistani women, it symbolised the beginnings of a painful and long-drawn out struggle against the use of state apparatus to promote a coarse and unashamedly chauvinistic Islamic world-view.

Downgrading women's legal status was part of the regime's decided policy to trawl for political support by administering ideological starch to the whims of a male-dominated society. Offended by the shifting boundaries of gender relations in the public realm, most Pakistani men could be relied upon to back state policies aimed at reinforcing patriarchal structures of authority within the family.

It mattered little whether the women who actually joined WAF, or preferred to support it from the sidelines, were all conscious of the complex dynamics shaping their relationship with the state. More important for them was the growing evidence of discrimination against women needing or aspiring to something more than the bracing securities of the *chardivari*. There were reports of women professors being molested, dismissed or harassed simply on account of their political beliefs. Those in public employment were expected to adopt the 'Islamic' dress code,[71] i.e. the *chador*; and while many did so with alacrity, others saw it as an unnecessary infringement. But if life for employed women had become more difficult than ever before, fears that the regime might buckle under pressure and do away with the Family Laws of 1961 also galvanised some middle- and upper-class housewives.

Within a short span of time, WAF chapters had been set up in key urban centres (Lahore, Islamabad, Peshawar, Bahawalpur, Lyallpur and Quetta). A number of women's organisations, most notably APWA, while retaining their autonomous existence decided to give WAF their unqualified support in advancing women rights, including employment, physical security, the choice of marriage partners, family planning, abortion and non-discrimination.[72] But WAF and women's groups associated with it faced many of the same dilemmas and constraints that had earlier prevented urban, educated middle- and upper-class women from piecing together a package of demands which were beyond the state's will or capacity to satisfy. So in formulating a strategy to counter the Zia regime's policies, these women were reluctantly compelled to reiterate their fundamental loyalty to Islam and the state. It was a tactical decision. Overriding serious dissension within its ranks, WAF introduced Quranic classes for its members and enlisted the support of those *ulema* who were out of sympathy with the General's intepretations of the Holy Book and the *Sunnah*. In the words of two founding members of WAF, 'it seemed pointless to oppose the supposed word of God with the mere words of women'.[73] Left with little choice but to play according to the rules of the game, WAF decided to avoid questioning the legitimacy of the military regime's ban on parties and politics. While conceding the intrinsically political nature of their activities in private, WAF's key strategists chose to define themselves as a non-political 'lobby cum-pressure group'.[74] Its members co-operated with the Women's Division in preparing a special report on women's rights, interests and welfare with a view to influencing the Planning Commission in the drafting of the sixth Five Year Plan.[75] On the grounds that none of the opposition political parties had taken an official stance against the Hudood Ordinance and the Law of Evidence, WAF maintained an equivocal stance towards the Movement for the Restoration of Democracy – a conglomerate of parties determined to force Zia's hand to lift martial law and hold free elections on a party basis.

These tactical decisions, however pragmatic, have had large consequences, both in terms of how WAF sought to articulate women's rights at the level of the state, and for what it has actually been able to achieve. By operating within the confines of their class accommodations with the state, by opting to use the Islamic idiom to redress the adverse effects of Zia's laws, and by making very tentative attempts to broaden their organisational bases of support,[76] WAF members succeeded in winning support from some of the more enlightened Pakistani men as well as a handful of orthodox *ulema*. Given the hurdles WAF had to overcome in being treated seriously, these are not insignificant achievements. But by the same measure, WAF's compromises served to limit its impact on state policies. Unable to mount a frontal attack on the very concept of a state-sponsored 'Islamisation' programme – there was never any sign of a groundswell of feeling for the General's policies outside a very narrow political constituency[77] – WAF's urban, educated women for all their good intentions and laudable determination singularly failed to stem the tide of social conservatism. This gave the regime an opportunity to exploit the ideological divide between the so-called 'Islamic' and 'secular' orientated Pakistani women. The women's wings of the fundamentalist *Jamaat-e-Islami* and its student appendage, the *Jamiat-i-Tulaba*, banded together with the newly formed *Majlis-e-Khawatin Pakistan* to stymy WAF's campaign against Zia's Islamisation policies. Buoyed by support from the fundamentalist quarters, it proved infinitely easier for the regime to cull passages from the Quran to counter the arguments of women demanding their rights within the Islamic framework. Above all, the actual number of women concerned about their status under Zia's 'Islamic laws' remained woefully small; reason enough for the state to make light of organisations like WAF.

The 12 February 1983 demonstration in Lahore against the proposed Law of Evidence by WAF and other women's groups illustrates the point. Hundreds of protesting women were subjected to tear-gas and a baton-charge by the police; several were arrested. Yet within a month the *Majlis-i-Shura*, Zia's version of the Islamic parliament, had adopted the Ordinance. Zia dithered for a year before signing the bill, and then too after restricting its application to financial transactions alone. However, the mere fact that the General went ahead with placing the law on the statute book suggests that in his eyes the sight of angry women in the streets was no more than a storm in a tea-cup.

All said and done, WAF and other women's organisations played a vital role in keeping some sort of check on the regime's attempts to gain quick results from its 'Islamisation' policies. Some government ordinances that tried to impose restrictions on women were either not implemented or quietly swept under the carpet. Women were not, however, able to force the government to retract from positions that had become integral to the perpetuation of the General's rule. Despite a highly charged and well orchestrated campaign against both the eighth and the ninth amendments, WAF and its affiliates encountered sullen defeat. Under the eighth amendment no action of the military regime could be challenged in any court of law. This complicated efforts to repeal the Hudood Ordinance and the Law of Evidence[78], while the ninth amendment aimed at placing the Family Law Ordinance of 1961 and other legislation pertaining to the family under the menacing purview of Shariat Courts. The mere existence of discriminatory laws towards women and the potential threat to the hard won Family Law Ordinance of 1961 is a sad comment on the movement for their rights in Pakistan.

This is the more so because the movement for women's rights has been hampered by contradictions internal to it quite as much as by the framework in which it has operated. Pragmatic responses are not always the most effective in an unaccommodating and rigid socio-political context. Admittedly, the proponents of women's rights have been constrained by the uses made of Islam to obfuscate the more proximate and materially based causes of the strains in the relationship between the state and large sections of society. Wielders of state power in Pakistan, with varying degrees of emphasis, have sought to secure a semblance of social legitimacy by resorting to an Islamic ideology rather than by renewing the popular mandate. The frequent suspension of the political process and the consequent gap between state policy and increasingly complex social dynamics has seen the expedient equation of Islam with state legitimacy. But there has never been any direct correlation between Islamic sentiments and political affiliations – Islamic parties have done poorly in electoral contests against parties promising redistributive reforms. By failing to exploit the contradiction between the state's use of Islam as ideology and the uncertain advantages of Islam as politics in Pakistani society, women's orgnisations such as APWA and WAF have left unscathed some of the more contrived affinities between Islam and the Pakistani state. WAF's pragmatic and seemingly principled decision to chalk out an independent course from political parties questioning the very legitimacy of Zia's military regime betrays a concern for the class accommodations of its mainly urban middle- and upper-class membership that cannot be squared easily with specific questions of gender. Given the peculiarities of the Pakistani context, gender-related strategies are unlikely to succeed without a conscious forging of political alignments based on the socio-economic interests of the subordinate classes, rather than those of the dominant classes for whom Islam has been a convenient umbrella to legitimise their accommodations with the state. WAF's Karachi chapter has been the only regional unit to have at least taken some steps towards mobilising broader socio-economic interests and forging links with rural women through the *Sindhiani Tehrik*.[79] The choice between class and gender interests may be painful, perhaps unacceptable. But short of resolving the contradiction internal to their own movement for rights, the many exceptional and highly competent women comprising WAF and other such organisations cannot expect to overcome the obstacle posed by the nexus between Islam and the Pakistani state as presently construed.

This is why Zia's death in August 1988 and the emergence of Benazir Bhutto as prime minister has been only superficially fortuitous for the proponents of women's rights in Pakistan. In the absence of a broadly based alliance between women's organisations and political currents deriving strength from the support of the marginalised strata of society, gender issues are not a priority for the members of the newly elected parliament. And this despite the fact that women's issues did find a place in the manifestos of parties belonging to such opposite ends of the ideological spectrum as the Pakistan People's Party and the fundamentialist *Jamat-i-Islami*. The PPP's promise to repeal Zia's discriminatory laws against women is seen more as a negation of a policy associated with its principal rival than an indication of its Co-Chairperson's single-minded commitment to the feminist cause. Many WAF activists expressed disappointment at Benazir Bhutto's efforts to present herself as a national leader rather than as an advocate of women's rights. They were quick to point out that apart from Benazir Bhutto, Nusrat Bhutto and Begum Ashraf Abbasi, no other woman secured a PPP ticket from the general constituencies. Benazir's retort that this was because no other women applied for PPP tickets failed to cut any ice. Certainly, the PPP manifesto's section on women's rights is nowhere near as elaborate as the WAF's ten-point charter issued on the eve of the general elections in November 1988.[80] WAF's contention that a certain proportion of party tickets for general seats be allocated to women went largely unheeded; of some 1300 candidates contesting from over 200 general constituencies, a mere 13 were women. A further demand that women be inducted at the policy-making level has been partially met by the prime minister's appointments to the federal cabinet. Yet despite a firm commitment in the PPP's manifesto to repeal the Hudood Ordinance and the Law of Evidence, Benazir Bhutto's government seemed in no obvious hurry to delete them from the statute book.

This is largely because the nexus between the state and Islam which helped promote gender biases during the Zia era has yet to face a challenge from a style of politics that effectively links issues of class and gender. Women who led the vocal protests against the Islamic laws were also the ones least likely to suffer their consequences. Under the leadership of these urban middle- and upper-class women, the movement for gender equality has so far proceeded in fits and starts. For the vast majority of Pakistani women in the rural areas little is likely to change, so long as their urban sisters continue to tolerate a modicum of subservience in public affairs in return for state policies that leave their not inconsiderable social privileges untouched. On the face of it the election of Benazir Bhutto as prime minister and the conspicuous role of Begum Abida Hussain as the most eloquent spokeswoman of the opposition might well suggest that the march of history has dramatically changed course. Yet even the most visible symbol of a woman successful in the public domain has been compelled to win social approbation with measured nods to the orthodox and fundamentalist galleries. For a woman who has struggled courageously to the apex of political power, social accommodations enhancing the political inheritance that had already come with daughterhood may be a small price to pay, but for the more typical woman of Pakistan who remains unempowered in almost every sense of the word, accommodations with existing social norms amount to abject physical and mental subservience. Until such time that urban middle- and upper-class women grasp the contradiction between an attachment to social privileges flowing from the class accommodations of their families and the social subservience which is their fate *qua* women, the gender balance in Pakistani society is unlikely to be restored. An early recognition, if not resolution, of this fundamental contradiction may emerge in the event that the classic test case of the Benazir Bhutto era reveals that social subservience does indeed have its inconveniences for politically assertive Pakistani women of the future!

NOTES

I would like to thank Deniz Kandiyoti, the moving spirit behind the entire project and this article, for providing insightful criticisms with patience, tenacity and humour. Comments by many interested readers have contributed towards the final version of this paper. Sugata Bose in particular was a good sounding board for my ideas.

1. Cartoon entitled 'The First Female Leader of a Muslim Nation takes Revenge' by Tony Auth in the in the *Philadelphia Inquirer* (Philadelphia), 18 November 1988.
2. Government of Pakistan, *Report of the Pakistan Commission on the Status of Women* (Islamabad: Government of Pakistan Press, 1986) p. 31. Public dissemination of the report, restricted to official circles during the Zia era, has been ordered by Benazir Bhutto's government.
3. During 1977 and 1983 the rate of female participation actually declined by 3 per cent (Ibid., p. 10)
4. *Appendix to Education Commission Report* (Calcutta, 1884) pp. 299–300, cited in Sarfraz Hussain Mirza, *Muslim Women's Role in the Pakistan Movement* (Lahore: Research Society of Pakistan, second edition, 1981) p. 7 [emphasis added].
5. See Hanna Papanek, 'Purdah: Separate Worlds and Symbolic Shelter', in Hanna Papanek and Gail Minault (eds), *Separate Worlds: Studies of Purdah in South Asia* (Misouri: South Asia books, 1982) pp. 3–53.
6. Maulana Ashraf Ali Thanawi, *Bihishti Zewar*, in Urdu (Lahore: Taj Company, 1344 hijri [1923]). The book remains a best seller in Pakistan to this day. Special 'marriage' editions are available at corner bookstalls. Portions of the book will soon be available in English. See Barbara Daly Metcalf, *Perfecting Woman: Maulana Ashraf Ali Thanawi's Bihishti Zewar: a Partial Translation with Commentary* (Berkeley: University of California Press, 1990).
7. *Zamindar* [Lahore], 2 February 1924, cited in Mirza, *Muslim Women's Role in the Pakistan Movement*, p. 27.
8. See Gail Minault, 'The Extended Family as Metaphor and the Expansion of Women's Realm', in Gail Minault (ed.), *The Extended Family: Women and Political Participation in India and Pakistan* (New Delhi: Chanakya Publications, 1981) p. 9.
9. Gail Minault, 'Sisterhood or Separatism? The All-India Muslim Ladies Conference and the Nationalist Movement', ibid., p. 87.
10. Mirza, *Muslim Women's Role in the Pakistan Movement*, pp. 16–19.

11. Michelle Maskiell, 'Social Change and Social Control: College-educated Punjabi Women, 1913–1960', *Modern Asian Studies* 18 (1984) 2, pp. 9 and 25, fn. 38.
12. Javed Iqbal (ed.), *Stray Reflections: A Note-Book of Allama Iqbal.* (Lahore: Sh. Ghulam Ali and Sons, 1961) pp. 64–5, cited in Sheila McDonough, 'Metaphorsof Change in Early Iqbal' in C. M. Naim (ed.), *Iqbal, Jinnah, and Pakistan: the Vision and the Reality* (Syracuse: Maxwell School of Citizenship and Public Affairs, 1979) p. 116.
13. Gail Minault, 'Sisterhood or Separatism? The All-India Muslim Ladies' Conference and the Nationalist Movement', pp. 83–108.
14. *Inqilab*, 16 June 1932, cited in Mirza, *Muslim Women's Role in the Pakistan Movement*, p. 36
15. This is apparent in the writings of both Begum Jahan Ara Shahnawaz, *Father and Daughter: a Political Autobiography* (Lahore: Nigarishat, 1971) and Begum Shaista Akhtar Banu (Suhrawardy) Ikramullah, *From Purdah to Parliament* (London: Cresset Press, 1963).
16. Syed Sharif-ud-Din Pirzada, *The Pakistan Resolution and the Historic Lahore Session* (Karachi: Pakistan Publishers, 1968) p. 35 and Mirza, *Muslim women's Role in the Pakistan Movement*, p. 45.
17. See Shahnawaz, *Father and Daughter* and Ikramuliah, *From Purdah to Parliament*.
18. See Ayesha Jalal, *The State of Martial Rule: the Origins of Pakistan's Political Economy of Defence* (Cambridge: Cambridge University Press, 1990), Ch. 6.
19. David Gilmartin, 'Kinship, Women, and Politics in Twentieth Century Punjab', in *The Extended Family*, pp. 165–9.
20. Gilmartin is too quick in concluding that the Shariat Application Act of 1948 'at a stroke, almost wholly superseded' a system of customary law it had taken the British over a century to weave together (ibid., p. 169). The frequency of court decisions based on customary law squarely refutes this view.
21. In April 1949, the Indian Deputy High Commissioner charged the Pakistan Government for failing to assist in the rehabilitation of abducted women (*Nawa-i-Waqt*, [Lahore] 17 April 1949).
22. Ibid., 20 April 1949.
23. Even within the seemingly secure environs of their homes, educated women do not always escape the humiliation of economic dependency and the risk of male repudiation that comes with subordination under a patriarchal society.
24. It was on 19 February that women members of the League staged their walk-out; by 22 February APWA had been established.
25. This was the opinion of the British High Commissioner to Pakistan (London: India Office Library, L/WS/1/1600, opdom no. 8, part 11, 18–24 February 1949).
26. APWA has retained its relative autonomy – financial as well as administrative – by refusing anything more than token grants from the state. But

its links with officialdom are undeniable.

27. Government of Pakistan, *Report of the Pakistan Pay Commission* (Karachi: Government of Pakistan, 1949) p. 46.
28. Dr Ishtiaq Hussain Quereshi's statement to the constituent assembly. Government of Pakistan, *Constituent Assembly Debates* (Karachi: Government of Pakistan, 1952) IX, 24 March 1951, pp. 216–17. (Henceforth *C.A.D.*, followed by volume, date and page number).
29. See *C.A.D.*, VII, 6 October 1950, p. 156.
30. Ibid.
31. *C.A.D.*, IX, 23 March 1951, p. 113
32. Ibid., [emphasis added].
33. See Khawar Mumtaz and Farida Shaheed (eds), *Women of Pakistan: Two Steps Forward, One Step Back?* (London: Zed Press, 1987) p. 54
34. *Dawn* [Karachi], 11 February 1951.
35. Sylvia Chipp-Kraushaar, 'The All Pakistan Women's Association and the 1961 Muslim Family Law Ordinance', in *The Extended Family*, pp. 265–73.
36. West Pakistan Government, *The Muslim Family Law Ordinance, 1961* (Lahore: West Pakistan Press, 1968) section six.
37. Ibid., section nine.
38. Ibid., sections ten and twelve.
39. For an account of APWA's role in persuading the state to issue the Ordinance see Chipp-Kraushaar, 'The All-Pakistan Women's Association and the 1961 Muslim Family Law Ordinance' in *The Extended Family*, pp. 273–4.
40. On the imperatives of state intervention regardless of ideological leanings, see Molyneux in this volume.
41. In July 1963 the West Pakistan provincial assembly passed a resolution requesting the national assembly to abolish the ordinance, But on 26 November 1963, not without considerable pressure from General Ayub, the national assembly defeated the bill. A similar attempt in 1965 was also quashed. (Chipp-Krauhaar, 'The All-Pakistan Women's Association and the 1961 Muslim Family Law Ordinance' in *The Extended Family*, pp. 276–8.)
42. Government of Pakistan, Pakistan Manpower Institute, Khalida Shah, 'Women's Participation in the Labour Force in Pakistan – a Macro Level Profile', in *Employment for Women in Pakistan* (Islamabad: Government of Pakistan Press, 1983) p. 49.
43. Government of Pakistan, *Pakistan Population Census* (Karachi: Government of Pakistan Press, 1962), bulletin no. 4, cited by M. Sabihuddin Baqai, 'Some Considerations of the Impact of Education of Women on Development of Human Resources', in Aquila Kiani (ed.), *Sociology of Development in Pakistan* (Karachi: Social Research Centre, University of Karachi, 1971) p. 65.
44. Government of Pakistan, *Central Statistics Office Survey, 1964* in ibid., p. 67.

45. See Rashida Patel, 'Cultural Transition and Employment of women', in ibid., p. 72.
46. See Kabeer in this volume.
47. In 1973, Mian Tufail Mohammad, the leader of the religious fundamentalist party, the *Jamat-i-Islami*, declared Bhutto's regime to be an illegitimate expression of Pakistan's Islamic ideology and called upon the army to seize power. (Maliha Lodhi, 'Politics in Pakistan During the Bhutto period', unpublished manuscript, p. 150.)
48. Mumtaz Ahmad, 'Ideology, Power, and Protest: Toward Explaining Islamic Revivalism in Pakistan' (Georgetown University; Centre for Stategic and International Studies, unpublished paper for a workshop on Islamic revivalism, 4 January 1983), pp. 18–19.
49. See Jalal, *The State of Martial Rule*, chapter seven.
50. For a discussion of similar tendancies in Bangladesh and India, see Kabeer and Chhachhi in this volume.
51. M. Sabihuddin Baqai, *Changes in the Status and Roles of Women in Pakistan (An empirical study in Karachi Metropolitan Area)* (Karachi: Department of Sociology, University of Karachi, 1976) pp. 15–24.
52. Shahnaz J. Rouse, 'Women's Movements in Contemporary Pakistan: Results and Prospects' (University of Michigan, working paper no. 74, December 1984).
53. Government of Pakistan, *Constitution Act of 1973* (Islamabad: Government of Pakistan Press, 1973) article 25 (1).
54. Ibid., section 27 (1).
55. Ibid., article 34.
56. Chapter two, article 37 (C).
57. According to Begum Ashraf Abbasi, a member of the national assembly, the Constitution 'fully protected' women's rights and it was their 'duty' to 'work hard for the progress and welfare of the country and discharge their duties without laxity [sic]' *Morning News*, [Karachi], 21 January 1973). Alas, if things could only be that simple for women shackled by centuries of tradition.
58. Lodhi, 'Politics in Pakistan During the Bhutto Period', p. 221.
59. Government of Pakistan, *Report of the Commission on Women's Rights*, in Urdu, in *Musawat Siyasi Edition* [Lahore], 20 August 1976.
60. A nine-party coalition representing a broad political spectrum – from the extreme right to the left – it included the *Jamat-i-Islami*, the *Jamiat-ul-Ulema-i-Pakistan*, the *Jamiat-ul-Ulema-i-Islam*, the Muslim League, the *Tehriq-i-Istiqlal*, the Pakistan Democratic Party, the National Democratic Party, the *Khaksar Tehriq* and the Muslim Conference.
61. Ahmad, 'Ideology, Power and Protest: Toward Explaining Islamic Revivalism in Pakistan', p. 11.
62. Government of Pakistan, *A Collection of the Islamic Laws* (Islamabad: Government of Pakistan Press, 1980) Hudood Ordinance, 1979, VI, 1–9.
63. Ibid., VII, 9–15.

64. Ibid.
65. See Anita M. Weiss, 'Women's Position in Pakistan: Sociocultural Effects of Islamization', *Asian Survey*, XXV (August 1985) 8, and Mumtaz and Shaheed (eds), *Women in Pakistan*, pp. 103–105.
66. For a detailed account of the Women's Divisions objectives and achievements see Michelle Maskiell, 'The Effects of Islamization on Pakistani Women's Lives, 1978–83' (Madison: University of Wisconsin, paper prepared for the South Asia Conference, 1983).
67. As Chhachhi notes in this volume, there is no necessary contradiction in the simultaneous adoption of discriminatory laws and development programmes for women. The irony is nevertheless striking.
68. Weiss, 'Women's Position in Pakistan', *Asian Survey*, XXV (August 1985) 8, p. 872, and the report of a meeting of nineteen women's organisations – welfare, professional and others – 11 February 1981, WAF papers, Lahore chapter.
69. J. Henry Korson and Michelle Maskiell, 'Islamization and Social Policy in Pakistan: the Constitutional Crisis and the Status of Women', *Asian Survey*, XXV (June 1985) 6, p. 600.
70. Rouse, 'Women's Movements in Contemporary Pakistan: Results and Prospects', p. 8.
71. Ibid and Mumtaz and Shaheed (eds), *Women of Pakistan*, pp. 77–81.
72. Rouse, 'Women's Movements in Contemporary Pakistan: Results and Prospects', p. 9.
73. Mumtaz and Shaheed (eds), *Women of Pakistan*, pp. 130–31.
74. 'Aims and objectives of the Women's Action Forum' (WAF papers, Lahore chapter). For an overview of WAF see Mumtaz and Shaheed (eds), *Women of Pakistan*, chapters five through eight.
75. See Maskiell, 'The Effect of Islamization on Pakistani Women's Lives. 1978–83', pp. 3–5; and 'Sixth Plan and Women's Development: WAF's Position' (WAF papers, Lahore chapter).
76. In 1983, the issue of membership rights resulted in a temporary split within WAF's Lahore chapter. Fearing penetration by women of the fundamentalist ilk, a section of WAF wanted more effective screening rules for new members. This was opposed by those seeing advantages in enlarging the membership.
77. In december 1984 when the General held a referendum to get a mandate for another five years by equating himself with Islam, the turnout was embarrassingly low.
78. This was challenged by members of WAF, who maintained that the Hudood Ordinance and the Law of Evidence was not protected by the eighth amendment. (Lahore: conversation with Hina Gilani and Asma Jehangir, January-February, 1989.)
79. Formed in 1983, the *Sindhiani Tehrik* is led by lower-middle-class women from *mofussil* (country) towns in Sind. Its populist message has been targeted at rural women. Mumtaz and Shaheed (eds), *Women of Pakistan*, pp. 153 and 161, fn. 10.

80. Calling for a 'radical change in the national policy on women', WAF listed a series of wide-ranging demands. These included a guarantee of women's constitutional rights as equal citizens; a repeal of discriminatory laws; a commitment to the International Convention on the Elimination of Discrimination against Women; larger budgetary allocations towards women's health, education and social welfare in place of defence and non-development expenditure; removal of gender biases in media projection; equitable compensation for work; fair access to employment; the right to own and control property; protection against violence and, finally, a commitment to peace and non-proliferation of nuclear weapons. *Viewpoint* [Lahore], 3 November 1988.

5 The Quest for National Identity: Women, Islam and the State in Bangladesh

Naila Kabeer

INTRODUCTION

This chapter examines the complex interactions between religion and culture in constructing definitions of national identity in Bangladesh and in shaping the political projects of recent regimes. It also attempts to throw light on certain features which differentiate current Islamisation processes in Bangladesh from those in Pakistan and Iran described elsewhere in this volume. In all three countries, official Islamisation programmes were begun in the latter half of the 1970s. In both Iran and Pakistan, however, these programmes went further than in Bangladesh and, despite clear differences in the political forces behind them, had important features in common. Of particular significance was the central place accorded by both to the position of women. Islamic norms of behaviour were enforced more strictly for women through a variety of religious laws as well as the state's pronouncements on female apparel and conduct in the public sphere.

In comparison, official Islamisation policies in Bangladesh have been altogether more cautious and hesitant and have not so far entailed any sustained attack on women's rights, deportment or dress. Nearly a decade separates the deletion of secularism from the country's constitution and the recent amendment which made Islam the state religion. Despite pressure from the country's fundamentalists, Bangladesh remains a People's Republic rather than an Islamic one. Women have benefited from this lack of confidence which characterises official attempts to promote Islamisation. They have also benefited from the presence of different and contradictory ideologies, both within state discourse as well as in the wider polity, whose effect has been to impede any systematic curtailment of women's rights in the name of Islam.

The contradictions and uncertainties which have dogged the state's Islamisation policy in Bangladesh stem partly from a central ambivalence in prevailing notions of national identity, an ambivalence which relates to the significance attached by different political constituencies to the place of 'Islamic' versus 'Bengali' values in determining national identity. A historical perspective is necessary to comprehend the nature of this ambivalence because it is rooted, in the first place, in the manner in which Islam was introduced and absorbed into Bengali society and, in the second, in the processes by which Bengali Muslims were incorporated into the wider Islamic community.

The next section discusses the concept of the national entity and illustrates its complexities in the case of the Bengali Muslim collectivity. It is followed by an examination of the effects of state policy in the Pakistan era in heightening the contradictions between official definitions of nationhood and the cultural identity of the Bengali Muslims. Finally, the continuing quest for national identity in post-liberation Bangladesh is analysed. Particular attention is paid to the interactions and conflicts which surfaced at different phases of the nation's history between official constructions of nationhood and the state's position on the 'woman question'.

THE NATION AS IDEOLOGICAL CONSTRUCT

Anderson's conceptualisation of the nation as an 'imagined community' is helpful in pointing to the *ideological* construction of national communities and therefore to their historical contingency.[1] National identities come into existence as a consciousness of specific forms of difference. The boundaries of demarcation are frequently transitory and fluid, drawing on a diverse array of forms: 'a myth of common ancestry, a sense of common territoriality, a common language and body of cultural symbols and/or common phenotypical appearance, in physique or in garments . . . '[2]

The case of Bangladesh will serve to illustrate the fluid and contingent nature of the national community. The demarcating principles of the Bengali Muslim collectivity have been reshaped several times during this century in response to diverse ideological and political forces.[3] When Pakistan came into existence as a homeland for the Muslims of the Indian subcontintent, Islam was inevitably invoked as the unifying principle of national identity, capable of transcending all differences between its geographically and culturally divided population. It continued to figure prominently as the *raison d'être* of the subsequently truncated Pakistani state. Unable to ignore or unify its dissatisfied minority nationalities,

Pakistan's rulers still relied on Islam to keep the nation intact: in the words of the late President, Zia-ul Haq, 'Take Islam out of Pakistan and make it a secular state; it would collapse'.[4]

Since liberation from Pakistan, the search for a national identity in Bangladesh has been driven by a different set of forces. Bangladesh is relatively homogeneous in cultural, linguistic and ethnic terms. It has a sizeable (10 per cent), but politically weak, minority of Hindus as well as a small tribal population. The problem of national identity for the Muslim majority today focuses less on forging the basis for internal unity and more on establishing its difference from the Hindu Bengalis of India, thereby justifing its claims to an independent state and, more recently, to a closer alignment with the oil-rich nations of the Middle East. The quest for the defining principles of 'Bengali Muslim' nationhood is complicated, however, by the fact that while Islamic religion and Bengali culture are the very essence of the community's separate identity, its historical experience has prevented the two from being successfully moulded into a coherent unity. In fact, the country's persisting preoccupation with its own identity may reflect its uncertainty that such a cohesion can ever be achieved. It may also contribute to the current lack of political stabilty in Bangladesh.[5]

THE RISE OF THE MUSLIM COMMUNITY IN BENGAL

Bangladesh consists of the eastern, deltaic districts of the province of Bengal and roughly approximates the areas of Muslim majority in the eastern section of the Indian subcontintent. In 1947 it became the eastern wing of Pakistan, the new homeland for the Muslims of India, which was carved out from the eastern (East Bengal) and northwestern extremities of the subcontinent. Islam was the basis for the creation of this geographically, culturally and ethnically divided state, separated by a thousand miles of hostile Indian territory. The bloody war for Bengali liberation in 1971 proved that religious ties were too fragile, uneven and tenuous in themselves to hold the two wings together.

The Islam of Bengal was not the Islam of Pakistan; it bore the imprint of very different historical and social forces. There are some suggestions that the original settlers of Bengal were migrants from south-east Asia who introduced their own agrarian practices and animist belief-systems into the region.[6] Hinduism, Buddhism and then Islam have each in turn been imposed on the pre-existing 'little tradition' and were permeated and transformed by it.[7]

The resilience of the early folk beliefs has been related to the 'extraordinary geography' and 'frontier' character of Bengal.[8] Situated at the far eastern periphery of India, at the delta of its two largest rivers, and cut off from the rest of the subcontinent periodically by massive floods, Bengal was isolated for several centuries from the dominant cultures of the region. The Aryan conquerors did not establish Brahmanical Hinduism in Bengal until the fifth century. The Brahmin elite, which based itself in the more accessible western part of Bengal, incorporated the local Bengali tribes into the Brahminical hierarchy as a ritually inferior caste. The indigenous Bengalis responded by enthusiastically embracing every major anti-Brahminical movement that flourished in the region – Buddhism, Vaishnavism and finally Islam.[9]

Islam came to Bengal in the wake of the Muslim conquest in the thirteenth century. Its egalitarian principles made for massive conversions among the despised low-caste population of Bengal, but it did not live up to their expectations. A caste-like division emerged within the Muslim community between the *ashraf*, those of noble or foreign extraction, and the *ajlaf*, indigenous converts of lowly origins. Bengali Muslims found themselves integrated into the Islamic *umma* (community) without transcending their former subordinate status. They sought solace in the preachings of the Sufis, holy men and mystics of Persian origin, whose respect for Islamic principles of equality brought them into closer contact with the artisans and cultivators of rural Bengal, making them more effective leaders than the distant urban-based *ulema* (Islamic clergy). The Sufi traditions co-existed easily with other devotional cults in Bengal, and came to represent non-conformity and rebellion in opposition to the established centres of *ulema* orthodoxy.[10]

Thus two forms of Islam flourished in Bengal. There was the Islam of the villages, a fusion of Hindu and Muslim traditions among cultivators and artisans who had lived and worked together for centuries and who shared the cultural legacy of the early pioneers of the delta. Within this syncretic system, it was impossible to disentangle the origins of various beliefs and customs about the land and the seasons, about pollution, seasonality and birth, about kinship and fate, about ghosts, demons and holy men which were shared by Muslim and Hindu peasant alike and were essentially Bengali beliefs.[11]

In marked contrast was the faith practised by the urban-based, foreign-born Islamic elite who strongly resisted assimilation into indigenous Bengali culture. They maintained their distance from the local population, as much from low-born Muslim converts as from Hindus, by stressing their foreign extraction, by adhering closely to orthodox Islamic practices and by speaking only Persian, Arabic and, later, Urdu.

It was this Islamic elite who became the leading Bengali representatives of the Muslim League and the most vociferous supporters of the demand for a separate Muslim homeland. Although they claimed to speak for all Bengali Muslims, they were from the outset made up of people, like Syed Amir Ali, Nawab Abdul Latif and Nawab Salimullah, who spoke in languages that were not understood by the majority of their 'imagined' constituency, who looked to West Asia for their cultural references and who regarded local culture and customs as irremediably Hinduised.[12]

This, then, was the situation at the time of partition. Two parallel belief-systems, both claiming to be Islam, co-existed uneasily within the Bengal delta: the orthodox Islam of the elite and the more syncretic and personal version of the Bengali peasant. Erected on this 'quicksand of a persisting identity problem between the self-image of Bengali Muslims and Muslim Bengalis'[13] was the solid weight of the state of Pakistan, brought into existence on the basis of Muslim separateness. The experience served to intensify, rather than resolve, the problematic nature of the Bengali Muslim identity.

NATIONAL INTEGRATION AND CULTURAL DIFFERENCE IN THE PAKISTAN ERA

From its inception, state power in Pakistan was monopolised by a Punjabi-based, military-bureaucratic oligarchy whose policies towards the east wing reduced it to the status of a colony and sowed the seeds of the country's subsequent disintegration. While these policies took the form of both economic and political discrimination,[14] it was probably the state's activities on the cultural front that finally brought home to Bengalis the full extent of their alienation from the Islamic Republic and accelerated their passage to independent nation-hood.

The assault mounted by the Pakistani state on Bengali culture met little resistance from Bengal's Islamic elites, who shared the attitudes of the ruling oligarchy. However, West Pakistani antipathy to Bengali culture was further intensified by racial arrogance towards the smaller and darker Bengalis and nourished by the suspicion that, though nominally Muslim, their 'relatively recent' conversion from low-caste Hindu status made them unreliable co-religionists.[15] The cultural and linguistic affinity between the Hindus and Muslims of Bengal was also profoundly threatening to a state which had only Islam to hold together its fragmented and divided people. Reluctant to rely on religious allegiance alone, successive regimes in Pakistan embarked on a strategy of forcible cultural assimilation towards the Bengalis.

The process began soon after partition and was targeted on the Bengali language, the primary vehicle for the specific identity and separate culture of the Bengali people. Urdu, with its echoes of the sacred language, had come to symbolise the movement for a Muslim homeland and in 1948 was declared its state language. The Bengali resistance to this move was spearheaded by the student movement, which did not share the Pakistani antagonism to Hindu culture, but chose rather to emphasise the common *bhadrolok* ('respectable classes') values and aspirations which informed the middle-class way of life for Bengalis on both sides of the political divide with India. The Language Movement resulted in the death of six student protestors and the overwhelming defeat of the Muslim League in the 1954 provincial elections. The victors were the United Front, led by the Bengali nationalist Muslim Awami League founded in 1949. The new party subsequently dropped the 'Muslim' epithet and henceforth became the voice of the disenfranchised middle classes of East Bengal. Bengali was finally given equal status with Urdu as state language in the Constitution of 1956.

However, the language issue symbolised a struggle about power, rather than speech, and the essential problems remained unresolved. Cultural issues came to the forefront again under Ayub's regime. A Bureau for National Reconstruction was set up to purge the Bengali Language of Sanskrit/Hindu elements and purify it with Arabic, Persian and Urdu. The songs of Tagore were banned from the state-controlled radio and television. Restrictions were imposed on the dissemination of Bengali literature, and grants offered to artists and literati who were prepared to work for 'national integration'. A policy of assimilation-through-miscegenation made its first appearance in the system of financial incentives for inter-wing marriages.[16]

Alienated by the regime's attempts to appropriate the mantle of Islamic purity for its own cultural traditions, the Bengali middle class was forced to confront more clearly the dilemmas of identity: were they Muslims first or Bengalis first? Resistance to Pakistani cultural hegemony helped to crystallise what was exclusive to the Bengali Muslim community: its common history and distinct way of life, reaffirmed continuously through shared cultural references, rituals and modes of communication. Although initially the province of the middle classes, Bengali nationalism had become a mass movement by 1971.

BENGALI WOMEN AND THE PAKISTANI STATE

Despite the significance attached to Islam as the basis of nationhood, the political leadership in Pakistan regarded itself as Muslim modernist, prepared to make pragmatic use of Islam for political ends but prepared also to reform its more anachronistic features. It was through Ayub Khan's initiative that the Family Law Ordinance, which modified the right of men to marry and divorce at will, was passed in 1961. On this occasion Bengali women united with women from West Pakistan in defending the bill against its detractors among the *ulema*. They united again in the 1960 presidential elections, to challenge the decision of the Combined Opposition to Ayub Khan to adopt the demand for a 'true' Islamic state and the abrogation of the Family Law Ordinance as a concession to the fundamentalist *Jamaat-e-Islami* presence in the coalition.

As a result of the modernist posture adopted by ruling groups, there were few direct attempts by the state to reshape the behaviour of Bengali women in accordance with orthodox notions of Islam. The official policy of purging Bengali culture of its 'Hindu' elements was fuelled by the fear that cultural differences could destroy the foundations of the national collectivity, rather than by a drive towards Islamisation *per se*. If Bengali women experienced official disapproval, they did so as part of the generalised attack on their culture rather thas as its specific targets.

Nevertheless, the dress and deportment of Bengali women took on increasing symbolic value as expressions of their cultural difference. On one level, it led to the politicisation of normally uncontroversial aspects of everyday middle-class life. The right to sing the songs of Tagore and to wear *bindis* [17] became acts of political dissent because they conflicted with the values of official Islam, as did the practice of the Bengali middle classes of training their daughters in the arts – singing, dancing and drama – and allowing them to perform in public.[18]

Bengali women celebrated their cultural identity within the conventional political sphere as well. Over the years, 21 February, formally observed as the Day of the Language Martyrs, had come to be enacted as an annual reaffirmation of Bengali identity. Women wearing white saris (the colour of mourning among both Hindus and Muslims in Bengal) joined in processions to lay wreaths at the monument to the martyrs. As the nationalist movement gathered force in the months preceding the declaration of Bangladesh's independence, massive demonstrations were held in Dhaka in which large contingents of women, dressed in traditional festive yellow and red saris, wearing *bindis* on their foreheads and singing Bengali nationalist songs, including the banned songs of Tagore, spearheaded what was effectively a cultural resistance to the Pakistani regime.[19]

The affronted sensibilities of the Muslim fraternity were avenged in the bloodbath that was unleashed on Bangladesh. In the nine months of occupation that followed, Bangladeshi civilians were picked up for interrogation by Pakistani soldiers with the question that haunted them with increasing intensity: are you a Muslim or a Bengali? Perhaps the most tragic victims of Pakistani hatred and suspicion were the estimated 30 000 Bengali women who were raped by Pakistani soldiers, purportedly in their mission to 'improve the genes of the Bengali people'[20] and thus populate Bangladesh with 'pure' Muslims. The policy of assimilation-through-miscegenation revealed the terrible deluded logic of racial supremacy.

THE POLITICS OF THE POST-LIBERATION STATE

Bangladesh emerged from the nightmare of 1971 as an independent state. It has been ruled ever since by an unstable alliance between an underdeveloped national bourgeoisie and the military and civil bureaucracy. Shifts in the balance of power within the ruling alliance have generated persistent contradictory pressures on national development strategies and have led to periodic conflicts and reversals in state policy. The post-liberation years in Bangladesh have been marked by coups, counter-coups, growing impoverishment and an increasing dependence on external assistance. During this time, the state has completed a full ideological circle which has taken it from a position of official secularism to one of giving constitutional recognition to Islam, only a step short of the Islamic Republic status of pre-liberation days.

The Awami League, under the leadership of Sheikh Mujib, led the nationalist movement against Pakistan and formed the first government after Independence. It won a massive mandate from the people, first in 1970 and then in 1973, and Mujib himself enjoyed tremendous personal popularity. Its political support was derived mainly from the salariat classes – the managers, bureaucrats and professionals – who had been deprived of opportunities for advancement under the Pakistani regime. It was also backed by the rich peasantry who, with sufficient state patronage, could be relied on to contain unrest among the rural poor and to muster votes at election time.

The Awami League government sought to implement a moderately socialist programme, nationalising banks and key industries and imposing controls over foreign exchange, imports and foreign investment. In the area of foreign policy, it opted for a non-aligned status for Bangladesh, negotiating aid and assistance from diverse sources, including India and the socialist countries.

However, its socialist rhetoric and nationalisation policies were not popular with the United States. One of the factors behind the devastating famine of 1974 was the US decision to withhold food shipments (over the question of Bangladesh's trade relations with Cuba) at a time when the country was suffering from floods of catastrophic proportions.[21] The government was forced to accept financial help from the newly formed Aid-to-Bangladesh Consortium, chaired by the World Bank, subject to conditions which sought to reverse government policy through greater stress on economic liberalisation and the private sector.

Within the country, the government's popular base was progressively eroded. Corruption and mismanagement of the economy by the Awami League and their cronies, the shortfall of essential goods, rapid growth in inflation rates, the government's glaring failure to utilise the foreign aid flowing into the country for productive purposes and, perhaps most importantly, the hostility of the traditionally anti-Indian army to a pro-Indian ruling party all combined to bring a loss of credibility and support by influential sections of society.[22] . Mujib was assasinated in August 1975 by a small group of junior army officers, who justified their action on the grounds of the corruption and incompetence of the Awami League government and its alleged subservience to India.

After a brief succession of coups, Zia-ur Rahman took power as the man most acceptable to the different factions within the military establishment and set the country firmly on its present pro-Islamic and pro-US course. Zia's political survival depended on distancing himself ideologically from the Awami League as far as possible in order to generate his own civilian base. He projected himself as a modernist, espousing a progressive version of Islam and committed to the enhancement and prosperity of private capital. The rapid de-nationalisation of the economy under Zia created a newly-rich class of entrepreneurs and traders whose interests were tied to those of the government in power and who became its allies.

However, electoral victory represented the acid test in his bid for domestic and international legitimacy; it was the most effective demonstration that the Awami League was not the sole party with a popular base. A broader-based political support was also necessary to insure him against the likelihood of a future coup by some aspiring military rival. Zia used the breathing space afforded by martial law to found his own party – the Bangladesh National Party (BNP) – using the various forms of patronage available to a government in power.

In the end, Zia's quest for civilian legitimacy proved to be his downfall. The military resented sharing power and resources with his newly established allies in the BNP and increasingly distanced themselves from him. He was assassinated in 1981 and succeeded by General Ershad. Ershad has imitated many of Zia's tactics – to the extent of founding his own political party and seeking electoral legitimation – but has not repeated his mistakes. The presence of the military is now more extensive and more overt: in industry, in commerce, in the diplomatic service and within central and local government. Ershad, in other words, is not going to risk being alienated from his military power base.

In the midst of the political turbulence and shifting strategies of the post-independence years, two consistent features have been in evidence. First, there has been increasing impoverishment and social differentiation. The rural development strategies pursued by successive governments emphasised yield-enhancing rather than redistributive effects, and recent studies indicate that the growth of landlessness is accelerating and that the standard of living has deteriorated for most rural families since the 1960s.[23]

The other consistent feature is an increasing dependence on aid. Aid disbursed as a percentage of GDP rose from 10 per cent in 1972/73 to 14 per cent in 1981/82.[24] However, there have been significant changes in the sources of aid. Aid from India and the socialist bloc decreased after the assasination of Mujib, whereas aid from the developed capitalist countries became much more important as did aid from the OPEC countries, particularly Saudi Arabia.

The magnitude of aid donated to Bangladesh has given the international donor community a far-reaching influence over the country's affairs. Both at the national level through IMF/World Bank conditionality, and at the local level, through the implementation of development programmes and projects, the effects of aid are evident in almost every sphere of people's lives. By 1982, most of the earlier nationalist policies had been modified or reversed, and the developmental emphasis had shifted to the private sector and export-orientated economic growth.

The preoccupation with national identity has not been abandoned in the post-liberation era; there are continuing tensions between the claims of *Din-ul-Islam* and *Bangla Samaj*, the sacred and the cultural community. However, different forces shape the ideological construction of national boundaries in the post-liberation era; it is now spearheaded by the state's search for political legitimation rather than by the politics of anti-colonialism. In this continuing process, women have entered the public arena in new, explicit ways that are often directly linked to the political projects of the post-liberation regimes.

THE AWAMI LEAGUE, STATE SECULARISM AND WOMEN'S RIGHTS

The increasing significance assigned to women in official discourse and state policy did not become apparent until after the assassination of Mujib. The liberation struggle had been fought on the grounds of Bengali 'culture-as-nationalism'. Women participated in the movement for Bangladesh, but raised no challenge to their position within the cultural community. Most middle-class women appeared willing to rely on the good intentions of the nationalist government to represent their interests and remedy social injustices.

Unchallenged in its paternalistic vision of gender relations, the good intentions of the post-liberation government towards 'the womenfolk' were circumscribed within narrow limits. The 1972 Constitution of Bangladesh recognised for the first time the equality of the sexes in all spheres, but went on to reserve for members of one sex some classes of employment or office on the grounds that 'it is considered by its nature to be unsuited to members of the opposite sex' (Clause 3, Article 29). Fifteen parliamentary seats were reserved for women, to be filled through nomination by the ruling party rather than through the electoral process. While the importance of education for women was recognised, it was seen strictly in terms of their domestic role: according to the First Five Year Plan, 'The level of schooling of women determines the efficiency of household management. Educated women pay better attention to nutrition, health and child-care than the uneducated . . . '

Mujib's regime was mainly preoccupied with coping with the ravages of war, famine and deteriorating law and order. It had little scope to deal specifically with the situation of women, except in connection with the rehabilitation of women who had been raped, widowed or otherwise affected by the war. Despite a variety of measures towards this end, it is likely that Mujib will be best remembered for declaring women who had been raped *birangona* (war heroines). The term was an attempt to disguise the sexual violence of the crime so as to make social ostracism of its victims less severe. However, it merely highlighted the social hypocrisy and unease surrounding the issue of female virtue in Bangladesh and many of the women were rejected by their families. A 5 per cent quota of government employment reserved for rape victims was, needless to say, never filled, since it merely served to identify them.[25]

In the broader policy arena, there were few initiatives for women under Mujib's regime. Women continued to be perceived in development planning efforts primarily in relation to fertility control and their critical role in realising population objectives; the only reference to women's income-generating activities in the country's First Five Year Plan is in connection with such objectives.

Nevertheless, at the ideological level the longstanding commitment to secularism by the Awami League must be regarded as more compatible with the ideas of women's emancipation than the theocratic rhetoric of the Pakistani state. Secularism in this context was taken to imply not the absence of religion, but equal status for all religions in the eyes of the state. The spheres of marriage, divorce, inheritance and guardianship for each religious community remained under the jurisdiction of its own personal status laws. What was new was the constitutional ban on communalism, on religious discrimination in any form, on state bias in favour of any religion and on political parties based solely on religion. Secularism was made a basic principle of the new constitution and Bangladesh was declared a People's Republic rather than an Islamic one. The choice of a national anthem, composed by Tagore, and of a national flag devoid of Islamic symbolism, were other signifiers of the secular leanings of the Awami League government.[26]

The Awami League's espousal of secularism as state ideology was, of course, derived from its analysis of the divisive role played by religion in the nation's history rather than from any particular commitment to gender equality. But it can be argued that there is a fundamental contradiction between official secularism and the extreme forms of gender discrimination which may be countenanced within a state-sanctioned religious framework. The Awami League's secularism effectively favoured the 'customary, communal, pliable' version of Islam which made up the folk traditions of Bengali Muslims over the 'divine, centralist and establishment-based' version favoured by theocratically-run states as well as by fundamentalists within the country.[27] Secularism removed the power of enforcing religious codes of conduct from the Muslim clerical establishment and permitted less rigid and immutable models for women's behaviour to emerge, models which were more open to change through contest and struggle.

WOMEN AND DEVELOPMENTALISM IN THE BANGLADESH STATE

By the time Mujib was assassinated, changing currents in the international donor community were converging to form new strands of donor policy. The influence of the international women's movement was making itself felt in the politics of foreign aid. It challenged the assumptions and priorities that had so far dominated development aid and demanded that women's interests be specifically taken into account rather than left to a dubious trickle-down process or be interpreted entirely in terms of their reproductive roles. The effects of these new trends were visible in the policies of aid donors to Bangladesh who began to earmark separate budgets for women's programmes and for research on women's issues. These developments had their positive effects in the Bangladesh context by introducing a new and potentially progressive vocabulary – the vocabulary of women's emancipation – into official discourse on women, by giving women's productive contributions a greater visibility and by increasing the number of development projects directed at women.

The coup that brought Zia-ur Rahman to power coincided with the United Nations International Women's Year (1975) and the declaration of the United Nations Decade for Women. Zia took up the cause of Women in Development (WID) with great public zeal. The second Five Year Plan (1980–85) was the first in two decades of development planning in the country to give explicit consideration to strategies for integrating women into the development process. A full-fledged Ministry of Women's Affairs was set up, the number of parliamentary seats reserved for women was doubled to 30 and 10 per cent of public sector jobs were to be reserved for women. Resources were channelled to rural women through the Women's Rehabilitation Foundation, mandated to assist poor women, and through various rural public works, women's co-operatives and as an expanded range of population-linked programmmes.

These efforts to improve the condition of women did not spring from entirely disinterested motives. On the contrary, Zia was able to make considerable political capital out of his championship of Women and Development policies. Having come to power by military means, he was faced with the problem of generating a political base for himself. The strategy of using state patronage to persuade rural interest groups to support regimes in power was not pioneered by Zia. But the opportunities for patronage inherent in the distribution of foreign development resources, together with the additional funding now available for women's projects, offered new and different channels of patronage to offer to the rural power brokers.

Zia's display of concern for women's welfare had other practical pay-offs. It helped mobilise an important constituency for himself and his newly founded party in their bid for electoral legitimation.[28] As the enormous potential contained in state championship of WID became apparent, he moved rapidly to nail its colours to his party's mast. The *Bangladesh Jatiya Mahila Sangshtha* (National Women' s Organisation), for instance, was initially set up in 1976 to co-ordinate organisations and programmes dealing with women and children and to run its own programmes in training and service delivery for women. Its membership was nominated through the district bureaucracies, ensuring a fairly broad spectrum of the rural middle-classes rather than a narrow faction within the political spectrum.

By 1979, however, all its most important members had joined Zia's newly founded political party, including its Chairwoman who also became Minister for Women's Affairs. During the parliamentary elections of 1979, the *Sangshtha* used its powers of patronage to mobilise truckloads of women for political rallies in support of Zia. Recruitment onto *Sangshtha* committees was subsequently changed to nomination by the new women members of parliament who were themselves appointed by Zia's ruling party; the politically-neutral character of the BJMS was thus abandoned and it became a vehicle for Zia's political ambitions.

So closely identified with the BNP did the *Sangshtha* become that when Ershad came to power, he opted to channel official resources through the redesigned Ministry of Social Welfare and Women's Affairs and to transform the *Sangshtha* into a subordinate, government-sponsored agency. In other respects, Ershad has continued Zia's policy of public commitment to WID policy. In addition to the conventional range of development activities for women, he has also pushed through certain legal initiatives. Family courts have been set up since 1985 with exclusive jurisdiction to deal with cases relating to parental and conjugal rights, thereby expediting their resolution. A number of ordinances have also been enacted which make crimes against women (abduction, trafficking, rape, acid-throwing and dowry-murder) subject to capital punishment.

To sum up, there is no doubt that both Zia and Ershad attached considerable significance to the place of WID in state policy. It is evident in their frequent and public declarations on the subject, generally couched in the WID language of 'ensuring women's participation' and 'integrating women into development'. It is also evident in the variety of projects and legal measures devised to advance women's welfare and provide them with incomes.

THE LIMITS OF DEVELOPMENTALISM: SOCIAL WELFARE AND THE MORAL ORDER

A more detailed examination of the state's WID policy is necessary before the gap between stated intention and actual implementation becomes apparent. While the public declarations are indeed impressive, they obscure the very specific, and ultimately limiting, ways in which women have been incorporated into state policy. They divert attention, for example, from the gross inadequacy of public sector funding for women's programmes: 0.06 per cent of the budget under the First Five Year Plan and around 0.2 per cent under the Second and Third.

Official efforts remain trapped within the paternalistic assumptions and class bias of the Bangladesh state and certain persistent themes connect present state policy with the past. One unifying theme which links the policies of different regimes derives from their common concern with political stability and the social order. The continuing priority given to population control, for instance, has been described by some writers as a form of 'crisis-managment' by an alliance of national elites and international donors who regard population growth as the key threat to the existing political order.[29] Other have described development projects for women as an essential element of the state's attempts to contain potential political unrest, by helping to meet, if only temporarily, the immediate needs of a growing section of the poor.[30]

However, bolstering the economic order is only one aspect of the state's defence of the status quo. Another aspect relates to the way in which its policies anticipate, embody and reproduce a particular, class-based paradigm of gender relations. This gender subtext is evident in the way in which women are positioned in state policy. While men enter in a variety of occupational, political and civil roles, women continue to be brought in primarily as wives and mothers and are persistently bracketed with children in both administrative structures and development plans. Family planning programmes are the only category of targeted development programmes which manage to reach more than 10 per cent of women, while income generating projects offered to women are designed to satisfy middle-class notions of female propriety rather than poor women's needs for financial security.

Tacit normative pressure gives way to overt moral coercion when the state turns its attention to the rehabilitation of women who have somehow slipped from their place in the social – and moral – order. Women singled out for special attention in rehabilitation efforts by the state have shifted periodically in response to changing public concerns; 'destitute' women (i.e. widowed or abandoned) in the period prior to independence; 'war-affected' women (those who had been widowed or raped) in the aftermath of liberation. More recently, media outcry over the traffic in women has highlighted 'socially handicapped' women (prostitutes) as the latest target for official rehabilitation. All these categories have one important feature in common: they are women who have been displaced through various processes from the protective custody of 'private patriarchy'. They present, in other words, the disturbing spectacle of women on their own, a deviation from the 'normal' order. Rehabilitation programmes in effect place such women in the protective custody of the state until they have been taught how to conform more closely to the social norms of poor-but-virtuous womanhood. The rhetoric of 'integration' and 'participation in development' that characterises state WID policy is abandoned here in favour of the language of 'moral upliftment' and 'normalisation'.

The main hallmarks of rehabilitation strategy are training in a range of 'appropriate' female skills (not remarkably different from those offered in WID projects), religious education and strict discipline. Women cared for by the Rehabilitation Foundation, for instance, are forbidden to visit friends or family without prior authorisation, locked into their hostels by five o'clock in the evening and sent to bed by seven. (Not surprisingly, 'psychological resistance . . . . to rehabilitation programmes' was cited as one of the major problems encountered by staff at such centres.)[31]

The most striking aspect of the state's rehabilitation efforts is, however, its anxious preoccupation with female virtue. This is evident, for instance, in the provision of hair-oil, comb and a copy of the Quran to women prisoners to ensure their decent appearance and moral education.[32] It is also evident in the title of a seminar organised after the media outcry over prostitution by the Directorate of Women's Affairs – 'Correction and Social Reclamation of Women from Moral Danger' [33] – as well as in the state's highly publicised, but largely unsuccessful attempts to rehabilitate prostitutes through marriage to local tradesmen. A recent proposal by the Directorate[34] for a new training and rehabilitation complex for prostitutes offers the familiar package of compulsory religious education, physical exercise, prison-like discipline and the usual forms of training, but in addition proposes a social worker/ counsellor to provide every 'inmate' with 'repeated counselling as and when necessary for their moral rectification'. It also recommends that women who successfully complete the rehabilitation programme be issued with a trade course certificate by the government in official recognition of their status as 'useful normal social being(s)'.

THE DRIFT TO THE ISLAMIC STATE

In its preoccupation with female purity, present state policy reproduces many of the attitudes of past regimes: paternalistic as long as the boundaries of social respectability are maintained, repressive when they are transgressed. However, the moral role of the state is being given a new edge by the attempts of recent regimes to revive the place of Islam in defining national identity. The search for a popular mandate by rulers who captured state power by military means has brought to the surface once again the old tensions between Bengali and Islamic definitions of national identity, fought out this time between liberal and orthodox forces within the national community.

The electoral victory needed to boost Zia's standing in the national and international arena required an ideology to counter the official secularism of the Awami League and to undermine its still considerable support. Islam offered an obvious and powerful alternative to win over right-wing Islamic elements who had been discredited by their pro-Pakistan politics in 1971, but who had re-grouped since the Awami League lost its hold on state power.

The process of dismantling state secularism was started by Zia in 1977 through Proclamation Order No. 1. This inserted the declaration *'Bismillah-ar-Rahman-ar Rahim'* (In the name of Allah, the Beneficient, the Merciful) at the beginning of the constitution; deleted the principle of secularism and replaced it by 'absolute trust and faith in the Almighty Allah'; and added a new clause which stated 'The state shall endeavour to consolidate, preserve and strengthen fraternal relations among Muslim countries based on Islamic solidarity'. Zia also proposed the designation of 'Bangladeshi', instead of the previous one of 'Bengali', to describe citizens of Bangladesh (reported in *Bichitra*, 27 April 1981). The redefined term played down the cultural aspects of the national identity, with its unavoidable connotations of a common heritage with Hindu West Bengal, and imposed instead a territorial definition which clearly demarcated the two communities. The ban placed on religious parties by the Awami League was lifted and many ex-Muslim Leaguers now aligned themselves with Zia's Bangladesh National Party.

Attempts to close the gap between state and religion have been continued by Ershad. A *Zakat* fund was established with the President at its head.[35] All television broadcasts have to be preceded by the call to prayer and female television presenters are required to present a modest appearance. Although a signatory to the World Plan of Action of the UN Decade for Women, the Bangladesh Government refused to ratify a number of clauses (relating to inheritance, marriage, child custody and divorce) in the Convention on the Elimination of All Forms of Discrimination Against Women, on the grounds that they conflicted with the *Shari'ah*.

Ershad, even more than Zia, needs to provide himself with a mantle of legitimacy. Zia was at least able to base his nationalist credentials on his active role in the liberation struggle. Ershad, by contrast, spent the entire period of the struggle interned in West Pakistan. His new party, *Jana Dal*, has a similar programme to the BNP, but has not succeeded in wresting away support for the BNP, which remains unified under the leadership of Zia's widow, Begum Khaleda Zia. Ershad's strategy is to play the Islamic card, without having to share power with the fundamentalist parties. This has not proved to be an easy task and accounts for his irresolute path to Islamisation.

In January 1983 he declared to a meeting of Islamic scholars that 'the place of Islam as a religion will be maintained above all in the constitution of the country. Our struggle is to fight the enemies of Islam and turn Bangladesh into an Islamic state'.[36] This was followed by a proposal that the Martyrs Day celebrations on February 21 be opened with readings from the Quran. This was immediately denounced by students belonging to the secular opposition parties as a negation of the achievements of the February 21 Movement, as 'changing basic state policy and promoting the interests of a group and a person in the name of religion'.[37] Twenty-three opposition leaders also issued a statement warning that declaration of an Islamic State would lead to civil war and communal strife. Ershad beat a hasty retreat and there were no readings from the Quran. He later told reporters that he realised it was a mistake to have allowed his emotions to have carried him away on those occasions.

In November 1987 a fresh wave of political activity nearly brought the government down. Incensed by a proposal to introduce military representatives into the newly-decentralised local government structure, the three main oppositional alliances led a series of general strikes and demonstrations, demanding fresh elections under a caretaker government. Ershad agreed to hold elections, but rejected the idea of a caretaker government. The elections were held in March 1988 and while Ershad's party swept the polls, it was a meaningless victory. The main opposition parties boycotted the elections and it was estimated that less than 3 per cent of the electorate turned out *(The Daily Telegraph,* 5 March 1988) in what was dubbed 'the voterless election'.

Ershad's first act in the new Parliament was to push through the Eighth Amendment in which Article 2A declares: 'The state religion of the Republic is Islam, but other religions may be practised in peace and harmony in the Republic'. Justifying the Amendment, Ershad declared that the distinct identity of the people of Bangladesh in their culture, language, geographical entity, independent sovereignty and other spheres of nationalism could only be defined through Islam *(Daily Ittefaq,* 21 June 1988). However, the move was widely seen as a cynical political act, an attempt to contain the secular opposition and to make inroads into the fundamentalist constituency. A large number of rallies and demonstrations were held in protest against what was seen as a violation of the liberal nationalism which brought Bangladesh into existence – 'the spirit of '71'. They were supported not only by the mainstream opposition parties and trade unions, but also by a wide spectrum of women's organisations, student groups, the Supreme Court Bar Association, the Combined Professionals' Action Committee, the Federation of Bangladesh University Teachers and various prominent intellectuals and ex-freedom fighters.

It is still not at all clear what the longer-term implications of the Amendment are going to be. According to Justice Sobhan, a constitutional expert,

At present, it might be a simple declaration, but in later phases of implementation it may call for certain very negative measures. For example, it may imply added constraints on women, including the imposition of the *purdah* system, end to demands for equal rights for women, certain amount of judicial discrimination and religious injunctions in various spheres of personal life *(Courier, 22 April 1988)*.

On the other hand, it may be a merely cosmetic decision. The alternative view reported in the same issue of *Courier* was that 'the declaration would be as good or as bad as choosing *doyel* [local species of robin] as the national bird'. According to this view, 'the government is not interested in theocracy. Its motives are more political than religious. It would never go for further "Islamising" the Constitution'.

THE ISLAMIC COMMUNITY: INTERNATIONAL SUPPORT AND THE INTERNAL CONSTITUENCY

The restoration of Islam to a central place in state ideology has been analysed so far as the strategy of military rulers in search of an ideology, but there were other considerations which assisted the process. Official Islamisation was also an attempt to create and capitalise on forces which would help to contain the secular and liberal opposition within the country.

During Mujib's ban on religious politics, the main fundamentalist party, *Jamaat-e-Islami*, had continued its activities unofficially through various social and community organisations such as the Masjid Mission and the Bangladesh Islamic Centre. Initially through clandestine and subsequently through open recruitment, it expanded its base from 425 full members and 40 000 associate members in 1968/69 to 650 and 100 000 respectively by 1980.[38] It continues to operate through a combination of well-organised proselytising and social welfare work (mobile clinics, medical services, education and charity). It has been particularly successful in recruiting a youthful cadre through the operations of its Youth and Student *Shibirs* (Encampments) and, significantly, it is for the first time successfully recruiting among women through a separate women's front.

A growth in non-political grassroots religious consciousness is also discernible. It is exemplified by the *Tabliq-Jamaat*, one of the largest but least known religious movements in the Muslim world today, whose annual assembly in Tongi (Bangladesh) draws together over a million people from all over the world. The *Tabliq-Jamaat* has no organisational structure or political aspirations, but assists the fundamentalist cause by creating an environment of revivalist Islam.

Various reasons have been advanced for this growth in Islamic conscious-ness. To some extent, it represents a rise in anti-Indian sentiment in reaction to Indian intransigence on the Farakka Barrage, its naval presence in the Bay of Bengal and other acts of hostility which have periodically disrupted the relationship between the two countries. Another reason offered is the import of conservative values by Bangladeshi migrants returning from the Middle East.[39] Another undoubtedly important reason can be termed the Saudi factor. The West is, after all, not the only source of funds for Bangladesh. The OPEC countries, most importantly Saudi Arabia, entered the ranks of major aid donors since the oil boom of the early 1970s. While it is not clear to what extent moves to reassert Islamic values were in deference to Saudi sensibilities, it should be noted that Saudi Arabia refused to recognise the new state of Bangladesh until the assassination of Mujib and Zia's accession to power. The change of regime expedited the flow of aid from the Middle East, with Saudi Arabia as the most important source.

The main vehicles identified by the Saudis to disseminate Islamic values have been the Islamic non-governmental organisations, the *madrassa* (religious education) system and the fundamentalist parties, all of which are believed receive a great deal of official and unofficial aid from Saudi Arabia. The outcome of Saudi munificence has been the creation of alter-native networks of patronage (scholarships, vocational training, student accommodation, employment and medical aid) which materially bolster the appeal of the Islamic constituency. Particularly noteworthy has been the remarkable expansion in the numbers and influence of community-oriented 'Islamic NGOs' – *Chattagram Al Jamiya Islamia, Jamat al Sabah, Dakheli Complex, Masjid* Mission, *Rabitat-ul-Islam, Mashjid Samaj* – all of whom draw on funds from the Middle East.[40] The training of imams by the Islamic Foundation to carry out village administration, basic health care, including maternity courses, and agricultural extension work exemplifies the entry of religious forces into the field of community development.

Various research organisations have also been set up to propagate Islamic values and build up a cadre of Islamic intellectuals to service the expansion in religious centres and the educational system. They seek to challenge head-on the ideology and rhetoric of developmentalism, clearly labelled 'Western'. The publications of the Islamic Foundation, for instance, are sold at unprofitably low prices to counter 'the fact that tons and tons of books on other ideologies in the best print and finest paper . . . are being distributed free in this country'.[41]

Predictably, the rising Islamic intelligentsia pays special attention to the conspicuous place accorded to women in the state's developmentalist discourse, denouncing 'the so-called progressive intellectuals' who 'in symphony with their Western masters' attempt to argue for equality between the sexes.[42] The Islamic Economics Research Bureau recently published a collection of papers presented at a seminar on Islamic Economics (to which the Saudi ambassador was invited as Special Guest). Three papers dealt specifically with women, all of them focusing on the issue of employment. One common feature of these articles is their attempt to subvert WID arguments to provide support for their own very different positions. Thus, in common with many feminists within and outside Bangladesh, one article contests the 'Western' idea that housewives do not work, but draws from this the conclusion that women do not require further employment opportunities.[43] The other aspect of these articles is their overriding fear of the sexual chaos which might result from women and men working together: 'the close proximity of opposite sexes arouses lust and love for each other which on many occasions lead to immoral and scandalous affairs'.[44] The message is simple: tampering with the 'natural' principle of separate spheres for men and women can lead to the total collapse of the moral order.

CONTRADICTIONS AND TENSIONS IN STATE POLICY

Clearly, state attempts to win the support of the Islamic constituency have different gender implications from those associated with promoting Women and Development policy. In contrast to goals of women's emancipation and economic participation, the Islamic lobby in Bangladesh seeks to confine women to a domestic role and to impose controls on their mobility. Zia's strategy, and that of Ershad after him, has been a blatant balancing act between the conflicting gender ideologies implicit in different aid packages and a refusal to acknowledge their inherent contradictions.

Women have not benefited, for instance, from the money being poured into the religious education system by the government and the *Madrassa* Board. They are generally excluded from the new *madrassas*, the Islamic Centre for Vocational Training and the Islamic University currently being set up by the government. Such discriminatory provision of education clearly contravenes the commitment to sexual equality still contained within the Constitution as well as the declared intention of the state to increase educational opportunities for women.[45] Measures curtailing women's visibility in the public domain also contradict the state's declared policy of encouraging women's employment in the public sector and women's participation in competitive sports. Thus the earlier policy of recruiting women into the metropolitan police has been gradually modified so that women are now restricted to roadside traffic booths or check points: obviously maintaining a female police force which operated on the streets 'did not quite tally with the values being cultivated by an aspiring Islamic state'.[46]

These shifts and contradictions within state policy are possible because the state regards the issue of women's rights – and of Islam itself – in essentially instrumentalist terms. It is significant that the most organised political force on the religious right – the *Jamaat-e-Islami* – has remained in the opposition, unimpressed, it would appear, by the government's Islamic posturing. Some degree of coherence in overall government policy is made possible by the fact that both the Saudis and the US have the long-term interests of private capital at heart. Consequently, while Saudi influence is apparent in some public sector policy and within the community, it has generally refrained from interfering with the workings of the private sector.

THE EMERGENCE OF WOMEN'S MOVEMENTS

When the totality of successive policies of the Bangladesh state is taken into account, its championship of women's rights can be seen in an extremely cynical light. In its pursuit of political legitimacy and international aid, it professes to believe in both the emancipation of women as well as in its opposite. The clash is most evident in the sphere of gender relations because the position of women is a key factor distinguishing the two ideological packages. At the same time, it is precisely the existence of these conflicting

interests and pressures on the state that has permitted some genuine advances
to be made in women's interests. The WID influence has helped to challenge
the monopoly of archaic ideological preconceptions about women at all
levels of Bangladesh society. It has also opened up new possibilities for
organisation and struggle around women's interests.

Since Liberation, political activities around women's rights have emerged
as a distinct area of mobilisation. The women's wings of the two main
parties – the BNP and the Awami League – are primarily active around
welfare issues but also support equal rights for women. However, since
they operate with a limited view of women's roles, their demand generally
translates into putting pressure on the state to reform family and personal
status law.

Women's rights are given a broader interpretation by the women's
organisations associated with various left-wing parties. The most active
of these is *Mahila Parishad* linked to the Communist Party, which now
has over 30 000 members. *Mahila Parishad* has been active on a wide
range of issues: it has fought for the rights of women workers both
in factories and in middle-class occupations like banking, kept up the
pressure on the government to implement the 10 per cent quota for
women in employment and (in contrast to the BNP and Awami League)
opposed reserved parliamentary seats for women as an anti-democratic
ploy to strengthen the party in power. More recently, it spearheaded a
campaign against the practice of dowry and against violence against women
and opened up shelters for women who had been victims of violence. Some
of the laws passed by the government on these issues were a consequence
of *Mahila Parishad's* campaigns.

Despite its undeniable strengths, *Mahila Parishad's* institutional links
with the Communist Party have prevented it from giving an independent
significance to women's oppression. The struggle for women's rights tends
to be subsumed within the 'wider' struggle for socialism and democracy;
the politics of gender in personal relations and everyday life and the
ideological bases of women's subordination receive scant attention from
its members. This was evident, for instance, in the national campaign
against male violence which reached its peak in the summer of 1985.
While *Mahila Parishad* took a leading role in denouncing male violence,
it joined forces with the left opposition in linking it with the breakdown of
law-and-order under Ershad's regime and focusing its efforts on bringing
down the government. Protests by other women's groups that women were
being portrayed in *Mahila Parishad's* campaign as passive victims and that
the issue of domestic violence (reported in the press far more frequently
than recognised in the law-and-order explanation) was being side-stepped,

were generally dismissed by *Mahila Parishad* as divisive, irrelevant and likely to alienate male support.

The other main location of struggles for women's rights is in grassroots development organisations which flourish outside the confines of official efforts. A significant number of these non-governmental organisations allocate a central place to women's oppression in their programmes for change. Rather than reproduce the welfarism that characterises most development initiatives, NGOs such as *Proshika, Nijera Kori* and *Saptagram* have shifted their primary objective from meeting the immediate needs of poor and landless women and men to that of their longer-term empowerment.

These NGOs work with a collective rather than individual concept of empowerment. Landless women and men are organised into groups, often on the basis of welfare or economic activities: health delivery, credit, cultivation of collectively-leased land and so on. Through a process of 'consciousness-raising' , they are encouraged to analyse the roots of their oppression and to break the 'culture of silence' which is part of the condition of poverty.[47] The training sessions include analysis of feminist issues – such as male violence, dowry, polygamy, verbal repudiation – as well as the more usual class-based ones of wages, land rights, corruption and clientelism.

These progressive NGOs and their strategies represent an important break with past efforts to change women's lives. They are primarily rural-based and thus able to reach the vast section of the population who fall outside the orbit of most political women's organisations. They also give greater primacy to the power of ideology in maintaining gender subordination. By acknowledging that the struggle against oppression also requires the transformation of individual consciousness, the progressive NGOs have extended the arena of the women's movement beyond the perimeters of conventional left politics.

Aside from political and development organisations, there are also a large number of independent women's organisations such as professional organisations (e.g. the Federation of University Women, the Federation of Business and Professional Women), the Bangladesh Women's Rights Movement (mainly working around legal discrimination), *Naripokkho* (For Women, an autonomous feminist group) and various women's research groups such as Women for Women and *Nari Shongoti* (Women's Collective). It is unlikely that women could have been active in such numbers and on such a range of issues if the state had been a more monolithic presence and displayed a firmer commitment to its Islamic programme.

Significantly, the first demonstrations and rallies in opposition to the government's Eighth Amendment were called by women's groups: as a leading newspaper commented, 'This time the women have taken the lead' (*Holiday*, 19 April 1988). The same article commented that women's opposition to the Amendment drew its moral roots from the humanistic values which had inspired the liberation struggle. In the words of a resolution adopted at the end of one of the rallies called by women's groups: 'the war was fought to ensure the continuity of the culture and tradition of the Bengali people. The war was supposed to guarantee freedom of speech, freedom of thought, women's rights' (*Holiday*, 29 April 1988).

As one of the women's groups that initiated the protests against the Amendment, *Naripokkho* declared its opposition to any attempt to mix religion and politics on the grounds that it strengthened the fundamentalists' hand and invested every man with the moral authority to police women's behaviour. The organisation has now issued a writ against Ershad on the grounds that his Amendment contravenes the equal rights guaranteed to women and to religious minorities by the Bangladesh Constitution, by the Charter of the United Nations and by the Universal Declaration of Human Rights. Its example has been followed by other women's groups and by legal and professional organisations who are contesting the Amendment on similar grounds.

CONCLUSION: WOMEN, ISLAM AND THE *AD HOC* STATE

This chapter set out to analyse the fluctuating definitions of Bengali Muslim identity in connection with the resistance encountered by official Islamisation programmes since their inception in the late 1970s. The syncretic form of Islam that flourished among the Bengali Muslims, and the common cultural legacy they shared with Bengali Hindus have often made them suspect in the eyes of the 'true' believers. A brutal war of liberation was fought in 1971 to defend what Bengali Muslims believed to be their own distinct national identity: a fusion of Bengali culture and humanist Islam.

Bangladesh's history since independence has been one of political instability, as different factions of the ruling class struggle to control state power. In their quest for an internal constituency and external legitimacy, successive military regimes have sought to reconcile apparently contradictory political programmes. The contradictions are most apparent in the sphere of women's rights, since state policy has, on the one hand, championed WID values and the emancipation of women, and on the other, set in motion a 'creeping' Islamisation process, thereby encouraging those who would snatch back the gains that women have made.

Women have been able to capitalise on the *ad hoc* politics of a politically insecure state. The contradictions and tensions that characterise state policy have opened up a new ideological space within which a nascent women's movement has come into existence. Women have also benefited from the resistance of liberal and secular forces to the state's attempts to restore Islam as a basic principle of Bangladeshi nationhood. Such resistance has helped to moderate the extent to which official Islamisation can be translated into a direct attack on women's rights, as was possible in Pakistan and Iran. The women's movement will continue to find allies outside its own ranks as long as political Islamisation is seen as a negation of the spirit of '71. In the words of one writer on the place of Islam in Bangladesh:

... since Bangladesh came into being certain issues have been reopened, which one thought were buried in the ashes of the war of liberation. We had established our identity as Bengalis, as a nation that embraces various religious communities ... We have learnt the hard way the difference between religion and nationhood. Let us not unlearn it.[48]

NOTES

This paper expands on certain issues which were raised in an earlier article 'Subordination and Struggle: Women in Bangladesh', *New Left Review* no. 168 (April/May 1988). I am grateful to Deniz Kandiyoti for editorial advice and to Rokeya Rahman Kabeer, Ruby Ghuznavi and Shireen Huq for their valuable comments on the paper.

  1. Benedict Anderson, *Imagined Communities: Reflections on the Origin and Spread of Nationalism* (London: Verso Press, 1983).
  2. Nira Yuval-Davis, 'National Reproduction: Sexism, Racism and the State'. Paper presented at the British Sociological Association Conference (Manchester 1982) p. 3
  3. The first partition of Bengal in this century took place in 1905 in an attempt by the British Raj to weaken the power of Indian nationalism in the region and play up Hindu-Muslim differences: as H. H. Risley, Home Secretary to India, asserted, 'Bengal united is a power. Bengal divided will pull in different ways' (cited in Premen Addi and Ibne Azad, 'Politics and Society in Bengal' Robin Blackburn (ed.), in *Explosion in a Subcontinent* (London: Penguin Books, 1975) p. 111). The Muslim

League was founded in Dhaka in the following year with the objectives of advancing Muslim interests in the subcontinent and promoting loyalty to British government. However, protest against partition shook not just (Hindu) Bengal, but the rest of India and it was annulled in 1911.

4. Tariq Ali, *Can Pakistan Survive? The Death of a State* (Middlesex: Penquin Books) 1983, p. 133.
5. David Kopf, 'Pakistani Identity and the Historiography of Muslim Bengal' in Richard L. Park (ed.), *Patterns of Change in Modern Bengal* South Asia Series Occasional Paper no. 29 (Asian Studies Centre East Lansing, Michigan State University, 1979) p. 111.
6. See for instance Clarence Maloney, K. M. Ashraful Aziz and Profulla C. Sarker, *Beliefs and Fertility in Bangladesh* (Dhaka: ICDDRB, 1981); A. M. A. Muhith, *Bangladesh: Emergence of a Nation* (Dhaka: Bangladesh Books International Ltd., 1978).
7. Examples of this for Bangladesh can be found in Therese Blanchet, *Meanings and Rituals of Birth in Rural Bangladesh* (Dhaka: University Press Ltd, 1984). For West Bengal see Lina M. Fruzetti, 'Ritual Status of Muslim Women in Rural India' in Jane J. Smith (ed.), *Women in Contemporary Muslim Societies* (London: Associated University Press, 1980).
8. See Blanchet, *Meanings and Rituals* . . . . and also Ralph W. Nicholas, 'Vaishnavism and Islam in Rural Bengal' in David Kopf (ed.), *Bengal Regional Identity* (Asian Studies Centre, Michigan State University, 1969).
9. Addi and Azad 'Politics and Society . . . '.
10. Romila Thapar, *A History of India Volume 1* (London: Penguin Books, 1968).
11. See, for instance, Blanchet, 'Meanings and Rituals' and Fruzetti, 'Ritual Status of Muslim Women'. See also contributions in Rafiuddin Ahmed (ed.), *Islam in Bangladesh: Society Culture and Politics* (Dhaka: Bangladesh Itihas Samiti, 1983).
12. In relation to Amir Ali, for instance, Kopf comments, 'His *Short History of the Saracens* (1900) illustrates clearly the heterogenetic identity of the Muslim Bengali intelligentsia; so intense was Amir Ali's concern with the temporally remote happenings of physically remote Arabia, that if one did not already know his Bengali origins, one could easily imagine the author to have been born an Arab' (in 'Pakistani Identity and . . . ', p. 120).
13. Kopf, 'Pakistani Identity . . . ', p. 112.
14. See Keith Callard, *Pakistan: A Political Study* (London: George Allen and Unwin Ltd, 1957), for an analysis of the political devices by which the Punjabi oligarchy secured its hegemony over the rest of the country. An analysis of the economic exploitation of East Pakistan is contained in Richard Nations, 'The Economic Structure of Pakistan and Bangladesh' in Blackburn, *Explosion in a Subcontinent*.
15. Tariq Ali, *Can Pakistan Survive*.

16. Zillur Rahman Khan, 'Islam and Bengali Nationalism' in Rafiuddin Ahmed (ed.), *Bangladesh: Society Religion and Politics* (South Asia Studies Group, University of Chittagong, 1985).
17. The vermilion spot traditionally worn by Hindu women as symbol of their marital state, but now widely adopted by both Muslim and Hindu Bengalis as a cosmetic feature.
18. Rehnuma Ahmed, 'Women's Movement in Bangladesh and the Left's Understanding of the Women Question', *Journal of Social Studies*, no. 30 (1985), pp. 27–56
19. Rehnuma Ahmed, 'Women's Movement . . . '.
20. Tariq Ali, *Can Pakistan Survive*, p. 91.
21. Rahman Sobhan, *The Crisis of External Dependence: The Political Economy of Foreign Aid to Bangladesh* (London: Zed Press, 1982).
22. Rounaq Jahan, *Bangladesh Politics: Problems and Issues* (Dhaka: Dhaka University Press, 1980).
23. Rahman Sobhan, *The Crisis of External Dependence*.
24. See, for example, Shapan Adnan, Mahmud Khan, Malik Md. Shahnoor, Hussain Zillur Rahman, Mahbub Ahmed and Mahbubul Akash, *A Review of Landlessness in Rural Bangladesh: 1877–1977* (Department of Economics, University of Chittagong, 1978); Harry W. Blair, 'Ideology, Foreign Aid and Rural Poverty in Bangladesh: Emergence of the Like-Minded Group', *Journal of Social Studies*, vol. 34 (1986), pp. 1–27; F. Tomasson Januzzi and James T. Peach (eds), *The Agrarian Structure of Bangladesh: An Impediment to Development* (Boulder, Colorado: Westview Press, 1980). See also Rahman Sobhan, *The Crisis of External Dependence*.
25. Sigma Huda, 'Women and Law: Policy and Implementation', paper presented at a seminar on Women and Law organised by Women for Women, 13–15 September 1987, Dhaka.
26. The Awami League's gestures towards secularism stand in marked contrast to Bhutto's stance in Pakistan during the same period. Despite his left-wing populism, Bhutto's version of socialism carried the prefix of 'Islamic' , he retained the status of Islamic Republic for Pakistan and declared Islam the state religion. A list of the symbols incorporated by Bhutto in his 1973 Constitution, which went beyond those in the Constitutions of 1956 and 1962, are cited in Khawar Mumtaz and Farida Shaheed, *Women of Pakistan: Two Steps Forward, One Step Back* (London: Zed Press, 1987).
27. B. K. Jahangir, *Problematics of Nationalism in Bangladesh* (Dhaka: Centre for Social Studies, 1986) p. 79.
28. Meghna Guhathakurta, 'Gender Violence in Bangladesh: The Role of the State', *Journal of Social Studies* no. 30 (1985), pp. 77–90.
29. Farida Akhtar, *Depopulating Bangladesh* (Dhaka: UBINIG, 1986).
30. Shelley Feldman and Florence E. McCarthy, *Rural Women and Development in Bangladesh: Selected Issues* (Oslo: NORAD/Ministry of Development Co-operation, 1984).

31. Roushan Jahan, 'Situation of Women Deviating from Established Social Norms' in Women for Women Research and Study Group (eds), *Situation of Women in Bangladesh* (Dhaka: Women for Women Research and Study Group, 1979) p. 364.

32. Meghna Guhathakurtha, 'Gender Violence in Bangladesh'.

33. Firdaus Azim and Shireen Huq 'The Shabmeher Story Reconsidered'. Paper presented at the workshop on Media and Women's Oppression in Bangladesh, Dhaka 29/30 January 1987.

34. This information is from a project proforma issued by the Ministry of Social Welfare and Women's Affairs proposing a new Training and Rehabilitation Complex for Socially Handicapped Women.

35. *Zakat* represents the charitable obligations of wealthy Muslims sanctioned by Islam. The President's prominent role in the distribution of this fund serves to emphasise his association with a particular form of public patronage while simultaneously establishing his Islamic credentials.

36. Peter Charles O'Donnell, *Bangladesh: Biography of a Muslim Nation* (Boulder, Colarado: Westview Press, 1987) p. 255.

37. Ibid.

38. Talukder Maniruzzaman, 'Bangladesh Politics: Secular and Islamic Trends' inRafiuddin Ahmed (ed.), *Islam in Bangladesh*.

39. Rehnuma Ahmed, 'Women' s Movement . . .

40. Tanvir Mokkamel, *Samrajyabader Pancham Bahini* (Dhaka: Jatiya Shahitya Prakashini, 1987).

41. K.M.Mohsin, 'Trends of Islam in Bangladesh' in Rafiuddin Ahmed (ed.), *Islam in Bangladesh*.

42. Zohurul Islam, 'Women's Employment: Problems and Prospects' in *Thoughts on Islamic Economics*, Proceedings from a seminar on Islamic Economics held by the Islamic Economics Research Bureau, Dhaka, 1980, p. 250.

43. Shah Abdul Hannan, 'Women's Employment: Its Need and Appropriate Avenues' in *Thoughts on Islamic Economics*, Proceedings from a seminar on Islamic Economics held by the Islamic Economics Research Bureau, Dhaka, 1980, p. 240.

44. Muhammad Musharraf Hossain, 'The Employment for Women' in *Thoughts on Islamic Economics*, p. 270

45. Salma Khan, *The Fifty Percent Women in Development and Policy in Bangladesh* (Dhaka: University Press Ltd, 1988).

46. Meghna Guhathakurtha, 'Gender Violence in Bangladesh'.

47. Paulo Freire, *Pedagogy of the Oppressed* (Harmondsworth: Penguin Books, 1972).

48. A. T. M. Anisuzzaman, 'Comments on Ghulam Murshid's paper' in Rafiuddin Ahmed (ed.), *Islam in Bangladesh*, p. 152.

6 Forced Identities: the State, Communalism, Fundamentalism and Women in India

Amrita Chhachhi

This chapter examines the process through which communal identities have been created in India and its implications for women. It argues that processes affecting Muslim women in India cannot be understood in isolation but must be set in the broader context of communalism, emerging fundamentalism and the dynamics of the relation between the post-colonial state, capitalist development and patriarchal control.

A commonly accepted definition of communalism presents it as an ideology which projects the 'belief that because a group of people follow a particular religion, they have as a result, common social, political and economic interests'.[1] Given differences of class and caste which divide the 'community', communalism has been presented as a form of 'false consciousness' and is posed in opposition to nationalism which is seen as necessarily more progressive. This view makes a distinction between religion and communalism stressing the political use of religion in conflicts over access to economic resources, and political power as the main distinguishing feature of communalism. Studies on communalism have therefore emphasised that people following a particular religion do not necessarily have common interests and have highlighted the significance of communalism as an ideology. Although this definition has been useful, especially in countering communal interpretations of history, the implication that communalism is a form of false consciousness which distorts the true interests of class solidarity and nationalism has been criticised.[2] Currently there is an attempt to re-evaluate the phenomenon of communalism on its own terms rather than as a 'negative' phenomenon counterposed to nationalism. There is a search for the material basis of communalism in contemporary India, and its interconnections with the economy, culture and political structures, and a need to problematise nationalism itself. It is recognised that, notwithstanding class/caste cleavages, communal identities can become objective forces resulting in a common articulation of interests.

In the last few years a number of studies of communal riots and ethnic tensions have stressed that such an identity is not inherent but is constructed. The process of identity creation involves the downplaying of internal divisions like caste and class differences and the construction of a common communal identity. Communalism in its contemporary form in India is a product of the nineteenth and twentieth centuries, when ethnic and community identities took on separatist and intolerant forms as a result of colonial policy and economic developments in the colonial economy. None the less, many commentators continue to see the South Asian region as torn by inherently antagonistic religious communities, with the roots of this antagonism traced to the medieval past. Similarly, studies on Muslims in India tend to take the Muslims as a self-evident community with its specific characteristics deriving from the inherent nature of Islam. The myth of the homogeneity of Indian Muslims has been countered through the evidence not only of class and caste differences but also of considerable regional differences among Muslims in the practice of marriage, kinship structures, inheritance and the custom of veiling.[3] Others have pointed out that the Muslims form a community only in an emotional sense, and that only when there is a perceived threat to them.

> If one is talking about the bond of Islam, then one should remember that the bond is quite tenuous, like all religious bonds, it accquires salience only when threatened; otherwise, it operates more at a sentimental rather than substantive level, and for real life issues it gets weak if not cancelled, once it comes into contact with other more basic bonds of socio-economic cohesion.[4]

In this chapter, rather than taking the Muslims as a self-evident community, I examine the processes arising out of the minority status of Muslims in India and draw out their implications for the status of Muslim women. Muslims in India constitute around 12 per cent of the population. Since the 1980s tensions between Muslims, Hindus and Sikhs have heightened. Two examples are examined to highlight the implications of the creation of communal identities for women; the Shah Bano case and the conflict over Muslim personal law and the defence of the recent incident of *sati* (widow immolation) in the name of Rajput/Hindu identity in the province of Rajasthan, Western India.

In 1985 the Supreme Court of India passed a judgement granting a 73-year-old woman, Shah Bano, the paltry sum of Rs. 179 per month as maintenance from her husband. Shah Bano had been thrown out of her husband's house in 1975 after forty-three years of marriage. In 1977 he stopped paying her maintenance of Rs. 200 and she filed an application under Section 125 of the Criminal Procedure Code for maintenance at the rate of Rs. 500 a month.[5] In the meantime, her husband divorced her and paid her Rs. 3000 as his final settlement. The judicial magistrate, however, ordered him to pay Rs. 25 as maintenance and this sum was later raised to Rs. 179.20 by the High Court of Madhya Pradesh. The husband appealed to the Supreme Court on the grounds that under Muslim Personal Law, he did not have the responsibility to maintain his wife after divorce. The Supreme Court dismissed his appeal and, in addition to maintenance, ordered him to pay legal costs. This judgement, provoked widespread reactions and led to mass demonstrations, strikes and petitions presented by Muslims calling for a reversal of the judgement which was seen as violating Muslim Personal Law. The issue of women's rights turned into a major confrontation of majority and minority interests. In 1986 the Indian Parliament passed the Muslim Women's Protection of the Right to Divorce Bill which withdrew the right of Muslim women to appeal for maintenance under the Criminal Procedure Code.

In 1987, an 18-year-old, recently married girl, was immolated on the funeral pyre of her husband in Deorala, Western India. This incident was lauded as a great act of wifely devotion, and *sati*, although banned since 1829, was resurrected as the hallmark of the traditional Hindu woman. This incident sparked off an agitation in which the Rajput community formed an organisation called the *Sati Dharm Raksha Samiti* (defenders of the religio-ethical ideal of *sati*) to celebrate *sati* as a symbol of warrior ideals of valour and honour. Crowds arrived on pilgrimage, a Trust was set up, the production of a paraphernalia of trick photographs, mementoes and music cassettes soon turned Deorala into a fairground. The provincial government took no action and several politicians, including some members of the ruling party, even arrived at the spot to pay homage. Opposition by feminists, reformist Hindu organisations, and civil liberty groups was seen by the Rajputs as an attack on them as a community. Temple priests and Hindu fundamentalist organisations entered the fray and quoted from ancient texts to show that *sati* was not only the noblest act of self sacrifice and wifely devotion for the Rajputs, but for Hinduism as a whole. The central government finally passed another law (since *sati* was already illegal) which contained many ambiguities and was not seriously implemented.[6]

Both these incidents involved women as symbolic representations of the community. Granting a Muslim woman maintenance was seen as violating Muslim personal law, which implied a direct threat to 'Muslim identity'. Preventing a Hindu widow from being immolated was seen as an attack on tradition and a threat to Rajput identity, which soon extended to a threat to Hinduism in general. Muslim and Hindu women were found on both sides of the confrontation – supporting the fundamentalists and opposing them. Both issues revived the old debates of the nationalist movement between tradition and modernity, the nature of state ideology and the specific implications of communal identities for women in India.

Recent feminist theories have questioned the category of 'women', given the differences in the experience of women of different classes, races, castes and communities. The contradictory and historically specific impact of patriarchy, colonialism and capitalism has resulted in a fragmentation and wide diversity in women's experiences.[7] Instead of adopting an essentialist position, it seems more useful to examine the multiple identities which women and men possess. These identities do not only rest on certain 'objective' criteria of colour, class or caste. Although these objective structures are significant, very often identities are constructed on an imagined commonality which is then given an objective existence. Anderson's study of nationalism has pointed out how the 'imagined community' of the nation is constructed and generates passion and sacrifice, in spite of the contingency of commonality at other levels.[8]

A more significant factor is the selective mobilisation of certain identities as a response to economic, political, social and cultural processes.[9] Identities are therefore constantly shifting, not only historically but also at any given point in time. Faced with racism, a black woman may assert her blackness but when faced with male chauvinism she may assert her rights as a woman, and again when confronted with upper-class privilege she may mobilise her identity as a working-class woman. She therefore possesses all these identities and yet is not reducible to any one of them. The mobilisation of identities often implies a lack of choice; that is, these identities are forced upon individuals. Forced identities do not imply that they are false or coerced – it simply implies the lack of real choice in a particular situation. In a communal riot, for instance, an individual identified as a Muslim, or a Sikh, is a target for attack, irrespective of her/his religious convictions or political views. In the context of the general communalisation of society, with regular outbreaks of violence, communal identities are increasingly forced upon individuals of various communities. In such a context, while it is true in general that 'the assertion of one's

Muslimness is an option available to an individual who may articulate, underplay or stress this form of identity . . . ,'[10] this is not always a freely chosen option.

There is thus a difference between an identity which is forced upon one and an 'identity which is a self consciously contructed space that (affirms). . . on the basis of conscious coalition, of affinity, of political kinship'.[11] This distinction is useful particularly in relation to the situation of Muslim women in India. Subject to contradictory political and economic pressures, they have defined themselves and been defined and redefined in their identities as women, as Muslims, and as a Muslim minority.

There is a tendency to see Muslim women as passive objects of this triple oppression, but in fact there have been continuous attempts by Muslim women and men to redefine women's rights since the mid-nineteenth-century, attempts which were scuttled or squashed due to the pressure of existing vested interests and political calculations. The logic of communal politics forced these progressive forces to retract and succumb to the logic of a threatened minority community, which clung to 'traditional' customs and practices. This progressive-regressive movement in the determination of Muslim identity in India is often glossed over in discussions about the 'Muslim community'. A clear illustration of this tendency to respond and act on the assumption that Muslims constitute one community is the way in which the government, media and politicians responded to the case of Shah Bano in 1986.

This case was picked up by the media, and by Hindu fundamentalists as well as the liberal intelligentsia as an illustration of the unchanging oppression of Muslim women, inherent in their Muslimness rather than in the particular socio-economic conditions of Muslims in India and the role of the state in fostering communal identities. Newspaper headlines focused on Muslim women as victims of Muslim law, with headlines like 'Legion of the Maimed and the Damned' (*Indian Express*, April 1986), 'Bill will throw Muslim women to the wolves' (*Sunday Observer*, February 1986) with gruesome stories of divorced and deserted women.[12] Hindu fundamentalists 'picked up the *burkha*, *talaq* and other discriminatory aspects of Muslim personal law and practice to prove how barbaric Muslims and Islam is . . .'.[13] Many feminists inadvertently adopted the same discourse and found themselves side by side with the Hindu fundamentalists in demanding a uniform civil code without a clear elaboration of what such a code should entail to distinguish their position from the fundamentalists'. The government disregarded the views of many Muslim politicians, intellectuals, and women's groups who opposed the Bill, thus according legitimacy to a small Muslim fundamentalist constituency as the representatives of the Muslim community.

A recent article analyses the legal, political, religious and feminist discourses generated by the Shah Bano case and argues that these were unified by the common assumption of an ideology of protection.[14] The thrust of the new bill was to push Muslim women back to a total dependence on their natal family thereby reasserting the private sphere, the family, as the protector of women. The resistance to this from a broad coalition of feminist and Muslim reformist groups, the authors argue, managed to reconcile the contradictory issues of women's rights with minority rights and kept the issue in the public realm. However, it is necessary to extend their argument on the conflict between the state and the patriarchal family over the rights of women beyond the private/public dichotomy.

The relationship between the state and women's subordination is a newly emerging area of feminist theory. Moving from studies on the various aspects of state policies which define women as mothers, wives or workers, recent work has highlighted the ways in which 'citizenship' itself is a gendered construction.[15] Others have pointed out that it is debatable whether the private/public distinction reflects the autonomous spheres of family and the state, given the evidence of state intervention into the so-called 'private' arena in advanced capitalist countries.[16] Eisenstein, for instance, argues that the state has always actively defined and constructed the realm of the family, and the welfare state has made this intervention even more explicit. The mystification of the state lies precisely in appearing to be public and thus unrelated to the family as the private sphere, whereas in fact 'the private sphere is defined and regulated in relation to the state realm'.[17] According to her, the state is relatively autonomous in relation to the capitalist class, but the fact that the state is patriarchal in structure and content acts as a constraint on its relative autonomy. This arises because there is a systematic representation of patriarchal interests in the state apparatus; that is, 'the governing or ruling class is made up of men who represent the sexual-class needs of men.'[18] This formulation is problematic since it identifies patriarchy with the persona of men rather than a structure of control over women, which benefits men. However she does raise the importance of examining the dynamics of the relation between state, capital and patriarchy in understanding the institutionalisation of women's subordination. Yuval-Davis and Anthias provide further theoretical insight into the ways in which the political project of the state incorporates women in particular ways. They argue for a move away from functionalist and essentialist explanations of the state to an approach which does not reduce state practices to 'a given primary source nor .. (to its) unitary effects.'[19]

The analysis of the state therefore implies taking into account the historical specificity of the social forces which construct as well as resist state practices. Women participate in crucial ways in the construction as well as the opposition to ethnic, national and state processes.[20]

In post-colonial societies, the relationship between state, capital and patriarchy becomes even more complex. Although the construction of anti-colonial nationalism and its realisation in an independent nation state has taken different forms, it has been argued that the general form of the transition from colonial to post-colonial nation states in the twentieth century has been along the Gramscian model of 'the passive revolution'.[21] The characteristic pattern involved a series of alliances between the bourgeoisie and other dominant classes, along with mass support from subordinate classes. As a result, the new state does not directly dismantle the colonial structures of administration, law, education and other areas of civil society, nor does it undermine the power of pre-capitalist dominant classes. The post-colonial state is interventionist only in the sphere of production, to create conditions for the development and expansion of capital. The essential character of the 'passive revolution' is, therefore, its subjection to the contradictory pressures of revolution/restoration. This analysis has been applied to an examination of the ideological currents and changes in the realm of ideas which accompanied the process of the constitution of the post-colonial state.[22] Further work needs to be done on the relationship between the state and other areas of civil society, in particular the relationship between the state and patriarchy. In this chapter aspects of the interation between state, capital and patriarchy will be examined. It is argued that, while the preservation of a traditional patriarchal family through the maintainance of separate personal laws could be explained as a result of the restorative element of the post-colonial Indian state, in the present context there is increasing state intervention in all areas of civil society. The state's commitment to capitalist development has led to the undermining of traditional patriarchal structures, generating contradictions between capitalist and patriarchal interests. This is occurring in a context of pervasive 'communalisation' of society, where fundamentalist groups of different communities are exerting pressure on the state to reassert traditional patriarchal controls. State practices *vis à vis* the family in the contemporary situation have to be seen as an attempt to mediate these various interests.

Since the 1960s there has been a tremendous increase in communal violence, now involving not just Hindus and Muslims but also members of other communities and creating new divisions, for instance between Hindus and Sikhs. These incidents have occurred mainly in urban areas but have recently also spread to rural hinterlands. In the 1980s close to 4 000 people were killed in communal riots. The number of districts involved increased from 61 in 1961 to 250 in 1986–87.[23]

Two major explanations have been put forward for this phase of communalism in India. At a political level, the general argument is that the secular consensus wrought in 1947 broke down in the 1960s as the ruling Congress Party began to play the Hindu communal card for electoral gains. The Nehru legacy was undermined, particularly after Mrs Gandhi returned to power in 1980 and began to woo the Hindu vote openly. Departing from its earlier stand as the protector of minority interests, the ruling party responded to the growing incidence of communal riots by refusing to allocate blame to the Hindu organisations responsible for instigating them or to acknowledge the complicity of the police and the administration. In 1983, for instance, in spite of evidence against the provincial armed constabulary of Uttar Pradesh in the riots of Moradabad, Meerut and Allahabad, no action was taken.[24] Visits to temples, the banning of beef tallow, the adoption of Hindu rituals and symbols in state affairs, leniency towards Hindu fundamentalist organisations as they organised to 'Save Hinduism', and the assertion of the 'rights of the majority' were all seen as increasing state identification with the Hindu majority.[25]

In addition, others have emphasised the petty bourgeois basis of communalism. In the last two decades Muslim-Hindu riots have occurred mostly in medium-sized towns where Muslims have attained a measure of economic success.[26] This economic prosperity led Muslims to expand their business. For instance, in Aligarh Muslims in the lock business moved into the construction industry, in Bhiwandi Muslims bought up small scale textile units, in Meerut Muslim weavers moved into furniture manufacture, scissor making and lathe operations.[27] A report on the riots in the walled city of Delhi concludes with the statement: 'Hindus tend to raise their eyebrows at the assertion of an equal status by a community which they have been used to look down upon as their inferiors in the post independence era.'[28] During the riots, the main attacks were on the business and industrial establishments newly aquired by the Muslims.

Another significant factor has been the emergence and expansion of Hindu, Muslim and Sikh fundamentalist organisations in the last two decades. Hindu fundamentalism is often depicted as a reaction to the flow of Gulf money to the Muslims and the threat percieved by the Hindus in the mass conversions of *dalits* (untouchables) to Islam in Tamilnadu in 1981.[29] Far deeper levels of enquiry are required to understand the basis for fundamentalism. It is important to stress that an examination of the economic and political processes affecting Muslims in India reveals that fundamentalism has received a response from Muslims only in recent years.

Muslims in independent India did not respond as a community in spite of attempts by sections of the traditional Muslim elite to mobilise around the demands for Urdu, Muslim Personal Law and Aligarh Muslim University. After partition and the departure of leading industrial families and professionals, and the dissolution of the Muslim League, the Muslims left behind were primarily weavers, artisans and craftsmen, i.e. economically depressed classes. In the 1960s and 1970s the expansion of handicraft industries and Gulf employment for skilled and semi-skilled workers led to the emergence of economically better off Muslim 'backward castes'. These strata were more interested in pushing their economic demands, for instance for looms and sheds, than mobilising around the old communal issues.[30] In fact as late as 1980, at the Muslim Convention at Lucknow, the attempts at forcing the 'old symbols of community unity' were rejected. Apart from this, the Muslims also had the position of a privileged minority and had linked their future with the ruling Congress Party. At the regional level, for instance in Kerala and Hyderabad, Muslim political organisations had some support but at the national level, Muslims voted on a non-communal basis.[31] In the mid-1960s a Muslim electoral front was formed but did not survive for long.[32]

Towards the middle of the 1960s the situation began to change as a spate of Hindu/Muslim riots broke out, the worst year being 1964 with over 1170 incidents. Communal attacks against Muslims were often led by volunteers of the *Rashtriya Swayamsewak Sangh* (RSS), a Hindu fundamentalist paramilitary group. This period witnessed the growth of Hindu fundamentalist organisations. Over 500 fundamentalist organisations exist today, the main ones being the *Hindu Manch*, *Vishwa Hindu Parishad*, *Virat Hindu Sammellan*, *Shiv Shakti Dal*, while the older RSS and *Shiv Sena* in Maharashtra have expanded their membership. These organisations are highly authoritarian in structure, have paramilitary wings and an ideology of Hindu expansionism. They are male-dominated, if not exclusively male organisations. Apart from organising all-India pilgrimages, and reconverting Muslims to Hinduism, in the last few years they have focused on reclaiming temples which they claim are birthplaces of mythical religious figures and which have been appropriated by the Muslims and turned into mosques.

A recent report shows that the RSS has adopted an increasingly militant posture, issuing pamphlets titled 'Warning: India in Danger' which attacked Muslims and Christians. The organisation sells inland letter cards which show India, Afghanistan, Pakistan, Nepal, Sri Lanka and

Bangladesh under a saffron flag.[33] While earlier Hindu fundamentalist organisations had excluded *dalits* and tribals, now there are well-organised campaigns to draw them into the Hindu fold. They are however rabidly anti-Muslim. In a recent by-election in Maharashtra, Bal Thackeray, the leader of the *Shiv Sena*, called the Muslims and Sikhs 'cobras' and stated: 'The population of Muslims was $2\frac{1}{2}$ crore at the time of independence but has now crossed 14 crore. We (Hindus) were practising family planning but they (Muslims) kept on producing children. Those children were being ungrateful.'[34]

This aggressive stance by Hindu fundamentalist organisations, and the shift in the ruling party strategy mentioned earlier, has created a tremendous sense of insecurity amongst Muslims. It is in this context that Muslim fundamentalist organisations have moved in, and this time found a response to the old symbols of communal unity. Today there is increased support for the Muslim League in Kerala, the *Itehadul Muslimeen* in Hyderabad and the *Jamaat-e-Islami*. The *Jamaat-e-Islami* has an extreme position on personal law, arguing that a ban on polygamy would be 'the first step in the direction of erasing every symbol of a separate Muslim culture in India'.[35] In 1974 an All India Muslim Personal Law Board was set up to monitor and resist any changes in personal law. The Shah Bano case galvanised this coalition into action. It was given further impetus as an ongoing conflict between Muslims and Hindus over the mosque Babri Masjid in Ayodhya resulted in the government conceding to the claims of Hindu organisations that the mosque was the original birthplace of the mythical warrior king Ram (Ramjanambhoomi) and the temple was opened in February 1986. Muslim reaction escalated as Syed Shahabuddin, MP and editor of *Muslim India* gave a call to Muslims to boycott Republic Day celebrations; strikes and demonstrations and forcible entry into several national monuments to offer prayers occurred all over North India. A paramilitary organisation called the *Adam Sena*, was formed by the Imam of Delhi's *Jama Masjid* along the lines of the Hindu fundamentalist groups. The same coalition of fundamentalist forces pressurised the government to ban Salman Rushdie's *Satanic Verses* in October 1988.

The continued increase in communal violence, the growth of fundamentalist organisations and the increasing identification of the ruling party with the Hindu majority has suggested another level of inquiry which locates the problem in the crisis of the nation state. This has led to a reassessment of nationalist thought and the so called secular consensus of the first twenty years of independence. The next section will explore some ways in which notions of womanhood and gender relations formed part of the nationalist project. The symbolic representations of femininity and masculinity

delineated the boundaries of the nation and community. In addition, certain
institutional structures were created and maintained which preserved both
women's subordination and the seeds of communalism.

POST-COLONIAL STATES, THE NATIONALIST PROJECT AND NOTIONS OF WOMANHOOD

Feminist scholarship has begun to consider the ways in which the woman
question was a crucial element in the formulation of anti-colonial nationalism. Kandiyoti has shown how the debates on women's emancipation
formed part of the ideological construction of Turkish national identity.[36]
Kumari Jayawardena's work on feminism and nationalism pointed out the
dual objectives of the nationalist intelligentsia in establishing a system
of 'stable, monogamous nuclear families with educated and employable
women such as were associated with capitalist development and bourgeois
ideology' and at the same time trying to ensure that women remained
subordinate within the family.[37] Studies of nationalism have focused on
the deeply contradictory character of anti-colonial nationalism as it tried
to constitute itself in opposition to the alien dominator as well as to certain
indigenous cultural traditions. In the 1970s historians in India questioned
the assessment of nineteenth and twentieth century nationalist thought
in terms of the conflict between tradition and modernity. Based on a
shared assumption of the inherent virtues of rationality, modernisation and
universal values, these studies tended to assess proponents of these views
as modern and progressive.[38] However recent studies have highlighted the
difficulty in making clear distinctions between a traditional and a modern
trend in nineteenth century intellectual history. Many liberal, secular and
rational attitudes were backed by concessions or sanctioned by resort to
scriptural or canonical authority. On the other hand, nationalist ideas often
sprang from a deep faith in the goodness of the colonial order and the
unBritish rule of the British in India.[39]

Partha Chatterjee in a recent study puts forward the thesis that nationalist
thought was different from colonial discourse, yet dominated by it.[40]
The argument is based on a distinction between the problematic and
the thematic of nationalism. The problematic of nationalist discourse
concerns the claims made regarding the historical possibilities and the
practical steps to realise these; the thematic of nationalist discourse are
the appeals to logical, epistemological and ethical principles to provide
legitimation and justification for the claims of nationalism. This distinction
is useful in identifying the areas of continuity and discontinuity between
nationalist and colonial discourses. It also makes it possible to examine

the specific choice of certain cultural markers of national and communal identity, specifically notions of womanhood. Cultural nationalism in the early nineteenth century constructed an imagined glorious past in which women were valued highly and suffered from no discrimination. Studies of Bengali literature from the 1880s onwards, for example, show how the image of woman was made synonymous with the country.[41] Chakravarti argues that this construction was closely woven into a communalised writing of history as the collapse of Hindu civilisation was traced to foreign invasions and subsequent Muslim rule.[42] The value attached to wifely chastity in early Hindu mythology was now extended to include 'community' identity. The ability of a Hindu woman to commit *sati* became a symbol for independence. 'What does India have to fear? . . . When nobody except her women have the capacity to lie down beside their husbands on the funeral pyre with a laugh'.[43]

During the second half of the nineteenth century three strands emerged in which women were represented either as powerful mothers whose special energies would be released in crisis situations (Bankim Chandra), or as stockbreeders to regenerate the Hindu race (Swami Dayanand) or as the epitome of virtue and 'Eastern' sprituality (Vivekananda). Although there were a number of strands in the construction of womanhood, Chakravarti argues that by the third decade of the nineteenth century, in spite of regional models, a 'national' model of womanhood drawn from the Sanskrit tradition had appeared.[44] Sarkar points out that the appropriation and modes of representation of certain Hindu female goddesses like Kali who symbolised female power led to an inner tension in nationalism between the energising force of female strength and its violent and destructive power. Further investigation is needed as to the construction and representation of manhood. Chakravarti argues that the notion of a 'traditional' Hindu woman was forged before a corresponding construction of manhood came into being, possibly because traditional values as symbolic of a 'national' identity are more difficult to forge in the case of men.'[45] By the 1920s, however, a particular notion of masculinity based on virility was being articulated by Hindu fundamentalist organisations.[46]

The Indian national movement, then, though secular in its objectives used communal consciousness. There was an identification of nationalism with the revival of Hinduism. Modern literature in Bengali, Hindi and Urdu was often blatantly communal, depicting Muslims as foreigners and oppressive, lecherous tyrants, while Hindus were portrayed as heroes struggling for positive values. This construction was forged in the context of growing communalism as it became an important instrument of colonial policy in the effort to thwart the rising national movement. Communalists, especially in the Muslim League, were encouraged through the ready acceptance of their demands and official patronage. In the 1920s there was a growth of communal antagonisms on a large scale after a period of relative harmony. While communal electorates had been laid down earlier, it was the Act of 1919 which enlarged the scope of the legislatures, broadened the franchise and extended the scope of local bodies which fanned the communal divide.[47] This was the period when religious and cultural symbols were used to create a separate Muslim identity, which held meaning for all sections of the community.[48]

While Hindu and Muslim women had organised in separate associations during this period, they also worked together on issues of suffrage, education and legal rights and both attacked the system of seclusion. However, as communal divisions intensified, Hindu feminists began to see *purdah* (veiling) as a custom brought to India by Muslim invaders and a cause for the fall from women's high status in the Golden Age. Muslim women, fearing that they would be swamped as a minority in an India ruled by a Hindu majority, began to defend passages in the Quran about female modesty.[49]

Gandhi's intervention in the national movement marked a decisive shift in the romantic, utopian metaphors of early nineteenth century cultural nationalism. He mobilised popular classes in the cause of the anti-colonial struggle and women were drawn into the national movement on a large scale. Gandhi saw the participation of women in the national movement as a life-preserving and humanising force, given woman's essential nature of noble suffering. Recent feminist analyses of Gandhi's construction of womanhood have pointed out that although women were drawn into politics, they were still defined within the contours of their biological roles within the home. Gandhi's ideal was the Hindu widow and he saw women as a collective symbol of the superiority of indigenous tradition against modernity.[50] Apart from the practice of child marriage, Gandhi did not consider it necessary to alter relations of power within the family or traditional Hindu society. Gandhi used Hindu symbolism and his construction of womanhood drew from the same tradition. Nandy has argued that Gandhi's rejection of modernity was only selectively Hindu in that he drew on the folk tradition of mainstream Hinduism rather than its Brahmanical version.[51] However, Gandhi's endorsement of the principle of hierarchy and his mix of religion and politics leave open the question of how his message was understood by people. Historians have pointed out that the equation of nationalism with *Ramrajya* (the kingdom of the mythical Hindu warrior king Ram) corresponded with peasant communal consciousness and this made it possible for their demands to be transformed into 'the message of the Mahatama'.[52] Similarly, Gandhi's critique of hypermasculinity, celebration of femininity as sacred and magical, and the search for androgyny do not necessarily imply that his ideology was non-patriarchal. The links he made between Swadeshi and the protection of women, the spinning-wheel as the symbol of female chastity, and his discomfort at what public involvement in politics meant for women constitute elements of a benevolent patriarchy which honoured women but endorsed the traditional sexual division of labour. At the same time, Gandhi's religious faith was different from the fundamentalists' and he tried to broaden Congress nationalism to include the Muslims. Despite this Imtiaz Ahmed states:

> It is nevertheless evident that Gandhi's efforts to bring about Hindu-Muslim unity made little sense to the majority of the Muslims. His use of the religious terminology of Hinduism alienated the majority of the Muslims. They felt his primary sympathies lay with the dominant community and were unwilling to accept his leadership. They continued to rally under the banner of the Muslim League.[53]

The final moment in the construction of nationalism and its realisation in the nation-state is seen in Nehru's vision for India. Clearly supporting industrialisation which he saw as the key to economic and political independence of the nation, he too had to resort to symbols which he himself found steeped in religiosity. In spite of his commitment to a nation state which 'must embrace the whole people, give everyone an equal right of citizenship, irrespective of sex, language, religion, caste, wealth or education,'[54] Nehru had to go against his own convictions on two issues which showed the uneasy tension in Indian nationalism at its birth between secularism and communalism. To win Muslim confidence, he allowed the continuation of Muslim personal law rather than pushing for equality of all women before the law. In 1954 he stated that although he thought a unified civil code was inevitable, the time was not ripe to push it through in India. Secondly, he allowed a total ban on cow slaughter, and legislation was passed in the states of Uttar Pradesh, Bihar, Madhya Pradesh and Rajasthan which were all Congress ruled.[55]

The reassessment of nationalist thought and its final realisation in the nation-state in 1947, although still requiring further investigation, reveal the elements which linked particular notions of womanhood, a certain female identity, with a particularised community identity. This identity derived from a Sanskrit upper caste version of Hinduism, thus excluding the tribals and the *dalits* (untouchables). Indian nationalism, far from being the opposite of communalism, contained in itself the seeds of division. These then found expression in the maintenance of certain institutional structures such as personal laws. While a common criminal code was formulated for all Indian citizens, the areas of marriage, inheritance, divorce and adoption were governed by separate personal laws for Muslims, Christians and Hindus. Secularism in reality was 'the sum of many communalisms'.[56] During the drafting of the Constitution, many members opposed the inclusion of a provision on the freedom of religion on the grounds that if true secular principles were to be followed then no provision on religion should be included in the Constitution. A note of dissent in the minutes is all that remains of the attempt to counter communalism. M. R. Masani, Hansa Menta and Amrit Kaur wrote at that time: 'One of the factors that has kept India back from advancing to nationhood has been the existence of personal laws based on religion which keep the nation divided into watertight compartments in many aspects of life.'[57]

PATRIARCHAL/COMMUNAL STRUCTURES AND THE STATE: THE POLITICS OF PERSONAL LAW

The process by which personal laws were codified was in itself a political one through which not only a specific interpretation of each religion gained sanction, but also the assumptions of colonial administrators and native representatives were incorporated.[58] An example of this can be seen in a commentary on the Hindu Code Bill. An English legal commentator, J. Duncan M. Derret remarks: 'English ideas and English remedies were wedded to Hindu rules and Justice, Equity and Good Conscience played in the spaces which were left unfulfilled'.[59]

In 1772, the first interpretation of Hindu personal law was commissioned by Warren Hastings through the appointment of ten Brahmin pundits from Bengal.[60] The separate laws of different castes and communities (Nairs, Nambudris, Rulins, Jats etc.) were all absorbed into one Hindu code based on a specifically Brahmanical interpretation. Departing from the policy of non-interference, the first changes made from 1925 onwards were to matrilineal systems and then to the patrilineal and bilineal communities of Travancore, Cochin and Madras State.[61] The process of codification included reform which, as Derret states, 'began to benefit from the process of anlysis of customary law, elimination of elements *obiectionable to contemporary taste* and, largely for the latter purpose, regulation by means of fairly comprehensive statutes' (emphasis mine).[62] The final codification was made in 1941 by the Hindu Law Committee. Violent opposition to the Hindu Code Bill resulted in many amendments. In 1948 the *dalit* (untouchables who affirm their identity as the oppressed rather than using the paternalistic term *harijan* i.e. children of God, which Gandhi had called them) leader Dr Ambedkar prepared a third draft to which there was still opposition. Finally the bill was separated into parts and passed piecemeal after 1951. In fact the final clause on irretrievable breakdown of marriage as a ground for divorce is still pending in Parliament.

There were many clauses significant for their inclusion as well as for their exclusion. Although it was laid down that religion was not important and the definition of a 'Hindu' was so wide as to include everyone except Muslims, Christians, Parsis and Jews, conversion from Hinduism implied the loss of rights. If a person converted from Hinduism, s/he lost the right of guardianship of children, could be divorced, could not inherit from Hindu relatives, and could not adopt or give his/her child in adoption. A significant exclusion was the rights of the *dasis* (concubines) and illegitimate children. Another significant exclusion in the Hindu Succession Act, which gave women rights to property, was the lack of provision 'for the devolution of the property of persons of indeterminate or no sex', although such a provision existed in the Cochin Makathayam Thiyya Act.[63]

The aim was to bring the 'family' under state control and institute a particular family form. The relationship of the colonial and post-colonial state to the family is therefore not one of simple non-interference in the private realm. At various points colonial administrators and local men pushed for changes which transformed the family and women's position in particular.[64] It is important to stress, however, that the demand for legislation often came from women's organisations, who saw codification as better than the arbitrary implementation of diverse customary laws. Examination of the campaigns by women for codification highlight the limitations of interpreting this process as a simple patriarchal conspiracy. The law in its final form represented the results of the confrontation between these different interest groups. It is however not within the scope of this chapter to examine this confrontation, which could provide important insights into the link between women's movements and nationalism.

Also in 1773, there was an attempt to translate Arabic law treatises into English. Muslim law proved too complex and the translation was abandoned half way. Various attempts were made by the British to compile a digest of Muslim laws which were not accepted by Indian lawyers. The British court allowed custom to overrule religious law for both Hindus and Muslims. As a result, many Muslims followed Islamic law in certain matters and argued for customary law in others.

The choices were often determined by class and patriarchal interests. In 1847, a woman from the Memon community and another from the Rhoja community demanded their rights to inheritance under Muslim law. The families argued against them on the basis of custom, which did not grant women the right of inheritance. The courts decided to uphold customary law and decided against the women's right to inheritance. Numerous cases exist of women from landed and business families in Punjab, North West Frontier Provinces, Rajasthan and Oudh Kashmir, who were deprived of their inheritance rights under Islamic law in a similar manner.[65]

Subsequent developments among which were the legal changes initiated in Turkey, led to the demand for reforms in Muslim personal law. The Shariat Application Act of 1937 had as one of its objectives the reform of the status of women.

> The status of Muslim women under customary law is simply disgraceful. The Muslim women's organisations have condemned customary law as it adversely affects their rights and have demanded that the Muslim Personal Law (Shariat) should be made applicable to them. The introduction of Muslim Personal Law will automatically raise them to the position to which they are naturally entitled . . . [66]

This bill, which clearly laid out a Muslim woman's right to inheritance, was opposed by the landed gentry, and Jinnah also tried to make the application of the Shariat Act voluntary so as to maintain support of these classes (see Jalal in this volume). After numerous debates in the legislatures, some amendments were made and the bill was passed in 1937. It is significant that agricultural land was exempt from the Act.

Continuing the process of the codification of Muslim law, in 1939 the Dissolution of Muslim Marriage Act was passed.[67] The main reason for this bill was the discovery by the *ulemas* that a number of Muslim women were renouncing Islam to seek divorce which was not available under Muslim law. Although the bill was passed as a result of women's campaigns, it also denied rights to *mehr* (dower) and limited alimony. Its prime motivation was the fear of conversion to other religions by Muslim women. In both the Hindu Code Bill and Muslim Personal Law there were clear sanctions against conversion to another religion, and these functioned to further delineate and consolidate the boundaries of the communities.

This political process of codification, reform and institutionalisation of personal laws then laid out the boundaries of the community, and established a particular family structure – i.e. patriarchal, patrilineal, conjugal as the norm (the laws contained further proposals to undermine the joint family). Most importantly, it drew the family and crucial areas of gender relations under the jurisdiction of the state.

> The Acts are strongly biased in favour of freedom, but freedom of a very curious kind. The Hindu formerly was able to conduct most of his affairs without the aid of a civil court . . . But the 'Hindu Law Hindu', to coin a phrase, could marry, divorce (where applicable), adopt, deal with his own or his co-heirs property, or his wards' property, and make his will, without the intervention of any official . . . The Acts have taken the opposite line in each case. The sphere of jurisdiction of the Courts has been increased. The Court can concern itself with divorces; with all important guardianship matters, and finally in certain aspects of succession-law.[68]

It is ironic that these laws have become the battleground for the defence of 'authentic' Muslim/Hindu identity, when historical analysis shows that the process of codification contained a mix of various elements, ranging from interventions by colonial administrators, native interpreters, selected priests and mullahs to pressures from progressive men and women.

The post-colonial state inherited and maintained these institutional structures of separate personal laws to regulate the family. In spite of the proclamation of secularism, the nationalist legacy was full of ambiguities. The sanction given to religion extended even to certain civil laws. The Special Marriage Act of 1956 was passed to enable individuals to intermarry without having to change their religion or to resort to personal law. Even this secular law contains features which tend to favour Hindus. Under this Act, first cousins are not allowed to marry, which is a common practice among Muslims. In 1976 amendments to this Act and the Indian Succession Act 1925 stated that Hindus married under the Special Marriage Act could retain their rights of inheritance, while persons belonging to other religions would lose their rights of inheritance under their personal laws. An examination of the functioning of the Special Marriage Act reveals loopholes which are used to prevent inter-community marriages. The Act has a provision to allow objections to the marriage so as to prevent bigamy. However since the provision does not exclude religious grounds as a reason for objection, these could be used to prevent inter-community marriages. In Delhi, women's organisations discovered that a Hindu fundamentalist organisation, the Hindu Mahasabha, had appointed one of its members to inspect marriage notices everyday with a view to spotting inter-religious unions. The names and addresses of

such parties, particularly Hindu-Muslim marriages, were noted and the
organisation then pressured the person to stop the marriage. If it had taken
place then they even went to the extent of forcing the Hindu to remarry
another Hindu. In 1988 a Hindu woman married a Muslim man under this
Act; the woman and her parents were intimidated, she was pressurised to
marry a Hindu, then forcibly taken to a doctor to obtain an abortion. It
was only after a women's organisation filed a case in the Supreme Court
that the couple were allowed to live together. The irony of the Special
Marriage Act is that the practice of posting notices is based on the English
custom of calling the banns in church on three successive Sundays. Its
inclusion in civil law shows once again the absorption of colonial features
in post-colonial legal structures.[69]

This existing patriarchal/communal structure forms the background
against which the recent upsurge in communalism and the significance
of the family as represented in personal laws, and therefore as markers
of identity, can be understood. The assertion of communal identities is
accompanied by a process of intensification of controls over the labour,
fertility and sexuality of women in each community.

COMMUNAL IDENTITY AND CONTROL OVER WOMEN

Recent studies of fundamentalism have shown that it constructs particular
notions of femininity and masculinity as symbolic of the community.[70]
In both the incidents referred to earlier, *sati* and the agitation over Shah
Bano, women became crucial symbols of communal identity and markers
of 'tradition' and culture. The traditions that are resurrected are often both
invented and selective. A feature of contemporary Hindu, Muslim and Sikh
fundamentalism is a stress on a martial tradition. Hindu fundamentalists
have incorporated the notions of honour, militancy, virility and manliness
from the *Khatriyas* (warrior castes) as essential elements of Hinduism, as
is also the case in the incorporation of Rajput customs in relation to *sati*.
Historical research by two feminists shows that *sati* was not even a 'traditional' practice in the district where it was recently reported. Shekawat
was originally a small princely state which had semi-autonomous status
under the British. As it was integrated into the province of Rajsathan after
1947, the Rajputs began the practice of *sati* to assert their caste identity
and function as a political bloc in order to recapture lost privileges.[71]
The speeches made by Hindu priests at the Chunri *mahaotsav* (ceremony
held after the *sati*) at Deorala stressed the notions of honour and posed
a simple choice between a true Hindu woman who committed *sati* and

prostitutes. This act was projected as a crucial difference between Hindus and barbarians. The perceived threat to Hinduism resurrects again the ideology propagated by the RSS in the late 1920s and 1930s. The most explicit statement was made by Gopal Godse, the brother of Nathuram Godse, an ex-RSS member, who assasinated Gandhi:

> Our motive was not to achieve control of the government, . . . we were simply trying to rid the nation of someone who had done and was doing great harm to it. He had consistently insulted the Hindu nation and had weakened it by his doctrine of *ahimsa* (nonviolence). On his many fasts, he always attached all sorts of pro-Muslim conditions . . . He never did anything about the Muslim fanatics. We wanted to show the Indians that there were still Indians that would not suffer humiliation – that there were still men left among the Hindus. [72]

Similarly, in the Punjab today, Sikh fundamentalists have drawn on Jat culture and the warrior legacy of the tenth Guru, rather than the tradition of the earlier gurus which emphasised peace and reflection.

There is a similar selectivity in the choice of the female symbol. The ideal of 'Indian womanhood' is the passive, chaste, devout and faithful wife Sita rather than other strong, independent women found in Hindu mythology. It is this image which is projected through the performance of the Ramayana on television and films. The serialisation of the Ramayana on television was so popular that riots broke out in a northern town when the electricity failed during the show. Factory managers were forced to adjust overtime on Sundays to enable workers to watch the serial. These selective symbolic representations of masculinity and femininity are crucial to the process of communal identity formation. However, it is the projection, preservation and defence of the female symbol which appears to provoke the most violent reactions.

An issue which needs further exploration is the question of why women become the symbols and repositories of communal/group/national identity. Anderson has pointed out that nationalism describes its object in the language of kinship or the home, both of which denote something which is natural and given.[73] Just as colour, sex, parentage are not freely chosen – therefore conveying inevitability, obviousness and a taken-for-granted legitimacy – the synonymity of the nation, community or other 'imagined communities' with these natural and given identities makes it possible to die in defence of them. The merging of the nation/community with the selfless mother/devout wife evokes the obvious and necessary response to come to her defence and protection. In addition, women represent the domain of authenticity, precisely because of their restriction to the private sphere. Sarkar argues that in India, it was women and peasants who represented the ultimate site of purity, unsullied by Western education and the modern world. This notion readily extends to the purity of the female body itself.

> Very often, an implicit continuum is postulated between the hidden, innermost, private space, chastity, almost the sanctity of the vagina, to political independence at state level: as if, through a steady process of regression, this independent selfhood has been folded back from the public domain to the interior space of the household, and then further pushed back into the hidden depths of an inviolate, chaste pure female body.[74]

This element is clearly seen in the sexual imagery of communal riots. A Muslim is seen as dirty and driven by uncontrollable lust, being ever ready to seduce, abduct and assault Hindu women. In the Shah Bano case, this notion was extended to Muslim women as well, as politicians and Hindu fundamentalists argued for the protection of Muslim women from their own men. Alternatively, Hindus are seen as mild, emasculated vegetarians and as sexually repressed. These stereotypes are often transfered from one community to another. The sexual stereotype of the Muslim is now extended to the Sikhs, or the *adivasis* or *dalits*. The access to economic and political resources is extended to a fear regarding the open access to women. During the caste riots in Ahmedabad in 1981, for instance, statements like this were common:

> the *harijans* (untouchables) do not really want reservations, they want our women. Once they could only come as far as our toilets. Then we felt sorry for them and let them come into our homes. But now they want our women. We must beat them and teach them a lesson.[75]

The same principle is expressed in the fact that women are raped during communal riots. Often riots are sparked off by alleged acts of harassment of women by men of the other community. In 1961, for instance, the start of the spate of communal riots between Hindus and Muslims was sparked off by the fact that in Jabalpur the son of a local Muslim *bidi* (cigarette) magnate eloped with a Hindu girl. Speeches of communalists are similarly peppered with references to the 'violation of our mothers and sisters' and exhortations to take revenge and prove that the men of that community are still men.In the context of fear and concerns over downward mobility, the link between the honour of the family and the honour of the community leads to attempts to control their 'own' women. Threats to or the loss of control over their women, are seen as direct threats to manhood/community/family. It therefore becomes essential to ensure patriarchal controls over the labour, fertility and sexuality of women.

While this merging of notions of masculinity/femininity with the nation/community/family has occurred in many different contexts, in the present context of India there are certain other factors which have led to 'the fundamentalist obssession with women'. It has been pointed out that the real issue behind *sati* and the Shah Bano case has been a preoccupation with the condition of 'single women'. The section under the Criminal Procedure Code under which maintenance was sought for Shah Bano was primarily concerned with destitution and vagrancy. The destitute woman 'widow, divorcée, or abandoned wife – is envisaged as a potential threat to public peace'.[76] The threat of single women, however, arises more sharply in a context where they have the possibilities of independence, when as today a widow can assert her right to property and even remarry. Maintaining property within the family and controlling the widow's sexuality have been offered as the main reasons for *sati*. Similarly, the demand for a separate Sikh customary law at the height of the Khalistan agitation was again focused on the restrictions on inheritance of property by daughters, and the custom of levirate (marriage of widows to their husbands' brother) whereby widows remained within the family.

In the present context it could be argued that a contributory factor to the need to control women arises from the breakdown of traditional patriarchal structures as a result of capitalist development. Studies of participation of women in the labour force have shown an increase in the number of working women, in the organised and unorganised sector, in agriculture and industry.[77]

In many areas women are entering into competition with men, as male employment remains stagnant and growing demand is created for female labour in export industries. The traditional structure of male provisioning, particularly in lower income families, is breaking down. In addition, male migration and desertion have led to an increase in female-headed households. Women have taken on new roles of decision-making regarding money, investment, and education. A study of the effects of male migration to the Middle East in Kerala, points out that 'Since the length of absence of migrants has been increasing, women have started to take on a more active role in the management of family affairs and, as a result, have become less dependent.'[78] Gulati reports that the greater involvement of young wives in financial affairs has led to a questioning of their fidelity, and hostility from other male relatives.[79] Apart from the control over women's labour, fertility and sexuality, restrictions are enforced on their mobility. In Jalgaon, a district in Maharashtra, Muslim organisations banned Muslim women from watching films. When a woman activist, Razia Patel, along with other Muslim women protested, they were physically assaulted, their *burkhas* (a garment which covers the whole body of the woman) cut with blades and they were told that next time their bodies would be cut if they disobeyed.[80] Deviation from these attempts at community control lead to violent reprisals. Muslim women have already faced the violence of the community as seen in the incidents in Kerala, where Zulaikha Bibi was given 101 lashes and Shabana of Perunthura had her head shaved as punishment for violating Muslim personal law.[81]

As a generalised consciousness of women's rights has emerged, more and more women are demanding their rights to property, maintenance and divorce. It is interesting that while women from different classes and communities have begun to use or challenge laws on these issues, a number of cases of divorce and desertion have been filed by Muslim women in recent years against their husbands who are working in the Middle East. In many cases, migrant husbands have refused to send money home or have acquired more wives, leaving the first wife without any economic support.[82] Muslim women have been resorting to secular laws in the last few years. The Shah Bano case, for instance, was preceded by two other cases in the 1970s where maintenance was provided to Muslim women under the Criminal Procedure Code. In 1984, Shehnaz Sheikh, who was divorced verbally and denied the payment of *mehr* by her husband, filed a petition with the Supreme Court, challenging the discrimination in Muslim Personal Law on issues of polygamy, divorce, maintenance, custody of children and inheritance. She argued that these were un-Islamic and unconstitutional. The increasing assertion of legal rights by women confronts and threatens old and unquestioned male privileges.

This challenging of traditional patriarchal privileges – both at a material level and in the emergence of a generalised consciousness of women's rights – stimulates attempts to reassert traditional patriarchal control. Fundamentalism therefore provides an ideological justification for bringing women back under the authority and control of men.[83]

In such a context, state sponsorship of fundamentalism provides further legitimacy to the control of women. What is significant about the passing of the Muslim Women's Bill is not that women are being pushed back into the private sphere of the family, but that the state is intervening to prevent

Muslim women from recourse to secular law, and is imposing communal control over them. In fact, some of the provisions on functioning of the *Wakf* (Muslim pious foundation) funds imply greater state intervention in the management of Muslim affairs. It appears that rather than opposing state intervention in the 'internal affairs of the Muslim community', Muslim fundamentalists have in fact secured state backing to enforce control over Muslim women.[84]

As I argued elsewhere, state-supported fundamentalism reinforces and shifts the right of control over women from kinsmen to any man of the community.[85] The state emerges as the protector and regulator of the community and the family resulting in a change in forms of patriarchal control over women. A simple counterposition of the public/private spheres ignores the fact that the public is also patriarchal. As patriarchy is threatened in the family, the state moves in to institute a different form of patriarchal control over women. It is important to stress this changing form of patriarchal control since the Shah Bano issue was polarised into support for the previous seemingly fairer judgement under the Criminal Procedure Code and opposition to the Muslim Women's Bill, without any critical examination of the former. Hensman points out that its main concern was to keep women off the streets and it provided a pittance, denying a woman the right to a share in the marital home.

An understanding of how patriarchy operates at the level of the state makes it possible to assess the recent judgements in favour of women under the Muslim Women's Bill. In January 1988, Rekha Dixit, a woman magistrate, liberally interpreted the law's stipulation 'reasonable and fair provision' by granting two Muslim women generous divorce settlements. These judgements could have been the result of a response to the public outcry against the Bill, combined with the fact that the judge was a woman, but it could be argued that in fact these judgements were a validation of the prime minister's statement that the new Bill would give Muslim women more benefits. The difference lies in that today it is the state which emerges as the protector and ensurer of these benefits. The fact that the Bill uses the community as the mediator is not just due to political expediency but reflects the uneasy tension within the Indian state as it is being forced to intervene directly to restructure civil society. There are increasing contradictions between its rhetoric of equal rights for women, the demands of a developing capitalist economy, and the maintenance of structures inherited from the colonial state. In the present context the Indian state has opted for restoration of traditional patriarchal structures. This creates an uneasy balance between capitalist and patriarchal interests and the state can only maintain it by resorting to greater authoritarianism.

In the past few years numerous laws and ordinances have been passed suspending democratic rights, including an attempt to control the press. The women's movement in India, like the movement in Pakistan, is being forced to confront the state directly.

THE POLITICS OF IDENTITY AND THE WOMEN'S MOVEMENT

There has been widespread opposition to the Muslim Women's Bill from a broad coalition of reformist Muslim organisations, large sections of the Muslim intelligentsia, democratic organisations and feminist groups. Memoranda and petitions have been submitted to the government, there have been demonstrations and rallies, articles in the press, seminars and conferences have been held on the issue and a broad-based campaign of consciousness-raising through films, street theatre etc. has been initiated.[86]

The Bill has been challenged in the Supreme Court. In spite of this opposition, the Bill was not withdrawn. New developments have occurred in the women's movement as a result of the emergence of separate Muslim women's groups like the *Bharatiya Talaq Pidit Mahila Parishad* in Maharashtra, and the Goa Muslim Women's Association. The necessity of organising separately on the basis of a Muslim identity is highlighted by the traumatic experience of one of the earlier petitioners who challenged Muslim law. Shehnaz Sheikh's case brings out poignantly the dilemma of Muslim women in the context of communalism and fundamentalism. After the petition was filed, she faced death threats and had to go into hiding. Muslim fundamentalist organisations put up posters against her and accused her of being sponsored by Hindus. Subsequently, she discovered that in fact her lawyer was a member of the RSS and was pressurising her to continue the case. Similarly, Shah Bano was not only threatened but also made to feel responsible for the communal riots the judgement on her case had generated, and she herself asked for the judgement to be withdrawn.[87]

These women have found that it is only as Muslim women that they can raise issues and oppose the Bill and its implications. This arises in response to the threat of Hindu as well as Muslim fundamentalism. Although one of the most effective and sustained campaigns against the Bill was led by the All India Democratic Women's Association (a women's front linked with the Communist Party of India), they too initiated the formation of a Committee for the Protection of the Rights of Muslim Women and held a Muslim women's march in Delhi to protest the Bill. The necessity of breaking the myth of a monolithic Muslim community as well as the dangers of subversion by Hindu fundamentalism forces a struggle on the basis of a Muslim woman's identity.

A progressive-regressive movement has acted upon Muslim women since the 1920s. The Shariat Bill, although desired by Muslim women, was codified and passed in the context of a new phase of communal tension in North India. In the 1960s and early 1970s a debate was generated around the Family Code Law passed in Pakistan; a member of the Bombay Legislative Council introduced an anti-bigamy bill and a committee was formed to study the bill. Once again the escalation of communalism, aggressive statements by the *Jan Sangh* (a Hindu communal political party) and the general suspicion against the Muslims during the war with Pakistan, led to a withdrawal of progressive legislation.[88] By 1970–71 there were reports of Muslim women attending women's conferences where they stated that they were quite happy with polygamy.[89] In 1972, the *ulemas* of Deoband organised the All India Shariat Convention and passed a resolution that any change in Muslim personal law was a direct interference in their religion. In addition they demanded that the government scrap Article 44 of the Constitution which contained a commitment to an eventual uniform civil code. In the 1980s as individual Muslim women again began to demand rights within personal law as well as challenging it, a major communal/fundamentalist upsurge pushed them back into being loyal members of a Muslim minority. The opposition to the Bill by Muslim organisations as well as broader democratic rights organisations and feminist groups has been based on an assertion of women's rights. However there are divergences between these groups concerning the way in which women could obtain equal rights. The main difference is between those who feel this could be achieved through the reform of Muslim law and a reinterpretation of Islam, and others who argue for a uniform civil code applicable to women of all communities. Hensman argues that these are false options and that a uniform civil code could be a necessary complement to the reform of personal laws.[90]

Underlying these immediate political positions, however, is the much broader issue of the relation between the state and women's subordination. During the colonial period, the state had intervened to construct and bring under control a particular family form. The continued existence of personal laws in the post-colonial period ensured the persistence of patriarchal and communal structures. The state's intervention in the sphere of production, facilitating capitalist development, has today generated contradictions which require more direct state intervention into these areas of civil society. The consolidation of state patriarchy and fundamentalism in India implies that the struggle for women's rights, whether as Muslim,

Hindu, Christian or Sikh women or as members of a feminist collectivity, necessarily has to be part of a broader struggle for democratisation and decentralisation of political and economic structures.

NOTES

1. Bipan Chandra, *Communalism in Modern India* (Delhi: Vani Educational Books, Vikas Publishing House, 1984).
2. Gyan Pandey, 'Liberalism and the Study of Indian History: A Review of Writings on Communalism', *Economic and Political Weekly*, 15 October 1983; Randhir Singh, 'Theorising Communalism – A Fragmentary Note in the Marxist Mode', *Economic and Political Weely* (23 July 1988) 1541–8.
3. Imtiaz Ahmed (ed.), *Family, Kinship and Marriage among Muslims in India* (Delhi: Manohar, 1983).
4. Rasheeduddin Khan, 'Minority Segments in Indian Polity: Muslim Situation and the Plight of Urdu', *Economic and Political Weekly* (2 September 1978) pp. 1512.
5. The Criminal Procedure Code passed, in 1872 and modified in 1973, specifies in Section 125 that if any person neglects or refuses to maintain his wife who is unable to maintain herself, or his legitimate or illegitimate minor child, married or unmarried, or father and mother, a judicial magistrate can order him to make a monthly allowance not exceeding Rs. 500 to the party concerned. The Muslim Women's Protection of the Right to Divorce Law 1986 deprives Muslim women the right to appeal to this secular law for maintenance.
6. Radha Kumar, 'Tradition versus Modernity: The Agitation over Sati-dana in India', unpublished paper, IDS Sussex (1988), Special Issue on *Sati*, *Seminar*, no. 342 (1988).
7. Donna Haraway, 'Situated Knowledges: the Science Question in Feminism and the Privilege of Partial Perspectives', *Feminist Studies* vol. 14, (1988) no. 4, pp. 72–73
8. Benedict Anderson, *Imagined Communities* (London, New York: Verso, 1983).
9. In an interesting study on the formation of a 'Singh' (literally meaning "lion" denotes martial qualities) identity amongst the Sikhs from 1849 to the 1920s, Richard Fox shows how identities are not fully formed and available but are made as people learn what they can and cannot be, in terms of their individual identity as well as their membership in a collectivity through interaction with specific political, social and economic forces. He shows how the colonial state applied the concept of martial races to the Sikhs as part of nineteenth century British colonial racism which was based on biological differentiation, and the processes by which these beliefs not only rationalised colonial domination but also constructed it. British policies based on a recontructed Singh racial

tradition resulted in the internalisation of this identity by the Singhs themselves. However, this very same identity took on a life of its own and turned against the colonial state as the Singhs led a mass rural protest against British rule in early twentieth century Punjab. Richard Fox, *Lions of the Punjab – Culture in the Making* (Delhi: Archives Publishers, 1987).

10. Zoya Hasan, 'Minority Identity, Muslim Women Bill Campaign and the Political Process', *Economic and Political Weekly* (7 January 1989) p. 44.
11. Haraway 'Situated Knowledges', p. 73.
12. Nasreen Fazalbhoy, 'The Debate on Muslim Personal Law'. Unpublished paper, Third National Conference on Women's Studies, Chandigarh (1986).
13. Madhu Kishwar, 'Pro Woman or Anti Woman?: The Shah Bano Controversy', *Manushi*, no. 32 (1986) p. 4–13.
14. Zakia Pathak and Rajeshwari Sunder Rajan, 'Shah Bano', *Signs* vol. 14 (1989) no. 3, pp. 558–82.
15. Carole Pateman, 'The Fraternal Social Contract' in John Keane (ed.), *Civil Society and the State* (London: Verso, 1988) Nira Yuval Davis and Floya Anthias (eds), *Woman–Nation–State* (London: Macmillan, 1989).
16. Zillah Eisenstein, 'The Relative Autonomy of the Capitalist Patriarchal State', in Zillah Eisenstein (ed.), *Feminism and Sexual Equality* (New York: Monthly Review Press, 1984).
17. Ibid., p. 89.
18. Ibid., p. 92.
19. Yuval Davis and Anthias *Woman–Nation–State*, p. 5.
20. Yuval Davis and Anthias have made a significant contribution towards theorising the relationship between the state and women's subordination. However there remain problems with their definition of the state as a 'body of institutions which are centrally organised around the intentionality of control with a given apparatus of enforcement at its command and basis' p. 5. This tends to equate the state with the state apparatus and that too only with its repressive aspects. Secondly, while it is important to counter the notion of the monolithic nature of the state and the diverse sources which generate state practices, and therefore to stress historical specificity, the relationship between the structures of patriarchy, the state and the economic system has to be developed at a conceptual level as well. The form and content of this relationship will vary historically and cross-culturally, but the question remains whether there is a structural link between them or not.
21. Antonio Gramsci, *Selections from the Prison Notebooks* (ed.), Quintin Hoare & Geoffrey Nowell Smith (London: Lawrence & Wishart, 1971).
22. Partha Chatterjee, *Nationalist Thought and the Colonial World – A Derivative Discourse* (Japan, Delhi: Zed Press UNU,1986).
23. A. A. Engineer, *Communal Riots in Post Independence India* (Delhi: Sangam Books, Orient Longman Ltd., 1984); A. R. Desai 'Caste and

172   *Forced Identities: India*

Communal Violence in the Post-partitian Indian Union' in A. A. Engineer, 'Communalism: The Razor's Edge', CED Factsheet 2 (Bombay, 1984).
24. Mohammed Aslam, 'State Communalism and the Reassertion of Muslim Idenity' in Zoya Hasan, S. N. Jha and Rasheeduddin Khan (eds), *State, Political Processes and Identity* (London: Sage Publications Ltd, 1989).
25. Mushirul Hasan, 'Indian Muslims since independence: in search of integration and identity', *Third World Quarterly*, vol. 10 (1988) no. 2 pp. 818–42.
26. A. A. Engineer, 'Socio-Economic basis of Communalism', *Mainstream* vol. 21 (1983) no. 45, pp. 15–18; Javed Alam, 'Dialectics of capitalist transformations and national crystallisation', *Economic and Political Weekly* (29 January 1983) pp. 38–39.
27. Hasan, 'Indian Muslims since independence'.
28. *Walled city riots: A report on the Police and Communal Violence in Delhi 19–24 May* (Delhi, 1987)
29. In February 1981 an entire *dalit* village in the southern provice of Tamilnadu converted to Islam. This was followed by conversions from other villages. See George Mathew 'Politicisation of Religion – Conversions to Islam in Tamilnadu', *Economic and Political Weekly* (19 June 1982) pp. 1027–72 for an analysis of this incident.
30. Hasan, 'Indian Muslims since independence'.
31. Studies of voting patterns were earlier heavily influenced by the notion of communal consciousness. Recent studies by Paul Brass, Peter B. Mayer and Imtiaz Ahmed have shown that Muslim candidates increasingly stood on national party tickets and until the mid-1960s, communal organisations were rejected. Hasan p. 822.
32. In 1964 a coalition of diverse Muslim groups like the *Jamaat-e-Islami*, former leaders of the Muslim League and some members of the Congress Party formed the *Majlis-i-Mushawarat*. They put forward the 'People's Manifesto' which articulated Muslim grievances and included demands for revision of textbooks with a Hindu bias, introduction of proportional representation in elections, protection of Muslim personal law and preservation of the minority character of Aligarh Muslim University. Although it put forward Muslim interests, the coalition asked for support from democratic candidates.
33. 'Open Offensive' Special Report, *India Today* (30 June 1989) p. 311.
34. A. A. Engineer, 'Communal Propaganda in Elections', *Economic and Political Weekly* (17 June 1989) p. 1325.
35. Hasan (1988), p. 839
36. Deniz Kandiyoti, 'Women and the Turkish State: Political Actors or Symbolic Pawns?' in Yuval Davis and Anthias (eds), *Woman––Nation–State*.
37. Kumari Jayawardena, *Feminism and Nationalism in the Third World* (London: Zed Press, 1986) p. 15.
38. Chatterjee, *Nationalist Thought* (1986).

39. Chatterjee, p. 28.
40. Chatterjee, p. 36–43.
41. Tanika Sarkar, 'Nationalist Iconography: Image of Women in 19th Century Bengali Literature', *Economic and Political Weekly* (21 November 1987) pp. 2011–15, see also Jasodhara Bagchi; 'Positivism and Nationalism: Womanhood and Crisis in Nationalist Fiction', *Economic and Political Weekly* (26 October 1985) for an interesting elaboration of the influence of Comte's notion of Order and Progress on the nineteenth century Bengali intelligentsia.
42. Uma Chakravarti, 'Cutural Identity, Notions of Womanhood and Feminist Consciousness in a Post colonial Society'. Unpublished paper, XIIth IUAES Congress, Zagreb (1988).
43. Sarkar, 'Nationalist Iconography', p. 2014.
44. Chakravarti, Part III, p. 6.
45. Charavarti, Part II, p. 7.
46. Amrita Chhachhi, 'The State, Religious Fundamentalism and Women: Trends in South Asia', *Economic and Political Weekly* (18 March 1989) pp. 567–78.
47. Mushirul Hasan, 'Communalism in the Provinces: A case study of Bengal and the Punjab, 1922–26', *Economic and Political Weekly* (16 August 1980) pp 1395–1406.
48. Gail Minault, *The Khilafat Movement: Religious Symbolism and Political Mobilisation* (Delhi: Oxford University Press, 1982).
49. Geraldine Forbes, 'Caged Tigers: First wave Feminists in India', *Women's Studies International Forum*, vol. 5 (1982) no. 6.
50. Sujata Patel, 'Construction and Reconstruction of Woman in Gandhi', *Economic and Political Weekly* (20 February 1988) pp. 377–87; Madhu Kishwar, 'Women in Gandhi', *Economic and Political Weekly* (5, 19 October 1985).
51. Ashish Nandy, 'From Outside the Imperium: Gandhi's Cultural Critique of the West' in *Traditions, Tyranny and Utopias* (Oxford: Oxford University Press, 1987), p. 131.
52. Shahid Amin, 'Gandhi as Mahatma' in Ranajit Guha & Gayatri Spivak (eds), *Selected Subaltern Studies* (Oxford: Oxford University Press, 1988) pp. 289–342.
53. Imtiaz Ahmed, 'Secular State, Communal Society' in CED Factsheet 2, (n.d.) p. 20.
54. Chatterjee, *Nationalist Thought*, p. 146
55. Sarvepalli Gopal in Hasan,'Indian Muslims since independence'.
56. See: Mano Ranjan Mohanti, Securalism; Hegemonic and Democratic *Economic & Political Weekly* (3 June 1989) pp. 1219-1220.
57. Nandita Haksar, 'Campaign for a Uniform Code' in A. R. Desai (ed.), *Women's Liberation and Politics of Religious Personal Laws in India* (Bombay: C. G. Shah Memorial Trust Publication, 1986).
58. Lata Mani, 'Contentious Traditions: The Debate on Sati in Colonial India', *Cultural Critique*. (Fall 1987) and 'Production of an Official

Discourse on Sati in Early Nineteenth Century Bengal', *Economic and Political Weekly* (26 April 1986).
59. J. Duncan M. Derret, 'The Codification of Personal Law in India: Hindu Law', *The Indian Year Book of International Affairs* (Madras: University of Madras, 1957) p. 198.
60. Mani, 'Contentious Traditions'.
61. Derret, 'The Codification of Personal Law in India'.
62. Ibid., p. 194.
63. Ibid., p. 208.
64. K. Jayawardena, *Feminism and Nationalism in the Third World;* Carla Risseeuw, *The Fish Don't Talk About the Water: Gender Transformation, Power and Resistance among Women in Sri Lanka* (Leiden: Brill, 1988).
65. Ramala M. Baxamusa, 'A Historic Perspective on Muslim Personal Law in India'. Unpublished paper, Second National Conference on Women's Studies, Trivandrum, India (1984).
66. Tahir Mahmood, *Muslim Personal Law* (Delhi: Vikas, 1977) p. 30.
67. J. C. Forber in Nasreen Fazalbhoy, 'The Debate on Muslim Personal Law'.
68. Derret, pp. 203–4.
69. Madhu Kishwar and Ruth Vanitha, 'When Marriage is a High Risk Enterprise' *Manushi*, no. 47 (1988) pp. 34–6.
70. Haleh Afshar, 'Women, State and Ideology in Iran', *Third World Quarterly* (April 1985); Farida Shaheed, 'Legal Systems, Islam and Women in Pakistan', *Ethnic Studies Report*, vol. 3 (1985) no. 1; A. Chhachhi, 'The State, Religious Fundamentalism and Women'.
71. KumKum Sangari and Sudesh Vaid in R. Kumar, 'Tradition versus Modernity'.
72. Walter Anderson and Shridhar Damle, *The Brotherhood in Saffron – The RSS and Hindu Revivalism* (Delhi: Vistarr Publications, 1987): p. 28.
73. B. Anderson, *Imagined Communities* p. 131.
74. Sarkar, 'Nationalist Iconography', p. 2014.
75. Renana Jhabvala, 'Caste Riots in Ahmedabad-Women faced the Fury' *Manushi*, no. 9 (1981) p. 12.
76. Pathak and Rajan, 'Shah Bano', p. 576; see also Imrana Qadeer, 'Roop Kanwar and Shah Bano', *Seminar* no. 342 (1988).
77. Nirmala Banerjee, 'Trends in Women's Employment, 1971–1981: Some Macro Level Obsevations', *Economic and Political Weekly* (29 April 1989): pp. 10–22.
78. Leela Gulati, 'Male migration from Kerala-Some effects on Women', *Manushi*, no. 37 (1987) p. 14.
79. Ibid.
80. Vibhuti Patel, 'Status and Struggles of Muslim Women in India', mimeo (n.d.): p. 6.
81. Qadeer,'Roop Kanwar and Shah Bano'.
82. Gulati 'Male migration from Kerala'.
83. Chhachhi, 'The State, Religious Fundamentalism and Women'.

84. Rohim Hensman, 'Oppression within Oppression: the Dilemma of Muslim Women in India', Working Paper 1, Women Living Under Muslim Law Network, Combaillaux (1989).
85. Chhachhi, 'The State, Religious Fundamentalism and Women.'
86. Hasan,'Minority Identity, Muslim Women Bill Campaign and the Political Process'; Pathak and Rajan, 'Shah Bano'.
87. Hensman, 'Oppression within Opression'.
88. Hasan, 'Minority Identity . . . '
89. Baxamusa,'A Historic Perspective on Muslim Personal Law in India'.
90. Hensman, Oppression within Oppression'.

7   Elite Strategies for State-Building: Women, Family, Religion and State in Iraq and Lebanon

Suad Joseph

INTRODUCTION[1]

Investigation of the relationships among women, families, religions and states in the Middle East has been stimulated in part by the problematisation of the concepts of 'women',[2] 'the family',[3] 'religion',[4] and 'the state'[5] in political sociology, anthropology and feminist scholarship. The rethinking of these concepts has produced a body of case studies mainly focused on individual countries and with a contemporary emphasis. This has been a necessary process for building the empirical foundations for comparative and theoretical endeavours.

While much of the literature has been relatively descriptive, some scholars have launched comparative and theoretical projects. In particular, they have investigated the appropriateness of modernisation, dependency, neo-Marxist and structuralist theories, refined by feminist analyses.[6] The ensuing debates have reflected some of the general cautions raised by Sami Zubaida[7] concerning cultural essentialism as well as concerns about the uncritical application of these approaches to the study of the Middle East. More specifically, many feminist scholars have challenged the usefulness of Western feminist constructs for understanding Middle Eastern women.[8]

In this essay, I present two case studies in the hope of contributing to the empirical base from which comparative and theoretical work can be built. I focus primarily on the different strategies for state-building pursued by the Iraqi and Lebanese elites. From there, I venture into comparisons between these cases to sketch some of the theoretical concerns that must be addressed as we construct a fuller understanding of the relationships among women, families, religions and states in the Middle East. Further research exploring other perspectives and focuses would enrich the empirical base from which we can build theory.

Iraq and Lebanon provide interesting materials for comparative case studies of these relationships.[9] The Iraqi state has been controlled by a homogeneous ruling elite which has organised a disciplined political party able to penetrate or control major institutions of the society. The Lebanese state has been managed by a heterogeneous, factionalised and highly competitive ruling elite, with few disciplined political parties. The ruling elite of Iraq has evolved a relatively monolithic ideology on the basis of which it has attempted to moralise and legitimate its their rule. The ruling elite of Lebanon represented different, often conflicting, ideological stances. With the possible exception of the Kata'ib,[10] it has not produced systematic ideologies to legitimate its rule. While personalism and individual charisma have been moralising forces in both states, in Lebanon they have been more central vehicles of legitimacy, while in Iraq they have been situated within the ideological framework of the ruling Ba'th party.

Women and families have been important in the dynamics of states and religions in both countries. In Iraq, the ruling elite has pursued a programme for state construction that included courting the allegiance of the population away from the large family/ethnic/tribal groups. In Lebanon, the elite's strategy for rule bolstered primordial affiliations at the expense of national loyalties. The Iraqi elite generated extensive public sector programmes in education, social services, industry, agriculture and commercial services. The Lebanese strategies contributed to the elaboration of basic social and economic programmes in the private sector where leaders maintained more direct control over their individual following. The Iraqi elite has had extensive public resources from the nationalisation of oil to fund its programmes. The Lebanese elite had fewer public resources and funnelled much of what was or could have been public resources into the private sector. The Iraqi elite has used the state as an agent of legal reform, attempting to change family structure and the position of women. The Lebanese elite shied away from legal reform, affirming the authority of religious institutions over women and the family. The centralising state was the critical arena of action in Iraq; the private sector was key in the minimalist Lebanese state. In both states, institutions and social processes were reconstructed, social relationships reconfigured and local culture reconstituted to build the modern reality.

IRAQI ELITE STRATEGIES: CENTRALISATION AND CONTROL

Iraq is a heterogeneous country with a population of about 13 million. While the majority of Iraqis are Muslim, with the Shi'a outnumbering the Sunnis, about 25 per cent of the population is non-Arab, including Sunni Kurds, Sunni Turcomans, Christian Armenians, Assyrians and Indians of different religious affiliations.

Despite this religious, ethnic and linguistic heterogeneity, the Iraqi state has been ruled primarily by Sunnis. For over the past two decades (since the 1968 *coup d'état*), the Arab Ba'th Socialist Party has been consolidating its control over the state. The party has been run by a relatively homogeneous ruling elite of petty bourgeois origins, many of whom are from the northern Sunni town of Takrit. A number of the key figures in the party are consanguineal or affinal relatives.[11]

The party, rather centralised and disciplined, has been organised around an ideology of Arab socialism and pan-Arab nationalism.[12] The party has controlled the leadership of public formal agencies and penetrated institutions in many arenas outside the state. Given that the same leadership has controlled the party and the state, there has been a degree of coherence in the programmes and policies of both.

There is some controversy as to whether the Iraqi ruling elite can be called a class. Regardless of their current sociological status, the elite appear to have been using their control of the state to create or consolidate their class position.[13] The wealth of the state, since the nationalisation of oil in 1972, made available to them considerable resources both for state-building and for consolidating their own positions.

The scale of this wealth has given the ruling elite a certain degree of independence from other social classes and institutions. Control of this wealth through the institutions of the state has allowed the ruling clique to practically monopolise socio-economic political initiatives. As Batatu[14] has argued, the state has become the centre of social action in Iraq. The state, furthermore, has come to be personified in the image of its head, Saddam Hussein. In 1974 and 1980, I observed his larger-than-life pictures looming in public places. In schools children were taught to cite his achievements. In the General Federation of Iraqi Women, members sang their love and admiration of him. In the trade unions, armed forces and other public institutions, workers were instructed that improvements in their conditions were the consequence of Saddam Hussein's concern for them. Villagers received television sets as personal gifts from Hussein. In the context of this cult of the leader, the advantages citizens received from the state were represented less as rights of citizenship, and more as the benefits of loyalty to the head of the party and state. State building and personal clientage were closely intertwined.

Women have been important to the Ba'th agenda for state construction, for two key reasons: the need for labour and for re-aligning the allegiances of the population.

The Iraqi state was created by the European powers after World War I from three former provinces of the Ottoman Empire (Baghdad, Basra and Mosul). The peoples of these provinces had never lived together as an autonomous political entity and had little allegiance to the newly created state. In the rural areas, where the majority of the population resided at the time of the formation of the state, large tribal groups organised and claimed the loyalties of the different ethnic, religious and linguistic groups.

When the Ba'th took control of the state, they embarked on an extensive programme of economic growth, focusing on industry and services. Agriculture, which had begun to deteriorate before the Ba'th take-over, appeared to offer less to the masses than the expanding industrial and service sectors. The Ba'th emphasis on growth in the industrial and services sectors has contributed to urban growth. Since the 1960s, a large percentage of the population has been urbanised: 51.1 per cent in 1965, growing to 63.5 per cent in 1977,[15] giving an annual urban growth rate of 5.3 per cent during that period.

Despite the growth in the urban areas due to rural migration and natural population growth, Iraq continued to be short of labour. Some of the shortage was covered by the importation of labour from other Arab countries, from India, Pakistan, Korea and South East Asia. However, to the Ba'th, importing non-nationals was not a politically acceptable long-term solution to their labour requirements. Another strategy, that of offering Iraqi citizenship to Arabs (except Palestinians) from other states, has not increased their labour force significantly.

In the context of labour shortage and their desire to win over the allegiance of citizenry, the Ba'th have developed a rather complex set of programmes, a number of which have been aimed at women. The programmes directed towards women focus in part on mobilising them into state-controlled agencies where they can be resocialised into 'new Iraqi women'. The resocialisation process has included general, vocational and political education for participation in the formal economy and the polity.

Interviews with key leaders in industry, the Ba'th party, trade unions and other organisations offered important insights into the mechanisms being employed for this resocialisation. I interviewed top-level management in numerous state-run industries. One of the questions I asked repeatedly was whether they encouraged the hiring of kin in the same place of work and what kind of relationship they supported among kin members. The 'DGs' (Director General) were divided on whether they would hire close relatives to work in the same place. However, they were consistent in insisting that loyalty to management (read the party and state) came before loyalty to family. A few DGs even indicated that in their hiring they posed a scenario to potential employees in which there would be a conflict between these loyalties. The expected correct answer to give would have been to subordinate the primordial to the workplace loyalty. When I asked similar questions about ethnicity and religion, the DGs most often gave the same answer: 'Ethnicity and religion do not matter here, we are all part of the Arab nation.'

Speaking to Ba'th party officials about the process of political socialisation of party members, I received standard answers concerning the primacy of party and state above other loyalties. I had the occasion to observe meetings of Ba'th party cells and was struck by the authoritarian processes used to claim and control the thinking of the cadres. I also had occasion in 1974 to observe Iraqi students participating in a summer programme building a village near Baghdad for workers. The obligatory work-camp was run by Ba'th party officials. All day we worked building the houses and every evening were presented with entertainment and extensive political rhetoric. Each night I engaged in lengthy discussions with the Ba'th camp leaders. They articulated a clear vision of use of these work-camps to train the youth in party discipline, national service and love of the party and country.

Interviews conducted with trade union leaders clearly indicated that the trade unions were not 'oppositional' forces defending the rights of workers against management. Rather, they presented themselves as agencies of the party and state assuring the accommodation of workers to the requirements of the workplace. Indeed, candidates for trade union positions were slated by the Ba'th party. These were rarely opposing candidates. When I asked workers how the candidates were nominated, they did not seem to know (or would not respond if they did). But a number of trade union leaders were direct in telling me that the party nominated the candidates. I posed the same question to trade union leaders that I had posed to the DGs concerning the conflicting loyalties between primordial and workplace ties. Trade union leaders gave me a management answer: their job was to help employees learn how to become productive workers for the nation, which included restraint on the emotional bonds of primordial relationships.

Observing other groups left the similar impressions: the young children's 'Tali'a', paramilitary groups, student associations, science, sports, cultural clubs – all seemed to have as part of their design socialisation for discipline and political loyalty to party and state.

The resocialisation process has been many-pronged. Perhaps the strongest aspect of the Ba'th programme has been the campaign for formal education. Article 45 of the Ba'th Party constitution proclaimed education an exclusive function of the state, abolishing foreign and private educational institutions. Article 46 made primary and secondary education compulsory and education at all levels free to citizens. In their concern to retain ideological control over the socialisation of the young, the Ba'th, in Article 48 of their constitution, barred non-Arab citizens from teaching in primary and secondary schools.[16] They have rapidly built or expanded public schools, recruiting young females and males into the state-run curriculum. Prior to the Ba'th Revolution, of the almost 4 million females in the population only 23 000 had achieved secondary certificates or their equivalents; 8000 college or institute certificates; 200 graduate degrees or diplomas; and 90 doctorates. Sixty-seven per cent of the females were illiterate.[17] A decade after the Ba'th take-over, females constituted 43 per cent of the children in primary schools, 30 per cent of those in intermediate and preparatory schools, 45 per cent of university students, 25 per cent of those in vocational schools.[18] In the decade of the 1970s, female enrolment in primary schools increased 366 per cent, in secondary schools 314 per cent and in universities 310 per cent.[19]

School expansion helped to reach the youth, but not the adults. To educate the adults, the Ba'th embarked on a literacy campaign in 1978. They promulgated a law requiring illiterate adults, female and male, from the ages of 15 to 45 to participate for a two-year period in one of the many literacy programmes the government established. Literacy centres were built across the country, particularly in the rural areas where illiteracy was highest. Penalties were to be imposed on those who did not attend or those who barred others from attending.

While I do not have evidence of whether penalties were imposed, I did interview a number of women in 1980 in both rural and urban areas, who attended these centres, as well as some who did not – apparently without penalty. The Illiteracy Secretariat of the General Federation of Iraqi Women[20] claimed that in one year alone, 2.5 million women attended various literacy classes – a somewhat problematical claim since it exceeded those between 15 and 59 considered illiterate.

Nevertheless, the statistics appear to indicate a remarkable success in recruiting the young and old into state-run educational programmes. More difficult to assess is the success of the long-term goal of resocialising the population into the world view of the state leadership, and the degree to which the leadership has evoked identification with and loyalty to the state, although there are indications that this process has been problematic for the Ba'th.

Programmes for the production of 'new Iraqi women', and their institutional and ideological absorption into the state, extended in many directions. Perhaps one of the most interesting of the ruling elite's vehicles for resocialisation and mobilisation of women has been the General Federation of Iraqi Women (GFIW). The GFIW was created by the Ba'th in 1968, immediately after their take-over of the state, as a female arm of the party. The leadership of the GFIW have been party members appointed by the Ba'th. Its generous budget has come directly from the state and its programmes have been co-ordinated by the party.

The party outlined the goals of the GFIW in the Revolutionary Command Council's law No. 139 of 9 December 1972: 1) to work for and fight the enemies of a socialist, democratic Arab society; 2) to ensure the equality of Iraqi women with men in rights, in the economy and in the state; 3) to contribute to the economic and social development of Iraq by co-operating with other Iraqi organisations and by raising the national consciousness of women; 4) to support mothers and children within the family structure.

Towards that end, by 1980, the GFIW had, established 256 centres around the country organised in a bureaucratised structure that claimed over 177 000 active members, or 7 per cent of Iraqi women aged 15 to 59.[21] GFIW staff worked closely with the state-run industries to train women for factory work and to trouble-shoot when incidents arose on the job. They collaborated with the trade unions in educational and service programmes. They worked with the peasant co-operatives in the rural areas where women formed a significant segment of the labour force. The ruling elite also gave the GFIW an important role in the implementation of the changes in the laws of personal status. In the spring of 1980, I attended the annual meeting of the GFIW held in Baghdad. Activist women from all over the world had been invited, at Iraqi state expense, to attend the meeting. The objective was apparently to showcase the GFIW to the Iraqi population and to create networks among the leaders of the GFIW and women from other countries. The conference received a tremendous amount of daily coverage in the Iraqi state-run television, radio, newspapers and magazines.

The visitors, given a controlled view of the organisation, were allowed into certain sessions only. The lobbying of several of the visitors with close Ba'th connections eventually resulted in increasing the access of a small number of us to the non-public sessions. What I observed in those sessions was later borne out in more detailed research on the organisation the following summer.

The structure of decision-making in the organisation was quite hierarchal. Programmes and policies were decided at the executive level as were all candidates for office. One slate of officers (as with all other public organisations I observed in Iraq) was presented for elections, with few members knowing precisely how the slate was chosen. I gathered that the slates, like the programmes and policies, were determined in conjunction with the Ba'th party. GFIW members were considered cadres and were expected to be disciplined, respecting the authority and orders of the leaders. Above all, members were taught that they must serve and be loyal to the party and the state.

Extensive observation of units of the General Federation of Iraqi Women reinforced the view that the GFIW was attempting to resocialise Iraqi women into new loyalties and identities. In 1980 I interviewed leaders of the GFIW at the state and local levels. I travelled from Baghad to Basra to Arbil observing GFIW centres and their work. Leaders expressed respect for the family obligations of their members. However, they were clear in trying to manoeuvre around families to free individuals for GFIW work. GFIW centres became alternative homes for many women for whom the party/state-sponsored GFIW was a legitimate cause for being out of their homes in a public setting. The women in the centres spoke of their love for each other and for the leaders of the GFIW. In particular, GFIW staff spent considerable time encouraging, among the membership, affection and loyalty to the head of the party and state, Saddam Hussein, who made frequent pronouncements and public appearances lauding the work and leaders of the GFIW. Their songs for Saddam were sung often as love songs – songs to a father, a brother, a son, a lover.

In addition to the GFIW, the Iraqi ruling elite has created numerous other organisations into which women are mobilised. Trade unions attempted to recruit women, although in 1977 only 4 per cent of the membership and administrative leadership of the unions were female.[22] Young girls, along with boys, from elementary schools to college were organised through the school system into paramilitary organisations. Sports groups, music and art groups, literary clubs, scientific and professional associations, student organisations, hobby clubs, service groups, youth hostels were organised by the party and subsidised by the state. With the backing and legitimacy of the party and the state, women were encouraged to participate in an expanding public domain of social, cultural, political and economic activities. The women received experience in organisation, hierarchy, discipline, service. Commitment to the party, state, ruling elite and their ideology of Arab socialism and pan-Arab nationalism was taught in all these contexts. The organisational incorporation of women into party- and state-run agencies also offered women an alternative route for participation in the political community.[23]

The Ba'th have sought to redirect the allegiance of women towards the party and state not only by providing them organisational alternatives but also by extending rights and services to them. Legislative reform as well as programmes of immediate relevance to women have been developed towards these ends.

In the area of legislative reform, the Ba'th made some modest changes in the personal status laws in 1978. They merged what they argued were more 'progressive' aspects of Sunni and Shi'a laws and modified them. For example, in cases of divorce, mothers were given custody of their children until the age of 10 (previously 7 for boys and 9 for girls) at which time, at the discretion of a state-employed judge, custody could be extended to 15. At that age the child could choose with which parent to stay. The code widened the conditions under which a woman could seek divorce. The law also made the permission of state-employed judges necessary before a man could take a second wife.

During my 1980 interviews, some of the GFIW leaders seemed ambivalent or disappointed with the modesty of these reforms. However, they were quick to rationalise, to their members and to me, the reluctance of the Ba'th to make more radical reforms in terms of the necessity of placating religious conservatives. Several GFIW leaders told mc that while they personally would have preferred a direct secularisation of the personal status laws (including the outlawing of polygyny), the selective merger of Sunni and Shi'a laws allowed them to claim the legitimacy of the *Shari'ah* and thus enabled them to manoevre around the clerics.

This Ba'thist view of their own caution is consistent with the analysis developed here. The Ba'th, like leaders throughout the Arab world, have been concerned to retain the loyalty of religious conservatives within and outside their own ranks. As GFIW leaders repeatedly asserted to me, their goal never was the 'liberation' of Iraqi women in the Western meaning of the term. Rather, the Ba'th's central ambition was building the state and nation. GFIW leaders concurred in that priority. In so far as freeing women from familial controls to participate in the labour force and the polity was needed for the state-building programme, some revision of the personal status laws became necessary and useful. However, the loyalty (or acquiescence) of religious conservatives was also necessary for this project. Thus, the modest legal advances for women would be precariously balanced against the costs the Ba'th would incur by antagonising other constituencies. Their cautious approach in the late 1970s and early 1980s left doubt as to whether they were willing to pay this cost. [24]

In other areas of legislation, the Ba'th have legally extended the same rights in the workplace to women as to men, including areas of pay, pension, training, advancement, retirement, compensation and medical care. Women exercised the right to vote and run for office in national elections for the first time in 1980.

I witnessed the first national election in 1980, finding that women did turn out at the polls in large numbers. The party put nineteen women on their slate of candidates for the parliament – all of them were elected. Considerably publicity was given to the women candidates during the campaign – primarily a political socialisation event since there were few opposing candidates. Saddam Hussein was seen frequently with the women candidates, particularly the president of the GFIW and the two other members of the GFIW executive board who ran. Government officials assisted the illiterate in voting in the polling centres. In an interesting twist, I noticed that at a couple of the centres, the government employees (women) reading the list of candidates to the voters would periodically not read the entire list, but simply ask, 'Do you want Manal?' (the president of the GFIW). Often their menfolk accompanied the women into the open polling booths, telling them how to vote or marking their ballots for them.

The Ba'th also have extended services of vital importance to women, particularly women working in the wage labour force. Among the services has been the provision of free child-care to working women, often adjacent to the place of work. Nursing mothers have been given time off from work, mornings and afternoons, to attend to their infants. Since the Ba'th have been attempting to encourage women to have more children to increase the population, they have also offered women rather generous maternity leaves – one month prior to delivery and 6 weeks after at full pay, followed by 6 months leave at half pay. Women, like men, could qualify for child allowances – increases in their pay for each additional child they had. The Ba'th also have given free meals to schoolchildren during school hours. In addition, the state has subsidised low-income housing for workers, which women workers could apply for independently of their male kin. Free transportation to and from work has been available at many of the state-run industries. Medical care has been either free or subsidised.

The record of achievement and limitations of the Ba'th programme is rather mixed. It is unclear how many or how deeply women have been affected and it is too soon to evaluate the long-term implications of these programmes. However, some changes are evident for at least part of the female population. There has been an increase in female labour force participation: an increase from 2.5 per cent of the total labour force in 1957 to 12 per cent in 1977 according to one report[25], or an increase from 7 per cent in 1968 to 19 per cent in 1980 according to another report.[26] There has been an increase in women's education and literacy. Women have been participating in public organisations in larger numbers, including military and government agencies. Certainly for a sector of the female population, particularly some petty bourgeois and recent urban immigrants, the Ba'th programme has brought benefits and increased integration into the institutions of the state.

The limitations of the Ba'th programme can be seen partly in the resistance of the population to participation. For example, while some working-class women found the day-care centres useful, many women, particularly of the middle-class, refused to put their children in the centres, preferring instead the care of family members. Resistance was often expressed by absenteeism in places of work and what appeared to me to be work sabotage, wastefulness and/or inefficiency. Further, there has been extensive documentation of the on-going resistance to Ba'th rule that has been organised particularly, though not exclusively, on the basis of religious-ethnic groups, especially among the Shi'ites and the Sunni Kurds.[27] These groups and the secular political opposition have been brutally suppressed by the Ba'th, as they have tried to consolidate their control over the population.

Despite the attempts of the Ba'th to undermine the allegiance of the population to the large family/tribal/ethnic groups, these primordial groups, can still claim the loyalties of a significant sector of the population. One reason for this is the repressive political atmosphere. The repression in the regime and the lack of legal political alternatives to the Ba'th has driven opposition underground or into silence. I noticed in 1980 a general state of fear. Individuals rarely talked politics, even to friends, since they were afraid of informants. Friends visiting me at the hotel whispered if they wanted to say anything even mildly critical of the state. The on-going mistrust of the state generated by this political repression has reinforced the family as an important arena of trust and security.

Economic realities have also reinforced the dependence of individuals on their families. The assistance of the extended family has been necessary to support young couples as they work and try to raise children. Given the shortage of housing, young couples often begin their householding by adding rooms on to the homes of their parents. Many have been turning to their families for child-care, loans, labour exchange and other economic assistance.

Families have also continued to be strong in part because the Ba'th has subsidised them directly and indirectly. The pro-natalism of the Ba'th and the stress on marriage has contributed to an idealisation of the family. The nation has been depicted as a large family with the president as the father. Article 38 of the Ba'th party constitution asserts that the state is responsible for protecting and developing the family which is considered to be the basic cell of the nation. The Article continues that the state must encourage, facilitate and supervise marriage, which is a national duty. And finally, it states that offspring are entrusted to the state immediately after the family[28].

Indirectly, the Ba'th leaders have provided implicit legitimacy for maintaining the solidarity of large family groups by their reliance on members of their own Takriti clan to rule. A significant number of key state positions have been occupied by consanguinal and affinal kin of state leaders. In so using their own primordial groups, they may have reinforced the legitimacy of such affiliations in general.

Despite the apparently contradictory nature of the direct and indirect support of 'family', and the uncertainty as to the degree of success of their programme, I would argue that the thrust of the Ba'thist project has been to curtail the connections between individuals and their large family/ethnic/tribal groups and intensify loyalties to and identification with the state. It would not be necessarily contradictory for them to try to subsidise their own primordial groups while undermining those of others.

Jacqueline Ismael[29] argues that the Ba'th have merely expedited the undermining of the family as a unit of production that was already underway prior to 1968. The Ba'th, she contends, have attempted to subordinate family to the state by taking over family functions (child socialisation, health care and social control), transforming the family from a unit of production to a unit of consumption and subsidising the nuclear family in order to win allegiance away from kin/tribal groups to the state.

I find her discussion valuable. I would add to this analysis that the programmes directed at women (discussed above) have been vital avenues for this project. Furthermore, the project of undermining primordial ties has been connected to Ba'thist projects both of state construction and of economic development, as I have argued elsewhere.[30] It remains the case, nevertheless, that the Ba'th may have been working against themselves, to some degree, in that the direct and indirect consequences of their programmes and their rule may be forcing sectors of the population back into their families for social, economic and political security.

LEBANESE ELITE STRATEGIES: PRIVATISATION AND MINIMALISM

While small in territory and population, Lebanon has been historically one of the most heterogeneous of the Middle Eastern states. The Lebanese state has formally recognised the participation of 17 religious sects in the polity. Officially, the Christians and Muslims have been in a ratio of 6 to 5, with the Christian Maronites ranked the largest group (30 per cent of the population), followed by the Sunnis (20 per cent), Shi'ites (18 per cent), Greek Orthodox (10 per cent), Greek Catholics (6 per cent), Druze (6 per cent), Armenian Orthodox (5 per cent) and others collectively making up the rest (about 5 per cent). However an official census has not been undertaken since 1932. As the current war has made apparent, the official figures do not represent the reality. The Muslims probably account for 55 to 60 per cent of the population, with the Shi'ites now the largest sect in Lebanon.

Such heterogeneity in a population of about 3 million is remarkable in that, while there have been some sectarian territorial concentrations historically, the different sects were found residentially mixed throughout the country. Lebanon also has been, by Arab standards, rather densely populated in both urban and rural areas. It has been more urbanised than most Arab countries. Seventy per cent of the population lived in cities in 1975, with the capital, Beirut, accounting for about 40 per cent of the population.[31]

Unlike Iraq, the Lebanese state incorporated the religious/ethnic heterogeneity into the formal structure of the state. Lebanon did not spawn a revolutionary movement or party capable of taking over and reshaping the state, as did Iraq, despite attempts to do so. The structure of governance, now violently contested, was shaped during the French mandate period which lasted until independence in 1943.

Article 95 of the Lebanese constitution requires formal representation of the seventeen recognised religious sects in government. This has been complemented by an informal agreement, the National Pact, designed by the ruling elite at the time of independence. As a result of these formal and informal strictures, since 1943 the president has been a Maronite, the prime minister a Sunni, the speaker of parliament a Shi'ite and his deputy a Greek Orthodox. Seats in parliament and positions in formal government offices were allocated according to a formal definition (based on the 1932 census) of the proportions of the sects in the population.

The formal definition of sect demography (in the politically sectarian state), combined with the extensive powers of the presidency in the hands of one sect, produced imbalances in power and allocation of state resources. The Christians, especially the Maronites, were over-represented in government, controlling key ministerial and military posts and receiving disproportional amounts of benefits from the state. Among the Muslims, the Shi'ites in particular were under-represented and disadvantaged.

While scholars have evaluated at length various aspects of Lebanon's formal political pluralism, little systematic investigation of the dynamics of the relationships between the state and sectarianism, on the one hand, and women and family on the other has been carried out. Control over matters relating to women and the family have been central issues in Lebanon, although the processes and outcomes have been quite different from those in Iraq.

Questions of women and family may have eluded most scholars concerned with Lebanon's pluralism because these issues have been in large part, delegated to the private sector – in particular to the authority of the religious sects. The apparent absence of the state, however, does not imply an indifference or neutrality on the part of the ruling elite *vis-à-vis* women and family. Rather, I would argue, it has been a concerted stance of the Lebanese elite to relinquish control over these matters in the hands of the private sector.

The ruling elite has legitimated its rule primarily on the basis of a social structure assumed to be organised around the primacy of sectarian affiliations.[32] Women and the family have been vital to the reproduction of that sectarianism. I would argue that most of the ruling elite has supported the continued sectarian control over issues related to women and family as a part of a strategy of maintaining the balance of sectarian power in the state.

The Lebanese ruling elite, since independence, has maintained a relatively minimalist, non-interventionist state. Key social, economic and political matters have been left to the private sector, with the state often subsidising programmes undertaken by private agencies. For example, unlike the Ba'th who have attempted to build a cohesive system of national education, the Lebanese ruling elite extensively subsidised private education. In 1968–69, 68 per cent of Lebanese primary, intermediate and secondary level students were in private schools and 32 per cent in public. By 1972–73, the percentage of students in public schools had increased (45 per cent), but was still less than those in private schools (55 per cent).[33] The tuition of many of the students in private schools was paid by the state. Not only was there no national curriculum, but also many of the schools, including those considered to be the best, were run by foreign agencies, often with a primarily foreign teaching staff.

The structure of the school system helped to fragment the population on a sectarian basis. Most of the private schools were organised by religious sects serving their own membership. Private schools run by non-religious organisations often, nevertheless, served one sect or were predominately Muslim or Christian. To the degree that residential segregation occurred, public schools were often mainly Muslim or Christian. This was particularly important in its impact on the population in that the public schools were attended primarily by rural and urban working and lower middle classes. The middle and upper classes generally sent their children to private schools.

The schools contributed to social fragmentation in other ways. A large part of the curriculum focused on language instruction. Each school was known for its primary language of instruction, usually French or English, but also Italian, German and a few others (depending on the cultural orientation of the directors). Few of the private schools used Arabic as their primary language. School curricula varied tremendously, including which days they closed (Fridays, Saturdays or Sundays and other holidays, which affected whether children were available to play with each other). The impact on the population was profound. They were being systematically socialised in different social, cultural, linguistic, religious and political orientations.

The school system was only one aspect of the social fragmentation process. Rather than building a system of public social services, the elite, to the extent that it offered a coherent social programme, tended to encourage activities in the private sector. Most hospitals, clinics, social-work agencies, projects to assist the needy were operated by private, mainly sectarian, agencies. Many of these received state funds. Youth groups, men's groups, women's groups, cultural institutions, sports clubs were also mainly privately organised and mainly sectarian. While the government ran some social services and a few programmes for youth, these were minimal and designed not to compete with the private sector. Most of the religious sects were relatively well-organised to offer social and cultural services to their membership. In turn, most individuals looking for these services tended to go to agencies within their own religious sects.

The absence of a coherent national social programme was coupled with the absence of a coherent national economic development plan. Planning in Lebanon was surely made more difficult by the minimal public resources available. However, resources which were available to the state or could have been available were drained away by the elite into the private sector, where it had more individual control. As a result, despite the economic growth in Lebanon in the 1950s through the early 1970s, there was a constant brain-drain. Lebanon exported skilled and educated workers, while importing relatively unskilled workers.

Perhaps one of the most significant domains in which the absence of the state was felt was that of personal status laws. The Lebanese elite, unlike the Iraqi, did not legislate a national family code. Rather, all matters of personal status were left in the domain of religious law. Marriage, divorce, inheritance, child custody were regulated by the seventeen formally recognised religious sects. Given the absence of civil marriage, mixed marriages usually took place within the church of the man, with the woman often converting and the children raised in the religion of the father. The impact of this legal fragmentation was to create as many different legal realities as there were legally recognised sects. The difference in legal realities tended to encourage different social experiences. Muslim and Christian men and women I interviewed in the early 1970s in an urban working-class neighbourhood of Greater Beirut often indicated that their circumstances were fundamentally different because of the different laws they followed. Muslim women sometimes envied Christian women because divorce was harder for the latter, while conversely sometimes Christian men envied Muslim men   Whatever their feelings about their own religious laws, the men and women recognised that the laws helped to create or maintain differences. The absence of the state affirmed the power of the religious sects over these critical matters concerning women and family. Commonalities of social experience therefore, often were clouded by the legal differences. As Yolla Sharara, a Lebanese feminist, noted, women in Lebanon did not feel the presence of the state in their lives.[34] Rather, they felt more directly the effects of the men of their sectarian communities.

Leaving personal status laws to the religious authorities was consistent with the strategy of the ruling elite to maintain a minimalist state. This was part of a strategy of reproducing the basis of its own political leadership. Like the Iraqi elite, the Lebanese elite did not comprise a class. Highly factionalised, the elite included members of some old ruling landed families, some petty bourgeois families, merchants, compradores. They organised their power bases to a large degree through their own family groups and through vertical and horizontal alliances with other families, mainly within their own religious sects – a strategy based on the bolstering of social fragmentation.

Interviews and participant observation from 1971 to 1980 at local and national levels revealed that leaders at both levels were intent on separating citizens by primordial affiliations. For example, in 1978 a key advisor to Ameen Gamayel (later to become president) indicated to me that the

Kata'ib Party was aware that they had to 'purify' certain neighbours from non-Christian influences, even if it meant a high cost in lives lost. Leaders of the Armenian Dashnag Party were unambivalent in asserting their desire to keep the Armenians from assimilating. Several specified that one of the key motivations driving their extensive efforts at building low-income housing for Armenians was to remove them from heterogeneous neighbourhoods where their 'Armenianness' might be diluted. I interviewed wives of Shi'a leaders who were working hard to actively maintain ties between newly urbanised Shi'a and their rural political/social roots. It was clear they did not want 'their' people to assimilate. In the neighbourhood in which I conducted research, residents reported cases of clerics refusing to perform rites for individuals who wanted to marry outside their religious sects. Members of Armenian political parties told me they sent thugs out to 'dissuade' Arab men from marrying their women. Directors of Christian schools expressed their concern about the blending of the population in mixed neighbourhoods. While there were many Lebanese, including members of the elite, who stood for more secular identities and affiliations, the political pressures towards primordial affiliations were highly institutionalised and were continually reinforced by the mechanisms leaders employed to build their own power bases.

The *zu'ama'* (political leaders) established vertical alliances on the basis of patron-client relationships, some of which were with individuals, but most of which were on a family basis. That is, a *za'im* usually courted heads of families on the assumption that family patriarchs could deliver their kin into the following of the patron. Patriarchs, for their part, tried to control their kin because they were then in a better bargaining position with the *zu'ama'*.

The *zu'ama'* offered their clients protection and access to state resources and services, while the clients gave the *zu'ama'* votes, labour and loyalty. Given the minimalism and weakness of the Lebanese state, it was, in fact, prudent for individuals and families to be allied in a face-to-face personal relationship with a *za'im*. Individuals integrated into a cohesive family, additionally, stood a better chance of gaining the protection of a *za'im*. Access to most services in Lebanon required *wasta* – contact, brokerage. Jobs, housing, medical and social services, legal procedures and the like were obtained more easily if doors were opened by *zu'ama'*. Many of the *zu'ama'* maintained private militias, which collectively, prior to the outbreak of the 1975 war, outnumbered the volunteer Lebanese national army. The militias were used against the state as well as against competing factions to protect the position and following of the *zu'ama'*.

Few Lebanese considered the state's legal system as ultimate protection. Ultimate protection, most Lebanese felt, came from families and *zu'ama'*.

In addition to being organised heavily on family bases, most patron-client relationships tended to be within the same religious sect. This reinforced the link between families, politics and sects. Families, in general, could more effectively take care of their members' needs if they acted collectively. Further, they tended to have greater leverage if they acted as a bargaining unit in relationship to political and religious leaders of their own sects. *Zu'ama'* were similarly more powerful if their families were cohesively organised and if they could control large numbers of people through contact with a few patriarchs. In a politically sectarian state, claims of legitimacy tended to speak loudest when they appeared to have religious sanction. Religious sanction came from the support of the clerics as well as the assumptions (or myth) of commonality of culture within sects that underwrote the sectarian organisation of leadership.

The ruling elite won the support of the clerics, in part, by respecting their domain of power over personal status laws – a key to the power the clerics had over their following - and their control over a number of important social services. It was in the interests of most of the ruling elite to encourage social fragmentation on a sectarian basis among the population. Political, legal, religious and social fragmentation fed into each other.

Thus an alliance between political and religious leaders and key family patriarchs emerged historically, in which issues of crucial relevance to women and family were fundamental. Women were important in this arrangement because of their reproductive role. In a patrilineal system (characteristic of both Muslims and Christians in Lebanon), lineages lose membership primarily when women marry out. The Muslim pattern has been to encourage lineage endogamy, expressed in the preferred marriage choice of close parallel cousins. Christians, influenced by Muslim practices, often married within their lineages as well. Lineage endogamy became, *ipso facto*, sect endogamy. The fact that legal authority over marriage, divorce, child custody and inheritance remained in the hands of sectarian institutions affirmed the practice and ideology of endogamy. Thus family and sect affiliation reinforced one another, with an important mechanism for that dynamic entailing control over women and their progeny.

Paradoxically, while the Lebanese ruling elite was quite directly encouraging the cohesiveness of the large family groups, the economic and social transformations in Lebanon offered individuals social alternatives outside family groups, perhaps to a greater degree than was the case in Iraq. Because of a fairly open market economy, Lebanon, prior to the war and despite the efforts of the leadership, was moving toward a more secular society. The economic and political openness, in a period of relative economic growth and prosperity, allowed some individuals a degree of autonomy and mobility beyond family control. Additionally, Lebanese, unlike Iraqis, turned to their families for support in the face of a weak state rather than a strong oppressive state.

However, the challenge to the ruling elite of the increasing secularism, as I have argued elsewhere,[35] contributed to the events leading to the war in 1975. One of the outcomes of the war has been an increased politicisation of religious identity, and an increase in the importance of family. With the collapse of the state during the current war, individuals have had to rely increasingly on their families for support. In addition individuals and families have had to forge even closer relationships with the political leaders who, through their control over militias, regulate political, economic and social life. Finally, the militias, in their efforts to mobilise the populace, have relied heavily on the support of the clerics to gain legitimacy. Thus, the war has more deeply enmeshed family, religion and politics in Lebanon.

IRAQ AND LEBANON: TOWARDS THEORY AND COMPARATIVE RESEARCH

The Iraqi and Lebanese case studies raise a number of concerns which must be addressed as we lay the foundations for historically and culturally useful approaches to the relationships among women, families, religions and the states in the Middle East. Family, religion and state have been competitive forms of social organisation in many respects, as Jack Goody's provocative study of the development of marriage and the family in Europe demonstrates.[36] While at times they may reinforce one another, they often compete with each other for the allegiance of the population. Control over women and their progeny are often central to this contest. In this chapter, I have focused primarily on the implications for women and families of two different elite strategies for state-building. Comparative research into questions concerning these relationships from different perspectives and starting points could lay the basis for more encompassing theoretical frameworks.

Iraq and Lebanon represent different elite strategies for state-building. Both Iraq and Lebanon have ethnically and religiously mixed populations. However, while the Iraqi elite formally rejected the use of parochial identities in the system of governance, the Lebanese legally incorporated religious/ethnic identities as a basis for formal representation in the state. The Iraqi elite was itself relatively homogeneous, the Lebanese relatively heterogeneous. The Iraqi elite organised around a single political party with a relatively coherent ideological framework. The Lebanese elite organised around competitive political cliques with conflicting and minimally developed ideological stances.

Each required means for controlling the population, mobilising a following and gaining legitimacy. Personalism and individual charisma have been significant mechanisms for control, mobilisation and legitimacy for both sets of elites. In the Iraqi elite, manipulation of these political processes have been dominated by the single head of party and state, in the Lebanese, shared by the factions and state. Though the Iraqi elite nurtured a cult of the leader, it mobilised a following through a broad array of institutions organised by the party and state, making the public sphere the centre of initiative and action. The Lebanese elite mobilised highly personalised followings attached to themselves as individual leaders, making the private sphere the centre of initiative and action. The Iraqi elite had extensive public resources available, allowing them a degree of autonomy from the institutions of society. The Lebanese had relatively few public resources. The institutional framework elaborated by the Iraqi elite through party and state offered citizens a range of alternatives to primordial groups for meeting social, economic, and political needs. The framework elaborated by the Lebanese elite formally built upon primordial affiliations to meet basic needs. The Iraqi elite legitimated their positions by claiming to represent the population as a whole. The Lebanese elite drew legitimacy from their representation of particular sectarian groupings.

Each of the ruling elites developed programmes with important consequences for women and families. Iraqi programmes attempted to draw women into the state, away from kin/tribal/ethnic groups. Lebanese programmes attempted to keep women in kin/ethnic/sectarian groups. The Iraqi elite used the authority and structure of the party and state to pull women into schools, places of work, voluntary associations. The Lebanese elite encouraged women's continued affiliation with private schools, industries, associations, often using resources of the state to subsidise those opportunities. The Iraqi ruling elite reformed the personal status laws, thereby offering a uniform family code for all Iraqi women. The delegation of authority over Lebanese personal status laws to the religious sects, supported diverse family codes and legal conditions for Lebanese women. For better or worse, the Iraqi state has been a presence in the lives of Iraqi women. The Lebanese state has been felt more by its absence.

In exploring the relationships among women, families, religions and states in Iraq and Lebanon, I have argued that a driving force has been the nature and circumstances of the two ruling elites' projects for state-building. The Iraqi elite was organised to build a strong centralised state with institutions capable of penetrating most aspects of society. The Lebanese elite was organised to sustain a minimalist state, delegating significant areas of institution-building to the private sector dominanted by primordial (particularly sectarian) groupings. In each case, I have focused on the impact of these state-building projects on women and families.

In both cases, strategies of the elites for state-building have been significantly affected by variables not considered in detail here, such as market conditions, international political processes and popular resistance by women and their families. For example, while it may be in the interests of the Iraqi elite to redirect loyalties to the party and state, the direct and indirect consequences of its rule, particularly its repressiveness, may have reinforced primordial ties to some degree. Paradoxically, in Lebanon, economic and social transformations may have redirected the interests of sectors of the population away from primordial groups up to 1975.

These elites have been in power for too short a period to evaluate the long-term consequences of their programmes for women and families. Furthermore, the effect of wars in each of these countries have contributed to new dynamics which are difficult to assess at present. While it remains to be seen what the long-term consequences of these programmes, practices and processes will be, the outlines of the theoretical issues present themselves more immediately. Among the variables that have been at play in the Iraqi and Lebanese cases has been the circumstances of the ruling elite: their degree of homogeneity, coherence of ideology, systematisation of programmes and willingness and ability to suppress competing social groups. Availability of public resources has been critical in shaping the degree of autonomy the elites have had from other social classes and institutions. The particulars of the elites' strategies for state-building have had important consequences for policies and programmes directed at women and families: the nature of the state they were trying to build, the focus of initiative and action within the public versus private sectors, the degree of political and social freedoms tolerated, the degree of investment of public resources for direct economic and social development, the strategies for labour recruitment or exportation and the bases on which claims for legitimacy have been founded.

A fuller analysis of the relationships among women, families, religions and states in the Middle East must take into account an assessment of other variables, such as international economic and political processes, and most critically, the actions and reactions of women and families to the processes in which they are at once subjects and objects. Evaluation of the dynamics of these relationships may help shed light on such issues as the structure and dynamics of family processes, the circumstances which are conducive to the emergence of autonomous women's movements, and the development of notions of individual and citizenship rights in the Middle East.

NOTES

1. This is a revised version of my paper, 'Family, Religion and State: Middle Eastern Models' in Richard R. Randolph, David M. Schneider and May N. Dias (eds), *Dialectics and Gender. Anthropological Approaches* (Boulder, CO.: Westview Press, 1988). This revison owes much to the persistent interest of Deniz Kandiyoti. Helpful comments, and insightful suggestions were offered by Roland Marchand, Marion Sluglett and Aram Yengoyan. Afsaneh Najmabadi shared drafts of her article for this volume. The parallels and counterpoints were useful to my revisions.
2. Sherry Ortner, 'The Founding of the First Sherpa Nunnery and the Problem of "Women" as an Analytic Category,' in Vivien Patraka and Louise Tilly (eds), *Feminist Revisions: What Has Been and Might Be* (Ann Arbor, MI: Women's Studies Program, University of Michigan, 1983).
3. Rayna Rapp, Ellen Ross and Renate Bridenthal 'Examining Family History', *Feminist Studies*, 5 (1979) no. 1; Barrie Thorne (ed.), *Rethinking the Family* (New York: Longman, 1982); Jack Goody, *The Development of Family and Marriage in Europe* (Cambridge: Cambridge University Press, 1983); Christopher Lasch, *Haven in a Heartless World: The Family Beseiged* (New York: Basic Books, 1977).
4. Rosemary Radford Ruether, *Sexism and God-Talk: Toward a Feminist Theology* (Boston: Beacon Press 1984); Azizah Al Hibri (ed.), *Women and Islam* (Oxford: Pergamon Press, 1982); Yvonne Haddad and Ellison Banks Findly (eds), *Women, Religion and Social Change* (Albany: State University of New York Press, 1985).
5. Perry Anderson, *Lineages of the Absolutist State* (London: Version, 1974); Leonard Binder, *In a Moment of Enthusiam: Political Power and the Second Stratum in Egypt* (Chicago: University of Chicago Press, 1978); Peter B. Evans, Dietrich Rueschemeyer and Theda Skocpol (eds), *Bringing the State Back In* (New York: Cambridge University Press, 1985); Irene Silverblatt, 'Women in States', *Annual Review of Anthropology* 17 (1988) pp. 427–60; Theda Skocpol, *States and Social Revolutions: A Comparative Analysis of France, Russia and China* (Cambridge: Cambridge University Press, 1979); John Waterbury, *The Egypt of Nasser and Sadat: The Political Economy of Two Regimes* (Princeton: Princeton University Press, 1983).

6. Sondra Hale, 'The Wing of the Patriarch: Sudanese Women and Revolutionary Parties', *Middle East Reports*, 16 (1986) no. 1, pp. 25–30; Mervat Hatem; 'Class and Patriarchy as Competing Paradigms for the Study of Middle Eastern Women', *Comparative Studies in Society and History* 29 (1987) no. 4, pp. 811–18; Suad Joseph, 'Women and Political Movements in the Middle East: Agendas for Research', *Middle East Reports*, 16 (1986) no. 1, pp. 3–7; Rosemary Sayigh, 'Palestinian Women: Triple Burden, Single Struggle', *Peuples Mediterranéens* (February 1988); Judith Tucker 'Insurrectionary Women: Women and the State in 19th Century Egypt', *Middle East Report*, 16 (1986) no. 1, pp. 9–13.

7. Sami Zubaida, *Islam, the People and the State. Essays on Political Ideas and Movements in the Middle East* (London: Routledge, 1989).

8. Leila Ahmed, 'Western Feminist Theory and Middle Eastern Women' Roundtable Discussion, Middle East Studies Association Meetings (Baltimore, Md., 1987), Mervat Hatem, 'Western Feminist Theory and Middle Eastern Women' Roundtable Discussion, Middle East Studies Association Meetings (Baltimore, Md., 1987); Suad Joseph 'Western Feminist Theory and Middle Eastern Women' Roundtable Discussion, Middle East Studies Association Meetings (Baltimore, Md., 1987); Marnia Lazreg, 'Feminism and Difference: The Perils of Writing as a Woman on Women in Algeria', *Feminist Studies* 14 (1988) no. 1, pp. 81–107.

9. The material on Iraq is based on a project in 1974 and two in 1980 at the invitation of the Iraqi Ministry of Culture and Information. The material on Lebanon is based on a number of fieldwork projects carried out from 1971 to 1980. The analysis of the Lebanese state reflects the pre-civil war situation (up to 1975).

10. The Kata'ib is the predominately Maronite right-wing party founded by Pierre Gamayel.

11. Hanna Batatu, 'Class Analysis and Iraqi Society', *Arab Studies Quarterly*, 1 (1979) no. 1, pp. 229–44.

12. In the Ba'th ideology, Iraq is a *qutr*, region, of the Arab nation.

13. Joe Stork, 'State Power and Economic Structure: Class Determination and State Formation in Contemporary Iraq,' in Tim Niblock (ed.), *Iraq: The Contemporary State* (London: Croom Helm and Exeter Centre for Arab Gulf Studies, 1982).

14. Hanna Batatu, 'Class Analysis and Iraqi Society'.

15. Ministry of Planning, Iraq, *Annual Abstract of Statistics* (Baghdad, 1978).

16. T. Y. Ismael, *The Arab Left* (Syracuse: Syracuse University Press, 1976).

17. Ministry of Planning, Iraq *General Population Census* (Baghdad, 1965).

18. General Federation of Iraqi Women, *A Practical Translation to the Objectives of the Revolution in Work and Creativity* (Beirut: Dar Al Afaq al Jadidah, Dar-Lubnan, 1980).

19. Amal Sharqi, 'The Progress of Women in Iraq', in Tim Niblock (ed.), *Iraq: The Contemporary State*.
20. General Federation of Iraqi Women, 'Summary. The Report of the Illiteracy Eradication Secretariat' (Baghdad, 1980).
21. Manal Al-Alusi, Speech Delivered at the Ninth Conference of the General Federation of Iraqi Women (Baghdad: General Federation of Iraqi Women, 1980).
22. Ministry of Planning, Iraq *Annual Abstract of Statistics* (Baghdad, 1977).
23. Jacqueline Ismael, 'Social Policy and Social Change: The Case of Iraq', *Arab Studies Quarterly*, 2 (1980) no. 3, pp. 235–48.
24. A first version of this paper was written in 1985 and revised for this volume in 1989. In March 1990 a new law was promulgated by the Ba'th giving legal exemption to men for killing women of their families whom they suspect of adultery. At the time of this writing (April 1990), the text of this law was not available to me, nor were any commentaries. While I am reluctant to interpret this development with so little information at hand, at first glance, this new promulgation seems consistent with the patterns observed earlier. The Ba'th were interested in freeing women from familial controls in so far as that served their interests in building the state. Ba'th control over the population and their state-building programme have been seriously impaired by the human and material cost of the war with Iran. The new law may be an attempt to further placate religious conservatives and patriarchal interests. Minimally, the Ba'th appear to be backing away from some of their modest legal restraints on familial control over women in order to bolster their flagging legitimacy.
25. Ihsan Al-Hassan, *The Effects of Industrialisation on the Social Status of Women* (Baghdad: General Federation of Iraqi Women, 1980).
26. Sharqi, 'The Progress of Women in Iraq', p. 83.
27. Batatu, 'Iraq's Underground Shi'i Movement: Characteristics, Causes and Prospects', *The Middle East Journal*, 354 (1981) no. 4, pp. 578–694.
28. T. Y. Ismael, *The Arab Left*, p. 134.
29. Jacqueline Ismael, 'Social Policy and Social Change'.
30. Suad Joseph, 'Ruling Elites and the Young: A Comparison of Iraq and Lebanon', in Laurence O. Michalak and Jeswald W. Salacuse (eds), *Social Legislation in the Contemporary Middle East* (Berkeley: Institute of International Studies. University of California, 1986).
31. United Nations Department of International Economic and Social Affairs (UNIESA), *Demographic Indicators of Countries: Estimates and Projections as Assessed in 1980* (New York: UN, 1982).
32. Suad Joseph, 'Muslim-Christian Conflict in Lebanon: A Perspective on the Evolution of Sectarianism', in Suad Joseph and Barbara L. K. Pillsbury (eds) *Muslim-Christian Conflicts: Economic, Political and Social Origins* (Boulder, CO.: Westview Press, 1978).

200   *Elite Strategies: Iraq and Lebanon*

33. Ministry of Planning, Lebanon *Recueil de statistique libanaises: Année 1969* (Beirut, 1969); Ministry of Planning, Lebanon *Recueil de statistique libanaises: Année 1973* (Beirut, 1973)
34. Yolla Sharara, 'Women and Politics in Lebanon', *Khamsin. Journal of Revolutionary Socialists of the Middle East*, 6 (1978) pp. 6–15.
35. Joseph, 'Muslim-Christian Conflict in Lebanon'.
36. Goody, *The Development of Family and Marriage in Europe.*

8 Competing Agenda: Feminists, Islam and the State in Nineteenth- and Twentieth-Century Egypt

Margot Badran

In Egypt the 'woman question' has been a contested domain involving feminists, Islamists, and the state. This chapter explores their competing discourses and agenda in nineteenth- and twentieth-century Egypt and how they have shifted over time.[1] Divergent discourses arose in the context of modern state and class formation, and economic and political confrontation with the West. These multiple discourses have been sustained in strikingly different political and economic cultures as state and society continually negotiate changing realities.

From the second quarter of the nineteenth century, the state in Egypt tried to draw women into the economic and technological transformations underway. As a consequence it began to wrest women away from the more exclusive control of the family, threatening the authority and domination of men over their women. Earlier in the century, after freeing Egypt from direct Ottoman rule, the new ruler, Muhammad 'Ali, while consolidating his power, had placed the Islamic establishment centred at Al Azhar under the control of the state. The former broad purview of the religious establishment was eroded piecemeal in the drive towards secularisation of education and law. The only exception to this was the sphere of personal status laws.[2] For women this created an awkward dichotomy between their role as citizens of the nation state (*watan*) and as members of the religious community (*umma*). In a division that was never precise, the state increasingly came to influence their public roles, leaving to religion the regulation of their private or family roles. The structural contradictions and tensions this created have to this day never been fully resolved.[3]

While promoting new social roles for women, the state could not afford unduly to alienate patriarchal interests and has therefore made various accommodations and alliances. Whatever their competing interests, the state and religious forces have retained patriarchal forms of control over women. It is this patriarchal dimension that feminists have identified and confronted and for which they have been variously attacked, contained, or suppressed by state authorities and Islamists alike. However, in Egypt there has been sufficient space – albeit more frequently taken than granted – within state and society for women to speak out as feminists and activists. Moreover, the authorities have at times deliberately encouraged women's initiatives for their own purposes.

The earliest articulation of women's feminist consciousness, first discernable in occasional published writings – poetry, essays, and tales – by the 1860s and 1870s, preceded colonial occupation and the rise of nationalism.[4] It was more widely expressed from the 1890s with the rise of women's journalism and salon debates. This new awareness (not yet called feminist; in fact the term, 'feminism' was not used in Egypt until the early 1920s) was based on an increased sensitivity to the everyday constraints imposed upon women by a patriarchal society. Muslim, Christian, and Jew alike shared this sensitivity and they projected an understanding, implicit or explicit, that these constraints were not solely religiously based as they had been made to believe. Furthermore, from the rise of feminism in Egypt to the present, its advocates across the spectrum from left to right have consistently used Islam, as well as nationalism, as legitimising discourses. In this chapter, feminism is broadly construed to include an understanding that women have suffered forms of subordination or oppression because of their sex, and an advocacy of ways to overcome them to achieve better lives for women, and for men, within the family and society. I am using a definition of feminism broad enough to be all-inclusive without intending to suggest a monolithic feminism. I indicate divergences within this larger framework while keeping the primary focus on the interplay among three major discourses, those of feminists, Islamists, and the state.[5]

Feminist, nationalist, and Islamist positions on the 'woman question' have seldom been considered together in the literature.[6] Moreover, although women's views come from the inside, their voices – whether as feminists or Islamists – have been subsumed within 'larger' (male) discourses. Here, I pay particular attention to the agenda of women who are feminists across the political spectrum and of women Islamists. Focusing on what women have to say makes it possible to discern their departures from their male counterparts as well as their own internal differences.

The exploration of the competing agenda and discourses on women is organised within the following historical framework: 1) the modern state-building and colonial periods; 2) the period of the liberal experiment; 3) the period of the revolution, Arabism, and socialism; and 4) the era of *infitah* capitalism and populist Islamist ascendancy.

THE MODERN STATE-BUILDING AND COLONIAL PERIODS: NINETEENTH CENTURY TO 1922

During the nineteenth century, especially in the later decades, new contenders appeared in the shaping and control of discourse in general, and more particularly, discourses on women. With the broadening of opportunities for education and the rise of women's feminist consciousness, women who had previously been the objects of prescriptive pronouncements began to challenge patriarchal domination.

The expanding modern state promoted new educational and work opportunities for women, especially in health and teaching, but incurred resistance from families. In the early nineteenth century, for example, Egyptians did not initially allow their daughters to attend the new state midwifery school (Ethopian slaves were recruited as the first students).[7] In 1836, Muhammad 'Ali appointed a Council for Public Education to look into creating a state system of education for girls but it was found impossible to implement. Later, however, during the rule of Isma'il, one of his wives sponsored the first state school for girls which opened in 1873 serving the daughters of high officials and white slaves from elite households. Meanwhile, encouraged by the state, Shaikh Ahmad Rifa'i Al Tahtawi and 'Ali Pasha Mubarak published books in 1869 and 1875 advocating education for women, using Islamic justifications from the Quran and *Hadith*.[8] It was not easy, however, to draw women out of the realm controlled by the family.

Feminist discourse first emerged in the writings of women of privilege and education who lived in the secluded world of the urban harem.[9] Women gained new exposure through expanded education and widening contacts within the female world. They made comparisons between their own lives and those of women and men of other social and national backgrounds. Through their new education women also gained deeper knowledge of their religion. Some urban middle- and upper-class women began to contest the Islamic justification for their seclusion, *hijab* (meaning then the veiling of both face and body), and related controls over their lives.[10] In 1892, Zainab Al Fawwaz protested in *Al Nil* magazine, 'We have not seen any of the divinely ordered systems of law, or any law from among the corpus of (Islamic) religious law ruling that woman is to be prohibited from involvement in the occupations of men.'[11] When Hind Naufal founded the journal, *Al Fatah* (The Young Woman) in the same year, inaugurating a women's press in Egypt, women found a new forum for discussing and spreading their nascent feminism.[12]

This emergent feminism was grounded, and legitimised, in the framework of Islamic modernism expounded towards the end of the century by Shaikh Muhammad 'Abduh, a distinguished teacher and scholar from Al Azhar. 'Abduh turned a revolutionary corner when he proposed that believers, by which he meant the learned, could go straight to the sources of religion, principally the Quran and the *Hadith*, for guidance in the conduct of everday life.[13] Through *ijtihad*, or independent inquiry into the sources of religion, 'Abduh demonstrated that one could be both Muslim and modern and that indeed not all traditional practice was in keeping with Islam. In dealing with gender issues, 'Abduh confronted the problem of patriarchal excesses committed in the name of Islam. He especially decried male abuses of the institutions of divorce and polygamy.[14]

The opening out encouraged by *ijtihad* had a number of consequences. While Muslim women's earliest feminist writing may not have been immediately inspired by Islamic modernism, it was not long before it developed within this framework. The progressive discourse of Muslim men was, however, from the start situated within Islamic modernism. It was generated by men of the upper educated strata, mainly new secular intellectuals, often men of law.[15] Later, towards the middle of the twentieth century, *ijtihad* would also be evoked by men and women of the lower middle class to create a populist, conservative Islamist discourse (the method – that is *ijtihad* – rather than the content was inspired by Islamic modernism). Thus two marginalised groups, women and the lower middle class, entered into the debate.

After women had been producing their own feminist writing for some time, Murqus Fahmi, a young Coptic lawyer, published *Al Mar'a fi al sharq* (The Woman in the East) in 1894, criticising patriarchal tyranny over women in the home which he claimed no religion sanctioned. Five years later, a Muslim judge, Qasim Amin, published his famous book, *Tahrir al mar'a* (The Liberation of the Woman, 1899), attacking the practice of female seclusion and the *hijab*, by which he meant face veiling (not modest covering of the head and body). He argued that women in Egypt were backward because they had been deprived of the legitimate rights accorded to them by Islam. He insisted that for the nation to advance and become modern, women must regain these rights. This pro-feminist discourse generated from within the establishment, by a Muslim lawyer and judge, drew wide criticism, especially from religious conservatives and members of the lower middle class.[16] While it was perceived as more dangerous than women's feminist writing, less widely visible at the time, in the long run women's feminism would be more sustained and more threatening.[17]

Early in the twentieth century, women's feminist writing became more visible and reached a wider mainstream audience, when Malak Hifni Nasif, known by her pen name, Bahithat Al Badiya (Searcher in the Desert), began publishing essays in *Al Jarida*, the paper of the progressive nationalist party, *Al Umma*. These essays and her speeches were published by the party press in 1910 in a book called *Al Nisa'iyyat* (which can be translated as Feminine or Feminist Pieces, in the absence of a specific term for 'feminist' in Arabic). Women's feminism was becoming more explicit and was increasingly expressed within a nationalist idiom reflecting and fuelling the growing nationalist movement in Egypt.

Another principal producer of feminist ideas at this period was Nabawiyya Musa, who later published her essays in a book entitled *Al mar'a wa al 'amal* (The Woman and Work, 1920). These two women were both from the middle class: Bahithat Al Bad'iya from the upper and Nabawiyya Musa from the more modest strata. They were among the first graduates of the Saniyya Teachers School established in 1889, and both became teachers. In 1907, Musa was the first Egyptian woman to sit for the baccalaureate examination, and the last until after independence; the colonial authorities with their policy of training men for practical administration, were not prepared to subsidize women's secondary education. Meanwhile, these two young women carried on consciousness raising through their public lectures to strictly female audiences composed mainly of upper-class women and at special classes for women at the new Egyptian University (which soon were stopped and the money saved was used to send three men on study missions abroad).[18]

In 1911, Bahithat Al Badiya became a pioneer in feminist activism when she sent demands to the Egyptian National Congress for women's education and rights to employment and women's rights to participate in congregational worship in mosques.[19] While they were claiming women's rights to public space, feminists like Bahithat Al Badiya and Huda Sha'rawi early in the century actually opposed the unveiling of the face that male feminists advocated. As a tactical move, they wanted women to gain more education and to reclaim public space before they unveiled. While for progressive men unveiling had a key ideological and symbolic value, for women unveiling was a practical matter that they themselves would have to undertake, with the attendant risks of taunts and assaults on their reputations.[20]

The nationalists of the *Umma* Party led by Ahmad Lutfy Al Sayyid and other men of the upper-class supported feminism while those of the *Watani* Party, mainly men of more modest middle-class origins, headed by Mustafa Kamil, were antagonistic towards women's emancipation which they saw as an undermining Western influence. Unlike the *Umma* Party, which advocated a more secular society, the *Watani* party favoured an Islamic society supporting the notion of a caliphate. It was within these respective frameworks that men as nationalists situated their views on women's place and roles and their own attitudes towards feminism.[21]

During the national revolution from 1919 to 1922, the first priority for Egyptian feminists and nationalists of both sexes was independence. To a large extent feminist and nationalist positions temporarily united in favour of the common cause. The extent and harshness of colonial oppression were underscored when upper-class women, mobilised by feminist and nationalist leaders among them, left the seclusion of their harems to demonstrate, and when poor women also filled the streets in more spontaneous protest. Members of the Wafdist Women's Central Committee (WWCC), created in 1920 as the women's section of the nationalist party, the *Wafd*, insisted on fully participating in decision-making, not just in auxiliary activities. In the midst of the revolution, these women at times took public feminist stands. In 1920 for example, when the male nationalist leadership did not consult the WWCC on the independence proposal they were circulating, the women publicly announced their objections.[22] Yet during colonial occupation a feminism that called for greater female participation in society was upheld by progressive male nationalists and generally tolerated by others. Moreover, during the ferment of revolution, male nationalists enthusiastically welcomed women's militancy.

While Islamic modernism, liberal nationalism, and the feminism of progressive men prevailed in the early modern state-building and colonial period, women's causes found a positive and supportive environment. The attacks of conservative *ulama* during this period focused on Qasim Amin's books, while the opposition to feminist ideas by nationalists like Mustafa Kamil and Talat Harb did not create the broader conservative groundswell that expressions of anti-feminism would produce later in the century. During colonial occupation, women's feminism was not connected with a public, organised, movement; it was the articulation of a broad, new philosophy. Men's pro-feminism likewise expressed a philosophical position, and at the time was seemingly more radical than women's, for example in calling for an end to face veiling. Men's feminist rhetoric, however, reached a climax during occupation. In the next stage, we find the more radical development of women's liberal feminism while men's earlier expression of liberal feminism faded for reasons that will become apparent later in our discussion.

In the late nineteenth and early twentieth century, polemics were started that have plagued feminist and Islamist positions ever since and have had political reverberations in official discourse. These concern definitions of culture, authenticity, identity, and modernity – and their implications for women's roles around which a battle of legitimacy has raged. The debate has continued right up to the final decade of the twentieth century, as have the state's efforts to control competing discourses and to appropriate elements useful to itself.

THE LIBERAL EXPERIMENT: 1923–1952

Early in this period, the feminist positions of progressive men and women which had drawn closest during colonial occupation and in the pre-independence nationalist movement started to diverge. Women had a rude awakening when it became clear that liberal men were not prepared to implement their promise to integrate women into public life after nominal political independence in 1922. Feminists became openly militant, while most men who had been pro-feminist nationalists, in the forefront of whom was Sa'd Zaghlul, grew silent as their attention turned towards their new political careers. A few others responded with concrete positive actions, such as Ahmad Lutfy Al Sayyid, whose championship of university education for women will be noted later.[23] There were moments, moreover, when feminists would be beleaguered, especially in the early 1930s during the government of Isma'il Sidki, a political and social reactionary. In the 1950s, the new more radical, socialist feminists would be harassed outright. During the same period, a rising activist, Zainab Al Ghazali, would move from feminism to Islamic fundamentalism, beginning a conservative women's religious and political movement.[24]

With formal independence (British troops remained on Egyptian soil until 1956), nationalist men become part of the new state. At first the official discourse articulated in the new Constitution of 1923 seemed to fulfill their promises to women when it declared: 'All Egyptians are equal before the law. They enjoy equally civil and political rights and equally have public responsibilities without distinction of race, language, or religion.' However, the principle of gender equality was soon cancelled when an electoral law restricted suffrage to males only. The following year women were barred from attending the opening of the new parliament, except as wives of ministers and other high state officials. The idealism of nationalist men gave way to political pragmatism in the new independent 'liberal' era.

At this point, women's feminist stance became explicit – the word 'feminist' began to be used – and their feminism became tied to an organised, political movement led by *Al Ittihad al nisa'i al misri* (the Egyptian Feminist Union, EFU) created in 1923 and headed by Huda Sha'rawi. The first unequivocal use of the term occurred in 1923 when the EFU feminists employed the term, *feministe*, in French, the everyday language of most of them. (To this day Arabic lacks a precise term for feminism).[25] From 1923, feminism crystallised around a set of demands, a broad agenda of claims for political, social, economic, and legal rights. However, initial priority was given to women's education followed by new work opportunities and the reform of the personal status law. Some demands were granted relatively easily, such as equal secondary school education for girls and raising the minimum marriage age for both sexes (achieved in 1923 and 1924 respectively). The entry of women into the state university in 1929, was achieved, not without difficulty, by the Rector himself, Ahmad Lutfy Al Sayyid, one of the few nationalists who actively strove to implement his progressive ideas. Gains in the sphere of employment were mainly achieved in those areas which were most congruent with the immediate priorities of the state, such as in education and medicine. These were fields in which women professionals typically served the needs of other women and thus their new work also perpetuated gender segregation in public space. However, greater numbers of women were also drawn into employment in the expanding textile factories, where they worked more closely with men.

During the early 1930s, when the reactionary, Isma'il Sidqi was at the head of government, feminists encountered some setbacks, such as a conservative educational policy opposing higher education for women. With the change of government in 1933, however, the more characteristic liberal atmosphere was restored. Although feminists were able to conduct public activities, there were also to be disappointments. Most importantly, no headway was made in formal political rights for women, nor in the reform of personal status law. In addition, state-legalised prostitution was not abolished.[26]

During this period religious officials and feminists shared some common social concerns. When the feminists called for the prohibition of alcohol and the ending of state-licensed prostitution, the Shaikh of Al Azhar, Muhammad Abu Al Fadl wrote to the president of the Egyptian Feminist

Union (EFU) saying: 'We appreciate the value of your honourable association and its diligent efforts to spread virtue and combat vice. There are in Egypt now distinguished women whose impact on society is no less important than that of honourable men.'[27] However, when it came to demands for political rights for women, the same Islamic authorities pronounced them to be un-Islamic, both officially through *fetwas* (religious decrees) and through unofficial utterances.[28]

Official Islam was not the only Islamist platform during this period. A conservative popular Islamic movement emerged with the creation of the Muslim Brothers (*Ikhwan Muslimin*) by Hasan Al Banna in 1928. This movement drew on a wide base of support from the modest and lower strata of the middle-class, strongly opposing the continued British military presence and economic imperialism. The Muslim Brothers, connecting Egypt's ills with a deviation from the practice of true Islam, went to the sources of their religion for fresh inspiration. They emphasised individual reform as the first step towards improving society, but their ultimate more radical goal was the creation of an Islamic state. The ideology of the Muslim Brothers, laying stress on the moral foundations of society, articulated a conservative discourse privileging the patriarchal family, male authority over women, and clear-cut differentiation of gender roles.[29]

During the militancy of the 1919 revolution and its immediate aftermath, class differences between women as feminists and nationalists were of little importance in the face of larger common causes. However, in time, differences in class and culture produced cleavages between women and raised questions of cultural authenticity. The upper-class had adopted elements of Western manners expressed in dress, in everyday life, and in the use of the French language. Indeed, the language of the EFU journal founded in 1925 was French. Because the EFU leadership was upper-class and because its feminist ideas were mainly expressed in French, feminism came to be considered, especially by detractors, as foreign. The nationalism of Egyptian men who also spoke French and wore Western dress, was not, however, denigrated in the same way.[30] The importance assigned to cultural symbols was different for the two sexes. Men could change and retain authenticity (the *tarbush* or fez, the Ottoman head-dress was even forbidden to men by the state following the 1952 revolution) while the burdens of continuity were placed on women.

The tension between feminism and cultural authenticity is well illustrated in the case of Zainab Al Ghazali. The daughter of a prosperous cotton merchant with an Al Azhar education, she joined the EFU as a young woman in 1935. Around that time, Al Azhar initiated seminars for women

at the *Kulliyya Shar'iyya* (the Islamic Law College) under the direction
of Shaikh Ma'mun Shinawi (later, Shaikh of Al Azhar) which Al Ghazali
joined. Within the year, Al Ghazali formed the Muslim Women's Society
(MWS) – Shinawi was present at its inauguration – and left the EFU. In a
recent interview Al Ghazali said, 'The Egyptian Feminist Union wanted to
establish the civilisation of the Western woman in Egypt and the rest of the
Arab and Islamic worlds.' She also remarked that when she left the feminist
organisation, Huda Sha'rawi told her 'You are separating yourself from
me intellectually,' adding, 'I ask you not to fight the Egyptian Feminist
Union.' And Al Ghazali confesses, 'I never fought it.'[31] In fact, there
was occasional co-operation between the two organisations, mainly in
nationalist activism, as Hawa Idris, the head of the EFU's youth group,
the *Shaqiqat* (established in 1935) recalled recently.[32]

The division between feminist and fundamentalist women that originated in the late 1930s was to persist, and their divergent orientations,
perceptions, beliefs and agenda would be articulated in competing
discourses. While the EFU women found their feminist ideology and
programme compatible with Islam, and sought its legitimising force,
their overall ideological framework was secular rather than religious.
For Al Ghazali and the MWS, on the other hand, since the *Shari'ah*
regulates all aspects of life, a separate ideology of feminism was at best
redundant and at worst an undermining Western ideology. Al Ghazali,
who extols the absolute equality (*musawa mutlaqa*) between women
and men in Islam, finds women's liberation within the framework
of religion.[33] Fundamentalist men and women typically speak of
complementarity rather than equality and stress male authority over
women. The EFU championed greater access for women to public roles
while the MWS lauded women's family duties and obligations.

As a secular Egyptian organisation the EFU included under its aegis
Muslims and Christians alike, while the MWS as a strictly Muslim religious
organisation did not cater to all Egyptians. The issue of 'secularism'
(*'almaniyya*) has been contentious. Fundamentalist women called Egyptian
feminism 'secular', thus implying that it was outside the bounds of Islam.
However, Egyptian Muslim women distinguished their feminism which
they based on Islamic principles from the 'secular' basis of Turkish
feminism. An article in the EFU's journal, *Al Misriyya* (The Egyptian
Woman), in 1937 said for example, that 'while the Turkish woman has
attained her freedom by virtue of foreign laws [alluding to the 1926 Turkish
Civil Code based not on the Islamic *Shari'ah* but on a Swiss model] the
Egyptian woman will never ask for her rights except by basing her requests
on the Islamic *Shari'ah*.'[34] The EFU and most other feminists

later shied away from a secularism which severed all links with religion. This would be called *"almaniyya la dini'*, literally, secularism without religion, by some of today's fundamentalists. Women's fundamentalist leadership under Al Ghazali favoured an Islamic state with a theocratic ruler, while the EFU feminists accepted the notion of a secular state whose legitimacy was grounded in the basic principles of Islam.

Around the time of the creation of the MWS, Egyptian feminist activism broadened in response to the Arab Uprising in Palestine and to calls for support from Palestinian women to Egyptian feminists. Both Arab and religious – Muslim and Christian – identities were evoked in the drive to save Palestine. The EFU hosted the Conference for the Defence of Palestine in 1938, which religious and state authorities applauded equally. It was yet another instance when militant nationalism blurred gender lines. The feminists' collective nationalist action in 1938 led to the first pan-Arab Feminist Conference in 1944. Waving the banner of Arab unity, the pan-Arab feminist conference again won the praise of governments and the Islamic establishment for their nationalist actions. While the Conference resulted in the creation of *Al Ittihad al nisa'i al 'arabi* (the Arab Feminist Union) headquartered in Cairo, it would be some time before many of the more than fifty resolutions covering virtually all aspects of women's lives would be realised. Like Egypt, other Arab states were slow to reform the personal status laws and to give women equal political rights, but they welcomed and needed women's political support. Arab regimes were not politically strong enough to change family laws significantly and in so doing challenge patriarchal authority in the family as well as threaten the last legal bastion of the religious establishment. The earliest and most drastic change in family law occurred in Tunisia in 1957 under Bourguiba, who, because of his own political power base and the particular political culture of Tunisia, was able to promote significant change and still survive. Almost two decades later, within a Marxist-Leninist framework, the People's Democratic Republic of Yemen in 1974 also instituted a more secular law.[35]

Towards the end of the 1930s and in the 1940s, feminism in Egypt broadened its outreach and new organisations proliferated. The EFU began its Arabic-language journal, *Al Misriyya*, in 1937, aiming to 'elevate the intellectual and moral level of the masses and to create lines of solidarity between the different classes of the nation.' The Arabic periodical aimed at a wider audience than *L'Egyptienne* and projected a self-consciously Islamic tone heralded in the journal's motto: 'Take half your religion from 'Aisha.' It was to be 'the *minbar* [pulpit] for feminist demands' as well as 'the tongue of the most noble nationalist hopes'. However, while EFU leaders Huda Sha'rawi and Saiza Nabarawi tried to serve the needs of a broader constituency, the rank and file of the EFU resisted opening up the organisation membership to women of humbler extraction. On two separate encounters with this author in the late 1960s and early 1970s, Duriyya Shafiq, from a middle-class family in Tanta in the Delta, contrasted Huda Sha'rawi's welcoming encouragement to her when she returned from France in 1939 with her doctorate with the grudging reception of the EFU membership.[36]

EFU resistance to broadening its constituency and the political and economic changes following World War II in Egypt encouraged a proliferation of more populist feminist organisations headed by middle-class women. Wishing to accelerate the struggle for political rights for women, former EFU members Fatma Ni'mat Rashid and Duriyya Shafiq founded respectively the *Hizb al nisa'i al-watani* (National Feminist Party, NFP) in 1944 and *Al Ittihad bint al nil* (The Daughter of the Nile Union, DNU) in 1948. Along with the advocacy of political rights for women, both the NFP and DNU mounted literacy and hygiene campaigns among the poor. They also sustained the concern with family law reform, education and work rights for women. Duriyya Shafiq, a protégée of Sha'rawi, was the more dynamic leader of the two, whose DNU was larger, longer-lived and more effective with branches throughout the country, whereas Rashid's NFP was a strictly Cairene organisation with limited outreach. Unlike their political goals, the social projects of these two feminist organisations could scarcely have antagonised the Muslim Brothers or the MWS. [37]

Despite the widening class base of the feminist movement through new organisations led by women who had come of age during the first phase of feminist activism, this new strand remained essentially within the liberal framework evolved by the EFU. It was the younger generation of women, university students and graduates of the middle 1940s, who moved in a new direction as socialists and communists. For them the liberation of women was tied to the liberation of the masses and both necessitated the end of imperialism and class oppression in Egypt. A young leader of the new socialist feminists, Inji Aflatun, a landowner's daughter, discovered Marxism at the French Lycée in Cairo. After graduating from Fuad I University (later Cairo University) in 1945, she helped found the *Rabitat fatayat al jami'a wa al ma'ahid* (the League of University and Institutes' Young Women) which Latifa Zayyat, a student leader, soon joined. The League sent Aflatun and others to the first conference of the International Democratic Federation of Women, but it was closed down the following year in the drive to suppress communists. However, the socialist feminists went on to form other associations, such as the

Jamiyya al nisa'iyya al wataniyya al mu'aqata (The Provisional National
Feminist Association). Within the mainstream communist movement there
was no room to address women's liberation, which was subordinated to
the struggle against imperialist military occupation and class oppression.
Aflatun linked class and gender oppression, connecting both to imperialist
exploitation, and at the same time was careful to argue in her books
Thamanun milyun imra'a ma'na (Eighty Million Women with Us, 1948)
and *Nahnu al nisa' al misriyyat* (We Egyptian Women, 1949) that women's
liberation was compatible with Islam.[38]

Meanwhile, not only were secular leftist groups coming under siege but
the Muslim Brothers also experienced the heavy hand of the state. In 1948,
the formal organisation of the Muslim Brothers was dissolved. At that time
Zainab Al Ghazali, who a decade earlier had resisted the overtures of the
Muslim Brothers' founder, Hasan Al Banna, to include her new MWS
under the umbrella of his organisation, immediately joined forces with the
Brothers. From then on she became, in her words, 'a soldier' in the common
struggle for the creation of an Islamic state and the MWS changed their
name to the Muslim Sisters.[39]

Not only did the MWS, now the Muslim Sisters, side with the Muslim
Brothers, but the growing nationalist determination to expel British troops
from Egypt led to coalitions among feminist and fundamentalist women.
In 1950, the *Harakat ansar al salam* (the Movement of the Friends of
Peace) brought together EFU feminist and then president, Saiza Nabarawi
(Sha'rawi had died in 1947), and the young leftist, Inji Aflatun. The same
year, Nabarawi created the *Lajna al shabbat* (the Youth Committee)
attracting women like Aflatun who went to poor quarters of Cairo
to politicise women. In 1952 when violence broke out in the Canal
Zone the *Lajna al nisa'iyya lil muqawama al sha'biyya* (the Women's
Committee for Popular Resistance) brought together women from the left
and right including the socialist feminist, Aflatun, and the fundamentalist,
Al Ghazali. Once again, women joined ranks with male nationalists in
common cause and again men welcomed their support.

In addition to various moves to clamp down on socialist feminists from
the middle 1940s, out of fear of a communist threat, governments were
not always tolerant of the political criticism of liberal feminists either.
This was clear in 1942 when Nabawiyya Musa, a staunch nationalist for
more than two decades, attacked the prime minister, Nahhas Pasha, for
accommodating British war-time needs. An order was thereupon issued
closing her schools for girls and sending her to prison where she was
thrown in with prostitutes. Musa went to the feminist lawyer, Murqus
Fahmi (whose book on women's rights was mentioned earlier) who took

up her case; he observed that the prime minister's wife had been one of her students.[40]

During this period, the religious establishment as we have noted, at times supported women's demands and at other times opposed them. While fundamentalists did not support any of the feminists' demands, neither were they overtly anti-feminist. This changed, however, on the eve of the 1952 revolution when religious scholars held a conference to examine all aspects of women's status within the context of Islamic law. They now openly attacked the feminist movement, claiming it was influenced and supported by British imperialists, and saying that 'Colonialism had encouraged women to go out in order to destroy Islamic society.'[41] The conference condemned the Egyptian feminist movement for its disruptive effects on society and held Sha'rawi and Shafiq responsible. Evaluating the past, it attacked Murqus Fahmi and Qasim Amin and praised the (anti-feminist) stance of Mustafa Kamil.

The reactionary conclusions of the conference seemed to be in part a response to the growing numbers of women in the workforce. By the early 1950s, women were found in shops, factories, the professions and the social services in sufficient numbers to alarm the patriarchal sensibilities of male fundamentalists. The conference, wishing to turn the tide or at least to stem it, scorned women's forays into public life, lamenting that women 'wished to be degraded by going out to work and being seen by everyone.'[42] The conference reiterated the reactionary refrain 'a woman's natural place is her home', insisting that 'her entry into public life is unnatural.' The nub of the problem for these men was revealed in their declaration, 'The most serious threat facing our society is the oriental woman's refusal to obey men.' Although fundamentalist men raised the alarm in March 1952, it was not until 1978 that the conference proceedings would be published under the title, *Harakat nisa'iyya wa silatuha ma' al isti'mar* (Feminist Movements and Their Connections with Colonialism, edited by Muhammad 'Atiya Khamis). This occurred six years after Sadat had come to power, by which time religious fundamentalism in Egypt had won considerable public prominence. (Khamis in another book, *Mu'amarat didd al usra al muslima*, Conspiracies against the Muslim Family, n.d., charged that unveiling was a weapon of communism). But during the period of Arab socialism under Nasser, these sentiments were not overtly expressed.

The period of the liberal experiment was a time in Egypt when a capitalist economy with ties of dependency to a dominant Europe still operated largely within a neo-imperialistic framework. The feminist or pro-feminist ideology that had served the nationalist cause during colonial occupation was no longer seen by most men to be useful or desirable during this new period of albeit incomplete independence. Thus feminists achieved limited gains. Their successes did not threaten the ruling class. In fact, these limited gains could be said to have helped construct a more viable, modern society by harnessing women to the development goals of the state. Feminist discourse was allowed public expression for the most part by the state, except in its most radical socialist form, but even this managed to survive more surreptitiously. When this period ended, women still lacked formal political rights, a symbol of their secondary status as citizens, while the stalemate on the reform of personal status laws affirmed their unequal positions within the family.

REVOLUTION, ARABISM AND SOCIALISM: 1952 TO THE EARLY 1970s

This was a time when independent feminist voices would be silenced. Radical Islamists were also suppressed, although the Islam of the establishment and the apolitical discourse of religious scholars would be tolerated. In short, it was a time when the state heavy-handedly silenced all political competitors, and did so publicly. The masses, whose liberation the state championed, included rank and file fundamentalists among those muzzled. Women, whose cause the state also claimed to support, and did so in certain ways such as granting them the vote, were likewise suppressed as independent political actors. However the feminism of the leaders who had come of age in the previous period remained alive behind the scenes, while a rising generation of future feminists was nurtured as women took advantage of new state-sponsored opportunities in education and work. In this atmosphere of repression, feminists sharpened survival skills that would be useful in the battles they would encounter in the 1970s and 1980s.

The revolution of 1952, led by young military officers of the lower middle class supported in their struggle for power by members of the same class among the Muslim Brothers, promised to usher in a new era. Soon, however, the Muslim Brothers were suppressed as dangerous to the state, and the leader of the Muslim Sisters, Zainab Al Ghazali, was imprisoned. From the early 1960s Arab socialism, with its new economic measures such as land reform and industrialisation, challenged the old class system. It was an era of hope for the majority, including the leader of the next generation of feminists, Nawal Al Saadawi, a 1955 graduate of the Medical Faculty at Cairo University, who recently recalled the early enthusiasm and optimism of her generation.[43]

The Arab socialism of the state in the 1960s called for social equality and justice for all citizens and aimed at pan-Arab unity and wider Afro-Asian solidarity. While the tone of Arab socialism was secular, it accommodated religion. The 1962 Charter delineating the Arab socialist project declared: 'The essence of religious messages does not conflict with the facts of our life . . . All religions contain a message of progress . . . The essence of all religions is to assert man's right to life and to freedom.' The Constitution of 1964 stated in Article One: 'The United Arab Republic is a democratic, socialist state based on the alliance of the working powers of the people. The Egyptian people are part of the Arab nation.' Article Five declared Islam the religion of the state. The new state suppressed Islam as a political force but did not tamper with the Muslim identity of the society.

The stifling of competing discourses did not occur instantly. Feminist organisations continued their activism after the revolution of 1952. At this juncture, they made a final push for women's political rights in which Duriyya Shafiq of the DNU led the way. In 1953, when a proposed revision of the Electoral Law was under review, she published *Al Kitab al abiyad lil huquq al mar'a al misriyya* (The White Paper on the Rights of the Egyptian Woman), a compendium of pro-suffrage arguments by sympathetic secular liberals and politicians as well as pro and con views from within the Islamic establishment. For example, a constitutional lawyer, Sayyid Sabri, argued that laws must change as the conditions and needs of society change. Since women were now part of the public opinion of society (*al ra'i al 'amm*) they should be able to participate in the formal political system. He noted that the Electoral Law contradicted the Constitution, which declared Egyptians equal in civil and political rights. However, the state and official Islam came down firmly against political rights for women. The Constitutional Affairs Committee of the Senate rejected women's suffrage and the *Fatwa* Committee of Al Azhar issued a decree saying that Islam did not condone it. The *Mufti* of Egypt, Shaikh Hasanayn Makhluf, contended that Islam opposed political rights for women. Shaikh Allam Nassar, who, it should be noted, was then a former *mufti*, however made the opposite claim. The day after the *Fatwa* Committee made its announcement, Islamic organisations held a conference in the office of the Muslim Brothers. Included in their lengthy statement was the demand that the government close once and for all 'the door to this *fitna* (literally chaos, but here referring to political rights for women), claiming it had been proven that political rights for women were contrary to religion, the Constitution, and the public interest. Meanwhile Shafiq intensified her militancy in this heated battle through a sit-in at the Parliament and a hunger strike. Finally, in 1956, thirty-three years after

EFU feminists had first demanded suffrage, the revolutionary government in its fifth year granted women the right to vote.[44]

The intentions of the state, however, were made clearer in its actions than in its official discourse. Feminist leaders tried to continue their political struggle while the state put a final stop to their public activity. In 1956, the same year that the state granted women the right to vote, it paradoxically started to ban feminist organisations and to suppress public expression of feminist views, completing its task by 1959. The Egyptian Feminist Union, under pressure from the government, purged its membership of alleged communist Saiza Nabarawi. The state dismantled the old EFU, but allowed a truncated version to continue as a social welfare society under the name of the Huda Sha'rawi Association. Meanwhile, after suffrage had been achieved, feminists formed *Al Lajna al nisa'iyya lil wa'i al intikhabi* (Women's Committee for Electoral Awareness) to make poor women aware of their rights, but the authorities closed down the committee within a year. Around the same time, a coalition of women of different political tendencies came together in *Al Ittihad al nisa'i al qawmi* (The National Feminist Union, the NFU). The authorities, however, blocked their project by withholding a permit for the NFU and finally shut it down in 1959. Aflatun was sent to prison in the same year. By then, Shafiq was under house arrest. Nabarawi and Rashid were also silenced. The clampdown on feminists occurred within the wider context of political repression. The state apparently perceived feminists as more dangerous than fundamentalists since the Muslim Sisters did not suffer the same fate until 1964, when they were banned; the following year their leader, Al Ghazali, was gaoled. The same year, new laws forbade the formation of women's political organisations.

With the official suppression of its organisations and the silencing of its spokeswomen, feminism went underground but did not disappear. In 1967 I made contact with some of the older generation feminist leaders including Saiza Nabarawi, Inji Aflatun (released from goal in 1963) and Duriyya Shafiq, and I found that feminism was still alive behind the scenes. Nabarawi kept a low profile in Egypt but was active internationally through the leftist Democratic Federation of Women. The exception to the public censoring of feminists was Amina Sa'id, a former school girl protégée of Huda Sha'rawi and a member of the EFU's youth group. Although her support for education and work for women coincided with the state's agenda to extend opportunities to all citizens across class and gender lines, and she was therefore conveniently accorded a public voice, Sa'id was not merely the regime's 'token woman', as we shall see presently.

The ideology of the new regime was set out in the 1962 Charter. The official discourse shifted from the more formal rhetoric of parliamentary democracy of the previous period to a fervent championing of the rights of the masses and socio-economic development. The grip of the old feudal class system was to be broken and the final vestiges of imperialist domination were to be eradicated. The Charter heralded Arabism expressed in language, culture, and pan-Arab political links. Now, also for the first time, the official state ideology confronted patriarchal supremacy. The Charter stated: 'Woman must be regarded as equal to man and must therefore shed the remaining shackles that impede her free movement so that she might take a constructive and profound part in shaping life.' This was situated in the context of the development needs of the country. The Constitution promulgated two years later declared in Article 8, 'The State guarantees equality of opportunity to all Egyptians.' This was translated into free university education and a guaranteed job for every graduate. State support for fuller participation of women in public life would before long, however, trigger conservative reactions.

Meanwhile, official educational and employment policies opened up new opportunities for women. Women's literacy rate increased and greater numbers of women graduated from university and entered the labour force. A corollary of this was a rise in the percentage of single women in the 1960s and 1970s and a decline in fertility. (Lower fertility rates, however, were also connected with birth control programmes which the state supported.) Because of the state's interest in increasing its scientific and technical capacities, it enforced policies to encourage greater enrollment in the applied sciences at university. Larger numbers of women were accordingly attracted to these subjects and subsequently into the professions. Nearly all women medical students graduating in the middle 1960s were reported to be practising their profession.[45] The marked increase of women with training in applied subjects and in the scientific and medical professions during this period should be noted for, as we shall discuss later, it was women university students specialising in these areas who were at the centre of the new wave of young fundamentalists in the 1970s and early 1980s.

At a time when the state had suppressed the Muslim Brothers and contained the 'dangerous' Islamist populist discourse, Muslim religious scholars were highly vocal in keeping alive a 'safer' discourse on gender issues. The National Charter calling for the removal of impediments to women's 'free movement' and state policies to grant women free university education and guaranteed jobs constituted a direct challenge to traditional gender ideology and patterns of behaviour based on male authority over women. As the 1960s and 1970s unfolded, the numbers of women university graduates continued to increase, as did their entry into various sectors of the labour force.

As often happens historically, when objective conditions change there is a burst of idealist and prescriptive literature extolling the very roles that are being altered in the process. Historian Yvonne Haddad, reviewing the publications of male conservative thinkers and *ulama* in the decade following the proclamation of the National Charter of 1962, found attempts to circumscribe the public roles of women through a reaffirmation of the doctrine of divinely sanctioned biological differences between men and women, and the renewed exaltation of wifely and maternal roles. There was also a call for different education for the two sexes corresponding to their different 'natures' and roles. Conservatives recognised that women's economic independence would reduce their need and desire to remain dependent upon men.[46]

This period also witnessed the rare entry of a woman into the domain of scholarly religious discourse. 'Aisha 'Abd Al Rahman, known as Bint Al Shati (a name purportedly taken as a pseudonym to hide her life of scholarship and writing from her *fallah*, relatives) became a professor of Islamic thought at Cairo University and a prolific writer of articles and books, including a series on the lives of the wives and female relatives of the Prophet Muhammad, held up as paragons for the modern woman. Neither feminists nor fundamentalists within their respective perspectives would consider her radical enough. But widely differing regimes through the years have considered her both safe and useful. In the words of Hasan Hanafi, a founder of the Islamic left in the late 1970s, she belongs to the *fuqaha al sultan* (the sultan's men of jurisprudence). Nasser, Sadat, and Mubarak have all decorated her.[47]

While Nasser gave Bint Al Shati space and awards, the fundamentalist, Zainab Al Ghazali was imprisoned in 1965 only to be released after Nasser's death. Her brand of Islamist discourse envisioning an Islamic state and insisting on the implementation of social justice for all, rather than just rhetoric, could not be tolerated during the Nasser period. She would only be allowed back on the scene from 1971 under the Sadat regime when competing discourses would once again surface.

We have already noted that under Nasser, Amina Sa'id was the exception to the suppression of feminists. Two years after the 1952 revolution she founded *Hawa* (Eve), a popular magazine for women, published by the large publishing complex, *Dar Al Hilal*. In 1956 she became a member of the Board of the Press Syndicate and three years later its vice-president. Sa'id wedded the message of liberal feminism to the socialist state's 'gender-neutral' agenda for the mobilisation of its citizens. She used her pen to promote women's causes within the framework of the Arab socialist revolution. Speaking to a Beirut audience in 1966 she said, '(Women) as a group form the greatest obstacle to national progress to be found in our country today', echoing the same notion differently phrased by male progressives at the end of the 19th century. While noting that recent declarations concerning sexual equality in Egypt and other progressive Arab states had provoked public hostility, she assured her Arab sisters that the Egyptian state had 'assumed responsibility for the emancipation of women.'[48] Three years after this speech the influential semi-official daily, *Al Ahram*, on 13 September 1969 recalled the paper's mention seventy-five years earlier of Murqus Fahmi's then new book, *The Woman in the East*. *Al Ahram's* reiteration of the book's argument that lack of progress in the East had been caused by women's lack of education and that women's lives must change so that the entire society might change aptly reflected the message of the new regime in Egypt.

Although her own brand of feminism coincided in large measure with the agenda of the state, Sa'id was not simply its spokesperson but a feminist who candidly criticised the failure of the state, then and later, to remedy inequities embedded in the personal status laws. She also decried women's new double burden, that accompanied their expanding economic roles, which the state did little to alleviate.[49] In fact, it was feminists with a social mission like Hawa Idris, who devoted her life to providing child-care for mothers working in the state system, and women belonging to social service societies who attempted to alleviate the double burden of poor working women.[50]

The education and work opportunities created after 1952 brought large numbers of women from middle and lower class families into the ranks of the educated and employed. However, while the new policies altered class and employment structures, gender inequalities persisted. The legacy of this partial change is apparent in the lives of two women born in the 1930s and educated at university in the 1950s, who in the 1960s and 1970s emerged as new feminist and Islamist activists.

Nawal Al Saadawi, after graduating as a medical doctor in 1955 found a mission as a practitioner among the rural poor. She was faced with physical and psychological health problems afflicting women relating to such matters as the practice of circumcision and the obsession with female virginity. The connections she made between patriarchy, class, and religion in structuring the oppression of women led her to publish *Al Mar'a wa al jins* (The Woman and Sex) in 1971, the first year of the Sadat regime. With Al Saadawi feminist discourse took a new turn: she introduced the issue of sexual oppression of women connected with everyday customs as well as the prevalence of deviant behaviours such as incest that victimised women inside the family. The feminist physician broke a cultural taboo by exposing the sexual oppression of women. The following year she lost her job. Silenced in Egypt, with her books and writings blacklisted and censored by the state, she went into self-imposed exile.[51]

Safinaz Kazim studied journalism at Cairo University graduating in 1959. From 1960 to 1966 she studied in the United States where she received an M. A. from New York University while living and working in Greenwich Village as a theatre critic. It was in the United States that Kazim began to move from the political left to the right. The problem of identity nagged her. Around the same time she was inspired by the book, *Al 'Adala al ijtima' iyya fi al islam* (Social Justice in Islam), by the Muslim Brother, Sayyid Qutb who had himself become disenchanted with the West and looked to Islam as a force of revolutionary revival. The mentor whom she never met was killed not long after her return from the United States in 1966. Six years later, after a pilgrimage to Mecca, Kazim took up Islamic dress signalling her total commitment to Islam. In the 1970s she met Zainab Al Ghazali with whom she shared the view of Islam as '*din wa dawla*' (religion and state) and the desire to see an Islamic state in Egypt.[52]

Between 1952 and the early 1970s, feminist voices with the exception of Amina Sa'id whom the state found useful and safe, were muted. However, the state also created structures and conditions within which a new feminism incubated. The conservative pronouncements of Islamist scholars and thinkers were tolerated, even though they championed women's domestic roles at the very juncture when the state was encouraging women to join the workforce. However, radical Islam which aimed at a more drastic overhaul of state and society was quashed. Yet, as we have seen, although these plural discourses were suppressed, they were by no means eradicated.

INFITAH CAPITALISM AND POPULIST ISLAMIST ASCENDANCY: THE 1970s AND 1980s

This period, which spans the rule of Sadat and the regime of Mubarak, witnessed a resurgence of competing discourses. Women's feminism became public once more while Islamic fundamentalists also found scope for new expression. In fact, the state, itself became an agent in the promotion of forms of feminist and Islamist discourse to further its own objectives. At the same time, controls were imposed on the more independent or radical expressions of these two positions.

Under Sadat there was a fundamental shift from socialism and anti-western imperialist rhetoric to *infitah* (open door) capitalism and strong pro-western rhetoric. This was accompanied by a shift from pan-Arabism to an inward focus on Egypt sealed when Sadat made a separate peace with Israel in 1979 and Egypt was expelled from the Arab League.

When Sadat came to power in 1970 the country was in a condition people wearily called 'no war, no peace' and still traumatised by the defeat of 1967 in the war with Israel. Sadat capitalised on the popular religious resurgence that followed the war and encouraged it, in part as a counterpoise to Nasser's Arab socialism with its more 'secular' cast.[53] After the war of 1973 and the acclaimed victory, there was a noticeable upsurge in the Islamic fundamentalist movement. It was popularly believed that victory had come because Muslims had returned to the correct practice of religion. The state encouraged the new emphasis on religion fuelling the spread of a fundamentalism which it subsequently needed to contain. Later, towards the end of the Sadat regime the government's own pro-Islamic positions were meant to appease fundamentalists, though it was hardly successful in containing the more radical among them.[54]

Meanwhile, the advocacy of women's causes espoused by Jihan Sadat and inspired by the UN decade of women (1975–1985) was encouraged by the state. However, the more independent and radical feminism promoted by Nawal Al Saadawi and others was contained. This has been interpreted in part as a result of Jihan Sadat's drive, and her ability as the president's wife to style herself the supreme advocate of women's causes in Egypt and so to keep competing feminists out of the limelight.[55] However, on another front, the government could not tolerate independent feminist activism because of its need to appease conservative Islamist forces.

At the beginning of the Sadat period for the first time since independence in 1922, the state promulgated a constitution spelling out a dichotomy between women as (public) citizens and as (private) family members governed by the *Shari'ah*. Thus women's right to the prerogatives of full citizenship became subject to male control. The new constitution of 1971 stated in Article 40, 'Citizens are equal before the law; they are equal in public rights and duties, with no discrimination made on the basis of race, sex, language, ideology, or belief.' The unprecedented explicit declaration of no discrimination on the basis of sex would seem at first glance to represent a step forward. However, we must note the 1971 language: 'equal in public rights and duties' as opposed to the 1923 language: 'They enjoy equally civil and political rights and equally have public responsibilities.' Moreover, the 1971 Constitution declared:

'The state guarantees a balance and accord between a women's duties towards her family on the one hand and towards her work in society and her equality with man in the political, social, and cultural spheres on the other without violating the laws of the Islamic *Shari' ah.*'[56]

Meanwhile, Islamic fundamentalism continued to gain new adherents among women evidenced by the growing numbers of women wearing the *hijab*. Islamic groups became increasingly active on university campuses spreading their word and actively recruiting. They were successful in appealing to large numbers of women, especially of the lower and more modest middle-class. Many of the new recruits were among women studying medicine and the sciences who, moreover, tended to stay out of the workforce after gruaduation.[57] At the beginning of the movement to adopt Islamic dress, a young woman, Ni'mat Sidqi, published an account of her conversion to Islamic dress and an apology for the veil in a book entitled *Al Tabarraj* ((bodily) Display) 'published in 1971' which became a cult book among young women in the early 1970s. At the same time, Amina Sa'id mounted a counter-attack on veiling in the press, mainly in her magazine, *Hawa*.[58] However, the trend persisted and by the middle 1980s veiled women from the wealthier strata of society had appeared. Among these was Keriman Hamza, the first television announcer to wear Islamic dress, who has recounted her conversion in her book *Rihlati min al sufur ilal hijab* (My Journey from Unveiling to Veiling). Veteran feminist Sa'id had been the main opponent of veiling until recently when a young leftist, Sana Al Masri, attacked the practice and its wider implications in her book, *Khalf al Hijab* (Behind the Veil, 1989).

Released from jail in 1971, the veteran fundamentalist leader, Zainab Al Ghazali, could return to discrete activism. Her prison memoirs, now in their tenth edition, have attracted new generations to her cause.[59] The year after Al Ghazali's release, Safinaz Kazim, as already mentioned, took up Islamic dress, becoming active as a 'committed Muslim' which she calls herself, rejecting the term, 'fundamentalist'. An author of several books and drama critic for the weekly magazine, *Al Musawwar*, she has assumed the role of a crusading intellectual with a special concern for issues of culture, identity, and authenticity while Al Ghazali has been active as an organiser.

Both women wish to see an Islamic state in Egypt and both have experienced state surveillance and incarceration. Kazim was imprisoned three times under Sadat: in 1973, 1975 and 1981. Each time, interestingly, she was accused of being a communist.[60] This could be motivated by a wish to discredit a fundamentalist leader and demoralise the movement without being seen to challenge Islam.

The contradictory pressures on women under Sadat were enormous. The reversal of socialist policies became clear in the 1974 proclamation of the policy of *infitah* when the door was opened to foreign investment and the private sector was encouraged once again in Egypt. The state no longer promoted full employment but, on the contrary, propagated an ideology that curtailed women's public roles encouraging a retreat into the home. This was attempted in different ways, many of them illegal. Lawyers and other women prominent in public life exposed this in their recent booklet, *Al Huquq al qanuniyya lil mar' a al 'arabiyya bain al nadhariyyat wa al tatbiq* (The Legal Rights of the Egyptian Woman: Theory and Practice, 1988) writing, 'We have observed a retreat from the principle of equality regarding the woman at work . . . This has become clear in certain practices that are contrary to the Constitution and Egyptian law such as advertising in the newspapers for jobs specifying that applicants must be males.'[61] Meanwhile, rising inflation and the out-migration of men to neighbouring oil rich countries, leaving women behind to cope, have pushed more women into the workforce.[62] In fact, the spread of the veil has been connected in part with women's need to work and their wish at the same time to protect themselves from exposure to male harassment. This security however is sought at the price of engaging in passive rather than active resistance to male intimidation.[63] On a different front, in yet another of its contradictory moves, in 1979 the government unexpectedly enacted a law guaranteeing women thirty seats in parliament which led to an immediate increase of women in the legislature.[64]

However, the most dramatic and politically sensitive move was the presidential decree making fundamental changes in the personal status laws for the first time in fifty years. Excesses of patriarchal privilege were curtailed in an unprecedented manner with the expansion of women's ability to initiate divorce, added protection for women in divorce, and with controls placed on polygyny. The president's wife had pushed hard for the 1979 decree, issued when parliament was in recess which, indeed, became known as 'Jihan's law'. Many men, not only fundamentalists, were outraged, but for feminists the gains constituted an important, if still inadequate, step forward.[65]

The year 1979 was highly charged for Egypt abroad as well as at home. Egypt ratified the Camp David accord with Israel isolating itself from the Arab world and antagonising both leftists and conservatives at home. The decrees favourable to women within the family and in parliament provoked Muslim conservatives. Meanwhile, the revolution in Iran brought Khomeini to power ushering in a new Islamic state which heartened fundamentalists in Egypt. As Islamist forces gathered momentum, the Egyptian state made an important placatory move in 1980 when it amended the Constitution to read: 'Islamic jurisprudence is *the* principal source of legislation.' replacing the 1971 formulation that 'the *Shari'ah* is a principal source of law'.[66]

Egypt was in a period of new and dangerous tensions which the state could not control. In the fall of 1981, massive arrests were made of women and men across the political spectrum including feminists and fundamentalists among whom were Nawal al Saadawi and Safinaz Kazim.[67] Not long after these arrests, Sadat was assassinated by a Muslim fundamentalist and the two women were released along with others by the new president, Mubarak.

The early 1980s witnessed the renewed visibility and organisation of independent feminism. Al Saadawi, who had by then gained both a local following and international repute, was active in feminist organising and politics. There was a significant number of highly educated women espousing feminism practising law and medicine, teaching in university, working in business, and active as writers and journalists. A number of these women, under the leadership of Al Saadawi struggled to establish the Arab Women's Solidarity Association (AWSA). In AWSA's own words: 'We knew that the liberation of the people as a whole could not take place without the liberation of women and this could not take place without the liberation of the land, economy, culture, and information.'[68] The process of institutionalisation was not easy. The Ministry of Social Affairs refused a permit to the feminist organisation in 1983. It relented, however, at the beginning of 1985 and AWSA registered the same year as a non-governmental organisation with the United Nations.

In 1985 in the face of growing opposition to the 1979 decree law revising the Personal Status Law, the government cancelled it.[69] This galvanised feminists into collective political action. Finally, within two months a new law was passed restoring most, but not all, of the benefits to women provided by the 1979 law. This occurred just before a large delegation of Egyptian feminists went to the United Nations Forum in Nairobi marking the end of the Decade for Women. It would have been impolitic for the Egyptian delegation to attend with such a major grievance.

There was marked concern among feminists at the growing conservatism in Egypt evidenced in efforts we have already mentioned to curtail women's public roles and push them back into the home. In 1986, AWSA held its first conference. Under the banner of 'unveiling the mind', its theme was Challenges Facing the Arab Woman at the End of the 20th Century. The proceedings issued by the Associations's own publishing house declared: 'It has become clear that the traditional stance towards women and their rights undercuts progress in Arab societies. The present situation demands a deeper, more modern look at women's roles in society as well as in the family.'[70]

Meanwhile, the authors of *The Legal Rights of the Egyptian Woman* mentioned above, pooled their practical talents to advance the cause of women, reminding them of their constitutional and legal rights as well as their rights under international treaties and conventions ratified by the Egyptian state. They published an open letter warning against the retrograde trends threatening to curtail women's rights and calling for the establishment of a women's platform to counteract these trends articulated in mass publications.[71]

The proliferating popular conservative Islamist literature of the 1980s echoed writings from the 1960s. According to the Egyptian historian, Huda Lutfy, since the early 1980s an increasing number of Egyptian publishing houses have specialised in cheap editions of popular religious tracts. These tracts extol the domestic roles of women, held up as the cornerstones of a new virtuous society, and stress the need for male authority over women to guide them along the correct path.[72]

An important author of popular books with wide appeal is Shaikh Muhammad Mitwalli Al Sha'rawi, a former minister of *Awqaf* (Religious Endowments), who has spoken to Muslims since the 1970s through state television, which accords him prime time. In the quietist tradition he praises the virtues of obedience and patience for men and women alike while he preaches specifically to women about their family and domestic duties. In a reactionary vein, Sha'rawi has called the woman who works while she has a father, brother, or husband to support her, a sinful woman.[73] Shaikh Sha'rawi's tone supports the official line. In addition to enjoying continued television time, he received a state decoration in March 1988.

There is a different emphasis in the discourse of fundamentalist women leaders, Al Ghazali and Kazim who both play active public roles. Kazim finds no contradiction between women's public and private lives. Al Ghazali left a husband because he interfered in her Islamic activism. She told this writer, 'Woman companions (of the Prophet) have given as much to Islam as men, even more. The woman companion sacrificed herself, her husband, and her children while the male companion sacrificed (only) himself.' Yet, although Al Ghazali has carved out a public role for herself and has attracted working women to her cause, she continues to commend women's primary roles as wives and mothers.[74] In 1979, in an article in *Al Dawa*, Al Ghazali blamed feminists for encouraging women's public roles despite the dangers that await them in the public arena.[75] Fundementalist intellectual and professor of English at Cairo University,

Muhammad Yahia, in a recent interview said, 'The Islamic movement is seen as marginalising women but the Islamic movement, itself, sees attracting women to the movement (as public activists) to be its problem.'[76] It seems that the mixed messages delivered by the movement contribute towards keeping women out of the public struggle.

Meanwhile, towards the end of the 1970s, there appeared what might be called a neo-Islamic modernism articulated by Al Ghazali Harb, a graduate of the languages section at Al Azhar and a former journalist, in his book, *Istiqlal al mara' a fi al Islam* (Independence of the Woman in Islam). Harb, like 'Abudh a century before him, called for a return to the sources of religion for a correct understanding of Islam.[77] Saying that women should consider themselves equal to men, he extolled women's work roles not only to meet economic needs but as a guarantee of their independence. In this he attacked patriarchal supremacy in the family and opposed the expulsion of women from public space. Harb took on the fundamentalists when he declared that there is no such thing as Islamic dress saying that Islam does not require *hijab* whether veiling the face, or simply the head and body. He asserted that only a correct upbringing can protect women, not veiling. Harb was sternly criticised for these views by Muhammad Yahia who saw the ideas of Harb (who he noted was far from the calibre and stature of 'Abduh) as useful to the state as a counterpoise to fundamentalism.[78] A few feminists have welcomed this position on women's liberation, argued in Islamic terms, because it suits them personally, while others simply acknowledged its wider political utility.

The state, trying to contain the spreading Islamic fundamentalist challenge, however, tries not to antagonize fundamentalist forces alternating between tough and conciliatory attitudes with the result that it generally displays a conservative stance regarding gender issues. It also favours more moderate conservative Islamicists such as Bint Al Shati who advocate an Islamic society, but not an Islamic state. The government bestowed a decoration on Bint Al Shati in 1988. However, women like Zainab Al Ghazali and Safinaz Kazim who call for an Islamic state and Nawal Al Saadawi who advocates an end to patriarchal and class oppression make the state very wary.

CONCLUSION

The 'woman question' around which competing discourses have flourished in Egypt has been, as we have seen, about more than women. It has been about gender relations and sexual hegemony, and broader issues of power.

It has been a question through which the state, the religious establishment and Islamic movements have projected other designs. Women themselves, helped to formulate the question on their own terms both as feminists and as actors in Islamist movements. While as feminists they generated their own terms of debate and as Islamists they mainly reproduced male discourses, as actors in everyday life both assumed new roles, and in so doing gave further definition to the question. While there has always been room in Egypt for alternative positions on the 'woman question', - with the state, Islamists, and feminists all keeping it alive, - only feminists, for whom the 'woman question' is central, have meaningfully attacked patriarchal interests and opposed male supremacy.

The state has through different phases generated contradictory discourses and policies. It characteristically imposed its own agenda and in so doing attempted to define the 'woman question' to suit its own political ends. Thus we have seen that while the state has promoted new roles for women for pragmatic and ideological purposes, it has also upheld imbalanced gender relations and male authority out of political expediency. In the state-building, liberal, socialist, and *infitah* capitalist periods, there have been shifts in rhetoric and emphasis. But while the terms of discourse shift a substratum of basic gender inequality is retained which does not ultimately challenge patriarchal relations nor the state's own power bases. Because of the state's own ambiguities, official discourses on the 'woman question' have often been discourses of deception.

Islam, in modern Egypt, has been controlled by the state. The Islamic establishment has had to negotiate with and accommodate to the secular state. The last bastion of official Islam has been the regulation of family life. This is precisely the area where the state has allowed patriarchal control over women a free hand and where gender relations have been most unequal. Populist, fundamentalist Islam confronted the state but upheld conservative codes of gender relations and endorsed male supremacy. Uncompromisingly radical vis à vis the state, it has elicited a defensive reaction from the state taking the form of a show of 'Islamic toughness' in the area of gender relations, most notably demonstrated in conservative family laws. Women Islamists, normally excluded from the Islamic establishment, have joined the ranks of more radical, populist fundamentalist movements. Their leaders have taken on daring social and political roles while acquiescing in an ideology that contradicts their own conduct as activists.

Secular feminists have created the only discourse that insists upon radical changes in gender relations. Feminists have held their own despite repression by the state and feminist ideology in Egypt has always managed to survive. In more liberal political climates, feminism can be absorbed in what appears to be a more supportive environment as we have seen in the period of struggle for national independence. In more hostile contexts, when the agenda of the state and Islamists promote extreme conservatism such as that of contemporary Egypt, feminism emerges as an oppositional discourse.

This chapter on competing agenda on the 'woman question' in Egypt has attempted to give a sense of the complex choreography of these discourses, how space is given and taken, and how for all but feminists the 'woman question' in the end is a matter of political expediency.

NOTES

For their comments and suggestions regarding this paper I would like to thank Deniz Kandiyoti, the editor of this volume, Yesim Arat, John Esposito, Sarah Graham-Brown, Enid Hill, and Albert Hourani.

1. For general definitions of feminism (women's rights, women's emancipation, women's liberation) see Karen Offen, 'Defining Feminism: A Comparative Historical Approach', *Signs* (Autumn 1988) no. 14, pp. 119–47 and Gerda Lerner, *The Creation of Patriarchy* (Oxford: Oxford University Press, 1986), appendix. For definitions of feminism in the Egyptian historical context see Margot Badran, 'The Origins of Feminism in Egypt', in Arina Angerman *et al.* (eds), *Current Issues in Women's History*, (London: Routledge, 1989). In this chapter the various meanings of feminism should be gleaned from context and Margot Badran, 'Independent Women: Over a Century of Feminism in Egypt', *Old Boundaries, New Frontiers*, forthcoming; Margot Badran, 'Dual Liberation: Feminism and Nationalism in Egypt, 1970s–1985', *Feminist Issues* (Spring 1988).
2. See Margot Badran, 'Huda Sha'rawi and the Liberation of the Egyptian Woman', Oxford D. Phil thesis, 1977 and 'The Origins of Feminism in Egypt', and Judith Tucker, *Women in Nineteenth Century Egypt* (Cambridge: Cambridge University Press, 1985).
3. On this dichotomy see Nawal El Saadawi, 'The Political Challenges Facing Arab Women at the End of the 20th Century', pp. 8–26 and Fatima Mernissi, 'Democracy as Moral Disintegration: The Contradiction between Religious Belief and Citizenship as a Manifestation of the Ahistoricity of the Arab Identity', pp. 36–43 in Nahid Toubia (ed.), *Women of the Arab World* (London: Zed, 1988).

4. See Margot Badran and Miriam Cooke (eds), *Opening the Gates: A Century of Arab Feminist Writing* (London: Virago and Bloomington & Indianapolis: University of Indiana Press, 1990).

5. Badran, 'Over a Century of Feminism in Egypt', pp. 15–34.

6. See Deniz Kandiyoti, 'End of Empire: Islam, Nationalism and Women in Turkey', and Afsaneh Najmabadi, 'Hazards of Modernity and Morality: Women, State and Ideology in Contemporary Iran', in this volume and Margot Badran and Eliz Sanasarian, 'Feminist Goals in Iran and Egypt in the 1920s and 1930s', paper presented at the Middle East Studies Association Meetings, San Francisco, 1984.

7. See Laverne Kuhnke, 'The "Doctoress" on a Donkey: Women Health Officers in Nineteenth Century Egypt', *Clio Medica*, 9 (1974) no. 3, pp. 193–205.

8. The books are respectively: *Tariq al hija wa al tamrin 'ala qawa'id al lugha al 'arabiyya* (The Way to Spell and Practise the Rules of the Arabic Language), 1869, and *Al Murshid al amin lil banat wa al banin* (The Faithful Guide for Girls and Boys), 1875.

9. See, for example, selections by Warda al Yaziji, Aisha Taimuriyya, and Zainab Fawwaz in Badran and Cooke, *Opening the Gates*.

10. On the *hijab* in nineteenth-century Egypt see Qasim Amin, *Tahrir al mar'a* (The Liberation of the Woman) (Cairo, 1899). Bahithat Badiya has written on the changing modes of *hijab* in early twentieth century Egypt. She generally favoured retaining the face veil for the time being for pragmatic reasons, but was aware this was not required by Islam. On the subject see, for example, her 'Mabadi Al Nis'ai', in Majd al Din Hifni Nasif (ed.), *Ta'thir Bahithat al Badiya Malak Hifni Nasif 1886–1918* (The Heritage of Bahithat al Badiya Malak Hifni Nasif) (Cairo, 1962) pp. 318–20. On the historical and contemporary context of *hijab*, see Valerie J. Hoffman-Ladd, 'Polemics on the Modesty and Segregation of Women in Contemporary Egypt', *International Journal of Middle East Studies*, 19 (1978) pp. 23–50. For various interpretations in general of *hijab* see Mostafa Hashem Sherif, 'What is Hijab?' *The Muslim World* (July–October 1978, nos. 3–4, pp. 151–63.

11. Zainab Al Fawwaz, 'Fair and Equal Treatment', *Al Nil* no. 151 (18, dhu al hujja, 1892) trans. Marilyn Booth, in Badran and Cooke, *Opening the Gates*.

12. The early years of the women's Arabic press in Egypt are the subject of a dissertation by Beth Baron presented to the University of California at Los Angeles in 1988.

13. See Albert Hourani, *Arabic Thought in the Liberal Age* (Cambridge: Cambridge University Press, 1983) pp. 130–63.

14. See 'Abd Al Razek, 'L'Influence de la femme dans la vie de Chiekh Mohamed Abdue', *L'Egyptienne* (August 1928) pp. 2–7. Abudh's writings include: 'Hajjat Al Insan lil Zawaj', 'Fatwa fi Ta'adud Al Zaujat', and 'Hukum Ta'adud Al Zaujat', in Muhammad 'Imara, *Al 'amal al kamila li Muhammad 'Abduh* (The Complete Works of Muhammad

'Abduh) (Cairo, c. 1971), pp. 49–54, 111–18, and 127–35.

15. See Juan Ricardo Cole, 'Feminism, Class, and Islam in Turn-of-the-Century Egypt', *International Journal of Middle East Studies*, 13 (1981) pp. 397–407 and Thomas Philipp, 'Feminism and Nationalist Politics in Egypt' in L. Beck and N. Keddie (eds), *Women in the Muslim World* (Cambridge, Mass.: Harvard University Press, 1978).
16. On Qasim Amin see Hourani, *Arabic Thought*, pp. 164–70.
17. On women's feminist discourse from the 1860s to the present see Badran and Cooke, *Opening the Gates*.
18. On the public lectures see *Huda Shaarawi, Harem Years: The Memoirs of an Egyptian Feminist* (London: Virago, 1986) pp. 92–3. Writings and speeches of Bahithat Al Badiya and Nabawiyya Musa are found, among other places, in their respective books: *Al Nisa'iyyat* (trans. as either Women's or Feminist Pieces) (Cairo: Al Jarida Press, 1910) and *Al Mar'a wa al 'amal* (Woman and Work) (Cairo: 1920). Donald Reid communicated to me the information related here concerning the closing of the women's section and the new use of the funds saved.
19. See Majd Al Din Hifni Nasif, *Ta'thir*.
20. See Margot Badran, 'From Consciousness to Activism: Feminist politics in Early 20th Century Egypt', unpublished paper.
21. See Philipp, 'Feminism and Nationalist Politics in Egypt', and Cole, 'Feminism, Class, and Islam in Turn-of-the-Century Egypt'.
22. Badran, 'Dual Liberation'.
23. Progressive men including Lutfy Al Sayyid, for example, acted as advisers to the Egyptian Feminist Union in their various professional capacities.
24. Fundamentalist, like feminist, is a term that needs to be understood in historical context but broadly it signifies the person who returns to the fundamentals of Islam, especially the Quran and *Hadith*, and is associated with a conservative reading of Islam. Many persons generally referred to as fundamentalists reject the term, preferring to call themselves committed Muslims. In this chapter I use the term 'fundamentalist' in a broad way, aware of the inherent difficulties, hoping the contexts in which it appears add clarification.
25. In a paper published in Arabic, 'Nisa'iyya ka quwa fi al 'alam al 'arabi' (Feminism as a Force in the Arab World), in *Al Fikra al 'arabi al mu'asir wa al mar'a* (Contemporary Arab Thought and the Woman) (Cairo: Arab Women's Solidarity Press, 1989), pp. 75–90, I deliberately used *nisa'iyya* in the title to signify feminism, although this is not normal usage.
26. See Badran, 'Huda Sha'rawi and the Liberation of the Egyptian Woman', pp. 299–308.
27. *Mudhakirrat ra'ida al 'arabiyya al haditha Huda Sha'rawi* (Memoirs of the Modern Arab Pioneer Huda Sha'rawi) (Cairo: Dar Al Hilal, 1981).
28. See Duriyya Shafiq, *Al kitab al abiyad lil huquq almar'a al misriyya* (The White Paper on the Rights of the Egyptian Woman) (Cairo, 1953).

29. The most complete study of the Muslim Brothers remains Richard Mitchell, *The Society of the Muslim Brothers* (London: Oxford University Press, 1969).
30. On language, feminism, and cultural authenticity see Irene Fenoglio-Abd El Aal, *Défense et illustration de l'Egyptienne: aux débuts d'une expression feminine* (Cairo: CEDEJ, 1989).
31. Interview with Al Ghazali, Cairo, February 1989. On Zainab Al Ghazali see Valerie J. Hoffman, 'An Islamic Activist: Zaynab al-Ghazali', in E. Fernea (ed.), *Women and the Family in the Middle East: New Voices of Change* (Austin: University of Texas Press, 1985).
32. Interview with Hawa Idris, Cairo, April 1988.
33. Interview with Al Ghazali, Cairo, February 1989.
34. Fatma Ni'mat Rashid, 'Muqarana bain al mar'a al Misriyya wa al mar'a al Turkiyya', *Al Misriyya* (1 May 1937) pp. 10–13.
35. See Norma Salem, 'Islam and the Status of Women in Tunisia' in Freida Hussain (ed.), *Muslim Women* (London: Croom Helm, 1984), pp. 141–68; John Esposito, *Women in Muslim Family Law* (Syracuse: Syracuse University Press, 1982), p. 92; and Maxine Molyneux, 'The Law, the State and Socialist Policies with regard to Women: the Case of the People's Democratic Republic of Yemen', in this volume.
36. Interviews with Duriyya Shafiq in Cairo in 1968 and 1974.
37. See Badran, 'Huda Sha'rawi and the Liberation of the Egyptian Woman', and 'Independent Women: A Century of Feminism in Egypt', and Akram Khater and Cynthia Nelson, 'Al-Harakah Al-Nissa'iyah: The Women's Movement and Political Participation in Modern Egypt', *Women's Studies International Forum*, II (1988) no. 5, pp. 465–83.
38. Interviews with Saiza Nabarawi in 1968 and 1973 and with Inji Aflatun, 1975. On socialist feminism see Khater and Nelson, 'Al-Harakah Al-Nissa'iyya', pp. 473–77; Michelle Raccagni, 'Inji Efflatoun, Author, Artist and Militant: A Brief Analysis of Her Life and Works' unpub. paper, n.d.; Selma Botman, 'The Experience of Women in the Egyptian Communist Movement, 1939–1954', *Women's Studies International Forum*, 2 (1988) 2 pp. 117–26; Guiseppe Contu, 'Le donne communiste e il movimento democratico feminile in Egitto al 1965', *Oriente Moderno* (May–June 1975) pp. 236–48.
39. Interview with Zainab Al Ghazali, Cairo, February 1989.
40. Information on the legal case came from Andree Fahmy, the daughter of Murqus Fahmi, and from papers relating to the case in her possession. See also Safinaz Kazim, 'Al Ra'ida Nabawiyya Musa wa In'ash ddhakkira al 'umma', *Majallat al hilal* (January 1984). (*The Pioneer Nabawiyya Musa and the Reviving of the Nation's Memory*).
41. Muhammad 'Atiya Khamis (ed.), *Al harakat al nisa'iyya wa silatuha ma'al ist'mar* (Feminist Movements and Their Relations with Imperialism) (Cairo: Dar Al Ansar, 1978).
42. This and the following quotations in this paragraph from Khamis, ibid.
43. Interview with Nawal Al Saadawi, Cairo, February 1989.

44. Shafiq, *The White Paper*.
45. Kathleen Howard-Merriam, 'Woman, Education, and the Professions in Egypt', *Comparative Education Review*, 23 (1979) no. 2, pp. 256–71.
46. Yvonne Haddad, 'The Case of the Feminist Movement', chap. 5 in *Contemporary Islam and the Challenge of History* (Albany: State University of New York Press, 1982) pp. 54–70 and 'Traditional Affirmations Concerning the Role of Women as Found in Contemporary Arab Islamic Literature', in Jane Smith (ed.), *Women in Contemporary Muslim Societies* (Lewisburgh, Pa., 1980). For a broader look at Islamicist discourse see her 'Islam, Women and Revolution in Twentieth Century Arab Thought', *The Muslim World*, 124 (July–October 1984) nos. 3–4, pp. 137–60.
47. Bint Al Shati' wrote two autobiographies: *Sirr al Shati* (Biography of Al Shati) (Cairo: 1952) and *'Ala jisr: ustur al zaman* (On a Bridge: A Myth of Time) (Cairo, 1967). See also C. Kooij, 'Bint Al-Shati': A Suitable Case for Biography?' in Ibrahim A. El-Sheikh, C. Aart van de Koppel and Rudolf Peters (eds), *The Challenge of the Middle East: Middle East Studies at the University of Amsterdam* (Amsterdam: Institute for Modern Near Eastern Studies, University of Amsterdam, 1982). Hasan Hanafi's epithet was taken from Valerie Hoffman Ladd, 'Polemics'.
48. 'Amina Said' in E. Fernea and B. Bezirgan, *Middle East Muslim Women Speak* (Austin: University of Texas Press, 1978).
49. On the double burden see Mona Hammam, 'Women and Industrial Work in Egypt: The Chubra El-Kheima Case', *Arab Studies Quarterly* 2 (1980) pp. 50–69.
50. Interviews with Hawa Idris, 1968 and 1972.
51. Interview with Nawal Al Saadawi, Cairo, February 1989.
52. Interview with Safinaz Kazim, Cairo, February 1989.
53. Interview in Cairo, January 1989 with Sa'id Ashmawi, Judge in the High Court of Cairo, the High Court for State Security, and the High Court of Assize, and author of *Al Shariah al islamiyya* (Islamic Law) (Cairo, 1980) and *Islam al siyasi* (Political Islam) (Cairo, 1988) who spoke of Sadat's stress on Islam as a means to distance his regime from Nasser's.
54. General analyses of what is called the Islamic resurgence include: Hamied N. Ansari, 'The Islamic Militants in Egyptian Politics', *International Journal of Middle East Studies* 16 (1984) 1 pp. 123–44 Said Arjomand (ed.), *From Nationalism to Revolutionary Islam* (Albany: State University of New York, 1984); Alexander Cudsi and Ali Dessouki (eds), *Islam and Power in the Contemporary Arab World* esp. Ali Dessouki, 'The Resurgence of Islamic Organizations in Egypt: An Interpretation,' pp. 107–19; R. H. Dekmejian, *Islam in Revolution, Fundamentalism in the Arab World* (Syracuse: Syracuse University Press, 1985); Ali Dessouki (ed.), *Islamic Resurgence in the Arab World* (New York: Praeger, 1982), esp. Saad Eddin Ibrahim, 'Islamic Militancy as a Social Movement: The Case of Two Groups in Egypt'; John Esposito (ed.), *Voices of Resurgent Islam* (Oxford: Oxford University Press,

1983); Nazith Ayubi, 'The Political Revival of Islam: The Case of Egypt', *International Journal of Middle East Studies* (December 1981) pp. 81–99; Fadwa El Guindi, 'The Emerging Islamic Order: the Case of Egypt's Contemporary Movement', *Journal of Arab Affairs*, 1 (1981) pp. 245–61; Yvonne Haddad, *Contemporary Islam and the Challenge of History* (Albany: State University of New York Press, 1982); Hassan Hanafi, 'The Relevance of the Islamic Alternative in Egypt', *Arab Studies Quarterly*, 4 (1982) pp. 54–74; Saad Eddin Ibrahim, 'Anatomy of Egypt's Militant Islamic Groups', *International Journal of Middle East Studies*, 12 (1980) pp. 481–99; Gabriel Warburg and Uri Kupferschmidt (eds), *Islam, Nationalism and Radicalism in Egypt and the Sudan* (New York: Praeger 1983); and Fouad Zakaria, 'The Standpoint of Contemporary Muslim Fundamentalists' in Toubia, *Women of the Arab World*.

55. Nawal Al Saadawi mentioned this in her February 1989 interview. The need of Jihan Sadat to be the supreme woman – not just feminist – was mentioned by Safinaz Kazim in an interview in Cairo in February 1989.

56. On the 1971 Constitution and gender see Nawal Al Saadawi, 'The Political Challenges Facing Arab Women'.

57. The literature on women's turn to fundamentalism and veiling includes: Fadwa El Guindi, 'Veiling *Infitah* with Muslim Ethic: Egypt's Contemporary Islamic Movement', *Social Problems*, 28 (1981) no. 4, pp. 465–85; Fatima Mernissi, 'Women and Fundamentalism', *Middle East Reports* (July–August 1988) pp. 8–11; Zainab Radwan, *Bahth zahirath al hijab bain al jam'iyyat* (A Study of the Phenomenon of the Veil among University Women) (Cairo: National Centre for Sociological and Criminological Research, 1982) and John Alden Williams, 'A Return to the Veil in Egypt', *Middle East Review*, 11 (1979) no. 3, pp. 49–54.

58. See Amina Sa'id, 'Hadhihi ithahira ma ma'naha' (This Phenomenon, What Does it Mean), *Hawa* (18 November, 1972); ''Awda illi hadith al ziyy hadhihi al dajja al mufta'ana ma ma'naha?' (Back to the Issue of Dress, This Show of Fuss . . . What Does it Mean?), *Hawa* (2 December, 1972); and ''Id al sufur 'id al nahada' (Feast of Unveiling, Feast of Renaissance), *Hawa* (24 March, 1973). In the latter article, written to commemorate the fiftieth anniversary of the founding of the EFU and the public unveiling of Huda Sha'rawi and Saiza Nabarawi, she attacks the current return to the veil which is 'the greatest enemy of civilization'.

59. Zainab Al Ghazali, *Ayyam min hayati* (Days of My Life) (Cairo: Dar Al Shuruq, 8th printing 1986).

60. Interview with Safinaz Kazim, Cairo, February 1989.

61. A Group of Women Concerned with Affairs Relating to the Egyptian (Aziza Husain, Inji Rushdi, Saniyya Salih, Awatif Wali, Mervat Ittalawi, Muna Zulficar, Magda Al Mufti), *Al Huquq al qanuniyya lil mar'a al 'arabiyya bain al nadthariyya wa al tatbiq* (The Legal Rights of the Egyptian Woman: Theory and Practice) (Cairo: 1988).

62. On elite women in the work force early 1980s see Earl Sullivan, *Women*

in Egyptian Public Life (Syracuse: Syracuse University Press, 1986) and
for a general survey see Ann Mosely Lesch and Earl Sullivan, 'Women
in Egypt: New Roles and Realities', *USFI Reports*, 22, Africa (1986).

63. See El Guindi, 'Veiling *Infitah*', and Williams, 'A Return to the Veil'.
64. For an analysis of this see Kathleen Howard Merriam, "Affirmative
    Action" for Political Representation of Women: the Egyptian Example',
    Women and Politics, forthcoming. See also Sullivan, *Women in Egyptian
    Public Life*, on women in parliament.
65. See Aziza Hussein, 'Recent Amendments to Egypt's Personal Status
    Law', in E. Fernea (ed.), *Women and the Family in the Middle East*,
    (Austin: University of Texas Press, 1985) pp. 231–2 and Kathleen
    Howard Merriam, 'Egyptian Islamic Fundamentalism and the Law:
    Connecting the "Private" and the "Public", *International Journal of
    Islamic and Arab Studies*, forthcoming.
66. For more on this see Enid Hill, *Al-Sanhuri and Islamic Law* Cairo Papers
    in Social Science 10, monograph 1 (spring 1987) pp. 125–29.
67. For an account of her experience in prison see Nawal Al Saadawi,
    Mudhakkirati fi sijn al nisa (Cairo: Dar al mustaqbal al 'arabi, 1985)
    trans. by Marilyn Booth, *Memoirs from the Women's Prison* (London:
    The Women's Press, 1986); and for her reflections inspired by prison
    see Safinaz Kazim, *'An al sijn wa al hurriyya* (On Prison and Freedom)
    (Cairo: Al Zahra' lil A'lam Al 'Arabi, 1986). On women's prison experi-
    ence and writings see Marilyn Booth, 'Prison, Gender, Praxis: Women's
    Prison Memoirs in Egypt and Elsewhere', *MERIP* (November–December
    1987) pp. 35–41.
68. 'Challenges Facing the Arab Woman', in Badran and Cooke, *Opening
    the Gates*.
69. See Nadia Hijab, *Womanpower: The Arab Debate on Women at Work*
    (Cambridge: Cambridge University Press, 1988) pp. 29–35; Howard
    Merriam, 'Egyptian Islamic Fundamentalism and the Law', and Sarah
    Graham-Brown, 'After Jihan's Law: A New Battle Over Women's
    Rights', *The Middle East* (June 1985) pp. 17–20.
70. 'Challenges Facing the Arab Woman', in Badran and Cooke, *Opening
    the Gates*.
71. *The Legal Rights of the Egyptian Woman*, pp. 5–6.
72. On this phenomenon see 'A Study of Muslim Popular Literature on the
    Role of Women in Contemporary Egyptian Society', presented at the
    Conference of the Middle East Studies Group, London, 1988 by Huda
    Lutfy, who has studied the recent literature, and Valerie Hoffman-Ladd,
    'Polemics', for an analysis of the historical up to early 1980s debate on
    women in Islamicist literature, and the work by Yvonne Haddad cited in
    note 46.
73. See Mahmud Saif Al Nasr, 'Shaikh Sha'rawi wa imra'a al Khati'a'
    (Shaikh Sha'rawi and the Sinful Woman), *Al Ahali* (3 July 1985) 8.
    A popular book written by Sha'rawi is *Al Mar'a kama araduha allah*
    (The Woman as God Wanted Her to Be) (Cairo: Maktabat Al Quran,

1980). On Sha'rawi see Barbara Freyer Stowasser, *The Islamic Impulse* (London: Croom Helm, 1987).

74. Interview with Zainab Al Ghazali, Cairo, February 1989.
75. Zainab Al Ghazali, 'Al Jamiyyat al nisa'iyya' (Feminist Organisations . . .) *Al Dawa* (November 1979) no. 42.
76. Interview with Muhammad Yahia, Cairo, March 1989.
77. Al Ghazali Harb, *Istiqlal al mar'a fi al islam* (Cairo: Dar Al Mustaqbal Al 'Arab, n.d.). This book includes articles the author published in the Cairo daily, *Al Akhbar*, in the late 1970s.
78. Interview with Muhammad Yahia, Cairo, March 1989.

9 The Law, the State and Socialist Policies with Regard to Women; the Case of the People's Democratic Republic of Yemen 1967–1990

Maxine Molyneux

No discussion of state policies towards Islam and women would be complete without consideration of how attempts at socialist transformation have affected Muslim Societies.[1] While the great majority of the world's Muslims have lived under regimes opposed to socialism, there have been a significant number of cases in which revolutionary socialist states have ruled over Muslim populations. This has been true for the sizeable Muslim minorities in the USSR and China, and for two third-world states committed in the 1980s to a form of revolutionary change, officially termed 'socialist orientation', Afghanistan and the PDRY, where the populations were almost entirely Muslim. Between 35 per cent and 40 per cent of the population of what was one of the most important other 'socialist oriented' states, namely Ethiopia, was also Muslim. This commitment to revolutionary change turned out to be temporary: by 1990 all three 'socialist-oriented' states – Afghanistan, the PDRY, and Ethiopia – had abandoned their earlier policies. Their records of social transformation nonetheless merit informed analysis, if only because of the impact these policies had. Whatever the eventual fate of socialism and 'socialist orientation' it would appear that in the 1980s at least, between 10 per cent and 20 per cent of the world's Muslims lived under socialist or 'socialist-oriented' regimes.

The purely numerical importance of these Muslim populations under socialist rule would, in itself, be sufficient to warrant study of them. But there is an even more important reason, especially in the context of the

237

questions posed by this volume, why these cases merit distinct and close attention. This is that these states were, to a greater degree than in almost all other cases, examples of interventionist states, committed to a process of radical social and economic transformation, and they were, consequently, concerned to reform and direct areas of social life and belief constituted by Islam. They therefore raise a set of questions of broader relevance about forms of state intervention in Islamic society, and about the motives and mechanisms of such intervention.

The relationship between Islam and socialism is often posed in pre-dominantly ideological or doctrinal terms, as a conflict or competition between two sets of belief. Such competition is undoubtedly important, at both the societal and individual levels, but in the analysis that follows the relationship will be approached in a somewhat different manner. On the one hand, 'Islam' will be considered not as a set of abstract beliefs concerning relations between individuals and a putative divine being, but as an ideological system that enjoins and legitimates forms of social practice. While some forms of social behaviour are common to most Muslim societies, there are considerable variations in the social, economic and political forms assumed in Muslim societies, both historically and in the contemporary world. In these societies 'Islam' embodies the legitimation of an ensemble of political and social practices that may have little, in origin, to do with Islamic doctrine: the powers of tribal oligarchies and military dictatorships are cases in point. Confronted with such ensembles, socialist states were concerned not so much to alter belief, or to contradict points of doctrine, as to alter social practices and assert political control. The conflict between socialism and 'Islam' was not, therefore, essentially a doctrinal one, but concerned the degree to which revolutionary states could establish control of, and transform, areas of social practice that were hitherto outside state control and legitimated by reference to Islam.

The obverse of this revision of the socialism-Islam relationship pertains to the character of state policy itself. The policies of revolutionary, and especially socialist revolutionary, states must be seen in the context of the historic expansion of state power, through capitalism and beyond. Under capitalism, the influence of the state has extended into areas that were previously free from state intervention; the regulation of social life was achieved by other means, amongst them religious, customary and kinship sanctions. Revolutions were usually accompanied by an expansion of the reach and capacity of the state[2] since they were above all projects directed at the state, overthrowing one form of state and its associated power bloc, and establishing a new political and social system and a new state.

Beyond the assumption of state power, revolutions entailed the use of that power to transform society according to a revolutionary programme and in order to consolidate the post-revolutionary regime. In this context such states not only performed a coercive role, but also what has been termed an 'infrastructural' one [3], taking over economic and social functions as an extension of their institutional power. Because of their commitment to bringing about changes according to a new set of values and priorities, and the need to consolidate the foundations of a new political order, revolutionary states were particularly drawn to the use of their capacities, coercive and infrastructural, to change social relations, often in ways which had profound affects on the daily organisation of social life and the lives of the population. After social revolutions, control over the territory administered by the state was increased: governments sought not to expand control for its own sake, in response to some 'totalitarian' imperative, but to incorporate the population into the project of social transformation and national unification under centralised rule. The state was the impetus behind attempts at national unification and engaged in policies which drew the population into a progressive dependency on the state's larger role as the provider of goods and services. This was paid for, often reluctantly, in various forms of taxes, food quotas, labour and political allegiance.

The increasing levels of state intervention in the economy were evident in the development policies pursued by these governments; these ranged from the collectivisation of economic units to outright expropriation. At the societal level too, the expansion of education and health provision marked a significant increase in state activity. But of equal importance were forms of state intervention in the realm of personal relations – in particular in the structure and practices of households and families, which was connected to the wider processes of social and economic transformation. As has been argued elsewhere, women were centrally involved in efforts to regulate behaviour within households and to promote change in the structure of the family itself. On economic, ideological and demographic grounds, families, and the roles of women within them, were considered of central importance in all processes of social transformation, be these justified in progressive or traditionalist terms.

It was, therefore, these broad social, economic and political goals of state policy, not general programmatic or ideological commitments, that determined the policies of socialist states towards women and towards religion. These latter policies are derivatives of a general interventionist project. This explains why, despite considerable variations, there recur three typical features of socialist state policies which are of special significance when it comes to considering women's socio-economic position. First, in order to justify their interventionist policies towards women, these states were committed in their constitutions to the principle of equality between sexes, and adopted a range of policy measures designed to further this aim. Second, they sought to promote a process of rapid socio-economic transformation, one that entailed the dissolution of 'traditional' society, typically characterised in terms of 'feudal' or 'semi-feudal' social relations. Third, socialist governments were usually committed to a process of secularisation. Their relationship with religion, and in particular with organised, traditional religious expression, was historically less than tolerant and sometimes openly hostile: again, this was not so much because of a general doctrinal conflict, as because of the obstacles which organised religions, with their separate financial, educational and ideological powers, posed to state policies. For developmental reasons, and to legitimate the new social order they were creating, the aim of these states was to promote secular values and to reduce if not eradicate religion as an organised, influential social force. Depending upon policy considerations, and the success of specific interventions, state actions ranged from attempts to reform and even co-opt religious practice to-all out assaults on it: the *khuzhum* or 'attack' launched by Stalin in Central Asia in the late 1920s, the destruction of mosques and Tibetan temples during the Cultural Revolution in China and the outright abolition of religion in Albania in 1967 are perhaps the most extreme cases of this. In the case of the Muslim republics of the USSR, these early policies evidently did not succeed, and it was therefore as a result of practical and political obstacles, not doctrinal change, that Soviet policy towards Islam at home, and advice to their Afghan and South Yemeni allies abroad has, dispayed in more recent times, a far more conciliatory attitude.[4]

The argument so far has been intended to establish the context in which the particular relation between the state and Islam in the PDRY between 1967 and 1988 is to be studied. 'Islam' is treated as an ideological system organising and legitimating a set of social and political practices. State policy towards it is seen as part of the overall extension of state control in revolutionary states committed to social transformation. The focus of this chapter is upon a particular form of state intervention, and one which has the most clearly visible implications both for women and for religious practices, namely legal reform as this affects laws of personal status. Legal reform is considered here as a crucial instrument of state policy, designed to promote changes simultaneously in five areas: religious practice; juridicial relations between the sexes; family structure; socio-economic transformation; and state formation or, as it is sometimes called, 'nation-building'.

LEGAL REFORM AND WOMEN'S SOCIO-ECONOMIC POSITION

At first sight, legal reform may not appear to be of great importance in changing the position of women especially if it merely provides for formal rather than real equality between the sexes and if, as is often the case, evasion of the law is common. However, in other contexts and as part of a broader process of social transformation, legal reform can have profound effects on the position of women. In regions where gender inequalities are marked and women's rights are closely circumscribed, the law usually functions as an important means of positioning women as subordinate to men, restricting their freedom and limiting their access to resources. It also provides men with a series of legal sanctions over women. Thus the combined effects of removing certain male privileges and granting women a full legal status, and equal rights in property and inheritance can be far-reaching. In the socialist states where Islam retained a role in social and political life, the new codes involved major changes in traditional marriage customs and property forms; where many of the previous laws were derived from religion, legal reform also challenged the previous state forms as well as traditional religious belief and practices.

The legal reforms introduced by socialist states which were of particular significance for women living in Islamic societies are broadly of three types. First were those aimed at removing kin control over marriages and establishing free-choice unions. This entailed the abolition of customary practices such as the bride price and child marriages. Secondly were those aimed at re-defining relations between the sexes so that they henceforth rested on an equal footing. Women therefore acquired both equality of status and a set of new rights previously denied to them under traditional interpretations of Koranic Law, while men lost most of their legal privileges over women. Socialist legal reforms also granted men and women equal rights within marriage in matters concerning property and inheritance, while unilateral divorce, polygny and male custody over children were outlawed. The third type of legal reform involved the redefinition or introduction of laws which specifically affected women as child-bearers and rearers. Socialist states usually passed laws which provided benefits for women, including generous maternity leave arrangements, and they made a commitment to providing child-care facilities for the working mother. Various forms of protective legislation were also introduced which restricted women's entry into some areas of work and banned the use of women workers on overtime.

In the context of predominantly agrarian societies the first two types of reform were of crucial importance because they involved a process of liberalising pre-capitalist family forms and introducing radical structural changes. As historians of European capitalism have noted, a similar kind of 'liberalisation' also occurred with the spread of commodity relations in the pre-capitalist economy. This accelerated the dissolution of the old social relations and property forms, while patriarchal controls over women and younger men were often challenged and weakened. Under socialist state intervention we see an analogous process of 'liberalisation' taking place with the difference that the state, rather than the economy or the laws of motion of capital, assumed the leading role.

This chapter examines the legal reforms introduced in Democratic Yemen, after it gained independence from Britain in 1967, and focuses on attempts to improve the juridical position of women in accordance both with its egalitarian principles, and with its commitment to the revolutionary socialist transformation of state and society. In common with the Muslim republics of the Soviet Union and with Albania, the PDRY was a Muslim society that experienced a substantial period of rule by governments committed to 'scientific socialism'.[5] In its espousal of Marxist doctrine and in its economic policies, the PDRY differed from those other Muslim countries – Egypt, Algeria, Syria, Iraq and Libya – which also proclaimed themselves to be 'socialist'. In all these cases the ruling governments made clear that *their* socialism was an essentially local or 'Arab' variant and distinct from that of other regions. When this specificity was defined by Nasser, or by the Ba'ath, it was held to be based on two main characteristics: 'Arab socialism' was derived from the principles of Islam, and it tried to avoid, through an appeal to nationalism, what Nasser called 'class strife'. Moreover, despite an expansion of the state sector, capitalist social relations prevailed in these states and marked inequalities of wealth persisted.

The PDRY challenged this definition of socialism in the Arab world. The ruling party, formerly the National Liberation Front (NLF), and known after 1978 as the Yemeni Socialist Party, described itself as 'the vanguard of the Yemeni working class', and its official doctrine was not derived from the teachings of Islam but bore the explicit influence of the writings of Marx, Engels and Lenin. While, according to Party documents, the country was not yet 'socialist' but was 'socialist-oriented', it was 'scientific socialism' which provided the theoretical underpinnings of government policy, and the word 'scientific' was implicitly contrasted to the word 'Arab'.[6] For these reasons the legal system which emerged in South Yemen was distinctive in the Arab context and its laws, taken as a whole, were among the most radical in the Muslim world. Despite several outbreaks of intra-regime conflict, the most violent being in January 1986, the underlying policy orientation with respect to women remained within the same broad outlines from the late 1960s until the departure of the regime from socialist policies in 1990 as a prelude to unification on 22 May with the conservative state of North Yemen. At the time of writing it remains unclear what, if anything, of earlier socialist policies will remain in effect.

The discussion which follows falls into two parts: the first describes the transformation in the juridical system after independence and the social upheavals that accompanied it. It demonstrates how legal reform constituted an integral part of the process of transforming the economy and society, and secured some of the conditions of existence of that transformation. The second part describes how legal reform sought to regulate social relations within the family, both by creating new legal rights, subjects, and responsibilities, and by altering the character and form of the family itself. This, it is argued, was seen by the government as necessary for realising its development goals as well as constituting a matter of socialist principle in its aim to equalise relations between the sexes.

SOUTH YEMEN

In November 1967 the National Liberation Front came to power after five years of guerilla fighting and terminated 128 years of British colonial rule in South Yemen. Aden, the region's principal city and main port, had been ruled by the United Kingdom as a colony since 1839, and by the 1930s formal control was gradually extended over the twenty-four mini-states in the hinterland to encompass the region that became known as South Arabia. It had an area of around 114,000 square miles, but a population of only 1.6 million in 1967. The last two decades of colonial rule were marked by an unsuccessful attempt to forge a single state, a Federation of South Arabia composed of Aden and these smaller units of the interior. It was the defeat of this project and of a rival guerilla grouping, FLOSY, in an armed struggle that lasted for four years which brought the revolutionary National Liberation Front to power.[7] In March 1968 the Fourth Congress of the NLF laid down its guidelines for government policy. The main decisions were influenced by the left of the Party and committed it to destroying the old state apparatus and developing, in its place, 'people's power', creating a revolutionary people's army, implementing measures against foreign capital, adopting an anti-imperialist foreign policy, and carrying out a radical land reform.

However little was done by the first NLF government headed by Qhatan Al Sha'abi, to implement these measures. It was not until a more radical faction came to unchallenged power in the 'corrective move' of June 1969, over a year and a half after independence, that serious efforts to transform the economy and society along socialist lines were made, and the early guidelines began to be translated into policy. All foreign trading and banking concerns were nationalised in late 1969. A redistributive land reform was decreed in 1970. The first three year plan of 1971–74 embodied the Party's earlier nationalist objectives but went some way further than these. It stressed the urgency of stimulating the rapid development of the economy to overcome the extreme poverty and underdevelopment of the country, to raise per capita income (estimated in 1968 at £34 p.a.) and effect a policy of redistribution in favour of the most deprived sectors of the population. The state was to assume a leading role in economic life, the main sectors of the urban economy were to be nationalised, industrialisation given maximum support, and foreign trade was to be brought under government control. The agrarian sector was to be transformed following the expropriation of the larger private holdings, through the rationalisation of production, and, where possible, through the establishment of state farms and co-operatives. In broad outline, the policies amounted to the construction of a planned economy with a strong state sector (80 per cent of production in 1983), and considerable government intervention at the level of prices, wages, distribution and production – a model emulated in most of the countries within the pro-Soviet socialist bloc.

The 'destruction of the old state apparatus' and transformation of the relationship between state and people was formalised by the Constitution of 1970, which was the embodiment of what Soviet theorists called 'basic laws'. Among other things, it outlined the government's political principles, the organisation of the powers of the state, and the rights and duties of citizens and their representative organisations. The Constitution had been drawn up with the collaboration of East German jurists and it laid the basis for the establishment of a state and legal system similar to that which was first developed in the USSR and which later spread to other countries in the socialist bloc such as Vietnam, the DPRK, Cuba and China.[8]

As in these countries, state power in the PDRY was formally vested in 'the working people' and, according to the Constitution, it was exercised through their representatives in the Supreme People's Council, initially a one hundred and eleven member body charged with enacting laws and approving state policies. The new state, according to the Constitution, was to be 'democratic' both because it represented the interests of the working people and because state power was to be devolved through greater popular participation in decision making, especially through the mass organisations, and at middle and local levels of state power.[9]

In establishing a new state form, the 1970 Constitution, embodying what was now Party policy, also redefined the legal system and the place of law in society. It pledged the government to introduce new legislation in the areas of employment, the family and criminal law, and these measures were defined in accordance with the egalitarian principles laid down in the Constitution. In the new legal system, the separation of the juridical and executive powers of the state was rejected on the same grounds as those advanced by Soviet constitutional theorists.

Since in theory state power was based on popular sovereignty and state policy originated from popularly elected representative bodies, the delegation of legislative power was considered to be in violation of the principles of the socialist political order.[10] The institutions, practice and content of the law were henceforth to respond to the requirements of the 'national new Democratic Phase' of the revolution, and, as the Party Programme put it, to the needs of 'the broadest sectors of the population'.[11]

The promulgation of the Constitution marked the beginning of a new phase in the reconstruction of the legal apparatus. The period since Independence had seen the gradual introduction of the new laws and procedures on an *ad hoc* basis, while the process of codification and systematisation of the laws was carried out. During that period the previous legal systems and their laws prevailed. A decree passed in December 1967, shortly after the NLF's accession to power, stipulated that current laws be respected unless they were 'repugnant to the sovereignty of the state' or 'contrary to the aims of the revolution'. This clause was designed to remove the legal impediments to the government's interim reforms and abolished the rights of appeal to the colonial courts.[12] The delay in bringing about a more radical transformation was in part caused by the shortage of qualified legal personnel, a situation which had been exacerbated by the mass exodus of members of the professions after 1967. In part, it also resulted from difficulties in dealing with the complexity of the existing legal apparatus.

On gaining power, the NLF had to administer an area which had no unified national economy or political structure, let alone a common legal system. The newly independent state, first known as the People's Republic of South Yemen and then renamed the People's Democratic Republic of Yemen, comprised the former Aden colony and the formerly independent states of the interior. The hinterland had been constitutionally separate from Aden, and was politically and economically fragmented as a result of tribal segmentation and the local autonomy hitherto enjoyed by ruling sheikhs, sultans or emirs. In general the area outside Aden Colony was characterised by a marked division between town and country, and by a preponderance of pre-capitalist relations of production, ranging from the nomadic pastoralism characteristic of the Bedouin tribes to the more diversified class structure typical of the towns. Some areas, such as the Hadramaut, had developed a many-tiered caste system, which had survived decades of migration, increasing commercialism, and social differentiation in the wealthier inland areas.[13] This variety of social forms and the relative autonomy of regional potentates was reflected in the varying degrees of local legislation and practice incorporated within the prevailing legal systems. Outside Aden there was no legal profession as such, and within any one state, the highest judicial authority was the ruler. He appointed judges (*Qadi*) and the equivalent of magistrates, on the basis of their knowledge of Islam and of customary law, known as *urf*. However, religion provided the fundamental unity of these different regions and systems, and established the main principles and practice of the law, as laid down in the Quran, and interpreted by the Shafei school of jurisprudence([14]).

In Aden a different system of law prevailed, one imported by the British administration, and similar in its essentials to those which existed in its other colonies, especially India.[15] Although Islamic or *Sharia'ah* law remained in force in Aden Colony in matters pertaining to marriage, divorce and inheritance, the colonial legal and judicial system with its Supreme, Divisional and Magistrates Courts, tried all other cases of legal infringement, and heard them in English.

These regional variations were eroded in the period between 1970 and 1979. The small *Qadi* courts in the interior were gradually abolished and a centralised legal system was extended across the national territory. Six new regional and administrative divisions, known as governorates, were established and these were further divided into districts. Each governorate became the site of a Provincial Court where cases were heard by judges, and each district acquired one or more divisional magistrate's court.[16] Aden, the capital, contained the Supreme Court of the Republic, presided over by the Chief Justice.[17]

There occurred a move towards the professionalisation of legal personnel, but this went along with an effort to retain parallel organs of popular justice based on lay practitioners.[18] 'Mass organisations' such as neighbourhood associations (known as Popular Defence Committees), were empowered to settle petty disputes and enforce the rules of community life, considering cases involving drunkenness, marital conflict, disorderly behaviour and the like.[19] They worked in conjunction with other mass organisations such as the General Union of Yemeni Women and the Union of Democratic Youth. In some areas this work was assigned to 'Social Justice Committees' also known as 'Social Courts'. These resembled the Comrades' or People's Courts pioneered in the USSR after 1961, and were first established in Aden on an experimental basis in 1977. They were then extended in 1980 to the Third Governorate in the hinterland. The amended constitution of 1978 provided for the establishment of these courts in all six governorates, but progress was slow and the process incomplete by the mid 1980s.

After 1970 there were far-reaching changes in the law itself as well as in the legal system. These were justified as attempts to transform the law in accordance with the egalitarian principles of the Constitution and with the government's claim to represent the interests of working people. Frequently cited examples of popular justice were said to be the Family Law of 1974, which extended women's legal rights, the Land Reforms of the early 1970s and the various labour laws which sought to provide workers with better conditions, protection and welfare. The government emphasised both the 'popular' character of the laws and their derivation from democratic procedures in which some of the new laws were discussed in public meetings before being promulgated. The 1970 Constitution was also discussed in this way prior to promulgation. Indeed Article 77 of the amended Constitution of 1978 stipulated that: 'The most important draft laws connected with the activity of the state and the society may be subjected to wide popular discussions pursuant to a decision of the People's Supreme Council or the Presidium'. The most widespread discussions at public meetings on any matter of law attended the formulation of the Family Law, to which we will return later. These campaigns certainly performed an educative function in explaining the proposed reforms and the aims of the state. It is difficult in the absence of evidence, however, to assess the impact of the popular response on the re-formulation of the reforms, or the range of discussion involved in such public meetings.

Before proceeding to discuss the reforms which affected the position of women, two general points can be made about the changes which were made in the PDRY's legal system. First, it is clear that this process involved fulfilling what the bourgeois revolutions achieved in Europe, namely attempting to create a unified, state-administered legal system, by extending the central legal authority into rural areas where religious, customary, and tribal law prevailed. Moreover the creation of a new legal system and new laws was part of the process of constructing a national entity, in the course of which efforts were made to dissolve the old ties of allegiance, chief among them being tribalism. The new areas of regional jurisdiction, the governorates and districts were especially designed to cut across tribal divisions and provide a different principle of regional identification.[20] At the same time, the extension of citizenship rights through the Constitution implied a change in the state-people relationship and was an important step aimed at forging stronger national as opposed to regional or tribal identification. The pre-existing political and social system was not a derivative of 'Islam'; it justified, in Islamic terms, a set of tribal relations and power structures that differed markedly from practices found in the more industrialised Muslim countries, while in some specific instances it enforced practices common throughout the Muslim world; nevertheless Islam came to stand both for these latter, specifically Islamic elements and for other political and social structures that were also legitimated in Islamic terms. Secondly, and following from this, in common with other socialist states, Party leaders saw legal reform not just as an accompaniment to the process of social transformation, but also as an important instrument in achieving it. The official texts therefore justified reform in terms of three main arguments: that the previous legal order served colonial and feudal interests and therefore had to be abolished; that it was undemocratic in failing to respond to the needs of the 'broadest sectors of the population';[21] and that new legal instruments had to be created in order to 'deepen and accelerate' the revolutionary process.

This conception of the law was therefore one which saw law not merely as a reflection of existing social relations, favouring certain class interests over others, but as a means of intervention in the process of transition, with the capacity to further this process through some measure of popular participation. It is obvious that the transition from a free market economy to one based on centralised planning, and from private to state control of productive property crucially affected concepts of ownership, possession, and property, as well as definitions of the obligations of state functionaries and citizens in this regard. The relationship between the law and the plan, and between civil and economic law had to be re-defined in order to provide the conditions of existence of the new social relations, and their institutional forms. Collective property had to have legal recognition, if only in order that the state could allocate resources to it and enter into contract relations.[22]

In the PDRY as in other socialist states, changes in the law were also seen as a means of accelerating or deepening the struggle of oppressed social forces who were to benefit from the government's policies - peasants, women, and the industrial working class for example. The passing of the 1970 land reform was followed in 1970–72 by peasant uprisings against landlords and the seizure of their lands. The embryonic state lacked the means of effecting this popular transfer of resources without the mobilisation of the rural workforce, itself spurred on by Party activists. The legal reform was important for this process in two respects: it provided the legitimation for class struggle and at the same time withdrew state and juridical support from the previous system of ownership. Its effectiveness, however, crucially depended upon the capacities of its beneficiaries and opponents to achieve their different aims.

THE IMPACT UPON WOMEN OF REVOLUTIONARY CHANGE

For women in South Yemen the revolutionary upheavals and their after-math were to have far-reaching effects, but ones which were far from uniform, and reflected the degree to which women were themselves a highly differentiated social category. The pre-revolutionary position of women in South Yemen was subject to class and regional variations within the limits imposed by local customs and religious practices. These variations included the degree to which seclusion, segregation and veiling were practiced and whether bride-price or dowry systems, or both, prevailed. The existing differentials were exacerbated by the development of trade and commodity production in some areas, and in Aden, by the effects of urban development and contact with the international market.

On the eve of independence the following picture of the differential position of women emerges. In Aden the situation by the late 1950s had begun to change for certain classes of women. The rules of seclusion were slowly becoming more relaxed, although the veil and *sheidor* was worn by all but the women at the two extremes of the social structure – the handful of educated women and the very poor. The former, from some of the wealthier families, occasionally studied abroad in Beirut or Cairo and on their return took up work in those occupations which were beginning to open up to women, such as education and the medical profession.[23]

For the less privileged women in the city there were far fewer oppor-tunities, as areas of employment typically occupied by women in other developing countries, such as manufacturing, domestic, and clerical work, remained dominated by men and boys, most of them migrants from the interior, or North Yemen. One exception to this general rule was a specific category of women who were unveiled and did various forms of manual labour. These were migrant women, who, desperate for an income and freed from the restrictions of (and deprived of the status of) seclusion, formed a stratum of low-paid workers mainly sweeping streets and factory floors; in effect, doing work that was considered too debased for Yemenis whether women or men. These women were either Somalis or members of a caste called the *akhdam* (literally 'servants') allegedly descended from slaves. Both groups lived on the margin of society, generally in the shanties of the capital city.

In the countryside there operated the familiar disjuncture between social status and economic activity. Women were almost totally excluded from positions of social influence which were generally in the hands of elder males. But in some regions they played an important role in agriculture, and in many parts of rural Yemen were unveiled, although restrictions and segregation still operated. The division of labour was based on gender and this allocated to women activities such as gathering firewood and carrying water. In general women also tended animals and participated in certain agricultural tasks such as sowing and harvesting.[24] Indeed since men took the afternoon off to sit together chewing the local narcotic *qat*, an activity from which women were almost entirely excluded, women's contribution in some areas to agricultural production was probably greater than men's. This pattern of social marginalisation and economic centrality is, of course, one found in many peasant societies.

Despite these regional and class variations, women shared a common secondary status to men in the law and social life, and enjoyed fewer rights than men in marriage. Virtually all the population consisted of Sunni Muslims of the Shafei variety and, as in many Muslim societies, women and men led segregated lives articulated upon a clearly defined sexual division of labour and gender hierarchy, in which women were both separate and inferior in status. Whereas the public domain, the world of social responsibility and authority, belonged to men, women's domain was in the home, and even there, the authority that individual women exercised was contingent on their age and status within the female hierarchy. A young wife could be made the virtual servant of her mother-in-law, or in polygynous households, of the senior wives. In general, however, a women's status in the family and in society at large was directly bound up with her ability to produce male heirs; apart from the idea that it was humiliating to beget daughters, the failure to produce sons was often sufficient reason for a divorce, even after a relatively short period of time.[25]

The strict controls exercised over women meant that their independent initiatives were closely circumscribed. At the onset of puberty or even before, they were forbidden to have any social contact with men not covered by the incest taboo. A high premium was placed on virginity before marriage and on female sexual fidelity within marriage. The penalties for infringing such rules, or for being thought to do so, ranged from beating to death at the hands of husbands or relatives avenging the loss of honour (*'Ird*) which such actions were thought to incur. At the same time men's sexual freedom was less circumscribed; men were permitted polygynous marriages and, until the 1950s, concubines; and the existence in the pre-revolutionary period of open prostitution in Aden and Mukalla, the port towns of South Yemen, attests to the absence of strong legal or social disincentives against it.

This socio-cultural context meant that women along with the rest of the population were largely excluded from any involvement in the political life of the colony. It was only with the growth of Arab nationalism in the 1950s, which began to exacerbate some of the tensions already present in the society, that men and women were drawn into the arena of politics chiefly through opposition to the colonial presence. It is known that women played an active, but limited, part in the nationalist struggles. They began to participate in political demonstrations in support of Nasser during the Suez crisis of 1956; women school teachers went on strike in 1957 to protest against what they saw as pro-British curricula, and women began to be drawn into the political organisations which formed chiefly, but not exclusively, in the capital city, Aden.

Despite the increased involvement of women in political activities, the issue of greater equality for women was raised in only a few organisations. Even these operated with a limited conception of what this would entail, one overshadowed by the struggle for national liberation, regarded as the overriding priority. Some women's organisations did exist during the Independence struggle but these were political arms of nationalist tendencies rather than women's organisations as such. In the four years of the guerrilla struggle against British rule between 1963 and 1967, women played a more active auxiliary role. As in Algeria's independence movement, the two hundred or so women who worked with or in the NLF acted as informers, messengers, arms smugglers, and even led demonstrations. Women are also known to have participated in the rival guerrilla movement known as FLOSY but in far fewer numbers. In the mountains women played a back-up role in the rural guerrilla warfare, carrying military supplies and food, and a few women took part in the fighting. One, Hadiga al Haushabi, became a unit commander.

The NLF as a socialist party therefore did try to mobilise women. The women who joined the nationalist organisations were often from the better educated and better-off sectors of Aden society, and many of them were affiliated by ties of kinship to male activists and leaders. But there was little discussion of women's specific interests beyond a call in the 1965 National Charter of the NLF for 'the liberation of women from tradition'. Women who supported the Party at that time saw themselves in general terms as 'progressives', committed to modernisation and social reform as part of the programme of national reconstruction following independence. They considered that their interests as women were encompassed in the Party's commitment to education and social reform.

After independence the NLF drew up its proposals for changing women's socio-economic position. In its official documents the NLF viewed women's pre-revolutionary situation with a mixture of pity for the victims and contempt for the old order which imprisoned them. The combined effects of 'feudalism', colonialism, and a family structure based on female subordination were to blame for women's deplorable status, which the NLF would henceforth try to improve. Women would no longer be kept in isolation under the control of despotic husbands and fathers; they would be educated and instilled with 'a love of work' so as to contribute to the development of the new society. A crucial means of their emancipation and incorporation into socially useful work was to be the reform of the law.

Legal reform affecting women and the family has been seen by most government planners in the socialist countries as a necessary part of their principled support for women's emancipation. But it was also considered to be important in securing more general policy objectives. In the context of under-developed societies, such as Democratic Yemen, the fulfilment of government development programmes depended upon bringing about social changes of a major kind. The pre-revolutionary social order, which was seen as an obstacle to economic development and social reform, needed to be transformed, and replaced by a new social order, one more suited to the demands of economic development. The NLF like other revolutionary governments considered the mobilisation of women in the period of social and economic transformation as helping to accomplish at least three goals: to extend the political base of the regime; to increase the active labour force; and to help 'modernise' the family and harness it more directly to state goals. Legal reform was of fundamental importance in all three cases.

The first of these considerations was, to help consolidate the power of the state, involved drawing women into political activity – into organisations such as the women's union, the party, neighbourhood associations, and the other mass organisations. This kind of participation was only possible, however, if kin control over women was challenged, along with the practice of seclusion. As part of this process of encouraging women's entry into the political realm, women were given the vote for the first time in 1970 when universal suffrage was implemented, and a special effort was made to ensure that some women candidates stood for election in the first national poll of 1977.

The most important means of mobilising women was the General Union of Yemeni Women, established in 1968 soon after the NLF came to power, but active in the whole country only after 1974. The Union enjoyed the status of a mass organisation, under Party leadership, and was charged with the responsibility of mobilising women into socially necessary tasks. To this end it was an active supporter of the literacy campaigns and a promoter of women's employment opportunities. The Union was involved in administering a number of aid projects specifically targeted at women and supported by initiatives deriving from the UN Decade for Women. It never achieved a large active membership and was perceived by many women outside the capital city as run by urban women with little feeling for the specific concerns and interests of their rural or provincial sisters. For its part the GUYW trod a fine line between promoting women's greater integration into the changing social structure and respecting the status quo for fear of antagonising its opponents. Its target groups were carefully selected, and little attempt was made, beyond the literacy campaign, to mobilise women to advance their own specific interests.

The second way in which the mobilisation of women was regarded as important was more directly relevant to the economy. The education of women and their entry into employment increases and improves the available labour supply, a process which is a necessary concomitant to any successful development programme. In the period after independence the pre-existing scarcity of labour in the PDRY was exacerbated by the departure of some 20,000 skilled and professional workers, and by a continuing large-scale emigration of men to the oil-producing states. The World Bank estimated in 1980 that there occurred a loss of one third of the men in the 15 to 35 age group or 18 per cent of the total workforce.[26] Faced with this situation, the government was dependent on women to make up the shortfall in labour supply. The five year plan of 1981–85 included among its principal objectives the promotion of women's participation in economic and social activities and the emphasis was on mobilising 'housewives' into economic activity to help meet the goal of a 3.61 per cent annual increase in the labour supply. By 1984 women still made up only one fifth of the EAP, a low rate of participation resulting partly from the stigma attached to women performing income-generating activities, especially if these involved working outside the home.[27] These cultural disincentives to women taking up paid employment were further reinforced by the legal authority hitherto invested in male guardians which gave them the power to prevent their female charges from breaking the rules of seclusion.

This latter concern was one which also lay behind the third objective, family reform. For, as we have seen, if women were to become politically active and enter wage employment, they had to be freed from traditional familial and cultural constraints. But there were two other social policy objectives which family reform addressed. One of these was the attempt to hasten the transformation of the economy by eroding pre-existing social relations and practices. Women's subordination is an integral part of the reproduction of many forms of peasant and tribal property systems. The control of marriage alliances by kin groups, and systems of inheritance which discriminate against women frequently do so in order to preserve the integrity of the property system concerned.[28] Economic planners in socialist states have long recognised this coincidence of the goal of women's emancipation and socialist modernisation[29] and the Family Laws which they promoted soon after coming to power had this as one of their explicit aims.[30]

The family has been an important site of state intervention for a further reason. Seen as the 'basic cell of society', it has been considered responsible for helping to form the next generation of 'patriotic, socialist' subjects. By promoting greater equality between the sexes, the family reforms were seen as laying the basis for a new egalitarian socialist family. This would not only be stronger because it was more harmonious, but would also be better equipped to perform the roles assigned to it by the state.[31]

In Democratic Yemen, according to the preamble of the Family Law the 'traditional' or 'feudal' family was 'incompatible with the principles and programme of the National Democratic Revolution . . . because its old relationships prevent it from playing a positive role in the building up of society'. The role of the reformed family was envisaged in terms of educating the young into the ideals of the revolution so that they could participate in constructing and defending the new society. Women's role in this process was regarded as crucial, since it was they, as mothers and educators, who had primary responsibility for the care of the young. Family reform was therefore seen simultaneously as a pre-condition for mobilising women into economic and political activity and as an indispensable adjunct of both economic change and social stability.

These more general considerations about the value of legal reform, in helping to secure policy objectives as well as address issues of principle, were shared by most socialist governments. What was distinctive and problematic about the reforms introduced in South Yemen was that improvements in women's social and legal status involved reforming codes which were derived from Islam and were considered to be of divine inspiration. The NLF, as a consequence, was open to the accusation by its opponents of being 'atheistic', anti-religious, and worse. And yet its reforms also belonged within the Middle Eastern context of gradual secularisation.

Despite recent moves in some countries to reverse the process (Iran, Pakistan, Tunisia, Sudan, Algeria), most Muslim societies underwent a gradual loosening of the ties between religion and the state from the mid-nineteenth century onwards.[32] This was a slow and uneven process both across and within countries; but while there were differences between them in points of detail, most Muslim countries experienced a reform process whereby the institutions of the state, education, and the law acquired some measure of independence from the religious authorities. Following the early example of the Ottoman reforms, many Muslim countries secularised that part of their legal systems pertaining to commerce, finance, criminal, and penal law. However, family law remained the most resilient redoubt of orthodoxy throughout virtually all the Muslim world until the period after the mid-1950s. It was only then, under both internal and external pressure to 'modernise', that some Muslim states began to see the practical advantages of liberating women from some of their traditional constraints. The 1950s and 1960s saw a wave of reform initiatives, the most radical of which was the Tunisian Law of Personal Status brought into effect in 1957 and amended in 1959. It was this law which was instanced by South Yemen's jurists as providing the main inspiration for their own Family Law of 1974.

The introduction of this law in the PDRY, as elsewhere, involved challenging both the power of the Muslim clergy and orthodox interpretations of Islam. After 1969 the government sought to curb the institutional and economic base of the traditional clergy and transferred some of its responsibilities to agencies of the state. This process began during the liberation struggle when the revolutionaries moved against the *Sada* (an elite caste) and other religious leaders in the areas around Radfan where they were based, expropriating their lands without compensation and forcing the more conservative elements into exile. After the revolution, *waqf* (religious) lands were placed under state administration and those religious leaders who did not leave the country were given the option of either surrendering their posts or continuing to occupy them as employees of the state. At the same time, religious education in schools was scaled down and made the responsibility of lay teachers.

Yet the programme pursued was one of reform rather than one of *abolition* of the old codes along the extreme lines of Albania in the 1960s and 1970s or Turkey in the 1920s under Ataturk. Islam remained the state religion of the PDRY; religious belief, observance and holidays were respected. The government refrained from adopting a confrontationist or provocative stance, although it sought to reduce the influence of orthodox beliefs and practices by redefining religious discourses so that more progressive readings were emphasised. The legal reforms which were introduced were often legitimised, where possible, in terms of the canons of Islamic jurisprudence and carried out with the co-operation of prominent religious jurists before being debated in public meetings.

THE NLF AND WOMEN'S EMANCIPATION

We can now turn to consider the legal measures which were taken to improve the social position of women in the PDRY. Within the NLF it was the left-wing radicals who were chiefly concerned with women's rights, and it was after they came to power in 1969 that more concerted efforts were made to encourage women to participate in and benefit from, the revolutionary process.[33] The Constitution of 1970 outlined the government's policies towards women and provided the framework within which the ensuing legal reforms would be inscribed. The proposed reforms were phrased in the familiar language of other socialist countries and embodied many of the same provisions.[34] Women were referred to in terms of two main roles envisaged for them by the revolutionary government – as 'mothers' and as 'producers'. Article 7, which described the political basis of the revolution as an 'alliance between the working class, the peasants, intelligentsia and petty-bourgeoisie', went on to add that 'soldiers, *women* and students are regarded as part of this alliance *by virtue of their membership of the productive forces of the people*' (emphasis added). Women were thus recognised as forming part of the 'working people', and the Constitution, in giving all citizens the right to work and in regarding work as 'an obligation in the case of all able-bodied citizens', called upon women not yet involved in 'productive work' to do so. This was part of the attempt to promote acceptance of identities based on economic function rather than more traditional kinship or religious referents, and in particular to transform the legal and social identities of women. Moreover, calling upon women to enter 'productive work' implicitly challenged both the restrictions of seclusion and the male authority through which it was enforced. At the same time, the Constitution promised to 'strengthen the family status and (to) protect mother and child' (Article 29). Lest this concern to preserve the family and encourage women to enter social production be thought contradictory, certain provisions were to be made specifically for the working mother: Article 36 promised that 'The state shall also ensure special protection for working women and children by granting paid leave to expectant mothers . . . (and) . . . The state shall establish nurseries and kindergartens and other means of care and custody (for children . . .)'.[35]

These statutes and provisions marked a considerable advance on previous government policy in a number of respects, but it was the article declaring juridical and political equality for all citizens that provided the context for even more profound changes in the legal position of women. Article 34, which stated that 'All citizens are equal in their rights and obligations . . . (and) all are equal in the eye of the law', represented a break with previous laws and customs under which women had inferior rights to men, and did not have a full legal personality, being treated as minors and regarded as the charges of men. Constitutional reform in this case implied at the very least a radical change in legal status if only, as yet, a formal one. Article 36 went some way towards making it more than merely a formal commitment by affirming that 'The State shall guarantee equal rights for men and women in all fields of political, economic and social scope (sic) and shall provide in a progressive manner the conditions necessary for realising that equality'. Among these conditions provided for in the Constitution were the expansion of the General Union of Yemeni Women,[36] in order to assist women in gaining their new rights, the extension of education and literacy programmes to women, the encouragement of women's political participation and their mass entry into social production. In short, the Constitution embodied the conventional socialist programme for the emancipation of women, and provided some of the legal pre-conditions necessary for its realisation. As yet, however, there was no specification of the forms of enforcement which would make them effective.

These Constitutional reforms, and the progressive extension of new penal and civil codes to the hinterland, brought some immediate gains for women. Whereas in the past crimes against them were frequently regarded as family or tribal affairs, and harsh punishment could be meted out to disobedient daughters or wives by men who were never themselves brought to trial, women not only gained new rights, but also official support in demanding them from the mass organisations. Moreover the fact that this formal equality was inscribed in the Constitution gave legal support to women's demands for equality in the face of opposition from their families and the traditional social milieu.[37] The state and its goals thus became a higher authority than the kin group, even than religion, in matters pertaining to women's status. However, it was not until the promulgation of the Family Law in 1974 that significant progress was made in transforming women's legal position within the home.

THE FAMILY LAW

The Family Law, like the Constitution, was discussed in the press and in open meetings around the country before being promulgated. The draft Law was drawn up in 1971 and over a period of three years amendments were incorporated into it on the basis of the popular response and on the advice of the mass organisations and legal practitioners. In the manner of its adoption it was similar to the Family Laws which were passed in Cuba and Somalia a year later, in 1975.

The text of the law contained the official justification for the reforms: it began by denouncing 'the vicious state of affairs which prevails in the family' the ending of which opened up the possibility of unleashing 'vast (areas) of creative work and equal revolutionary relations which lead to the increase of production, development and innovation'. The Law went on to proclaim the end of some of the traditional inequalities in marriage:

> Marriage is a contract between a man and a woman who are equal in rights and duties, and is based on mutual understanding and respect with the object of building up the cohesive family which is regarded as the foundation stone of the society.

The specific reforms introduced by the Law included the following:

1. The principle of free-choice marriage was established. Families were henceforth forbidden to agree to engagements without the consent of the parties concerned. Although this was stipulated in one of the *hadiths* or sayings of the Prophet, it was almost never observed, and its re-incorporation in the Code marked an attempt to end kin control of marriages.

2. Whereas there had previously been widespread child marriage in the countryside, the minimum legal age was fixed at 16 years for women, and at 18 for men. (In 1984 this was under review and was to be raised to 18 and 20 years respectively.) In a further move to prevent the marriage of young women to much older men, the age difference was limited to 20 years for women under 35.

3. Whereas under the *Shari'ah* Codes men had previously been allowed to marry up to four wives, the Law now stipulated that men could have only one spouse, except in certain exceptional circumstances such as barrenness, or incurable disease.

4. In order further to reduce family control over marriage, the amount of the 'bride-price' or *mahr* was limited to 100 Yemeni dinars (about twice an average white-collar monthly salary). In this way it was hoped to remove a conventional form of class control over marriages while at the same time making it easier for women to escape from a bad marriage by repaying the betrothal settlement herself. The preamble to the Law stated that women in the previous situation had been 'in the hands of the highest bidder'. Officials justified this control by referring to the *Hadith*: they recalled Mohammad's remark that his daughter could marry for a 'mere ring of iron'.

5. Whereas men were expected to be the main breadwinners, Article 17 of the new codes stipulated that both spouses must bear the cost of supporting the family's economy. This clause, along with that on custody (below) finds no authority in the Islamic Codes and derives from the government's commitment to egalitarian principles.[38]

6. Under the new Law unilateral divorce was prohibited and all divorces had to be processed through the courts. The grounds for divorce were, with some minor differences to be discussed later, now applicable to both men and women.

7. Whereas on divorce, men previously had greater rights of custody, male children were henceforth to remain with their mothers until the age of ten years and female children until the age of fifteen years. In all cases the courts reserved the right to decide the outcome in terms of the best interests of the children.

The Family Law therefore established the basis for a quite different family structure and sought to alter the relations within it. It attempted radically to change pre-existing forms, reducing both the husband's authority and the control of the natal families over marriage. The new Yemeni family was to be monogamous and egalitarian, and the preferred institutional form was no longer the extended but the nuclear family.[39] It was hoped that this family form would be a more stable institution and thus perform its social functions as the 'basic cell of society' more efficiently. However likely this was in the longer run, the immediate consequence of the passing of the law had the opposite effect, namely a steep rise in the divorce rate.

Divorce rates were always high in South Yemen but in the past these were mainly initiated by men;[40] after 1974 women began to form an increasing proportion of those suing for divorce.[41] Among the main reasons were women's greater financial independence, and desertion by emigrant husbands who had remarried abroad and abandoned their families back home. The trend to divorce grew even stronger after 1978 when a civil law bill was passed which awarded the marital home to the wife on divorce if there were children from the marriage. This led to a steeper rise in the number of women petitioning for divorce and caused the Supreme People's Council (the Legislature) to revise the article to give the courts more scope in deciding these matters. The People's Defence Committees were also requested to play a role so as to arrive at a more equitable solution to the allocation of accommodation. To curb the high incidence of marital instability the government made divorce more difficult to obtain. Potential divorcees had to wait between several months and a year before their case was heard, in order to allow them time to reconsider whether they should continue to press their suit. In the meantime the women's union or the Popular Defence Committees acted as marriage guidance counsellors and tried to reconcile the couple. Before a case even went to court these bodies had to be persuaded that the litigant had a reasonable case; otherwise it did not go forward. But according to Yemeni legal practitioners, this did not result in any significant fall in the number of women petitioners. This was striking in view of the fact that alimony was granted for only one year and was in practice difficult to enforce. After that the chances of support from the state, although theoretically possible, were minimal; husbands were then under no further obligation, and a divorced woman (unless she was a wage earner) generally had to rely on the beneficence of her kinfolk, who, foreseeing this, were likely to try to dissuade her from divorcing in the first place. The kin network thus joined the government bodies in discouraging the break-up of the family.

Despite the radical changes in the law, it is worth noting that, even after the 1974 reforms, certain inequalities between men and women persisted as relics of Islamic and customary practices. A man, for example, could take a second spouse under exceptional and certified circumstances such as barrenness, whilst a woman could not do so on grounds of impotence. Similarly, a woman could be divorced for barrenness but nothing was said in the law as to whether a man could be divorced for impotence, although the courts would be likely to give a sympathetic hearing to a case brought on such grounds. A divorced woman was still prohibited for the stipulated period (known as *Iddat*) of ninety days from remarrying, an Islamic injunction designed to protect men from the loss of an heir who might have been conceived before the divorce and who, if the woman remarried, could be considered to belong to her new spouse.

Although arranged marriages were outlawed, the bride-price remained, albeit with a lower upper limit. Finally, as far as property transmission was concerned, *Shari'ah* law continued to prevail, and the discrimination against women that it embodied therefore persisted.[42] On the occasion of the tenth anniversary of the passing of the Law in 1984, a symposium was called to discuss its adequacy. Although largely a celebratory occasion, there was a move by some women present to have the *mahr* abolished and more egalitarian inheritance laws introduced. However these proposals were quashed and the existing law approved.[43]

The retention of certain provisions influenced by the Islamic codes must be understood in the regional context as well as in relation to the government's domestic policy on religion. As noted earlier, the official concern was to avoid provoking opposition on religious grounds, but even so, its reforms provided the government's adversaries with ammunition. Yemeni exiles in Saudi Arabia, and during periods of hostility between the two countries the Saudi state itself, tried to provoke internal opposition by beaming hostile radio broadcasts into the PDRY.[44] They accused the government of 'godlessness', and pointed in particular to the efforts to emancipate women as proof of the PDRY'S contravention of religious customs. Further evidence of the 'degeneracy of the regime' was said to be the appointing of women as judges; this was claimed to be in violation of the Quran which stipulates that 'masculinity' is among the ten qualities required of judges. Other conservative Arab states such as Kuwait joined Saudi Arabia in condemning the PDRY for encouraging gender desegregation and repeatedly called on them in pan-Arab congresses to re-segregate educational establishments. The dangers of a traditional and religious backlash were ever present, especially in the context of growing popular support in the Muslim world for fundamentalist movements, but up to 1990, when state policy changed, government officials insisted that it should not be exaggerated, both because the reforms were popular in many quarters and because traditional religious feeling in South Yemen was never as strong as in some other Arab states. Nevertheless, even before 1990, the PDRY was vulnerable to pressure from both inside and outside and for this reason was at pains to demonstrate its continued adherence to Islam, and its tolerance of at least some of its social practices. The underground opposition, organised by the Muslim Brothers and receiving funds from Saudi Arabia, was in the end to break into the open in 1990.

These considerations help to explain why the government refrained from using the law as a means of intervening in certain social practices associated with women's subordination, such as veiling or for that matter clitoridectomy (*khitan*). As far as the latter was concerned, the official view was that it was not a serious problem since it was not widely practised in the PDRY. Where it did exist it was thought that it would soon die out, with the extension of medical facilities to the rural areas and the erosion of the power of traditional doctors (*hakimi*). Male circumcision was, as would be expected, still encouraged as an acceptable, indeed desirable, Islamic custom. Veiling and the seclusion of women were similarly tolerated on the grounds that, as the then head of the women's organisation put it, they were 'merely anachronisms', which if left to objective forces would soon disappear.[45] Between 1970 and 1972, with the *intifadhat* or peasant uprisings following the land reforms in the interior, women were reported to have marched through the streets proclaiming the end of veiling, and whilst the government gave some support to this campaign, it later preferred to discourage veiling in a more indirect manner. Certainly stringent measures against the veil such as those adopted in Soviet Central Asia in 1927, or in Iran under Reza Shah, were never adopted. The policy was again to avoid provoking hostility by refraining from directly confronting the issue.[46] Indirectly, tacit support was given to eroding the practice by encouraging the wearing of school and workplace uniforms; many government officials and Women's Union cadres also went about their tasks in the urban areas unveiled, but wearing loose scarves and long-sleeved blouses as a token observance of the Islamic injunction to wear 'modest' dress.

As far as the issue of juridical reform was concerned, two main problems confronted the government: that of popularising the Law, and that of enforcing the new legislation – merely to promulgate laws was no guarantee that they would be effective. As far as the first issue was concerned, we have seen that in drafting and circulating the new laws for discussion, an effort was made, as in Cuba during a comparable period, to diffuse knowledge of the law at formulation stage through public meetings and to encourage some measure of popular participation. Even a decade after the promulgation of the laws, work went on to inform people about their rights and obligations through public meetings, newspaper coverage, television and radio broadcasts. In this way the government hoped to further the voluntary acceptance of the new codes through persuading people of their role in formulating laws and of the superiority of the new over the previous system.

Yet evasion of some of the new rules of conduct was common, especially in the rural areas where traditional and familial authority remained strong and where customary modes of procedure continued to be favoured. For example, one clause of the Family Law which was disregarded by most rural dwellers was that which restricted the *mahr* to 100 YD. In 1984 the richer families of the Hadramaut region were paying *mahrs* of 2–3000 YD, an inflation caused partly by earnings from the oil-producing states. Party officials in the region said it was impossible to resist the trend and that they took no punitive measures against it. The Law was in this case apparently treated as merely indicative of preferred conduct rather than carrying any real sanction. The payment of high *mahrs* continued, along with arranged marriages, sometimes with legal minors.[47] Likewise, although marriages were supposed to be registered by the state, and individuals were under no official obligation to undergo religious ceremonials, Yemenis in many regions continued to do so. Until 1983 there was no national registration system, and even in the regions where birth registers existed, they did not date back far enough to allow officials to prove that a marriage was illegal. Moreover, although the consent of both principals was required before a marriage contract was concluded by the state, marriage partners rarely defied their families' wishes. There was reported to be an increasing number of cases where the principals did resist, but these were in the minority and the control exercised by kin over marriage and the family was not, on the whole, surrendered.

However, the government occasionally resorted to severe measures against those who violated the law, as was illustrated by an episode which took place in the fourth Governorate in 1978. A young girl, from a prominent Sada family in Haban, refused to marry the man her grandfather had chosen for her.[48] Instead she eloped with a man of inferior caste. Her grandfather tracked her down, had her murdered and secretly buried: but some local people who suspected that a crime had been committed reported their suspicions to the authorities, who mounted a search for the young girl's body, and found it. The villagers on hearing of the crime seized the old man and dragged him through the streets in a procession; he was eventually brought to trial and sentenced to death. The whole episode was well publicised in the media and at public meetings so that appropriate lessons could be drawn.[49] The attitude of the authorities and of the villagers was significant in that it marked a radical change in mores as much as in understandings of legality; a few years earlier, such a murder would have gone unpunished and would indeed have been regarded as the natural prerogative of an elder whose will had been disobeyed by a woman,[50] and whose family honour was put in jeopardy.

As this episode suggests, some of the reforms may have been popular, at least among the poorer and disadvantaged sectors of the population. This was reportedly the case with the attempt to lower the *mahr*. But it is clear that there was resistance to them as well, although it is not known on what grounds, by whom, or how widespread it was. As already indicated, there was some opposition on orthodox religious grounds, although the government claimed that this was minimal and largely stimulated by outside sources.

CONCLUSIONS

The transformation in the structures and practices of law which were brought about in the PDRY had far-reaching implications for women, as well as for some other social groups. This was so despite the fact that the substantive impact of the reforms varied as between the specific laws themselves and as they affected different categories of social agents. As far as women were concerned, the legal reforms may be considered modest, but their radical significance was given by their regional context and by the place they occupied within the wider process of social transformation.

It is clear from the preceding discussion that understanding the significance of legal reforms in such contexts requires more subtle theoretical instruments than has informed much of the debate in the Marxist tradition on socialist legality. Recent theoretical work has rejected *simpliste* class reductionism and base/superstructure metaphors to describe the relationships between the law, the economy and the state. It has argued for proper recognition of the relative distinctiveness and independence of the law from these spheres and emphasises its heterogeneous and often contradictory nature and effects. While laws and legal systems generally help to provide the conditions of existence of determinate relations of production, and hence may define and embody class relations and other forms of inequality, it does not follow that they should be conceived of as a coherent entity with a determinate essence, a conception which itself entails the problematic notion of social formation as 'expressive totality'[51] Laws and legal systems perform a variety of different roles, which can be summed up as defining and regulating the public realm, as well as the capacities and conduct of social agents. These operations may be reformed, in the interests of greater equality, but they cannot easily be dispensed with, even (or especially) under socialism.[52] The case of Democratic Yemen, like that of other socialist states, demonstrates how the law was conceived of by the government as providing some of the conditions of existence of new forms of ownership and control, as well as constituting a form of intervention outside the economic realm to meet certain social policy objectives. Our main concern here has been to show how legal reform assisted in the social, political and economic repositioning of women as a concomitant of social transformation. In summary form five related but discrete forms of such legal intervention to achieve this can be identified. These are:

1. Relations between the sexes were redefined by conferring on women new rights, and providing them with new capacities. For example, women could now divorce, refuse arranged marriage, work and vote; they could seek the assistance of the mass organisations and the state in actualising these rights. By the same token, men lost certain rights and privileges that they previously enjoyed (polygyny, *talaq*).

2. Kin, class, and tribal control over women were outlawed and to some degree delegitimised. This was in part designed to meet the social policy objective of redefining the structure and affiliations of the family by reducing the incidence of polygamy and promoting the nuclear family form.

3. The legal authority of orthodox Islam and customary law was challenged and the state became the higher legal authority, bringing under its control certain ceremonial and juridical functions which were previously in the hands of religious entities (marriage), or voluntary agencies (divorce).

4. The law functioned to assist in the demarcation of a realm of legitimate struggle between women and traditional repositories of power over them. (This redefinition also occurred in the case of peasants through the provisions of the Land Reform.)

5. Within the realm of public law, women were interpellated in new ways (as workers, national subjects, political subjects) in order to help construct less private, traditional, identities. In this sense, as well as in that of the first point, they acquired new legal personalities. Legal reforms also made it more possible for women concretely to operate in these areas, as evidenced by women's entry into the legal profession and into political life. The extension of full citizenship to women can be seen as part of the process of creating a new state form with an extended area of support.

The substantive impact of these juridical changes on women was of course contingent on the degree to which they were matched by transformations in their material circumstances, on popular acceptance of the new codes, and failing that, on women's willingness and capacities to struggle for their observance. While changes took place in the areas of education and employment, with women's participation showing marked increases over the pre-revolutionary period, much remained to be achieved before women were able to attain an independent and equal place in a male-dominated society. Attitudes towards the reforms are more difficult to assess, especially since they were introduced 'from above' and as far as we know in the absence of any demands for legal change from below. While there was opposition to some of them on a variety of grounds (religious, practical), the available evidence seems to support the government's claims that with some exceptions the new codes were popular among many women, if less so among men. Official observers present at meetings called to discuss the draft laws reported that women generally exhibited more enthusiasm than men and in many cases called for more radical measures than those proposed by the original law.[53]

One index of the popular acceptance of new laws is the degree to which they are made use of. In many Islamic countries it is common to find that most rural women have little knowledge of their legal rights and, even if they are aware of them, they rarely initiate legal action to attain them. In the PDRY, partly as a result of the efforts to publicise the reforms, women in most areas made use of their new rights and brought their complaints to the courts within a few years of the passing of the Family Law. The sharp rise in female-initiated divorces was the clearest indication of this. It is none the less likely that some women may have perceived the increase in personal freedom and responsibility entailed by the Law as a threat to their security, particularly if the kinship system of responsibility was eroded and the gap was not filled by satisfactory alternatives.

In spite of these qualifications, the changes that were introduced can be recognised as important without exaggerating their overall impact or their contribution to 'women's emancipation'. Their limits in this latter respect are evident enough, and it is worth remembering that even where legal reform is considerably more advanced than it was in Democratic Yemen, the rules of jurisprudence do not by themselves define the entire spectrum of power relations which prevail to women's disadvantage. In the PDRY, legal reforms affecting the family helped to weaken some of the traditional loci of power and inequality, whether these were based on gender (patriarchy) or upon kinship and class. By most standards of historical change this process was an accelerated one; in the West, as in some Middle Eastern countries such power relations suffered some erosion through protracted and extensive changes in the economy, in some regions centuries before legal reforms were introduced in the more industrialised Arab States.[54]

The opposite was attempted in the PDRY with economic change accompanying and in some cases *following* the legal reforms. These transformations were seen by the government as a necessary part of constructing a socialist society, yet this was a process which barely began. According to official party policy, efforts in this direction' could only remain at the stage appropriate to the 'national democratic' phase of development. Despite the extension of citizenship rights, the elementary forms of democratic participation did not acquire a meaningful influence on the political life of the country, and the Yemeni Socialist Party's reforms are therefore best understood as attempts from above to promote 'socialist modernisation'. The conditional and limited character of the PDRY's social transformations must all the more be registered in the light of the regime's collapse in 1990. What union with North Yemen entails, and what effects this will have on policy on women, are questions that must, at the time of writing, remain unanswered.[55]

ACKNOWLEDGEMENTS

Thanks are due to Fred Halliday for his comments and help with translations from the Arabic and German, and to the numerous South Yemenis, juridical practitioners and otherwise who provided much of the information on which this article is based. The material was gathered on two field trips, one in 1977, the other in 1984, and supplemented by interviews in London. An earlier version of this article appeared in *The International Journal of the Sociology of Law*, no. 3 (1985).

NOTES

1. The term 'socialist' is used here for the sake of brevity to refer to those states which broadly adhered to Marxist doctrine and which were committed to the socialisation of a substantial proportion of the economy, while effecting policies of social redistribution. They were of course not socialist in the strict sense of the term, as they did not implement socialist democracy.
2. See Theda Skocpol, *States and Social Revolutions* (Cambridge University Press, 1979) for an elaborated discussion of this question.
3. Michael Mann, defines the 'infrastructural power' of the state as 'the capacity of the state actually to penetrate civil society, and to implement logistically political decisions throughout the realm'. See M. Mann, 'The Autonomous Power of the State: Its Origins, Mechanisms and

Results' in J. Hall (ed.), *States in History* (Oxford: Basil Blackwell, 1986).

4. On Soviet policy towards Islam see Shirin Akiner, *Islamic Peoples of the Soviet Union* (London: Kegan Paul, 1983); Gregory Massell, *The Surrogate Proletariat* (Princeton University Press, 1974); Alexander Bennigsen and S. Enders Wimbush, *Muslim National Communities in the Soviet Union* (Chicago: University of Chicago Press 1979); Edward Mortimer, *Faith and Power* (London: Faber, 1982); Fred Halliday, 'Islam and Soviet Foreign Policy', *Journal of Communist Studies* vol. 3 (March 1987) no. 1.

5. Fred Halliday, 'Yemen's Unfinished Revolution, Socialism in the South', *Merip Report*, vol. 9, no. 8 (October 1979).

6. PDRY, *Programme of the Unified Political Organisation, the National Front* (Nottingham: Russell Press, 1977), and PDRY, *Documentos del I Congreso del Partido Socialista de Yemen* (Editorial Moscú, 1979).

7. Fred Halliday, *Arabia without Sultans* (Harmondsworth: Penguin, 1974) gives the most detailed account of the national liberation struggle.

8. William Butler, *Soviet Law* (London: Butterworth, 1983); Robert Stookey, *South Yemen: A Marxist Republic in Asia* (London: Croom Helm/Westview, 1982).

9. An East German writer, although from a sympathetic perspective, comments that by 1980 this process had not proceeded very far; see Frank Weidnitzer, 'Grundzuge der Entwicklung der politisch–staatlichen Verhaltnisse in revolutionaren VDRJ' in *Asien, Afrika, Latein-amerika*, vol. 8 (1980) no. 6 (Berlin DDR).

10. Butler, *Soviet Law*.

11. PDRY, *The Political Report presented by Comrade Abdel Fattah Isma'il* (Aden: Government Press, 1975).

12. Appeals were previously heard by the Court of Appeal for Eastern Africa and by the Judicial Committee of the Privy Council. See N. A. Shamiry, 'The Judicial System in Democratic Yemen', in B. Pridham (ed.), *Contemporary Yemen: Politics and Historical Background* (London: Croom Helm, and Centre for Arab – Gulf Studies, University of Exeter, July 1983), also S. H. Amin, *Law and Justice in Contemporary Yemen (Glasgow: Royston, 1987)*

13. Abdalla Bujra focusing on the Hadramaut region, provides the only sociological analysis of social relations in the South Arabian Protectorate. See A. Bujra, *The Politics of Stratification: A Study of Political Change in a South Arabian Town* (Oxford University Press, 1971).

14. The Shafei school of jurisprudence is within the Sunni branch of Islam, one to which 95 per cent of South Yemenis belong. For a more detailed discussion of the colonial and post-colonial legal infrastructure, see the original article, M. Molyneux, 'Legal Reform and Socialist Revolution in Democratic Yemen: Women and The Family', *International Journal of the Sociology of Law* (1985) 13, pp. 147–172.

15. Aden Colony was administered from India until 1937.
16. In 1984, according to a former woman judge, one of the six judges of the Provincial Courts was a woman, and of the fifty magistrates, six were women.
17. See Shamiry, 'The Judicial System in Democratic Yemen'.
18. 'Popular courts' were in operation after Independence. They dealt with cases of a political nature, and according to the Minister of Justice, were dissolved after 1979.
19. A feature of this type of infringement is that it is conceived of as a violation of 'rules of socialist community life' which promote behaviour based on the idea of 'new socialist norms'. These are not laws as such but rules of conduct 'which are reinforced by public opinion and interact with and support legal rules' (Butler, *Soviet Law*).
20. See Fred Halliday, 'The PDRY: the "Cuban Path" in Arabia' in Gordon White *et al.*, *Revolutionary Socialist Development in the Third World* (Sussex: Wheatsheaf, 1983).
21. PDRY, *The Political Report . . .*
22. Butler, *Soviet Law*, and P.Q. Hirst, 'Law, Socialism and Rights', in P. Carlen and M. Collinson (eds), *Radical Issues in Criminology* (Martin Robinson, 1980).
23. Doreen Ingrams, *A Time In Arabia* (London: Cox and Wyman, 1970) and author's interviews.
24. This description of the sexual division of labour is corroborated by such diverse sources as the documents of the GUYW, and interviews by the author with rural women, 1977 and 1984.
25. According to Women's Union officials in Dhaleh (near the border with the Yemen Arab Republic), the birth of two daughters in a row was regarded as sufficient grounds for divorce in the area.
26. World Bank, *The PDRY: A Review of Economic and Social Development* (Washington D.C., 1979). World Bank, *Development Report 1980* (Oxford University Press, 1980).
27. For a detailed study of women and work in the P.D.R.Y. see Maxine Molyneux, *State Policies and the Position of Women Workers in the PDRY 1967–1977* (Geneva: ILO, 1982).
28. Maxine Molyneux, 'Women's Emancipation under Socialism: a model for the Third World?', *World Development*, vol. 9 (1981) no. 9/10.
29. Massell, *The Surrogate Proletariat*; Judith Stacey, *Patriarchy and Socialist Revolution in China* (Berkley: University of California Press, 1983).
30. Chinese and Soviet theorists are perhaps the most explicit about this relationship.
31. Ludwig Liegle, *The Family's Role in Soviet Education* (New York: Springer, 1970).
32. Neil Coulson, *Conflicts and Tensions in Islamic Jurisprudence* (University of Chicago, 1969) and Lois Beck and Nikki Keddie, *Women in the Muslim World* (University of Chicago, 1979).

33. General Union of Yemeni Women *Documents of the GUYW* (Aden: Government Press, 1976).
34. Most of these were formulated at the Second Congress of the Comintern in 1920 and have since formed the basis for ruling communist parties' provisions and policies on women. See PDRY, *The Constitution* (Aden: Government Press, 1975, and amended, 1978).
35. By 1984 there were twenty 'kindergartens' in the PDRY.
36. In 1984 the G.U.Y.W. claimed 'membership' of 8000. See Helen Lackner, *PDRY Yemen: Outpost of Socialist Development in Arabia* (London: Ithaca Press, 1985) for a discussion of the GUYW.
37. As one factory worker expressed it to me in 1977: 'If my father forbids me to go out to work I can tell him he is acting against the law. If he still stops me, I can get the women's union to leave me alone. After all I am in the right and he is in the wrong'.
38. Norman Anderson, *Law Reform in the Muslim World* (University of London: Athlone Press, 1976); Isam Ghanem, 'A Note on Law no. I, Concerning the Family, Peoples Democratic Republic of Yemen', *Arabian Studies*, no. III (1976) pp. 191–6. The Holy Quran, Translation and Commentary by Abdallah Yusuf Ali (London: The Islamic Foundation, 1975). S. H. Amin, *Law and Justice in Contemporary Yemen* (Glasgow: Roysten Press, 1987). The English translation of the *Family Law* was published by the Russell Press Ltd, Nottingham, 1978.
39. Nuclear families were considered by officials and many interviewees in the urban sector to represent the ideal of modern living, free from parents and in-laws. After the revolution modern apartments were usually built with this ideal in mind. See Molyneux *State Policies and the position of Women Workers' in the PDRY* for factory workers' attitudes towards family size and composition.
40. *Aden Colony Census Report* (Aden: Government Press, 1955) and *Adenisation Committee Report* (London, 1959).
41. As written sources on the PDRY are extremely rare, this information is based on interviews with the then Minister of Justice in London, in 1983, and with senior legal practitioners in the PDRY in 1984.
42. In the laws of 1957 and 1975, respectively, Iraq and Somalia tried to equalise inheritance between the sexes but with limited success and determination owing to the strength of religious opposition (Anderson, *Law Reform in the Muslim World*).
43. The case for maintaining *Shari'ah* inheritance was said by a South Yemeni woman advocate to rest on the fact that it is customary for men to bear the financial responsibility for aged parents and infirm relatives. As women are not expected to do so, nor wish to assume such responsibilities, they are generally allocated a smaller share of the inheritance. Defenders of the *mahr* pointed out that in some regions this payment was to the bride and remained hers as an insurance against divorce.
44. BBC Summary of World Broadcasts ME/35681A5, 21 December 1970.

45. See Maxine Molyneux, 'State Policy and the Position of Women in South Yemen', *Peuples Méditerranéens*, no. 12 (July/September 1980).
46. The same was true with regard to abortion and contraception. These practices had no legal status and the government's official view was that they could be justified where necessary on the grounds that Islam does not expressly forbid them.
47. Interview by the author with officials of the General Union of Yemeni Women, 1977, in Dhaleh in the Fourth Governorate.
48. The *Sada* (sing. Seyyid) were a highly respected and generally wealthy caste which claimed direct descent from the Prophet Mohammed. See Bujra, *The Politics of Stratification*, for a detailed account of their social position.
49. Author's interview with party officials in the Fourth Governorate, 1977.
50. The death penalty was in force and applied *inter alia* to cases of rape where the victim died as a result of the attack. It was reportedly resorted to infrequently.
51. Barry Hindess and Paul Hirst, *Mode of Production and Social Formation* (London: Macmillan, 1977).
52. P. Q. Hirst, 'Law, Socialism and Rights'.
53. Author's interview with an official rapporteur appointed to monitor the proceedings of the public meetings called to discuss the Family Law. His account was corroborated by other observers.
54. See for example, Judith Tucker, *Women in Nineteenth Century Egypt* (Cambridge University Press, 1985).
55. It is significant that the issue of unification was accompanied by the politicisation of women's place in social and economic life. Demonstrations by women in South Yemen called for a defence of their legal and social rights after unification, while in the North the Muslim Brothers led demonstrations calling for the immediate implementation of Shari'ah law in the new republic.

Index